SHAREPOINT® SERVER 2010 ADMINISTRATION 24-HOUR TRAINER

SharePoint® Server 2010 Administration

24-HOUR TRAINER

SharePoint® Server 2010 Administration

24-HOUR TRAINER

Bill Crider
Martin Reid
Clint Richardson

WILEY

John Wiley & Sons, Inc.

SharePoint® Server 2010 Administration 24-Hour Trainer

Published by
John Wiley & Sons, Inc.
10475 Crosspoint Boulevard
Indianapolis, IN 46256
www.wiley.com

Published simultaneously in Canada

ISBN: 978-0-470-93906-2
ISBN: 978-1-118-22152-5 (ebk)
ISBN: 978-1-118-23527-0 (ebk)
ISBN: 978-1-118-26001-2 (ebk)

Manufactured in the United States of America

10 9 8 7 6 5 4 3 2 1

For general information on our other products and services please contact our Customer Care Department within the United States at (877) 762-2974, outside the United States at (317) 572-3993 or fax (317) 572-4002.

Wiley publishes in a variety of print and electronic formats and by print-on-demand. Some material included with standard print versions of this book may not be included in e-books or in print-on-demand. If this book refers to media such as a CD or DVD that is not included in the version you purchased, you may download this material at http://booksupport.wiley.com. For more information about Wiley products, visit www.wiley.com.

Library of Congress Control Number: 2011928392

This is book is dedicated to my family. My wife Noele, and my three children Anna, Garrett, and Isabelle.

—BILL CRIDER

For Seamy McGivern, always remembered by his friends.

—MARTIN REID

For Michelle—My Crustacean Forevermore

—CLINT RICHARDSON

ABOUT THE AUTHORS

BILL CRIDER is a SharePoint architect and principal consultant at Ascendum Solutions in Cincinnati, Ohio. He is an active speaker, writer, and blogger on all things SharePoint. His current interests include mobile applications, social networks for businesses, and SharePoint in the cloud. You can visit his website at http://www.DrSharePoint.com for a variety of posts, podcasts, and videos on SharePoint administration, development, and architecture.

MARTIN REID is an analyst with the Queens University of Belfast where he works with a large SharePoint 2010 farm. Martin is married with six children and lives in Belfast, Northern Ireland. Martin's main interest is using SharePoint to solve business issues.

CLINT RICHARDSON has been working in the IT industry for more than a decade, and has focused exclusively on SharePoint for the last 5 years. His primary interest is in the deployment and administration of large scale farms. He has assisted multiple branches of the US military in locations around the world. Currently he runs his own SharePoint consultancy in the Ohio Valley area of the US.

ABOUT THE TECHNICAL EDITORS

TODD MEISTER has been working in the IT industry for over fifteen years. He's been a Technical Editor on over 75 titles ranging from SQL Server to the .NET Framework. Besides technical editing titles he is the Senior IT Architect at Ball State University in Muncie, Indiana. He lives in central Indiana with his wife, Kimberly, and their four great children.

MARTIN REID is an analyst with the Queens University of Belfast where he works with a large SharePoint 2010 farm. Martin is married with six children and lives in Belfast, Northern Ireland. Martin's main interest is using SharePoint to solve business issues.

CREDITS

ACQUISITIONS EDITOR
Paul Reese

PROJECT EDITOR
Jason Gilmore

TECHNICAL EDITORS
Todd Meister
Martin Reid

PRODUCTION EDITOR
Rebecca Anderson

COPY EDITOR
Sarah B. Kleinman

EDITORIAL MANAGER
Mary Beth Wakefield

FREELANCER EDITORIAL MANAGER
Rosemarie Graham

ASSOCIATE DIRECTOR OF MARKETING
David Mayhew

MARKETING MANAGER
Ashley Zurcher

BUSINESS MANAGER
Amy Knies

PRODUCTION MANAGER
Tim Tate

VICE PRESIDENT AND EXECUTIVE GROUP PUBLISHER
Richard Swadley

VICE PRESIDENT AND EXECUTIVE PUBLISHER
Neil Edde

ASSOCIATE PUBLISHER
Jim Minatel

PROJECT COORDINATOR, COVER
Katie Crocker

PROOFREADER
James Saturnio, Word One New York

INDEXER
Johnna VanHoose Dinse

COVER DESIGNER
LeAndra Young

COVER IMAGE
© iStock / Daniel Vice

DVD TECHNICAL PRODUCER
Focal Point Studios LLC

VERTICAL WEBSITES PROJECT MANAGER
Laura Moss-Hollister

VERTICAL WEBSITES ASSISTANT PROJECT MANAGER
Rich Graves

VERTICAL WEBSITES ASSOCIATE PRODUCER
Marilyn Hummel

ACKNOWLEDGMENTS

I would like to thank the staff at Wrox for giving me the opportunity to write my first book. Also my thanks go out to them for their patience along the way. The process of writing is much more difficult and time consuming that I imagined when I started this project. Many thanks to my wife, who put up with my 60 hour weeks turning into 80 hour weeks as I fought to cross the finish line with this project. Finally, I would like to thank my co-author Martin, who stepped in at the last minute and put forth an incredible amount of effort to bring this project to a successful close.

—BILL CRIDER

I would like to thank my wife, Patricia, for her usual support when I am working on these books. People always say it would not be possible without that support, in my case that is more than true.

—MARTIN REID

CONTENTS

INTRODUCTION

SHAREPOINT IS ONE THE MOST SUCCESSFUL products in Microsoft's history. It can be found in small businesses, universities, and Fortune 500 companies. SharePoint 2010, the latest release, contains many new areas for existing and new SharePoint server administrators and site administrators. This book will help you meet the new challenges SharePoint administrators face in their day to day deals with the product.

Existing SharePoint administrators will find there are a lot of changes in SharePoint 2010 with which they may not be very familiar. One of the major changes covered extensively is the move away from a single farm Shared Service Provider to a system of Service Applications which need to be configured and managed. For example Access Services, new to SharePoint with this release will allow your users to actually convert Access 2010 databases to run within the browser hosted by SharePoint.

Our intention in writing this book was to help you with what is, being honest, a complicated bit of Software to manage and one of the main requirements required with SharePoint is patience when things don't work out as expected! This book is there to guide you, to provide help when you need it. Each lesson looks at one particular area of administration giving you the tools and information to get a service up and running. Video files accompany each lesson, extending the information given in the book with real world experience and useful tips.

It would be an unusual day in the life of a SharePoint administrator to know the answer to every question encountered when managing this product. This book will go a long way to helping you understand the questions, provide many answers to common issues, and give you a thorough grounding in the skills required to manage what is in our view the best product ever released by Microsoft.

WHO THIS BOOK IS FOR

This book is aimed at both new and existing SharePoint Server and SharePoint 2010 Foundation server and site administrators. The book covers almost every aspect of SharePoint administration at the server level using Central Administration to working at the site collection level. No previous experience is required as the authors take you through each area using real world examples reinforced with Lesson DVD videos.

WHAT THIS BOOK COVERS

This book covers SharePoint 2010 and SharePoint Foundation 2010 Administration. We look at options available to you from Central Administration, looking at working with Service Applications, setting up search at the server level to working with Site Collection Administration features for example setting individual search scopes.

HOW THIS BOOK IS STRUCTURED

The book is divided into several sections each organized to provide you with a comprehensive guide to a particular SharePoint administrative area. The following areas of SharePoint Administration are covered included real work practical exercises accompanied by a video demonstration of both the exercise and extended information on the topic.

➤ Section 1—Administration at the Site Level

➤ Section 2—Administration at the Site Collection Level

➤ Section 3—Managing Search

➤ Section 4—Setting up Content Management Options

➤ Section 5—Managing Publishing Sites

➤ Section 6—Setting Users and Permissions

➤ Section 7—Managing Service Applications

➤ Section 8—Site Templates

WHAT YOU NEED TO USE THIS BOOK

In order to work with the examples in the book you will of course require access to SharePoint 2010 either the full version or SharePoint Foundation 2010. For some of the practical example you will also need access to Microsoft Office 2010, however Microsoft Office 2007 will work just as well to create some of the example files required. You will also need appropriate permissions to the Central Administration web site and Site Collection Administrator permissions to fully follow all the examples.

CONVENTIONS

To help you get the most from the text and keep track of what's happening, we've used a number of conventions throughout the book.

TRY IT

The *Try It* is an exercise you should work through, following the text in the book.

1. They usually consist of a set of steps.

2. Each step has a number.

3. Follow the steps through with your copy of the database.

Boxes with a warning icon like this one hold important, not-to-be-forgotten information that is directly relevant to the surrounding text.

The pencil icon indicates notes, tips, hints, tricks, or and asides to the current discussion.

As for styles in the text:

- ➤ We *highlight* new terms and important words when we introduce them.
- ➤ We show keyboard strokes like this: **Ctrl+A**.
- ➤ We show file names, URLs, and code within the text like so: `persistence.properties`.

SOURCE CODE

As you work through the examples in this book, you may choose either to type in all the code manually, or to use the source code files that accompany the book. All the source code used in this book is available for download at `www.wrox.com`. When at the site, simply locate the book's title (use the Search box or one of the title lists) and click the Download Code link on the book's detail page to obtain all the source code for the book. Code that is included on the web site is highlighted by the following icon:

Available for download on Wrox.com

Listings include the filename in the title. If it is just a code snippet, you'll find the filename in a code note such as this:

Code snippet filename

Because many books have similar titles, you may find it easiest to search by ISBN; this book's ISBN is 978-0-470-93906-2.

Once you download the code, just decompress it with your favorite compression tool. Alternately, you can go to the main Wrox code download page at www.wrox.com/dynamic/books/download.aspx to see the code available for this book and all other Wrox books.

ERRATA

We make every effort to ensure that there are no errors in the text or in the code. However, no one is perfect, and mistakes do occur. If you find an error in one of our books, like a spelling mistake or faulty piece of code, we would be very grateful for your feedback. By sending in errata, you may save another reader hours of frustration, and at the same time, you will be helping us provide even higher quality information.

To find the errata page for this book, go to www.wrox.com and locate the title using the Search box or one of the title lists. Then, on the book details page, click the Book Errata link. On this page, you can view all errata that has been submitted for this book and posted by Wrox editors. A complete book list, including links to each book's errata, is also available at www.wrox.com/misc-pages/booklist.shtml.

If you don't spot "your" error on the Book Errata page, go to www.wrox.com/contact/techsupport.shtml and complete the form there to send us the error you have found. We'll check the information and, if appropriate, post a message to the book's errata page and fix the problem in subsequent editions of the book.

P2P.WROX.COM

For author and peer discussion, join the P2P forums at p2p.wrox.com. The forums are a Web-based system for you to post messages relating to Wrox books and related technologies and interact with other readers and technology users. The forums offer a subscription feature to e-mail you topics of interest of your choosing when new posts are made to the forums. Wrox authors, editors, other industry experts, and your fellow readers are present on these forums.

At p2p.wrox.com, you will find a number of different forums that will help you, not only as you read this book, but also as you develop your own applications. To join the forums, just follow these steps:

1. Go to p2p.wrox.com and click the Register link.

2. Read the terms of use and click Agree.

3. Complete the required information to join, as well as any optional information you wish to provide, and click Submit.

4. You will receive an e-mail with information describing how to verify your account and complete the joining process.

> *You can read messages in the forums without joining P2P, but in order to post your own messages, you must join.*

Once you join, you can post new messages and respond to messages other users post. You can read messages at any time on the Web. If you would like to have new messages from a particular forum e-mailed to you, click the Subscribe to this Forum icon by the forum name in the forum listing.

For more information about how to use the Wrox P2P, be sure to read the P2P FAQs for answers to questions about how the forum software works, as well as many common questions specific to P2P and Wrox books. To read the FAQs, click the FAQ link on any P2P page.

SECTION I
Administration at the Site Level

- ▶ **LESSON 1:** Using the Site Administration Menu

- ▶ **LESSON 2:** Using the Site Actions Menu

- ▶ **LESSON 3:** Changing a Site's Look and Feel

- ▶ **LESSON 4:** Using Custom Themes

- ▶ **LESSON 5:** Managing Reporting Services

1

Using the Site Administration Menu

A SharePoint application is largely organized around the concept of the individual site. Every SharePoint site must have at least one owner who will have available to him or her the full range of administrative options at the site level.

In many cases the people responsible for building and maintaining a SharePoint site are not IT professionals. More often they are business users charged with organizing documents, posting meeting information, and uploading photos of the company picnic. The purpose of this chapter is to explain the basic administration functions that are available to a user who has administrative access to a site. Typically, this person is known as the *site owner*.

The SharePoint administration interface is displayed by a browser and is *security-trimmed*. This means that many of the menu options, links, and other parts of the interface can be viewed only by people who have a certain level of rights. If you are following the steps in this chapter and the accompanying video walkthrough, and you are not seeing the links and menu items described, it's likely that you do not have a sufficient level of rights to the site. Someone with a higher level of access will have to increase your security level.

ACCESSING THE SITE ADMINISTRATION MENU

Every SharePoint site includes a Site Settings page. This page consists of various link groupings that contain all of the various administration and configuration options available to a site owner. You can access the site settings page from any page on a SharePoint site using the site actions menu. The site actions menu is usually found in the upper left corner of a SharePoint site. If the page has been modified from its original layout, it could be located somewhere else.

Figure 1-1 shows the site actions menu and the drop-down list of choices. If you click the drop-down arrow on the Site Actions menu, you will see this list of options and links. The links in your environment may differ from the ones shown in Figure 1-1. The choices you see in this menu vary based on a wide array of settings, options, and other variables, but near the bottom of the list should be an option called Site Settings. Clicking this link takes you to the Site Settings page.

On the Site Settings page for any SharePoint site, you will find a large collection of links organized under several categories. See Figure 1-2.

For this chapter we focus on the links under the heading Site Administration. (Later chapters discuss the other headings.) These links deal with a range of functions and settings common to every SharePoint site.

You may notice that the links under your Site Administration heading are different from the ones in this book. SharePoint offers a dizzying array of options, features, and configuration settings. The links that appear on the Site Actions page depend on the version of SharePoint being used and the type of site that was created; in addition, optional features may have been activated.

Links that are the result of optional configurations will be discussed in later chapters. In this chapter we will deal strictly with the site administration options found on all (or at least most) SharePoint sites.

FIGURE 1-1

Reporting Services
Manage Shared Schedules
Reporting Services Site Settings

Site Collection Administration
Search settings
Search scopes
Search keywords
FAST Search keywords
FAST Search site promotion and demotion
FAST Search user context
Recycle bin
Site collection features
Site hierarchy
Site collection navigation
Site collection audit settings

Site Administration
Regional settings
Site libraries and lists
User alerts
RSS
Search and offline availability
Sites and workspaces
Workflows
Workflow settings
Related Links scope settings
Content Organizer Settings
Content Organizer Rules
Term store management
Content and structure
Searchable columns
Content and structure logs

FIGURE 1-2

A SharePoint installation typically contains a number of individual sites. Each option in the site administration menu must be set separately for each SharePoint site. Other items we will look at later have a larger scope and will affect the behavior of several sites at once.

In the following sections in this lesson, we will discuss the purpose of each link in the site administration menu. The links found in the Site Administration menu common to all SharePoint sites include:

➤ Regional Settings

➤ Site Libraries and Lists

➤ User Alerts

➤ RSS

➤ Content and Structure

➤ Content and Structure Logs

Exploring these administrative functions will be the focus of this lesson.

Setting the Regional Settings Options

The Regional Settings link in the Site Administration menu opens the Regional Settings page. The Regional Settings page is used by administrators to determine how SharePoint displays certain elements that change according to a user's time zone or location. Let's walk through the various options and discuss the effect each one has on the site. Figure 1-3 shows the Regional Settings page.

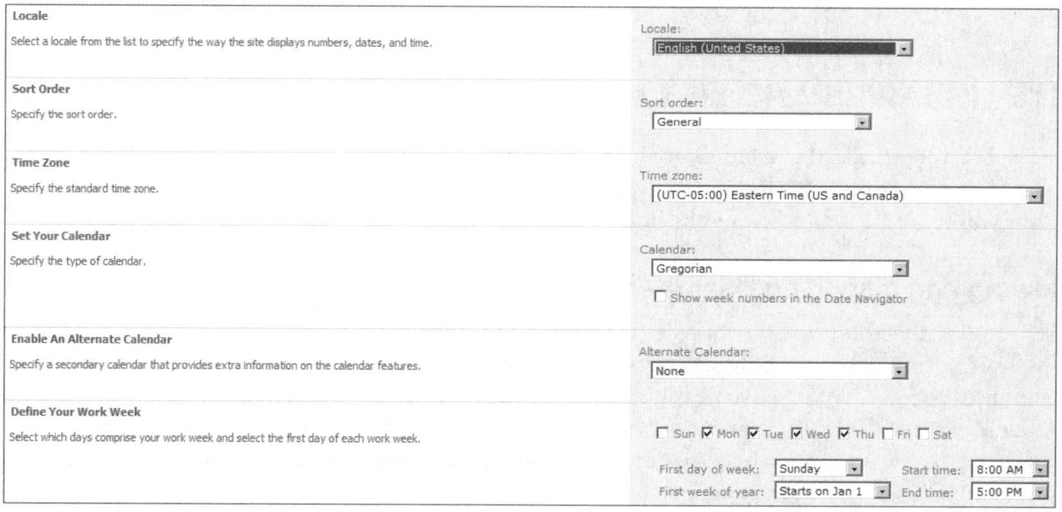

FIGURE 1-3

➤ **Locale:** Selecting a locale causes SharePoint to display numbers, dates, and time-related elements in the formats used in the locale selected. It will also cause some less obvious behaviors such as showing the names of months on a calendar view in the chosen locale.

➤ **Sort Order:** If you have the proper language pack installed for the selection you make in this drop-down box, items in lists and libraries are sorted in alphabetical order according to the chosen language. Language packs should be installed by a SharePoint farm administrator.

➤ **Time Zone:** This setting is important to set properly because often the users of a SharePoint portal are in a different time zone from the physical server that SharePoint is hosted on. Users expect time and date stamps on documents and items to reflect local time. If a server sits in California, but users are in New York, leaving the default setting here causes the time stamps of the users' documents to be three hours too early. If you are the owner of a site, make sure this setting is correct for the predominant location of your users.

➤ **Set Your Calendar:** This setting affects the presentation of calendar views (usually used for events lists). The default is the standard Gregorian calendar. To see how different settings change the presentation, complete the Try It walkthrough at the end of this chapter.

➤ **Enable an Alternate Calendar:** The alternate calendar presents an alternate month and year next to the month and year in the chosen format for calendar views. In addition, next to each day of the month shown in the calendar view, the alternate day is shown in parentheses to highlight differences between the chosen and alternate calendar formats.

➤ **Define Your Work Week:** This option is reflected in calendar views, as the weekday shown on the far left side of a calendar view will be the day chosen here as the first day of the week. Options for the work week and for the start and end times for the workday affect which days and times in the calendar views are shaded darker. Non-working days and hours are shaded, while working hours have a white background.

➤ **Time Format:** The 12-hour format shows time in the more common format, with a.m. and p.m. indicators. The 24-hour setting is military time, such as 15:00 for 3 p.m. (12 p.m. plus three hours).

SITE LIBRARIES AND LIST LINKS

The Site Libraries and Lists link provides a shortcut by which a site administrator can access the list and library settings page for all the lists and libraries on a site. This page presents a link for each list and library in the site. Clicking the link takes you to the settings page for that list or library.

Viewing and Managing User Alerts

Alerts are a method for users to receive notification when content in the site are added, changed or deleted. Users can voluntarily set alerts that will send e-mails to them when the contents of lists or libraries change. Note that you cannot set up alerts for other users using the browser interface provided in SharePoint. Users must elect to receive them and set the alerts themselves. However, this page enables you to view alerts that users have set up and to delete them at your discretion. Sometimes users decide they no longer wish to receive alert notifications and ask an administrator to remove them.

For alerts to work, the SharePoint farm administrator must have previously set up an e-mail server. Because alerts rely on the SharePoint server using e-mail, commands that enable users to set alerts are not visible unless an e-mail server has been set up and associated with the SharePoint farm. This must be done by someone with farm administration rights. Figure 1-4 shows the Share & Track toolbar on the ribbon. If the e-mail server has not been set, the Alert Me bell icon will not be visible.

FIGURE 1-4

Configuring RSS Feeds

RSS stands for Really Simple Syndication. As with most technical acronyms, the individual words don't have any meaning to people who aren't already information technology professionals. So what does Really Simple Syndication mean? RSS is a means people who have some content, usually on a website but not always, to publish that content and have it subscribed to on other websites, iPods, and a host of other medium. It enables updates to the source information to be reflected in all the locations that show the source content.

SharePoint lists can use RSS in a variety of ways. For instance, using the RSS Web part, content from other sites that have RSS feeds can be pulled into SharePoint. In addition, SharePoint lists and libraries can serve as sources of feeds for others to subscribe to. The Configuring RSS Feeds page deals with using SharePoint lists and libraries as feeds for others to subscribe to.

On the RSS Settings page you will see either one or two checkboxes, titled Enable RSS and (if applicable) Site Collection RSS (see Figure 1-4). You will see the Site Collection RSS checkbox only if the site is the top-level site of a site collection. The Site Collection checkbox enables or disables allowing RSS feeds for lists and libraries for every site in the collection. That includes the current site and any site below it. Disabling this checkbox overrides any setting that may be set on sites below it. The Enable RSS checkbox will allow or disallow feeds for the current site only.

In the Enable RSS setting you can allow RSS feeds for an individual site. If the Site Collection RSS setting is not enabled, the Allow RSS Feeds in this Site setting will be grayed out. If RSS is not enabled for a site or site collection, the RSS Feed option in the ribbon (see Figure 1-5) will be grayed out as well.

FIGURE 1-5

Finally, in the Advanced Settings section, you can enter some information about the RSS feed that will appear to someone who subscribes to the feed. The Time to Live setting affects how often the feed will update to subscribers. Decreasing the Time to Live will cause the feed to be updated more often and increase traffic on the site. See Figure 1-6 for an example of how these options appear.

Site Collection RSS	
	☑ Allow RSS feeds in this site collection
Enable RSS	
	☐ Allow RSS feeds in this site
Advanced Settings	Copyright:
Specify the site-wide channel elements for the RSS feeds.	
	Managing Editor:
	Webmaster:
	Time To Live (minutes):
	60

FIGURE 1-6

Managing Content and Structure

This feature and related links are available only if you have the licensed version of SharePoint 2010, SharePoint Server 2010, installed. If you are using SharePoint Foundation 2010, you will not see this link under Site Administration. In addition, you will have the publishing feature activated for these links to appear. Lessons 2 and 6 discuss the concept of activating features.

This feature consists of two separate links under the Site Administration heading: Site Content and Structure, and Content and Structure Logs. The first presents a tree view of the site collection, sites, and various site elements. Furthermore, it enables the user to view settings and permissions on the objects and move them around the hierarchy of the site collection. The second link (Content and Structure Logs) shows the same page but with an additional view of long running background processes.

TRY IT

In this lesson, you will review the Site Administration menu and how the options affect a SharePoint site. To participate in this walkthrough, you can either follow along with the accompanying instructional DVD or visit www.wrox.com/go/sp2010-24, or try a more hands-on approach via a SharePoint site using your Web browser.

Lessons Requirements

To perform this lesson you will need the following:

➤ Access to a SharePoint site

➤ Administrator rights to the site

Hints

This lesson is a survey of the Site Administration menu. It covers only the elements common elements to all (or most) SharePoint sites. Many optional features will be covered in other lessons in this book.

Step-By-Step

1. From the home page of a SharePoint Site, locate the Site Actions drop-down menu. You should find it in the upper left-hand corner of the screen. Select Site Settings. This will open the Site Settings page. You should be presented with a page full of various links under different headings. Look for the heading titled Site Administration. If you are following along on your own website the links you see may differ from what is displayed on the video or in the screenshots in this walkthrough. There are many factors that affect which links will become visible based on configuration choices, licenses, and a host of other options. Figure 1-2, from earlier in the lesson, shows the Site Administration menu as it is presented on the Site Settings page.

2. Click the Regional Settings link under the Site Administration heading. Make the following changes to the settings on the page (see Figure 1-7):

   ➤ Change the time zone to (UTC-9:00) Alaska.

   ➤ Change the Calendar setting to Japanese Emperor Era (a popular setting in Alaska).

   ➤ Set the checkboxes for the work week as Mon–Thu. Leave the others blank. (No real work gets done on Friday anyway.)

   ➤ Click the OK button at the bottom of the screen.

3. Create a list of type Calendar. You will see the calendar displaying Japanese characters reflecting your choices from Step 2.

4. Upload or create a file in a document library. You will see the time stamp on the Date Created field reflect the choice of time zone. In addition, the date portion of the time stamp will reflect the calendar setting from Step 2 (see Figure 1-8).

Time Zone	
Specify the standard time zone.	Time zone: (UTC-05:00) Eastern Time (US and Canada)
Set Your Calendar	
Specify the type of calendar.	Calendar: Gregorian ☐ Show week numbers in the Date Navigator
Enable An Alternate Calendar	
Specify a secondary calendar that provides extra information on the calendar features.	Alternate Calendar: None
Define Your Work Week	
Select which days comprise your work week and select the first day of each work week.	☐ Sun ☑ Mon ☑ Tue ☑ Wed ☑ Thu ☐ Fri ☐ Sat First day of week: Sunday Start time: 8:00 AM First week of year: Starts on Jan 1 End time: 5:00 PM

FIGURE 1-7

5. Return to the Site Settings page and click the Site Libraries and Lists link. This will open a page that will contain a link to the settings page for every list and library on the site, as shown in Figure 1-9. This page makes it easier for administrators to manage their lists and libraries.

Modified
平成 23/2/3 19:29

FIGURE 1-8

6. On the Site Settings page, click the User Alerts link to view the Alerts Management page. On this page you can view the current alerts and delete them at your discretion. Note that there is no way to set alerts for users in the interface. They must set their own alerts, or you can use programming to set them. To view alerts, choose a user name from the drop-down box and click the Update button. The details of the alert will be shown below on the page and you can delete it by selecting the appropriate checkbox and clicking the Delete Selected Alerts link. See Figure 1-10 for an example.

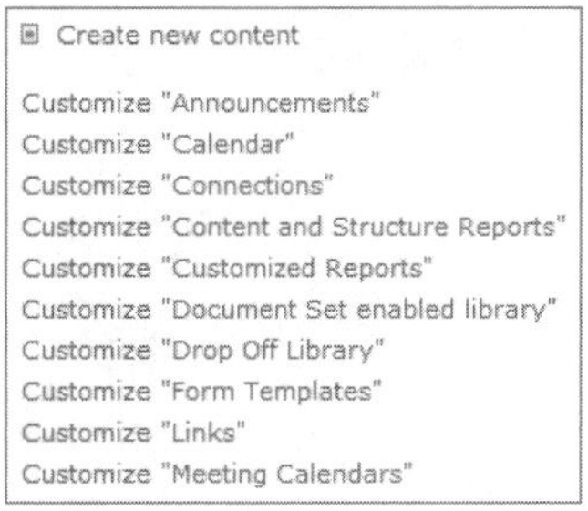

⊞ Create new content

Customize "Announcements"
Customize "Calendar"
Customize "Connections"
Customize "Content and Structure Reports"
Customize "Customized Reports"
Customize "Document Set enabled library"
Customize "Drop Off Library"
Customize "Form Templates"
Customize "Links"
Customize "Meeting Calendars"

FIGURE 1-9

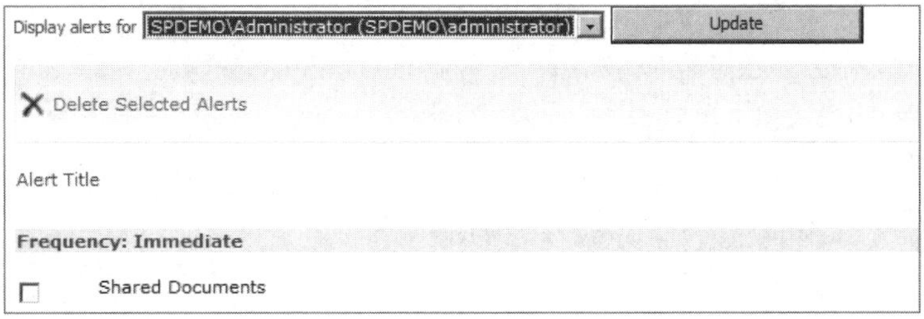

Display alerts for [SPDEMO\Administrator (SPDEMO\administrator)]   [Update]

✖ Delete Selected Alerts

Alert Title

Frequency: Immediate

☐   Shared Documents

FIGURE 1-10

 Please select Lesson 1 on the DVD or visit www.wrox.com/go/sp2010-24 to view the video that accompanies this lesson.

2

Using the Site Actions Menu

The Site Actions menu is another collection of administrative links on the Site Settings page and is open only to users with the Manage Web Site permission level. By default, this permission level is assigned to the Site Owner's group. It is also possible to assign this permission level separately, a topic we explore in Lesson 25. Most users typically have only Read or Contribute permissions and cannot access this menu.

The Site Actions menu contains a handful of important site-related functions that you need to learn just as you did the options in the Site Administration menu in Lesson 1. In this lesson we examine each of the features made available through the Site Actions menu. Figure 2-1 shows the Site Actions menu.

Site Actions
Manage site features
Save site as template
Reset to site definition
Delete this site
Site Web Analytics reports
Site Collection Web Analytics reports

FIGURE 2-1

MANAGE SITE FEATURES

Clicking the Manage Site Features link takes you to the `managefeatures.aspx` page. See Figure 2-2.

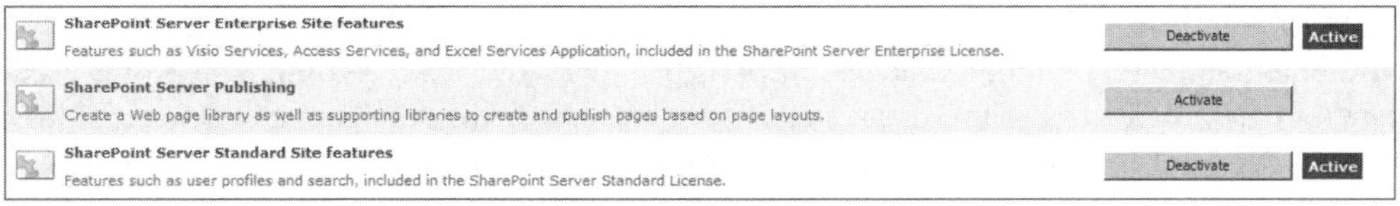

SharePoint Server Enterprise Site features
Features such as Visio Services, Access Services, and Excel Services Application, included in the SharePoint Server Enterprise License. — Deactivate | Active

SharePoint Server Publishing
Create a Web page library as well as supporting libraries to create and publish pages based on page layouts. — Activate

SharePoint Server Standard Site features
Features such as user profiles and search, included in the SharePoint Server Standard License. — Deactivate | Active

FIGURE 2-2

On the left side of the screen you can see the names and descriptions of various features, and on the right side is a toggle button for each feature that activates or deactivates it. If the feature is active, you see a blue box with the word Active in white text next to the button. The button displays the text Deactivate. If the feature is not active, the button text reads Activate.

As with everything else in SharePoint, the items you see in the feature list vary greatly based on the version of SharePoint you are running, how it is configured, and a host of other factors.

What is a Feature

A *feature* is a piece of functionality in SharePoint that can be activated (turned on) at different levels of the SharePoint farm. The concept of the feature was introduced in the 2007 version of SharePoint and it enables site owners to turn on certain functions on their sites and leave others off. Each time you activate a feature you turn on additional functionality. Site Features only affect the site where they are located. Other features can affect entire site collections or the whole SharePoint installation. Features in the Site Actions menu, however, only apply to a single individual site. In addition to the features supplied by SharePoint, developers can deploy their custom solutions using this same framework. Creating custom features and deploying them is a subject for a more developer-oriented book. Here the goal is merely to make you familiar with what features are and why you need to understand them.

One of the most important things to understand about features is the effects of turning them on or off. When features are activated, or when active features are deactivated, they can create a variety of changes on your site. One typical change is displaying menu items that were previously hidden. Another change is displaying previously inactive, gray items on the ribbon. These changes may affect the choices a user has when selecting, for example, the type of list to create on a site. Turning on certain features increases the list or site templates available to a user creating new content. As we discuss different functionalities we will mention which features need to be turned on to enable those functionalities.

If you cannot find links, list choices, or ribbon options that you have seen on other sites or expect to see on your site, one of the most likely culprit is a disabled feature. If you find yourself missing functions or links, always visit the Site Features page to determine if this is the problem. (If that doesn't work, visit Lesson 25, which discusses permissions. It may be you don't have rights to see the feature.)

To obtain a better understanding of how a feature works, you will turn one on and off as part of the Try It section at the end of this chapter.

Save Site as Template

Save Site as Template is a link on the Site Actions menu. The Save Site as Template link is used to create a site template out of the current site. Before we look at the details of this process, it is important to understand why you would want to create a site template.

When you create new sites you have a range of default options for site types. Each site type contains different pre-loaded lists, libraries, and other elements. However, most sites require additional elements to meet users' needs. Templates allow you to create sites with your own combinations of elements that you anticipate users will want and allow them to create a site that is pre-configured with those items. Items that users often want to recreate include:

➤ Custom lists

➤ Custom icons and company logos

➤ Page layouts

➤ Combinations of lists and libraries in a site

Site templates are used to save a site that can then be recreated with its layouts, lists, and other elements already present. Without templates, these elements would have to be manually recreated for each new site. Figure 2-3 shows the form used when saving a site as a template, the items on the form are discussed below.

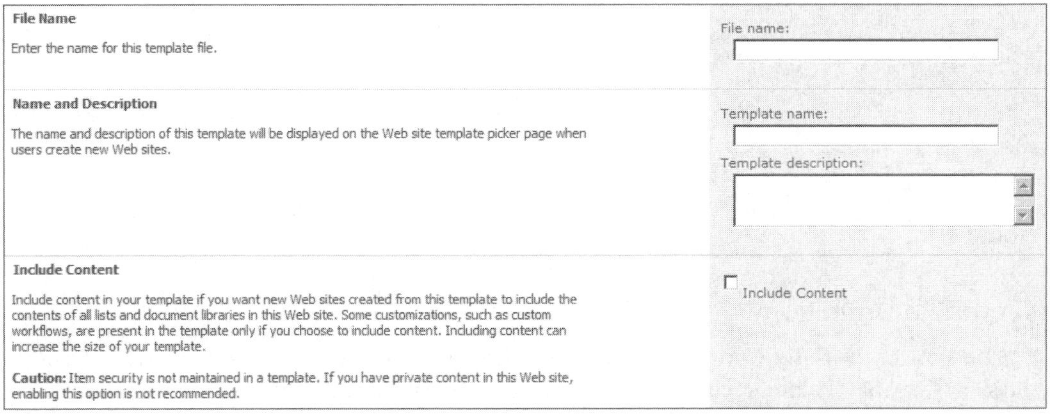

File Name
Enter the name for this template file.

File name:

Name and Description
The name and description of this template will be displayed on the Web site template picker page when users create new Web sites.

Template name:

Template description:

Include Content
Include content in your template if you want new Web sites created from this template to include the contents of all lists and document libraries in this Web site. Some customizations, such as custom workflows, are present in the template only if you choose to include content. Including content can increase the size of your template.

Caution: Item security is not maintained in a template. If you have private content in this Web site, enabling this option is not recommended.

☐ Include Content

FIGURE 2-3

➤ **File Name:** The template is saved as a file with the extension of `.wsp`. Enter the name for the file here.

➤ **Template Name:** When users create a new site using this template, the template name is what they see on the page where the new site is created and the list of available templates is displayed.

➤ **Template Description:** Next to the template name, users can see a description of what the template is for and what elements it contains. Fill out this item to provide the description. Figure 2-4 shows where the title and description are displayed on the Create Site dialog using a custom template.

➤ **Include Content:** Check this box if you want the list items added to lists and the documents added to libraries to be present in any new sites created from this template. Usually content is specific to the site on which it is created and you don't want to use this option. However, there are some scenarios where it makes sense:

    ➤ For lists that contain elements for drop-down options. Each site created from the template uses the same drop-down options.

    ➤ For custom pages you have created with custom branding.

    ➤ For other instances in which you want to keep Web Parts, list items, documents, or branding elements intact on each site.

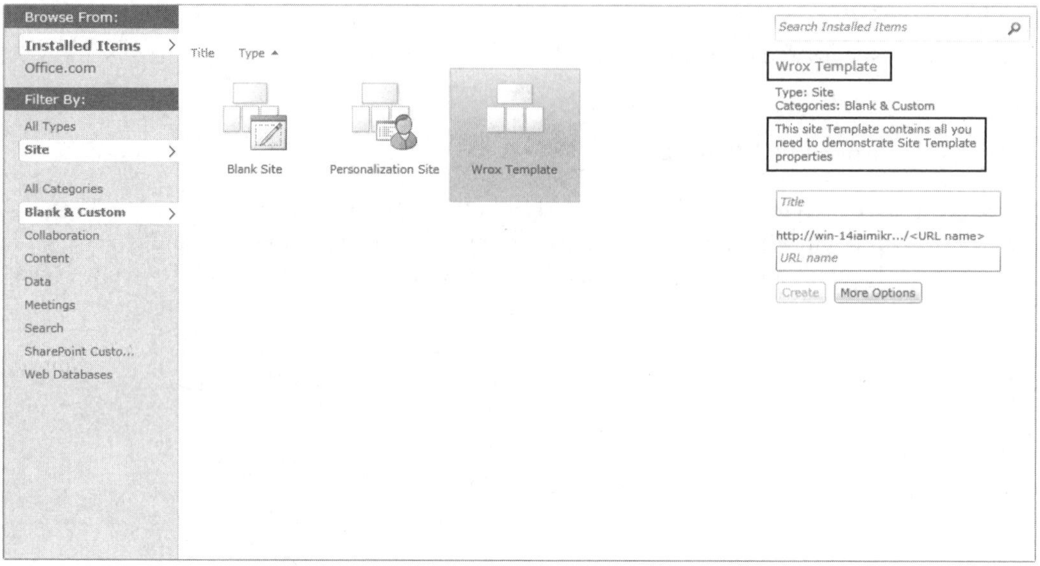

FIGURE 2-4

Reset to Site Definition

The purpose of the Reset to Site Definition link is to remove customizations that have been made to the site using SharePoint Designer. It is beyond the scope of this book to discuss the architectural implications of customizing a site with SharePoint Designer. Suffice it to say that if the farm administrators enable the use of SharePoint Designer on a SharePoint site, it is possible to create a wide range of customizations to that site. Sometimes these customizations cause unforeseen problems or the attempt just doesn't work out as planned. If you decide you want to revert to how the site looked when you first created it, clicking this link undoes any changes made to the site definition.

Note that not *every* change to a site is a customization that is undone by this command. Common changes to a site that can be reset this way include:

➤ Changes to the underlying layout pages and master pages of the site

➤ Data views

Examples of changes that cannot be undone by this command are:

➤ Web Parts added to pages

➤ Custom lists or libraries you have created

➤ Themes

➤ Changes made using the SharePoint UI

Using the Site Analytics Web Analytics Reports

Site analytics simply tell you how many people are looking at your site. SharePoint keeps statistics on how many pages are viewed, how many unique users visit the site, and various other metrics. To view these reports, an administrator has to turn on a service that collects the data. If this service is not set up, you will see the error in Figure 2-5.

Web analytics reports cannot be displayed because the web analytics service application is not provisioned
Contact the farm administrator to request that the web analytics service application be provisioned

FIGURE 2-5

In this case the SharePoint farm administrator needs to provision the Web Analytics service application. This function is beyond the rights level assigned to the average user in most SharePoint deployments. Once the service is provisioned, you will see the page in Figure 2-6.

Category	Metrics	Value (Current)	Value (Previous)	Trend
Traffic				
	Total Number of Page Views	134	2	6,600.00 %
	Average Number of Page Views per Day	4	0	-
	Total Number of Daily Unique Visitors	13	1	1,200.00 %
	Average Number of Unique Visitors per Day	0	0	-
	Total Number of Referrers	0	0	-
	Average Number of Referrers per Day	0	0	-
Inventory				
	Total Number of Sites	-	-	-

FIGURE 2-6

TRY IT

In this lesson we will review the items in the Site Actions menu and how they affect a SharePoint site.

Lesson Requirements

To complete this lesson, you will need the following:

➤ Access to a SharePoint site

➤ Administrator rights to the site

Hints

This lesson is a survey of the menu items in the Site Actions menu. The features you see in the video walkthrough and screenshots may be different from what you will see in your SharePoint farm. It is common for feature sets to differ from farm to farm.

Step-by-Step

First you will activate a site feature and see how it affects other elements of the site. Select the Site Settings option from the Site Actions drop-down menu in the upper left corner of the screen. Under the Site Actions header, select the Manage Site Features link.

1. Find the feature called Group Work Lists and click the Activate button. This feature creates some lists with some functionality for team and resource scheduling. Figure 2-7 shows this feature.

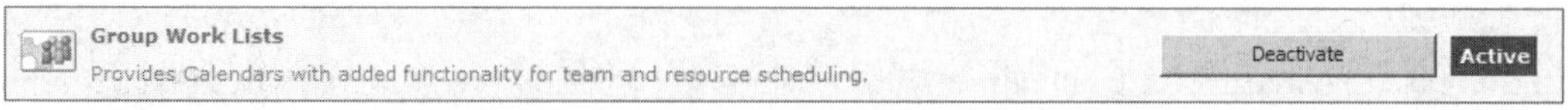

Group Work Lists
Provides Calendars with added functionality for team and resource scheduling.

Deactivate   Active

FIGURE 2-7

2. Select the View All Site Content link in the Site Actions drop-down menu, which remains in the upper-left corner of the screen. Notice in Figure 2-8 how three new lists have been created as a result of the feature's activation: Phone Call Memo, Resources, and Whereabouts. Every feature is different, but activating a feature frequently creates these kinds of changes to a site — creating new elements, adding new options to the toolbar, and so on.

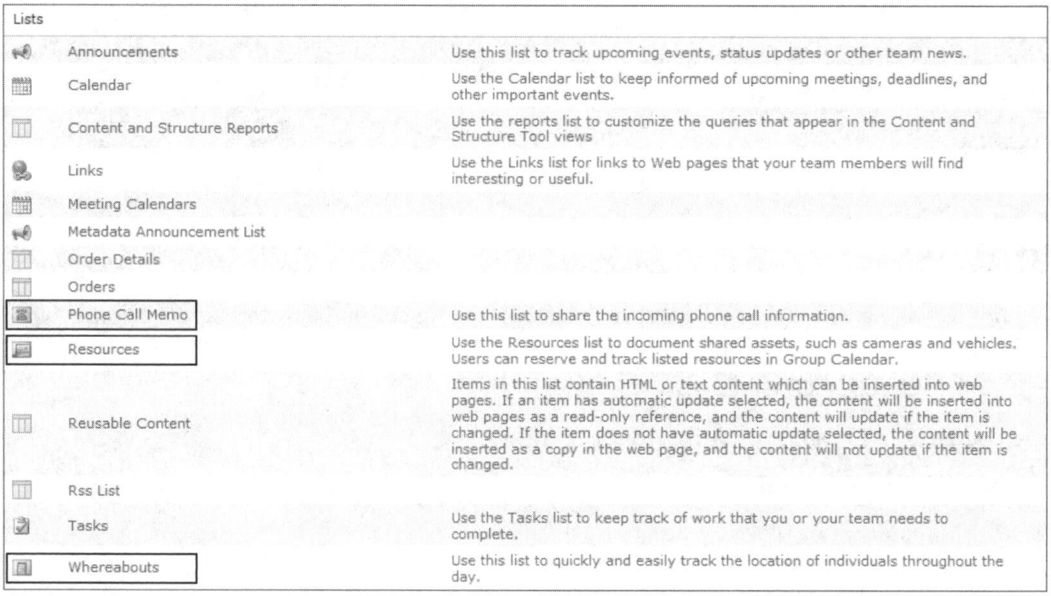

Lists	
Announcements	Use this list to track upcoming events, status updates or other team news.
Calendar	Use the Calendar list to keep informed of upcoming meetings, deadlines, and other important events.
Content and Structure Reports	Use the reports list to customize the queries that appear in the Content and Structure Tool views
Links	Use the Links list for links to Web pages that your team members will find interesting or useful.
Meeting Calendars	
Metadata Announcement List	
Order Details	
Orders	
Phone Call Memo	Use this list to share the incoming phone call information.
Resources	Use the Resources list to document shared assets, such as cameras and vehicles. Users can reserve and track listed resources in Group Calendar.
Reusable Content	Items in this list contain HTML or text content which can be inserted into web pages. If an item has automatic update selected, the content will be inserted into web pages as a read-only reference, and the content will update if the item is changed. If the item does not have automatic update selected, the content will be inserted as a copy in the web page, and the content will not update if the item is changed.
Rss List	
Tasks	Use the Tasks list to keep track of work that you or your team needs to complete.
Whereabouts	Use this list to quickly and easily track the location of individuals throughout the day.

FIGURE 2-8

3. The next action in the Site Actions menu is to save a site as a template. To save a site as a template, click the Save Site as Template link in the Site Actions menu.

4. Fill out the form and click OK. The site and all of its settings, lists, and options will now be available as a choice when you create new sites. The file is also available in the Solutions gallery as a .wsp file. The Solutions gallery is introduced in Lesson 7. You can take this file and use it in other areas of the SharePoint farm or upload it into completely separate SharePoint

installations. Figure 2-9 shows the template form you must fill out to save a site as a template. Galleries are discussed in more detail in Lesson 7.

File Name

Enter the name for this template file.

File name:

Name and Description

The name and description of this template will be displayed on the Web site template picker page when users create new Web sites.

Template name:

Template description:

Include Content

Include content in your template if you want new Web sites created from this template to include the contents of all lists and document libraries in this Web site. Some customizations, such as custom workflows, are present in the template only if you choose to include content. Including content can increase the size of your template.

Caution: Item security is not maintained in a template. If you have private content in this Web site, enabling this option is not recommended.

☐ Include Content

FIGURE 2-9

5. The next link in the Site Actions menu is the Reset to Site Definition link. This command will give you two options for resetting any customizations you have made to the page. The first option is to reset an individual page whose address you provide. The second option is to reset the entire site. Figure 2-10 shows this page.

Reset to Site Definition

If you want to remove all customizations from a page (such as changes to Web Part zones or text added to the page) you can use this feature to reset to the version of the page included with the site definition.

You can reset a single page within your site to use the version of the page included in the site definition, or you can reset all pages.

Caution: When you reset to the site definition version, you will lose all customizations made to the current version of the page. No backup copy of the page will be made before the page is updated, and no new version is created.

◉ Reset specific page to site definition version
Local URL for the page

Example: "http://server/site/default.aspx"

○ Reset all pages in this site to site definition version

FIGURE 2-10

6. Click the View the Web Analytics reports link.

There are two sets of analytics reports, one for the site and one for the site collection. You will see the site collection link only if you have Site Collection Administrator rights. If you are an owner for this site only and not for the site collection (the difference is discussed in Lesson 8) you will see only one link for the site-level reports.

Please select Lesson 2 on the DVD or visit www.wrox.com/go/sp2010-24 *to view the video that accompanies this lesson.*

3

Changing a Site's Look and Feel

On the Site Settings page is a heading titled Look and Feel. Under this heading are several links that are used to alter aspects of the SharePoint site's user interface. The Look and Feel commands give users with Site Owner or Designer permissions the ability to make some basic branding and navigation changes. In this lesson we examine these options. In Lesson 4 we discuss creating custom themes.

TITLE, DESCRIPTION, AND ICON

Clicking on the Title, Description, and Icon link under the Look and Feel heading takes you to the Title, Description, and Icon screen. This screen enables you to upload a custom logo to add some branding to your site. The title and description are displayed to the right of the logo. Figure 3-1 shows where the icon, title, and description elements are positioned on the page in the upper left corner of the screen.

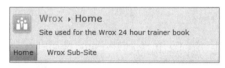

FIGURE 3-1

DISPLAYING NAVIGATION OPTIONS

A SharePoint site has two main navigation sections, a top link bar that usually displays sites below the current site and a left-side navigation element that is commonly referred to as the Quick Launch section. The Quick Launch section is normally used to display elements in the site, such as lists, document libraries, or web pages that have been created. Both menus are fully customizable by site administrators, and you can put links to anything you like on either the top bar or the Quick Launch section.

Figure 3-2 shows the menu for modifying the Quick Launch and Top Link bar navigation elements.

The tree view option shows the various lists, libraries, and sub-sites along the left side of the screen. This view can be used along with or in place of the Quick Launch menu. Unlike the Quick Launch menu, the tree view cannot be customized on the Site Settings screen. Figure 3-3 shows the tree view of a sample site. Notice that the last link is to a sub-site.

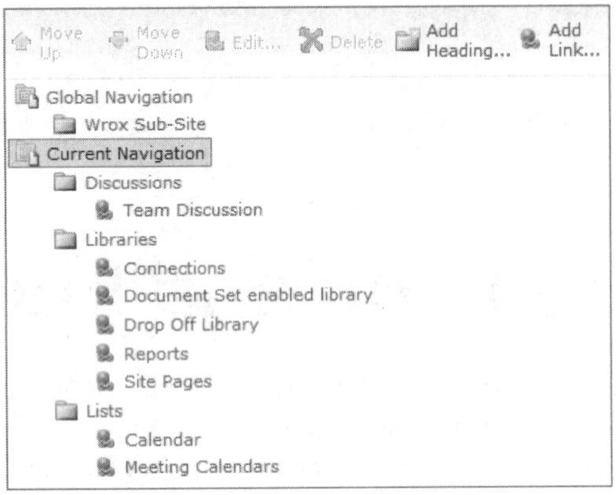

FIGURE 3-2

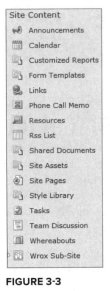

FIGURE 3-3

TRY IT

In this Try It, we will examine and configure the options available in the Look and Feel menu on the Site Settings page.

Lesson Requirements

To perform this lesson, you will need the following:

➤ Access to a SharePoint site

➤ Administrator or Designer rights to the site

Hints

This lesson is a survey of the Site Administration menu. It covers only the most common elements among all SharePoint sites. A lot of the links you see that are not covered in this lesson are related to optional features, some of which are covered in other lessons in this book.

Step-by-Step

1. Navigate to the Site Settings page and find the Look and Feel heading. Click the Title link, description, and icon. On the Title, Description, and Icon page (see Figure 3-4), enter a value for the title, the description, and a URL that is a link to an image that you want to place on the screen on your site. It is common to store the image you want to use on your site in a library on the site itself.

FIGURE 3-4

2. Figure 3-5 shows how the changes to the Title field, the Description field, and the Logo URL will show on the page. The Title field is circled. The description is underlined, and the logo is circled. One important thing to keep in mind is that if the URL you choose for your logo is not

FIGURE 3-5

accessible to a visitor to your site, the visitor will not see the site logo. In this case, she will see whatever you place in the description field below it, or a red X if you leave this field blank.

3. On the Site Settings page, under the Look and Feel heading, the Tree View link enables you to select navigation options for the left side of the screen. Enabling the Quick Launch option will show the Quick Launch links, which can be added for each element that you add to a site, such as a list, library, or picture. Enabling the Tree View option shows a collapsible view of every site element, grouped by type of content. Select the Tree View checkbox and return to the home page of your site to see how the selection affects the navigation. See Figure 3-6 for a screenshot of the tree view.

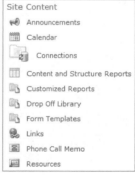

FIGURE 3-6

Please select Lesson 3 on the DVD or visit www.wrox.com/go/sp2010-24 *to view the video that accompanies this lesson.*

4

Using Custom Themes

A SharePoint theme is a quick means by which a user can apply some branding to his or her site, primarily with text and background color schemes. The advantage of themes is that they are available to any user with owner or designer rights on the site and do not require administrative or developer resources to create. Themes have changed quite a bit from previous versions of SharePoint, offering more flexibility in some areas and less in others. In this lesson we examine the process for creating a simple theme using the SharePoint UI and also walk through an example of creating a theme for your SharePoint site using Microsoft Office 2010 products.

ACCESSING THE SITE THEMES PAGE

Custom themes are created on the Site Themes page. The link to this page is located on the Site Settings page, under the Look and Feel heading. Access to the link requires either owner or designer permissions on the site.

First, access the Settings page by expanding the Site Actions menu. The Site Settings link is the last link on the Site Actions drop-down menu. See Figure 4-1.

On the Settings page, under the Look and Feel heading, click the link titled Site Theme. Figure 4-2 shows the options under the Look and Feel heading, including the link to the Site Themes page.

FIGURE 4-1

FIGURE 4-2

CREATING A THEME

The themes page is divided into three sections. Let's take a look at what you need to do in each to create your theme.

Select a Theme

Figure 4-3 shows the list of available themes. Each theme's associated color scheme is displayed on the left side of the screen.

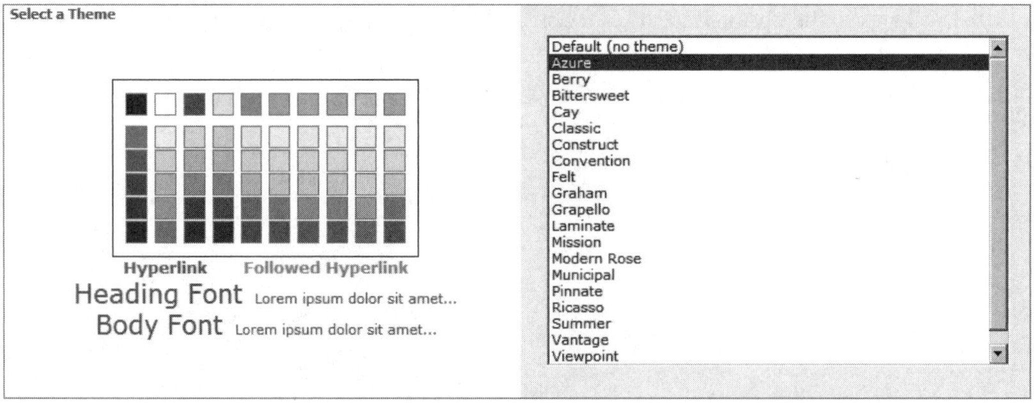

Select a Theme

Hyperlink   Followed Hyperlink

Heading Font Lorem ipsum dolor sit amet...
Body Font Lorem ipsum dolor sit amet...

Default (no theme)
Azure
Berry
Bittersweet
Cay
Classic
Construct
Convention
Felt
Graham
Grapello
Laminate
Mission
Modern Rose
Municipal
Pinnate
Ricasso
Summer
Vantage
Viewpoint

FIGURE 4-3

Changing your theme selection changes the color schemes. Later in this lesson we'll look at how the different columns displaying the color scheme correspond to various elements in the SharePoint site. For now, browse through the theme choices on the right and select one that looks appealing. For this chapter I'm using Azure.

Customizing Themes

After you have chosen your basic color scheme you can customize it for each major color category in the theme and for unselected and selected hyperlink colors. In addition you can choose the prevailing fonts for headings and body text on the site. You have a much greater ability to customize your theme than in previous versions of SharePoint, in which the color scheme was much more of a take-it-or-leave-it proposition, unless you were prepared to do some more serious customization work beyond the level of the average user. Figure 4-4 shows how the interface for customizing the color scheme is presented to the user.

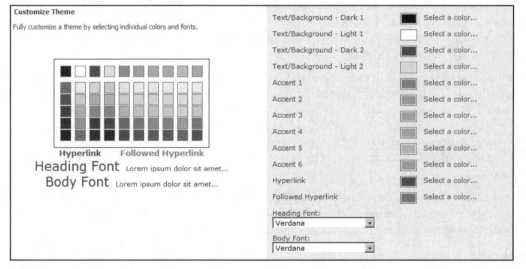

FIGURE 4-4

Notice the 10 columns in the color scheme squares on the left. (The page does not appear this way on the site; the color scheme squares have been transposed in this figure for clarity.) From left to right, the columns relate to the first 10 items on the right side of the screen, the four text/background colors and the six accents. In addition, you can modify the color of hyperlinks and previously selected hyperlinks. Finally, the two drop-down boxes enable you to change the font types of headings and the body fonts. A lot of the customization process is going to be trial and error to work out the shades of color you like for each column and where you want those colors to appear on the page.

Selecting Colors

When you click the Select a Color link next to a section, you are presented with the screen shown in Figure 4-5.

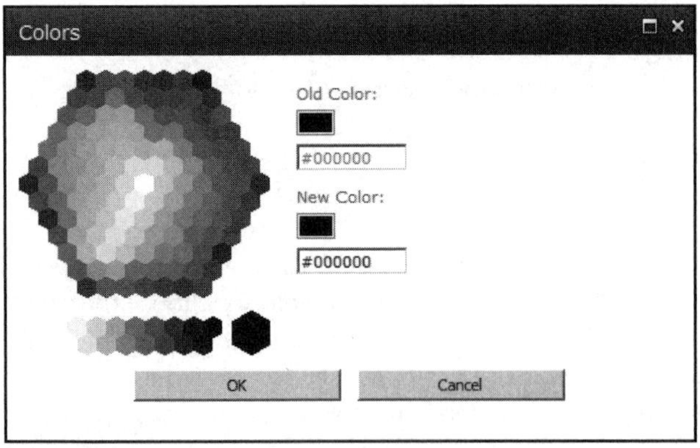

FIGURE 4-5

At this point you have two options for selecting a custom color. The first and simplest is to select a color on the color wheel and click OK. You will notice a box under the heading New Color, whose value changes as you select colors on the color wheel. The other color-selection option is to enter your own color value in this box.

The advantage of typing your own value in this box is that it enables you to choose from a vast array of shades far beyond what is available on the color wheel. The disadvantage is that the color box requires you to enter a value in hexadecimal format. This is why the number in the box is preceded by a number sign (#). However, unless you spent your high school and/or college years programming for fun and playing Dungeons and Dragons on the weekend, you may not have any idea what hexadecimal numbers are. Here is a crash course on picking colors using hexadecimal notation.

Notice that the color number consists of six digits. This does not represent one large number but in fact is three two-digit numbers, each with a value between zero and 255. The first two digits designate the level of red shading, the second green, and the third blue.

With normal numbers you enter the digits 0 through 9. With hexadecimal notation you can enter the digits 0 through 9 and the letters A through F. Don't worry about how it works, just understand that A is 10, B is 11, and so forth. The largest value you can enter for any two digits is FF (representing 255) and the smallest is 00. For example, if you want pure red you enter #FF0000. The number sign (#) is required for hexadecimal notation, the FF for the first two digits maxes out the red shading. The second two digits represent zero, or no green and the last two digits indicate no blue shading at all. From there you can create any shade you want by modifying the mix of red, blue, and green shades.

Preview the Theme

Figure 4-6 shows the Preview button at the bottom of the page. Use this button if you want to see what the theme will look like before you actually make the change.

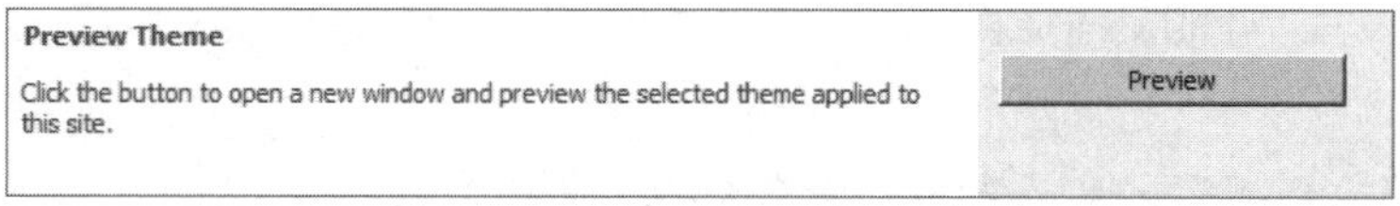

Preview Theme

Click the button to open a new window and preview the selected theme applied to this site.

Preview

FIGURE 4-6

This is also a good way to see how your modifications to color choices will look.

TRY IT

In this section, you open Microsoft PowerPoint 2010 and create a theme for a PowerPoint presentation from a list of available choices. Then you save that theme, import it into SharePoint, and apply it to a SharePoint site.

Lesson Requirements

➤   A SharePoint site and Microsoft Office PowerPoint 2010.

Hints

You can also use Microsoft Word to create custom themes similar to what is shown in this walkthrough.

Step-by-Step

1.   Open Microsoft PowerPoint 2010.

2.   Click the Design tab on the top menu bar.

3.   In the Theme group of toolbars, select a theme for the presentation.

4.   Click the File tab on the top menu bar, select Save As, and choose to save as type office theme. Save the presentation to your machine. The file will have a .thmx extension. The Save As dialog box is shown in Figure 4-7.

5.   Open your SharePoint site and browse to the Site Settings page. Under the Galleries page, select Themes. The Galleries menu is shown in Figure 4-8.

6.   On the Themes gallery page, select the Documents option under Library Tools. Then select Upload Document, as shown in Figure 4-9.

7.   Browse to where you saved the file in Step 4 and select it. Add a description if you wish, and then click Save. See Figure 4-10.

8.   Look at the list in the Themes gallery. You should now see the theme you just uploaded.

9.   Browse to the Theme selection page as described earlier in the chapter (Site Actions ➪ Site Settings ➪ Select a Theme link under the Look and Feel heading).

10. In the list of themes, you should see the theme you uploaded to the gallery. Select it and click Apply. Notice the change in color scheme on the page.

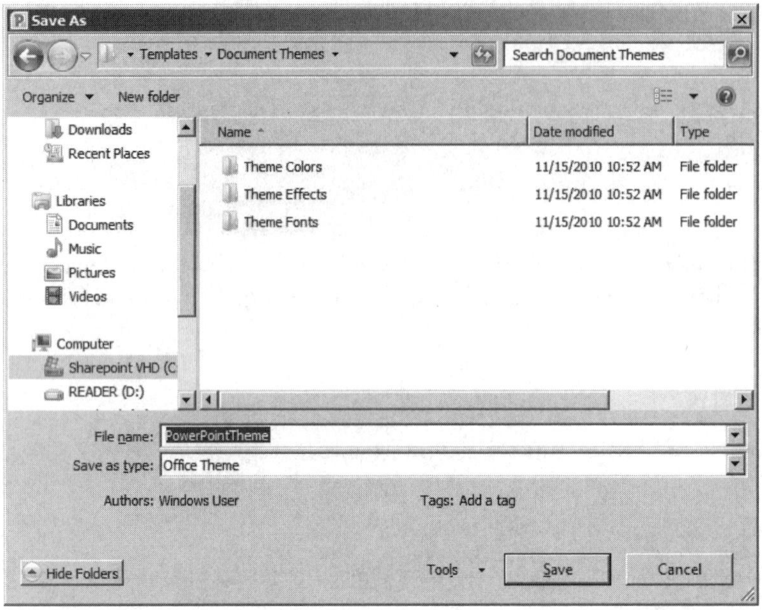

![Save As dialog box]

FIGURE 4-7

FIGURE 4-8

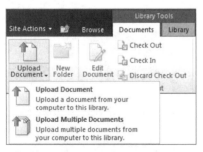

FIGURE 4-9

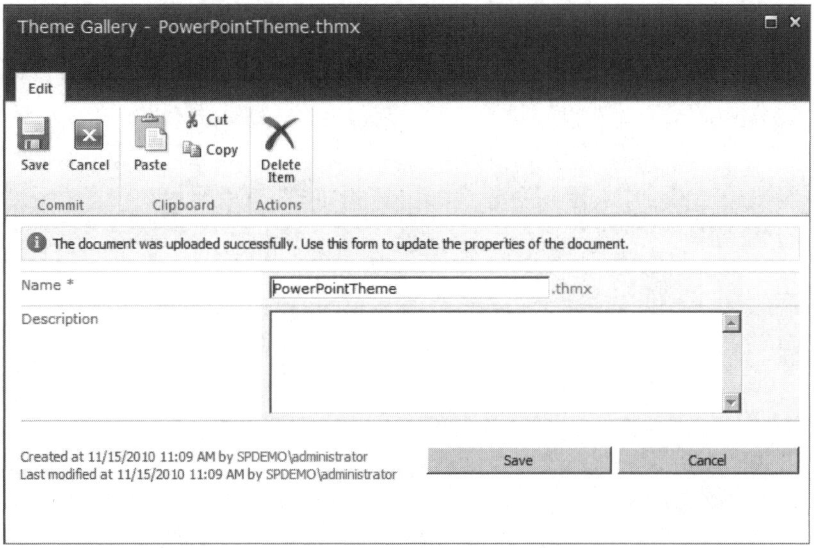

FIGURE 4-10

You can also select and export themes from Microsoft Word and you can import them into SharePoint.

Please select Lesson 4 on the DVD or visit www.wrox.com/go/sp2010-24 to view the video that accompanies this lesson.

Managing Reporting Services

On the Site Settings page of a SharePoint site is a heading called Reporting Services. SharePoint site administrators can use these settings to schedule and display reports created from a tool called Reporting Services. Typically the reports created from this tool pull data from an external data source or a SharePoint list, and present a view of that data on the report.

This lesson shows you how to use Reporting Services to schedule the report and display it in a document library. By scheduling the report, we mean periodically refreshing the information from the report's data source. This lesson assumes someone else has already configured the Reporting Services tool and created the report. What follows is a brief description of the Reporting Services tool, whose use is beyond the scope of this lesson.

Reporting Services is a feature of SQL Server that can be integrated with SharePoint. It enables a SharePoint site owner to make schedules for creating reports and for viewing reports via SharePoint that were created in Reporting Services. The initial setup and configuration of Reporting Services is quite complex: a SQL server database administrator and a SharePoint administrator must work together to enable SharePoint Server to act as a reporting portal.

After Reporting Services is configured, reports can be created in SQL Server and published to a location on a SharePoint Server site. Alternatively, they can be uploaded to a document library and placed on a schedule to run automatically. This lesson deals only with how to set a report schedule and enable some Reporting Services settings. It is beyond the scope of this lesson to discuss the setup and configuration of Reporting Services or to delve into the details of how the reports are created. The goal of this lesson is to show you the final product of the Reporting Services application and to walk through the configuration options open to SharePoint site administrators.

MANAGE THE SHARED SCHEDULE

The Shared Schedule page is used to create a schedule on which to run reports that are on the SharePoint site. After the schedule is created and named, it can be assigned to any given report. For example, a manager may wish to see an updated copy of a status report weekly. In SharePoint the report can be published to a document library, and items created in the library can use the schedule to automatically update according to the schedule assigned to it. Schedules are created under the Manage Shared Schedule link in the Reporting Services section on the Site Settings page. Reports used in this fashion are created using a program called Report Builder that is part of the SQL Server 2008 R2 Reporting Services toolkit. A completed report can be uploaded into a SharePoint library and assigned to a schedule. Incidentally, you can download Report Builder 3.0 for free from `http://www.microsoft.com`.

REPORTING SERVICES SITE SETTINGS

On the Site Settings Page page is a heading titled Reporting Services. Clicking on the Reporting Services Site Settings link under this heading reveals a small menu consisting of three checkboxes.

Enable RSClientPrint ActiveX Control Download

Check the Enable RSClientPrint Active X Control Download checkbox if you want to allow users to download an ActiveX control that can give them printing functionality for reports from their browsers. (An ActiveX control is a sort of mini-program that is downloaded to the browser and provides extra features.) A user must also take action to ensure the ActiveX control is downloaded and installed. If you do not check the Enable RSClientPrint Active X Control Download checkbox users will not have the option to download the additional control and take advantage of the print options.

Enable Local Mode Error Messages

In order to display information in reports on the browser, SharePoint uses a control behind the scenes called the Report Viewer. In previous versions of SQL Server before 2008 R2, your SharePoint farm had to be integrated with your Reporting Services server that processes the reports in order to view them in a SharePoint document library. New to SQL Server 2008 R2 is a method for rendering reports from Reporting Services without integrating the SharePoint farm with a Reporting Services server. Using the Report Viewer control to view reports from a Reporting Services server not integrated with SharePoint is referred to as being in *local mode*. If you wish to view detailed error messages from reports while using this disconnected mode, select the Enable Local Error Messages checkbox. Local mode can be useful for troubleshooting, but it is generally considered poor form for production applications to display detailed error messages, and in some cases it is a security risk. Reports using local mode are more likely to produce errors because of the additional configuration and security concerns. The purpose of this checkbox is to make this troubleshooting easier. It should be unchecked once the reports are working properly.

For additional information on local mode, refer to the following Microsoft documentation: `http://msdn.microsoft.com/en-us/library/ff487969(v=SQL.105).aspx`.

Enable Accessibility Metadata for Reports

Checking the Enable Accessibility Metadata for Reports checkbox will enable the report to output metadata that defines accessibility options for people with disabilities. For example, the report may be able to note the availability of Braille formats, audio descriptions, and other such features.

TRY IT

In this exercise, you will create a shared schedule and see how you can use it to set a schedule for a report to be run in a SharePoint farm that is using Reporting Services.

Lesson Requirements

To perform this lesson, you will need the following:

➤ Access to a SharePoint site.

➤ Administrator rights to the site.

➤ SharePoint Reporting Services set up in SharePoint integrated or local mode on SQL Server. This setup work is beyond the scope of this book. This lesson assumes that a SharePoint farm administrator or SQL database administrator has set up the prerequisite elements for making Reporting Services available on a SharePoint site.

Hints

The document library in this example has been configured to allow content types. There is a specific content type for these type of reports called "Report Builder Report" that should be added to the document library as an available content type.

Step-by-Step

Follow these steps to complete the lesson:

1. On the Site Settings page for your site, browse to the section titled Reporting Services (see Figure 5-1). If you do not see this section, you should verify that you have a Reporting Services service running in integrated mode on your SharePoint farm. Click the Manage Shared Schedules link.

Reporting Services
Manage Shared Schedules
Reporting Services Site Settings

FIGURE 5-1

2. Click Add Schedule in the command bar (see Figure 5-2).

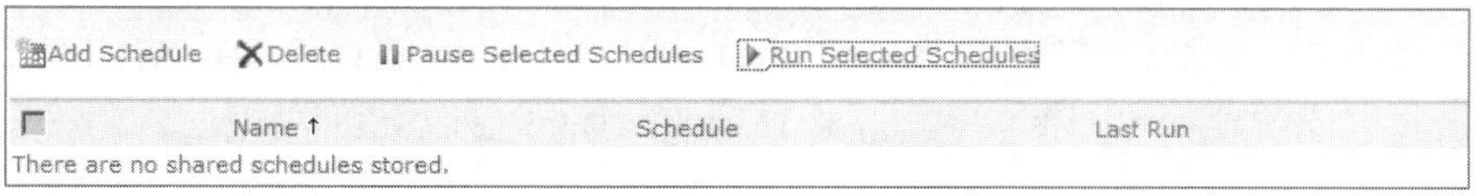

Add Schedule   Delete   Pause Selected Schedules   Run Selected Schedules

	Name ↑	Schedule	Last Run
There are no shared schedules stored.

FIGURE 5-2

3. Set the options (see Figure 5-3) for how often you would like the report to be processed. Click OK.

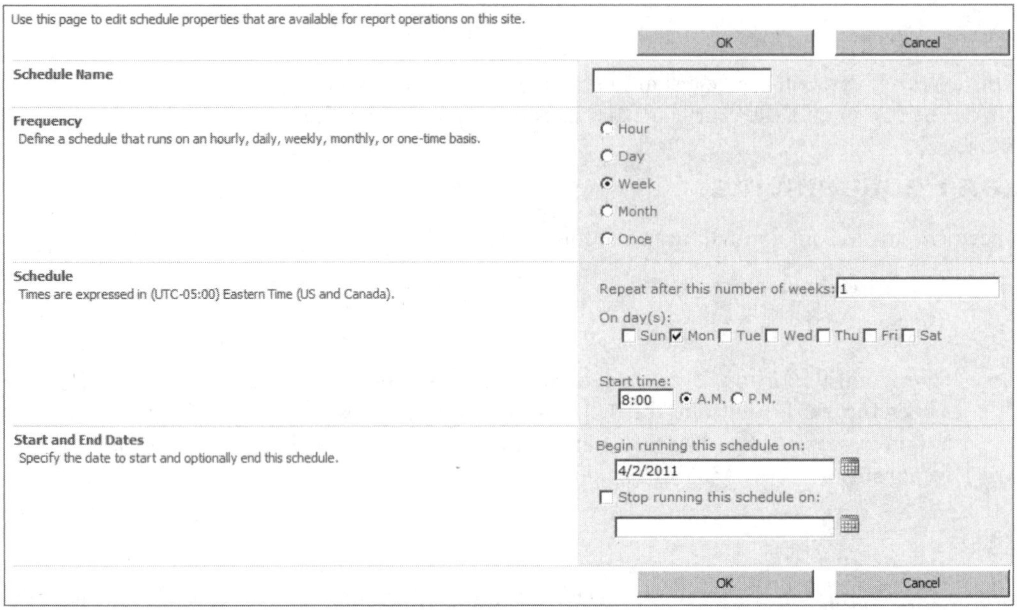

Use this page to edit schedule properties that are available for report operations on this site.

| OK | Cancel |

Schedule Name

Frequency
Define a schedule that runs on an hourly, daily, weekly, monthly, or one-time basis.

- ○ Hour
- ○ Day
- ● Week
- ○ Month
- ○ Once

Schedule
Times are expressed in (UTC-05:00) Eastern Time (US and Canada).

Repeat after this number of weeks: 1

On day(s):
☐ Sun ☑ Mon ☐ Tue ☐ Wed ☐ Thu ☐ Fri ☐ Sat

Start time:
8:00 ● A.M. ○ P.M.

Start and End Dates
Specify the date to start and optionally end this schedule.

Begin running this schedule on:
4/2/2011

☐ Stop running this schedule on:

| OK | Cancel |

FIGURE 5-3

4. Browse to a document library in which you have Reporting Services reports. It is possible to define the output to a SharePoint library automatically in Reporting Services. For the purposes of this walkthrough, the report has been manually uploaded to the document library, as opposed to the output of the report automatically appearing in the library after it runs. In addition, we have added the Report Builder Report content type to the library, which will enable scheduling and other options for our report document.

5. This example uses an uploaded .rdl file (a Reporting Services report) to our document library and assigned it the content type of Report Builder Report. In Figure 5-4 you can see the options available in the drop-down menu.

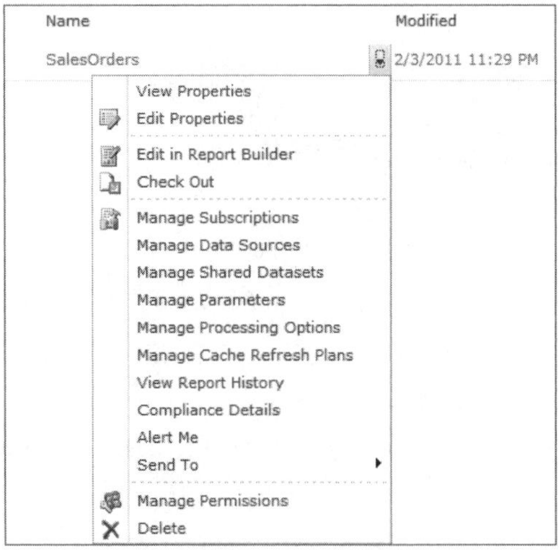

Name	Modified
SalesOrders	2/3/2011 11:29 PM

View Properties
Edit Properties

Edit in Report Builder
Check Out

Manage Subscriptions
Manage Data Sources
Manage Shared Datasets
Manage Parameters
Manage Processing Options
Manage Cache Refresh Plans
View Report History
Compliance Details
Alert Me
Send To ▶

Manage Permissions
✕ Delete

FIGURE 5-4

6. Select the option Manage Processing Options. Notice that under the History Snapshot Options (Figure 5-5) there is a checkbox titled Create Report History Snapshots on a Schedule. The schedule can be customized for this report or you can use the shared schedule that you just created in Step 3.

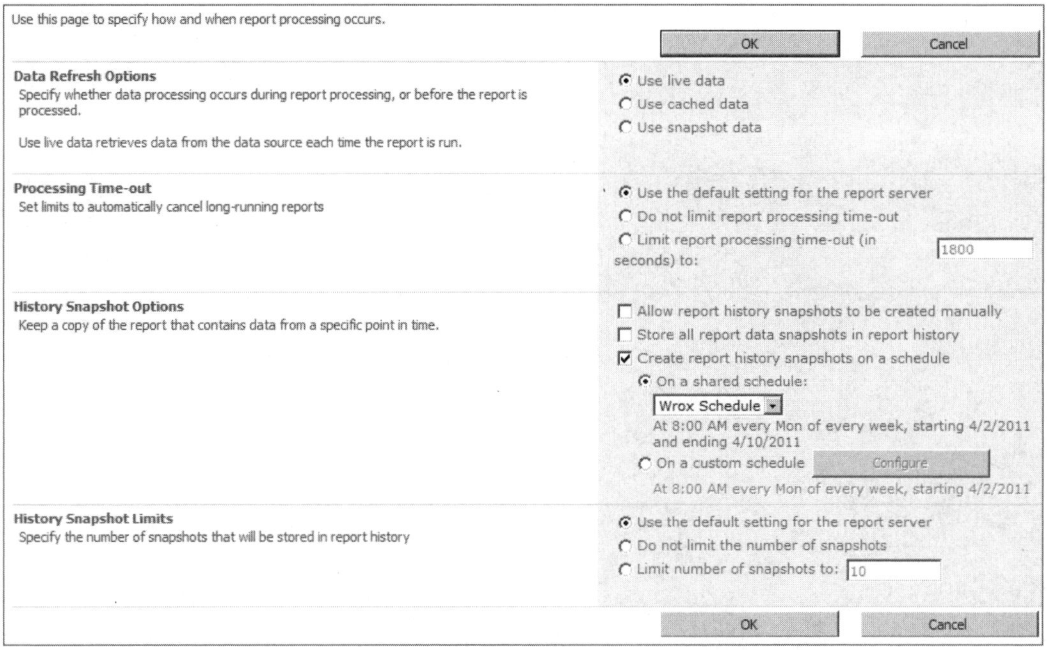

FIGURE 5-5

Please select Lesson 5 on the DVD or visit www.wrox.com/go/sp2010-24 to view the video that accompanies this lesson.

SECTION II
Administration at the Site Collection Level

6

Site Collection Administration Settings

Individual web sites are the main context, through which most people experience and think about SharePoint. A site is a visible part of the portal and is easy to understand. A site collection, on the other hand, is an abstract administrative entity. In this lesson we discuss the purpose of the site collection and cover some of the administrative options available at the site collection level. Many of the site collection administrative options not covered in this lesson, such as search settings, are covered in other lessons.

DEFINING SITE COLLECTIONS

A site collection is a group of individual SharePoint sites, grouped together to form a major administrative boundary. A lot of SharePoint features and functions are designed to work across sites but not across site collections. This boundary allows for different settings and configurations for groups of sites that have a clearly separate purpose. Site collections can be created at the farm level by farm administrators or, if the Configure Self-Service Site Creation option has been enabled by the farm administrator, site collections can be created by end users. The Configure Self-Service Site Creation option can be enabled in the Central Administration website in the Site Collections heading in the Application Management section of Central Administration.

Each site collection has a top-level site, also known as a *root site*. On the settings page of this site you'll find the site collection administrative options.

Following are a few examples of the SharePoint configurations that are restricted to an individual site collection. Each site collection will have its own set of configurations, named administrators, and other elements.

> ➤ **Site Collection Administrators:** A site collection administrator has absolute rights on any site within the site collection. These rights cannot be removed by the enforcement of unique permissions on sites, lists, or items at any level. The link to set site collection administrators is found under the Users and Permissions heading of the settings page of

the top-level site of the site collection. Figure 6-1 shows the
section of the Site Settings page where you can add site
collection administrators by clicking on the Site Collection
Administrators link.

FIGURE 6-1

➤ **Navigation:** Within a site collection, navigation items can be
configured to appear identically on every site. However, sites in
one site collection will not use the navigation items configured in another site collection.

SITE COLLECTION ADMINISTRATIVE OPTIONS

You can see site collection administrative options only in the
Site Settings page of the top-level site of the site collection. If you
visit the Site Settings page of any child site you will see only a link
to the site collection administrative options. If you don't see any
link at all, you are not listed on the site as a site collection admin-

FIGURE 6-2

istrator. Figure 6-2 shows a link on the settings page of a sub site to the Site Collection Administration
options on the root site. If you are on the root site you will instead see a full range of options.

Table 6-1 lists various options and the settings that are necessary for various Site Collection
Administration options to display on the screen. You will only see the link on the left side of the
table if the prerequisite is met on the right side of the table.

TABLE 6-1

SITE COLLECTION ADMINISTRATIVE LINK PREREQUISITES	
LINK	**PREREQUISITE**
FAST Search Keywords	FAST Search installed on the farm and SharePoint Server Enterprise Site Collection feature activated
FAST Search Site Promotion and Demotion	FAST Search installed on the farm and SharePoint Server Enterprise Site Collection feature activated
FAST Search User Context	FAST Search installed on the farm and SharePoint Server Enterprise Site Collection feature activated
Content Type Service Application Error Log	Content Type Syndication Hub feature activated for the site collection
Document ID Settings	Document ID Service feature activated for the site collection
Record Declaration Settings	In Place Records Management feature activated for the site collection
Variations Variation Labels Variation Logs Translatable Columns Suggested Content Browser Locations	SharePoint Server Publishing Infrastructure feature activated for the site collection

The following links do not have any prerequisites. They always display in the Site Collections Administration menu if you are using SharePoint Server. Many of these links do not exist if you are using only SharePoint Foundation.

➤ **Recycle Bin:** The recycle bin is used to allow Site Collection Administrators to restore content that has been deleted. The recycle bin at the site collection level is known as the "second stage" recycle bin. Items only end up here after they have already been removed from site level recycle bins.

➤ **Site Collection Features:** This page activates different functionality that will affect all of the sites in the current site collection.

➤ **Site Hierarchy:** This page that shows all of the sub sites in this site collection.

➤ **Site Navigation:** This page contains options for how navigation options can be displayed across the site collection.

➤ **Site Collection Audit Settings:** This page contains options for how the content of the site collection can be audited and the audit logs stored in a separate database.

➤ **Portal Site Connection:** It is possible to have several (even hundreds or thousands) of site collections. You can use the portal site connection page to link them to an overall corporate portal site. The main benefit of this is to have a breadcrumb navigation element that will always link to the top level portal site, no matter how far down into the navigation you may be. SharePoint designer settings: On this page you can restrict what a user can do on this site collection with the SharePoint Designer program.

➤ **Visual Upgrade:** If you have upgraded from the previous version of SharePoint, but have maintained the old user interface, this page contains options to upgrade the interface to the 2010 version.

➤ **Help Settings:** On this page, you can choose which topics to display on the help screens, when a user clicks the help icon on the screen.

TRY IT

In this walkthrough, you will configure several site collection level settings.

Lesson Requirements

To perform this lesson you will need the following:

➤ Access to a SharePoint site

➤ Site collection administrator rights on the site collection

Hints

This lesson is a survey of the Site Collection Administration menu. Some elements of Site Collection Administration, such as search settings, are covered in other lessons which are targeted to those features.

Step-by-Step

Follow these instructions to complete the lesson:

1. Navigate to the Site Settings page via the Site Actions menu. If you see a link as shown in Figure 6-3, it means you are in a subsite of the site collection, and not the top-level root site. You can only access the Site Collection Administration menu from the top-level site of a site collection.

FIGURE 6-3

Fortunately, if you click on the link, you will be taken to the root level Site Settings page and you will see the menu as shown in Figure 6-4. Note that the exact list of options should be similar, but not necessarily identical.

2. Click on the Recycle Bin link. That will take you to the Recycle Bin page as shown in Figure 6-5. The site collection level recycle bin is a second level recycle bin. When a user deletes an item, it is first stored in that site's recycle bin for a period of time as set by configuration options. After that time expires, or if a user empties the site level recycle bin, the content is moved to the site collection level recycle bin, where you have one more chance to reclaim it before it is permanently deleted. Notice on the recycle bin page at the site collection level you have 2 options on the left hand side, including End User Recycle Bin Items and Deleted from End User Recycle Bin. The former displays a view of items still in the site level recycle bin, while the latter displays items in the site collection level recycle bin. Restoring an item places it back on the site. Deleting it removes it permanently if in the site collection level bin. If in a site level bin, deleting it removes it from the site level to the site collection level recycle bin.

FIGURE 6-4

FIGURE 6-5

3. Click on the Site Collection Features link. Figure 6-6 shows a sample of the features listed on this page. The important thing to remember about this page is that many elements of SharePoint functionality must be activated at the site or site collection level, or both, in order to function properly.

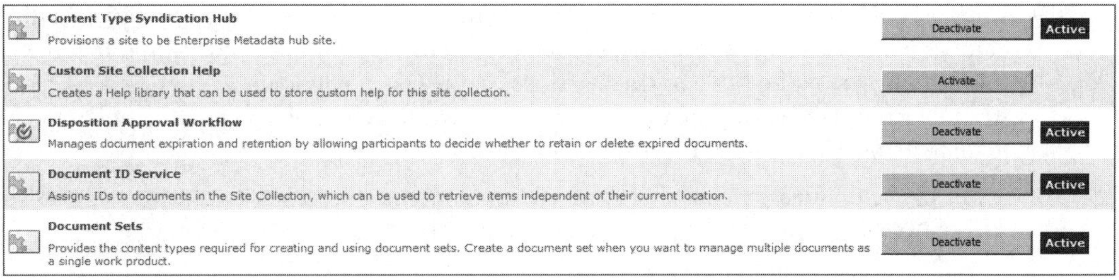

FIGURE 6-6

Some common points of confusion among inexperienced SharePoint users or administrators that are caused by inactive features include:

1. Not finding web parts in the web part list when trying to add them to a page.

2. Not having access to publishing features and web parts unless the publishing features are activated at both the site and site collection levels.

3. Not having access to site or list templates when creating new sites or lists.

Take a moment to look at the list of features on this page and how they may relate to functionality you want active on your site collection. Looking for inactive features should always be one of your first options when you cannot find a certain type of SharePoint functionality.

4. Click on the Navigation Settings link. This will open the Navigation Settings page as shown in Figure 6-7.

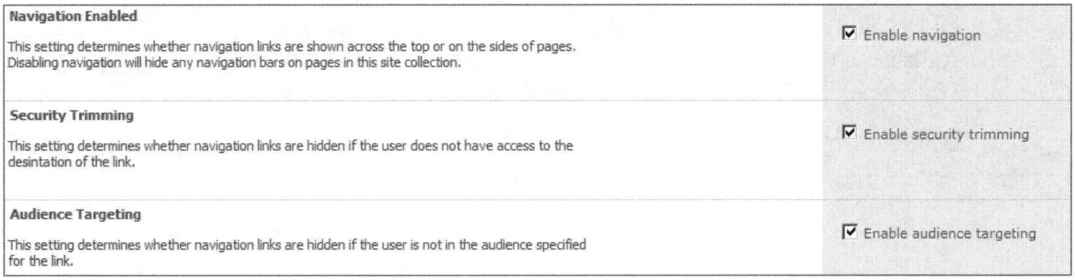

FIGURE 6-7

The Enable navigation button changes navigation behavior. Figure 6-8 shows a site with navigation enabled.

Figure 6-9 shows a site with navigation disabled. Note how the links across the top and left side are gone.

Disabling the security trimming button allows people to see links even if they do not have rights to the page it links to. This is sometimes desirable as a user may require access to a page and not realize it exists if they never see the link.

Disabling audience targeting will remove the ability to target navigation links to a certain group of users based on group membership.

5. Click on the link titled Site Collection Audit Settings. This will open the Configure Audit Settings page. This page allows you to configure auditing for the site collection. If you enable this feature, you will be able to track actions that users take in your site collection such as viewing documents, executing searches, or downloading items. Figure 6-10 shows the available options.

Many of the options for choosing events to audit are self-explanatory. The options at the top of the page are especially important:

➤ Automatically trim the audit results

➤ Specify the number of days to retain

➤ Specify a location to store audit reports

Auditing can occupy a large amount of disk space. A flaw with auditing in previous versions of SharePoint is that no viable option existed for removing auditing information from the database. It is important that you set the options for trimming if you are going to use site collection auditing. This will prevent the database from growing too large.

Auditing data can be viewed in one of two ways. First, the database can be examined to gather data. This type of task is usually performed by IT professionals. The other option is to use the link on the Site Collection Administration menu titled Audit Log Reports. The information from the audit logs is available in the form of Excel-based reports.

6. Click on the link on the Site Collection Administration menu titled Audit Log Reports. Figure 6-11 shows the page and the reports that are available to download. Click on a report to download audit data into Excel. You can use your Excel skills to further analyze the audit data.

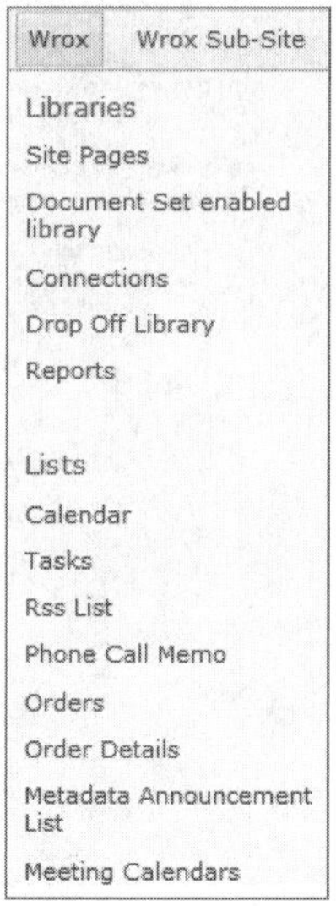

Wrox	Wrox Sub-Site
Libraries	
Site Pages	
Document Set enabled library	
Connections	
Drop Off Library	
Reports	
Lists	
Calendar	
Tasks	
Rss List	
Phone Call Memo	
Orders	
Order Details	
Metadata Announcement List	
Meeting Calendars	

FIGURE 6-8

Wrox	
Recycle Bin	
All Site Content	

FIGURE 6-9

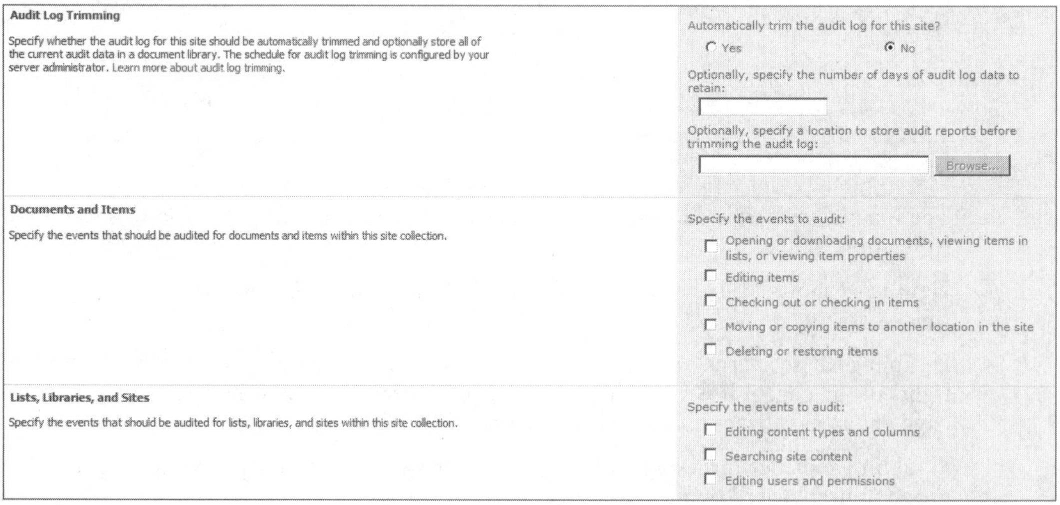

Audit Log Trimming

Specify whether the audit log for this site should be automatically trimmed and optionally store all of the current audit data in a document library. The schedule for audit log trimming is configured by your server administrator. Learn more about audit log trimming.

Automatically trim the audit log for this site?

○ Yes   ● No

Optionally, specify the number of days of audit log data to retain:

[ ]

Optionally, specify a location to store audit reports before trimming the audit log:

[ ] Browse...

Documents and Items

Specify the events that should be audited for documents and items within this site collection.

Specify the events to audit:

☐ Opening or downloading documents, viewing items in lists, or viewing item properties

☐ Editing items

☐ Checking out or checking in items

☐ Moving or copying items to another location in the site

☐ Deleting or restoring items

Lists, Libraries, and Sites

Specify the events that should be audited for lists, libraries, and sites within this site collection.

Specify the events to audit:

☐ Editing content types and columns

☐ Searching site content

☐ Editing users and permissions

FIGURE 6-10

7. Our final link in this walkthrough is the Portal site connection link. Figure 6-12 shows this page.

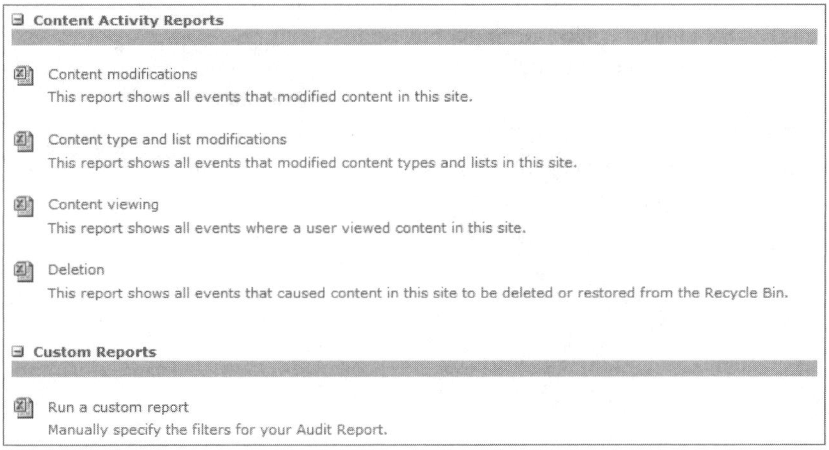

Content Activity Reports

- **Content modifications**
  This report shows all events that modified content in this site.

- **Content type and list modifications**
  This report shows all events that modified content types and lists in this site.

- **Content viewing**
  This report shows all events where a user viewed content in this site.

- **Deletion**
  This report shows all events that caused content in this site to be deleted or restored from the Recycle Bin.

Custom Reports

- **Run a custom report**
  Manually specify the filters for your Audit Report.

FIGURE 6-11

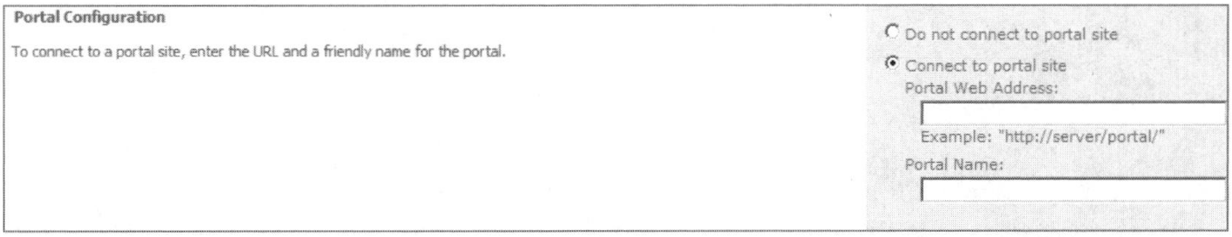

Portal Configuration

To connect to a portal site, enter the URL and a friendly name for the portal.

○ Do not connect to portal site

● Connect to portal site
  Portal Web Address:
  [   ]
  Example: "http://server/portal/"
  Portal Name:
  [   ]

FIGURE 6-12

Normally site collections are autonomous units. The settings and data of one site collection are not available to other site collections. This includes navigation structures. In many cases, however, portal designers want to provide separate site collections for different areas of their organization and still provide an integrated navigation experience without having to configure the navigation elements manually for each site collection.

The portal site connection option allows site collections to link back to a single parent site collection. This is provided via the breadcrumb navigation control.

In this example, we will select the radio button option Connect to Portal Site. Then we will enter the address of the top level portal we want to connect to. In this case `http://<servername>/sites/demo`. Then we give the more descriptive title "Top Level Portal Site" in the portal name box. Figure 6-13 shows the result in the breadcrumb control on the ribbon. Notice that the top

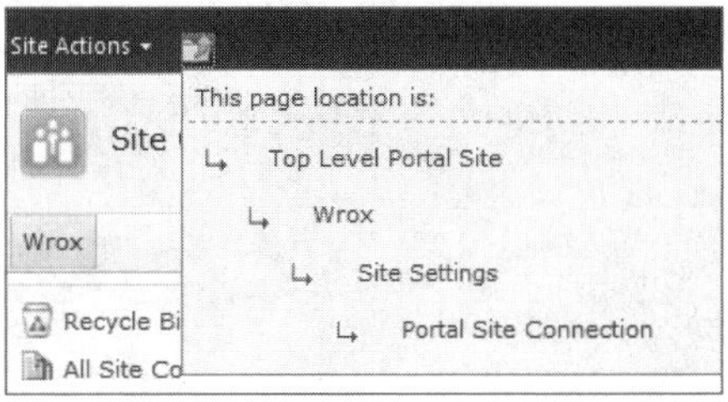

FIGURE 6-13

level of the breadcrumb is the "Top Level Portal Site". We can use this same connection on every site collection to provide this linkage.

Figure 6-14 shows the same breadcrumb without the portal connection. Notice how it stops at the top of the site collection.

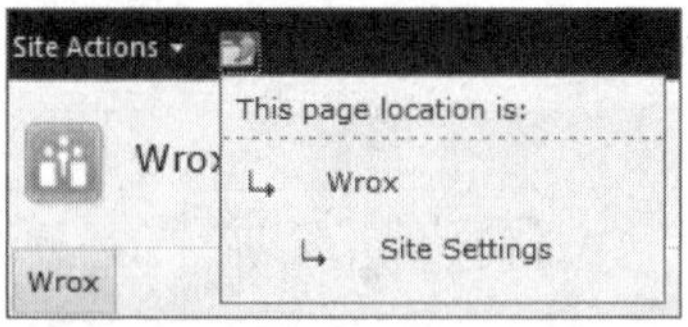

FIGURE 6-14

Please select Lesson 6 on the DVD or visit www.wrox.com/go/sp2010-24 *to view the video that accompanies this lesson.*

7

Managing the Solutions Gallery

Besides being a very powerful and full-featured collaboration tool out of the box, SharePoint is also a development platform. When you need to add capabilities to SharePoint that are not part of the deployed product, there is a mechanism for delivering that capability, formally called *solutions*.

The solutions gallery is used to hold elements of a SharePoint site that are repeatable and can be reused across sites. The gallery exists at the site collection level; therefore, anything placed in it is available on any site within the collection, but not in any sites outside the site collection. Items that can be placed in the solutions gallery include site templates created using the Save as Site Template command on the Site Settings page, and custom solutions written by developers that extend the capabilities of SharePoint. Once the element is created, it is deployed to the solutions gallery and becomes useable anywhere within the site collection. In this lesson we will be examining the ways a site collection administrator can use the solutions gallery.

The solutions gallery can be found on the Site Settings page under the heading Galleries. The main advantage of the solutions gallery is that it allows individual site collection administrators to deploy customizations that will not affect other site collections. This is a big deal because in days gone by, before this was possible, farm administrators would often disallow all site customization.

SOLUTION FRAMEWORK

The solution framework in SharePoint has been around since the 2007 version of the product. It was created to provide a rational method for deploying customizations to SharePoint. Solutions are made up of various files such as programming code, style sheets, images, and any other resources used to create the functionality that the solution provides. All the files are packaged into a single file that ends with the extension .wsp. In the previous version of SharePoint, only farm administrators could deploy solution files. In addition, it was possible for poorly written code to wreak havoc on the entire SharePoint farm or for solutions to create customizations that, while intended for one particular site or site collection, could contain elements that caused changes to the entire farm.

In SharePoint 2010, *sandbox solutions* enabled solutions that could be deployed by a site administrator to affect only the site collections in which they were installed. These solutions are limited in some ways compared to those deployed at the farm level by farm administrators. However, these limitations are the concerns of developers. As a site collection administrator, what you need to know is how to deploy a .wsp file and understand the role of a *resource quota*.

One thing to note about sandbox solutions is that they are possible only if the farm administrator activates the feature. Some farms may not want to enable site collection administrators to publish custom solutions, or enable any custom solutions in the farm at all. The rest of the content in this lesson assumes that the option is enabled at the farm level.

UNDERSTANDING RESOURCE QUOTAS

Farm administrators use resource quotas to limit the impact that site collection–level solutions can have on the rest of the farm. Each site collection is assigned a number of "points" that the administrator spends by activating and using the elements of a solution in the solutions gallery. Once the pool of points for that site collection is expended for the day, no more solutions can be run. You can track your daily point use on the solutions gallery page, as shown in Figure 7-1.

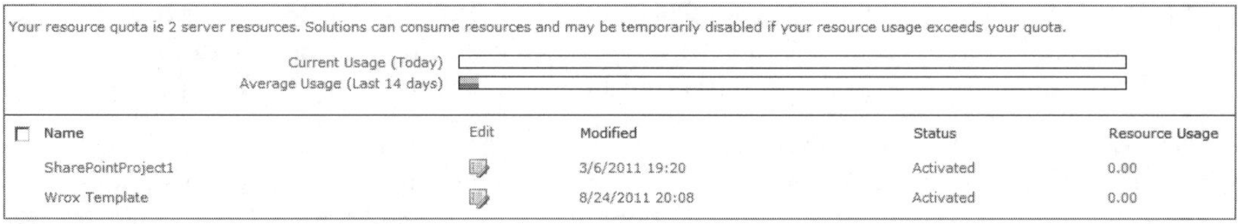

Your resource quota is 2 server resources. Solutions can consume resources and may be temporarily disabled if your resource usage exceeds your quota.

| | | Current Usage (Today) | | | | |
| | | Average Usage (Last 14 days) | | | | |

	Name	Edit	Modified	Status	Resource Usage
	SharePointProject1		3/6/2011 19:20	Activated	0.00
	Wrox Template		8/24/2011 20:08	Activated	0.00

FIGURE 7-1

Some commonplace occurrences which result in the expenditure of points include:

➤ Code that generates errors

➤ Code that taxes the server's processor

➤ Code that uses the database a lot

These criteria can be modified by a farm administrator but the underlying idea is that code that taxes the farm is going to be limited in how long and hard it can run. Again, most of the problems of point usage are concerns for developers rather than SharePoint administrators, but you should be aware of what these points mean and why a solution might use them too quickly.

DEPLOYING A CUSTOM SOLUTION

Deploying a custom solution is a simple process. A developer will provide a file having a `.wsp` extension. This file can then be uploaded into the solutions gallery. Deploying a solution is a two step process. Step one involves uploading the file, while step two involves deploying the solution. Once deployed, the solution will be made available via the solutions gallery. Activating the solution is what makes its features available in the site collection. Figure 7-2 shows the toolbar commands used in the solutions gallery for uploading, activating, and deactivating a solution.

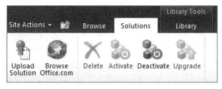

FIGURE 7-2

TRY IT

In this lesson you will be creating a very basic Web Part and deploying the solution to the solution gallery. Unfortunately, the code produces an unhandled exception. Unhandled exceptions burn a lot of points. You will see the effect of using up daily a resource quota.

Lesson Requirements

To complete this Try It exercise, you need the following:

➤ A SharePoint site.

➤ Visual Studio 2010, to build the Web Part. If you don't own a Visual Studio 2010 license, consider using Visual Studio Express Edition for this exercise, as the license is free.

Hints

This exercise does contain some coding, but does not really require any programming skills. You can cut and paste. In addition, if you are not familiar with Visual Studio, viewing the accompanying video with this lesson will be especially helpful.

Step-by-Step

1. Open Visual Studio 2010.

2. Select New Project.

3. From Installed Templates, under Visual C#, select SharePoint 2010.

4. Select the "Empty SharePoint Project" type. Leave the default name set to SharePointProject1. Figure 7-3 shows a project being added in Visual Studio.

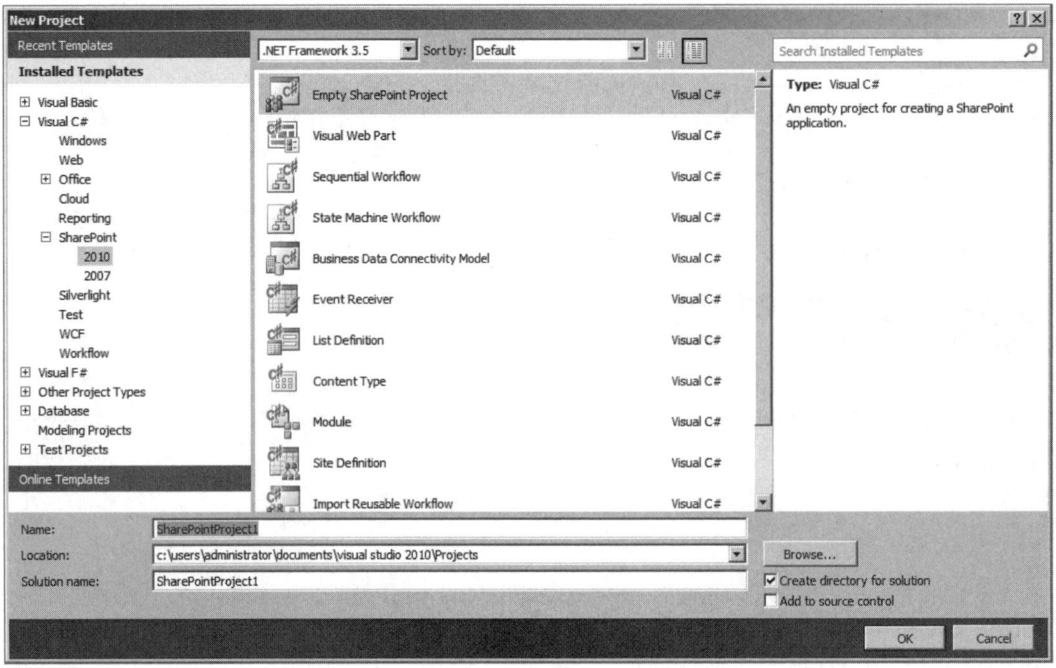

FIGURE 7-3

5. In the dialog that pops up, make sure the site collection listed is the one you are using. Select the sandboxed solution with the radio button. Figure 7-4 shows this dialog.

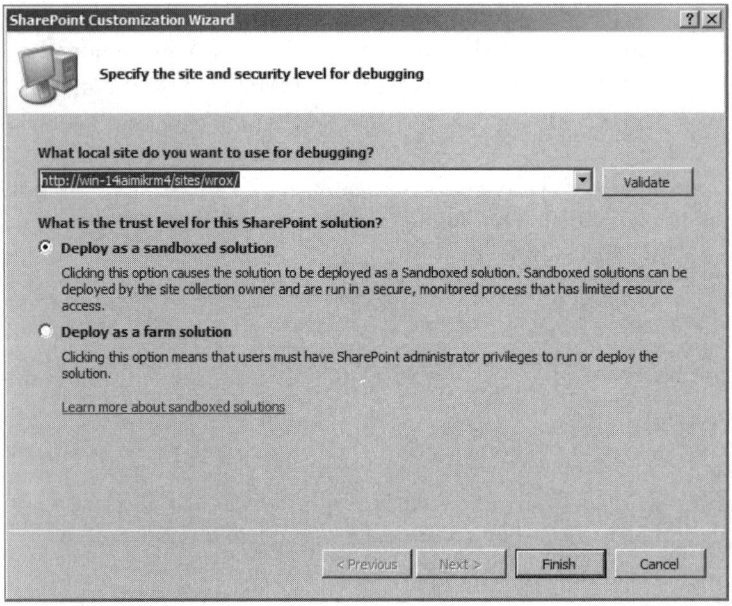

FIGURE 7-4

6. Right-click the project name and select Add. From the templates, select Visual C# and SharePoint 2010. From the list of projects, select Web Part. Figure 7-5 shows how to add a Web Part project.

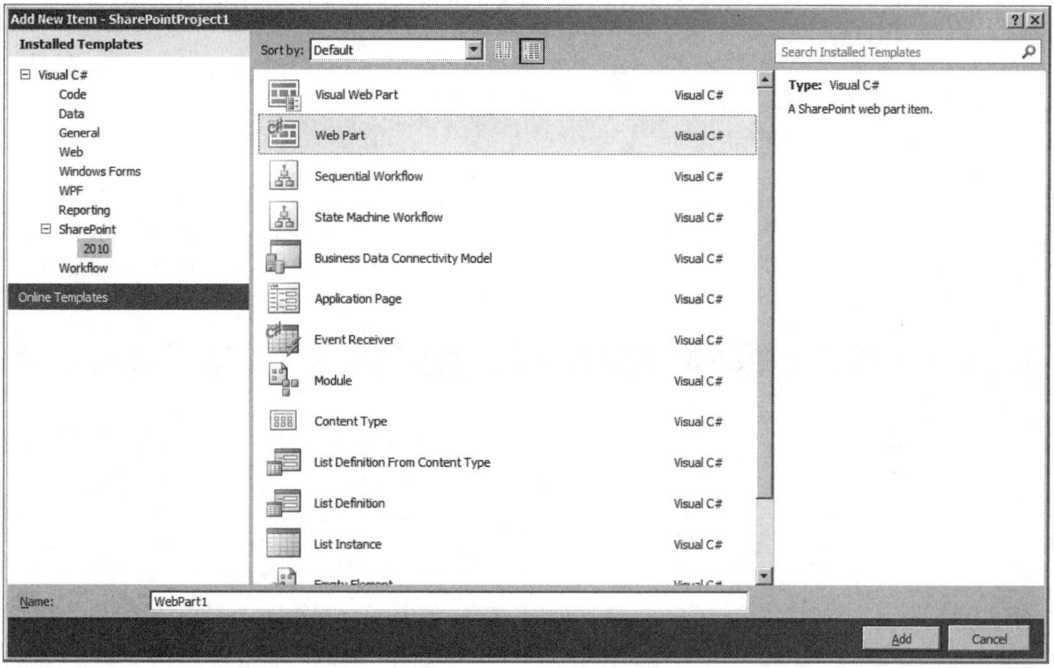

FIGURE 7-5

7. Copy and paste the following code. Some code will start on the screen. Overwrite everything on the screen from the word `namespace` to the final curly bracket (`}`). This code creates a button on the screen, and throws an error when you click it:

```
namespace SharePointProject1.WebPart1
{
    [ToolboxItemAttribute(false)]
    public class WebPart1 : WebPart
    {
        protected override void CreateChildControls()
        {
            var button = new Button();
            button.Text = "Create Error";
            button.Click += new EventHandler(button_Click);
            this.Controls.Add(button);
            base.CreateChildControls();
        }

        void button_Click(object sender, EventArgs e)
        {
            throw new NotImplementedException();
        }
    }
}
```

8. Right-click the project title and select Deploy. The code will run for several seconds and then, barring any errors, will be deployed to the solutions gallery. Figure 7-6 shows the title of the project as it appears in the solution explorer on the right side of the screen. If you do not see the solution explorer, you can open it in the view menu on the menu bar at the top of the screen.

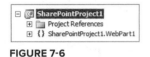

FIGURE 7-6

9. Now browse to Site Settings ⇨ Galleries ⇨ Solution Gallery. You should see your project in the Solutions Gallery. At this point it has consumed no resources, as indicated by the two white lines. Figure 7-7 shows the resource usage of 0.0 in the rightmost column.

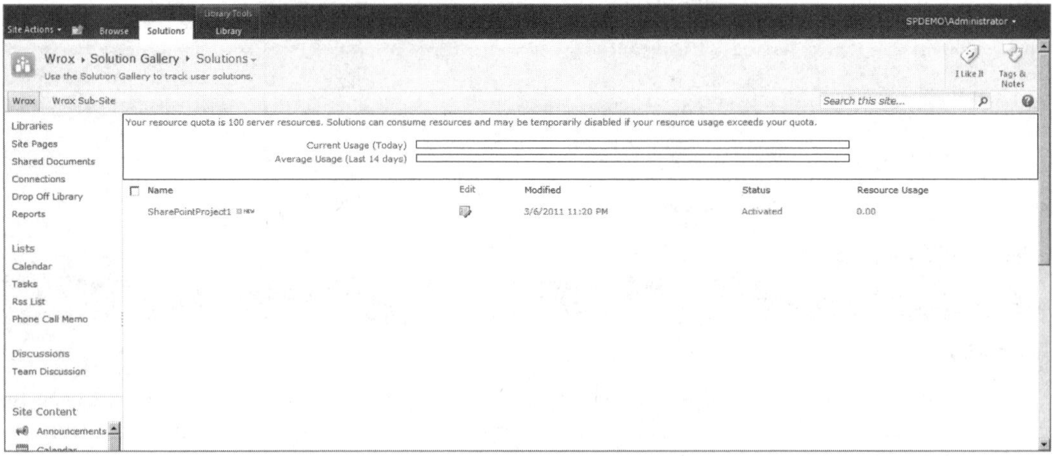

FIGURE 7-7

10. Now we will add the Web Part to a web page. Browse to a page on your SharePoint site that can have a Web Part added to it. (The home page of a test site would be a good choice.) To add a Web Part to the page, use the site actions menu and select the edit page option. This will put the page in edit mode and the Editing Tools section will appear on the ribbon. In the Editing Tools section, select the insert command. The ribbon will change to show the toolbar items that you can insert on the page. Select the web part option and insert the web part onto the page. It should look like the screen as represented in Figure 7-8. Figure 7-8 below shows the toolbar and the Web Part added to the page.

In this example you can see the Web Part, represented by a simple button that will create an error. After creating this error a few times, and waiting a few minutes, you can revisit the gallery to see how many resources an unhandled error consumes.

11. Click the Create Error button. You should see an error message show up on the Web Part. Click the button a few times to use up points. You may have to refresh or revisit the page several times.

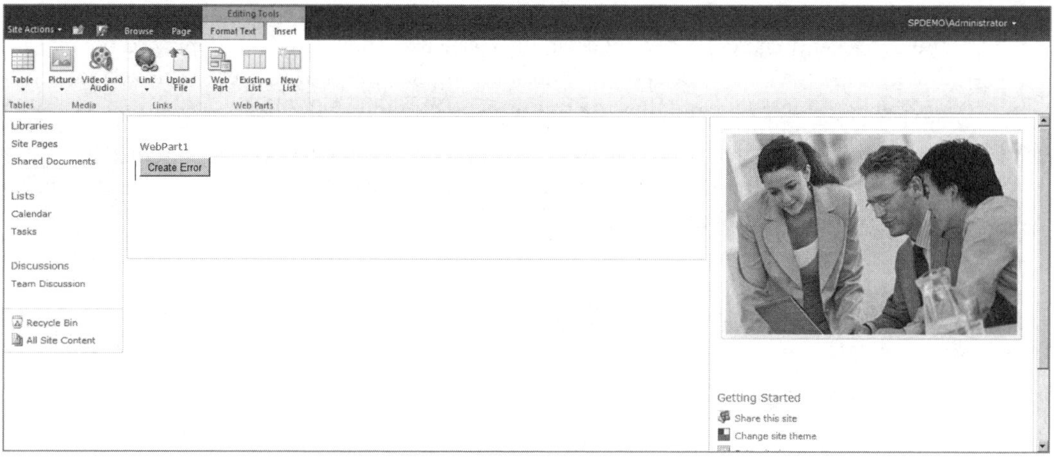

FIGURE 7-8

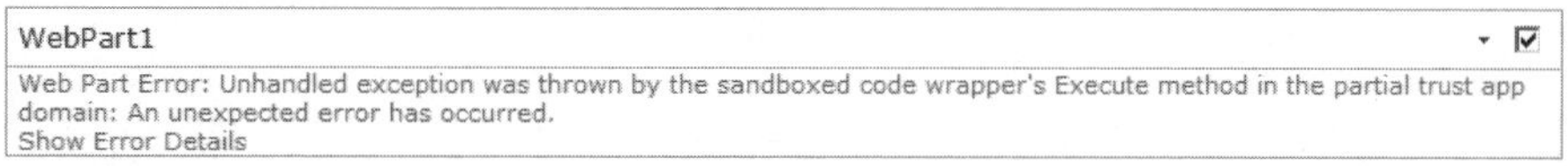

WebPart1

Web Part Error: Unhandled exception was thrown by the sandboxed code wrapper's Execute method in the partial trust app domain: An unexpected error has occurred.
Show Error Details

FIGURE 7-9

12. Return to the solutions gallery. By default, every 15 minutes the statistics for resource usage will be updated. It is possible for farm administrators to manually process these statistics or to update them more often. Figure 7-10 shows how the gallery page will look after you have used all your daily resources and the statistics have been updated. Your screen may look slightly different, or the orange bar may be of a different length, depending on the resource quota created by your farm administrator. In this case, it is set to the unrealistically low number of 2 to show a more dramatic usage bar. More common is a quota of several hundred points or more.

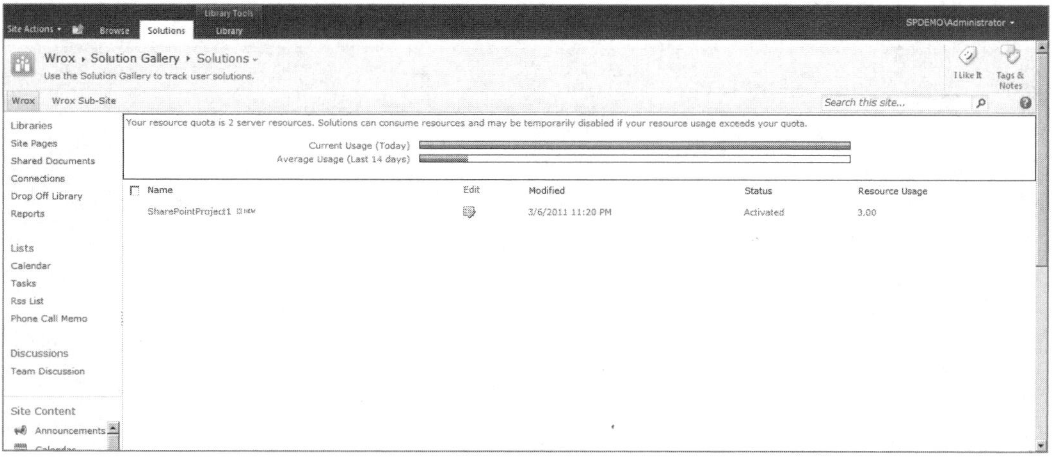

FIGURE 7-10

13. Although in this example Visual Studio was used to automatically deploy the solution, another scenario is that a developer hands you a `.wsp` file for you to deploy to the gallery. In that case browse to the gallery and, after clicking the Solutions tab in the ribbon, select the Upload Solution command, browse to the `.wsp` file, and click OK.

14. Once the file is uploaded, use the Activate command on the Solutions tab to activate the solution. Figure 7-11 shows the solution-deployment commands on the ribbon. Deactivate is used to remove solutions from the site collection.

FIGURE 7-11

 Please select Lesson 7 on the DVD or visit www.wrox.com/go/sp2010-24 *to view the video that accompanies this lesson.*

SECTION III
Managing Search

8

Setting Search Options at the Site Collection Level

Once you begin to use SharePoint to store documents and other content, you need a way to search through what's there and make it available. SharePoint Search provides you with a powerful tool to assist your users in finding information. Lesson 9 examines how to configure and use search scopes to help users find information. In this lesson you will look at the overall approach to working with Search on your site and how to configure it.

When you search within a site collection your results are displayed on a default search page, which is used by the entire site collection. This page `results.aspx` is actually stored on the SharePoint server. For example, searching a site with the URL `http://martinreidpc/sites/demo/SitePages/Home.aspx` will display results using a results page located at the URL `http://martinreidpc/_layouts/OSSSearchResults.aspx/Results.aspx?k=test&s=All%20Sites`.

Clicking the Home link on the results page will send you to the URL `http://martinreidpc/Pages/default.aspx`. This is not the site where you started searching. You are now outside the context of the site on which you started the search. This is because the search results page is located at the top level of the site collection not within the team site you started on. This can be confusing for your users, who can get lost in complex site structures. This is one of the reasons SharePoint enables you to customize the search results page and change its location. We'll look at doing this later in the lesson.

Search is managed by site collection administrators from the Site Settings page. From here you can work with scopes: you can create custom scopes, add or remove items from the search scopes drop-down list, add new items to the list, and more. In terms of search results you can create your own results page and customize its layout.

Figure 8-1 shows the top section of a newly created site collection. Notice the search box, which will enable you to enter a search term and get results.

FIGURE 8-1

Now look at Figure 8-2, which shows the same search box but with a configuration change made. In this case the search scopes drop-down list is now available. This enables your users to conduct searches restricted to specific areas of the site or indeed specific content types. In this case the search scopes drop-down has been configured to display Lesson 8.

FIGURE 8-2

Figure 8-3 shows the same list with the search settings changed again, this time to make more items available for targeted search.

FIGURE 8-3

People and All Sites are now available, enabling users to conduct searches within those specific categories. As you progress with SharePoint and search you will begin to understand what information your users search for and how, and you can then begin to customize search and scopes to make searching for common terms easier. This is discussed in Lesson 9 when you look at search scopes in more detail.

SEARCH RESULTS

SharePoint 2010 has also improved how results are displayed to the user. Figure 8-4 shows the results for a simple search using the word *test*. (Note that some areas of the screen that display user account information have been blanked.) The left-hand side of the results page enables you to further filter the results by:

➤ **Result Type:** Filter for all results, or for web pages, PowerPoint documents, or Microsoft Word Documents.

➤ **Site:** View results from all sites or specific sites listed.

➤ **Author:** Filter results by content author.

➤ **Modified Date:** Filter results by date modified.

➤ **Tags:** Filter results using metadata tags associated with content.

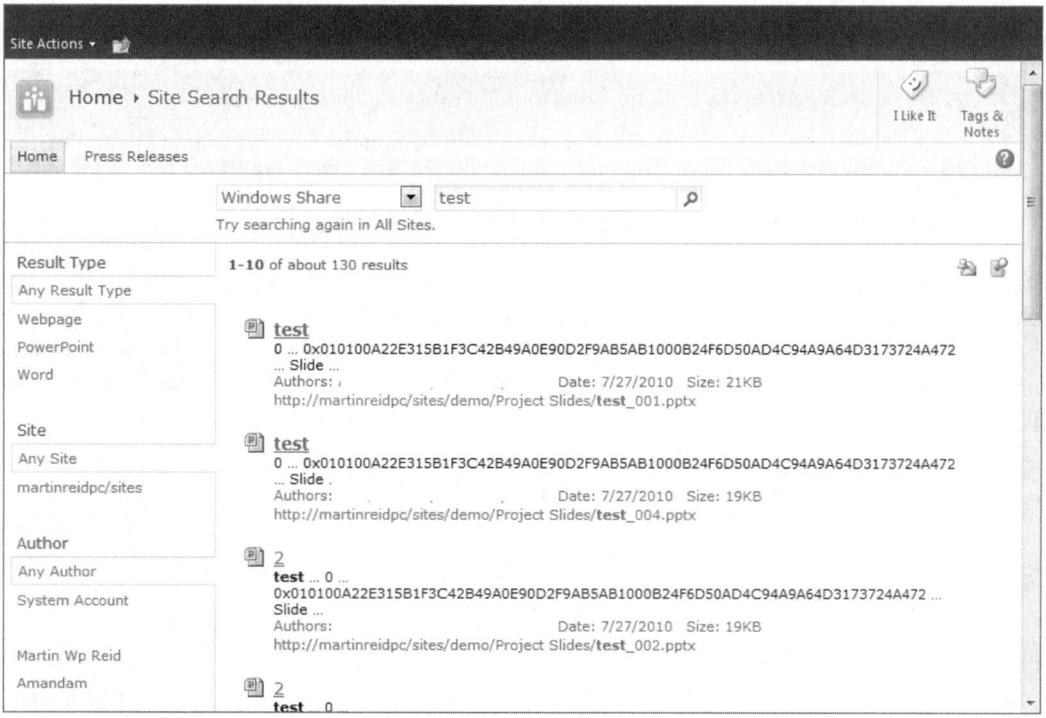

FIGURE 8-4

These options enable you to filter results directly on the screen according to your requirements. When working with a custom Search Center you can also change the way in which results are displayed to your users by editing the Search Core results Web Part. This is the main Web Part used to display results within the results page.

TRY IT

For this exercise you will be changing the search drop-down mode to display additional items to help users find content. You will also be examining the advanced searching and filtering results of the search results page.

Lesson Requirements

➤ A new site collection with default settings.

➤ Content copied into the Shared Documents library, such as Word, Excel, and PowerPoint files.

Step-by-Step

To change the Search scopes drop-down to include additional search scopes, proceed as follows:

1. Click Site Actions.

2. Click Site Settings.

3. Click Search Settings (Site Collection Administration).

4. Select the Show Scopes drop-down from the Site Collection Search Dropdown Mode drop-down list. Accept the rest of the defaults on this screen.

5. Click OK to save the changes and return to the site settings page.

Return to the home page of your site collection, where you may need to refresh the page to see the changes. In this case the search scopes drop-down should now be added just before the search text box. Figure 8-1 shows the drop-down list. In this case only a single scope has been made available. To add further scopes to the list you will change one other setting in the search configuration. To proceed, click Site Actions, Site Settings and return to your search settings page.

1. Click the Enable Custom Scopes radio button (such as All Sites) by connecting this site collection with the following Search Center. This option enables the custom scopes and allows you enter a new Search Center or use the existing one.

2. Click in the Site Collection Search Results Page text box and copy the URL.

3. Paste the copied URL into the text box below the Enable Custom Scopes radio button.

4. Click OK to save the changes.

5. Return to the homepage of your site and refresh the page.

6. There should now be three scopes available in the drop-down list: All Sites, This Site, and People.

When conducting a search from the home page users can now choose to search any of the following:

➤ **All Sites:** All SharePoint sites within the site collection.

➤ **This Site:** The current site only.

➤ **People:** Only people within the profile stores.

Results will be displayed on the default search results page within the top level of the site collection. Within the Shared Documents library I have uploaded four documents:

➤ Company marketing (PowerPoint)

➤ Company results (PowerPoint)

➤ Monthly budgets (Excel)

➤ Staffing report (Word)

Running a search for the word "Company" will return several sets of results, including these documents. The Search results page will permit you to further filter the results by using the Result Type filters on the page. In this example clicking PowerPoint in the Result Type area will narrow the results to PowerPoint files only. Figure 8-5 shows the results page filtered for PowerPoint results only.

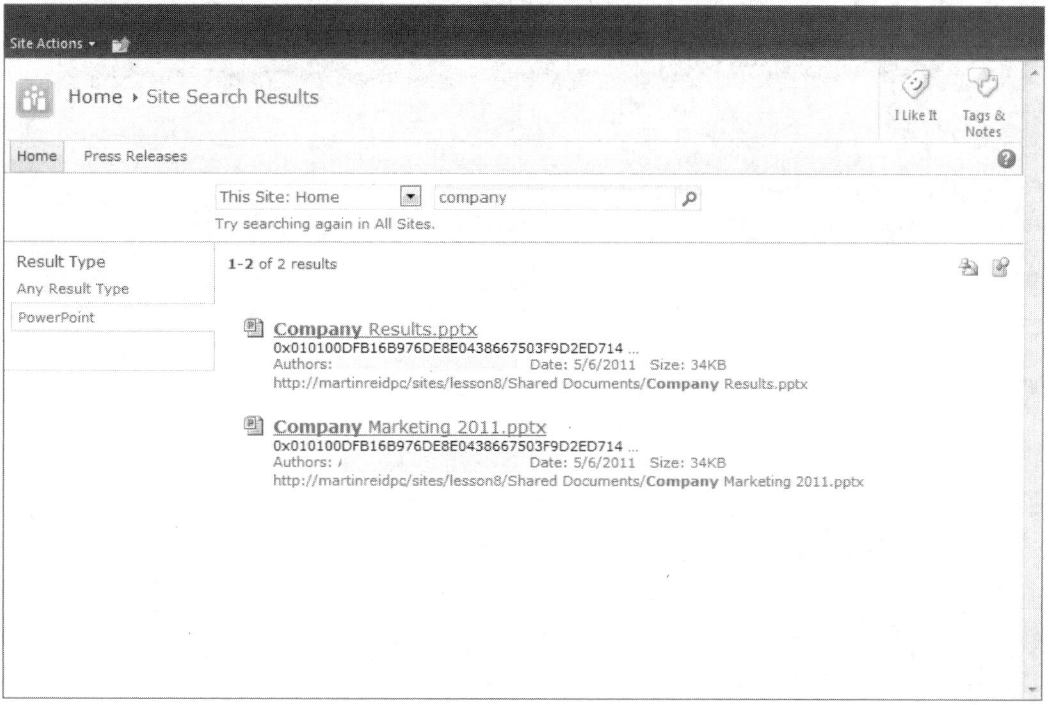

FIGURE 8-5

The search results page also enables you to set preferences and carry out advanced searches. The Preferences link located beside the search text box enables you set the search language and turn search suggestions on or off. To view the advanced search form click the Advanced link beside the search text box. Figure 8-6 shows the options available to you on this form.

Advanced search enables you to create highly targeted searches. You can search using the following document properties:

➤ Author

➤ Description

➤ Name

➤ Size

➤ URL

➤ Last modified date

➤ Created by

➤ Last modified by

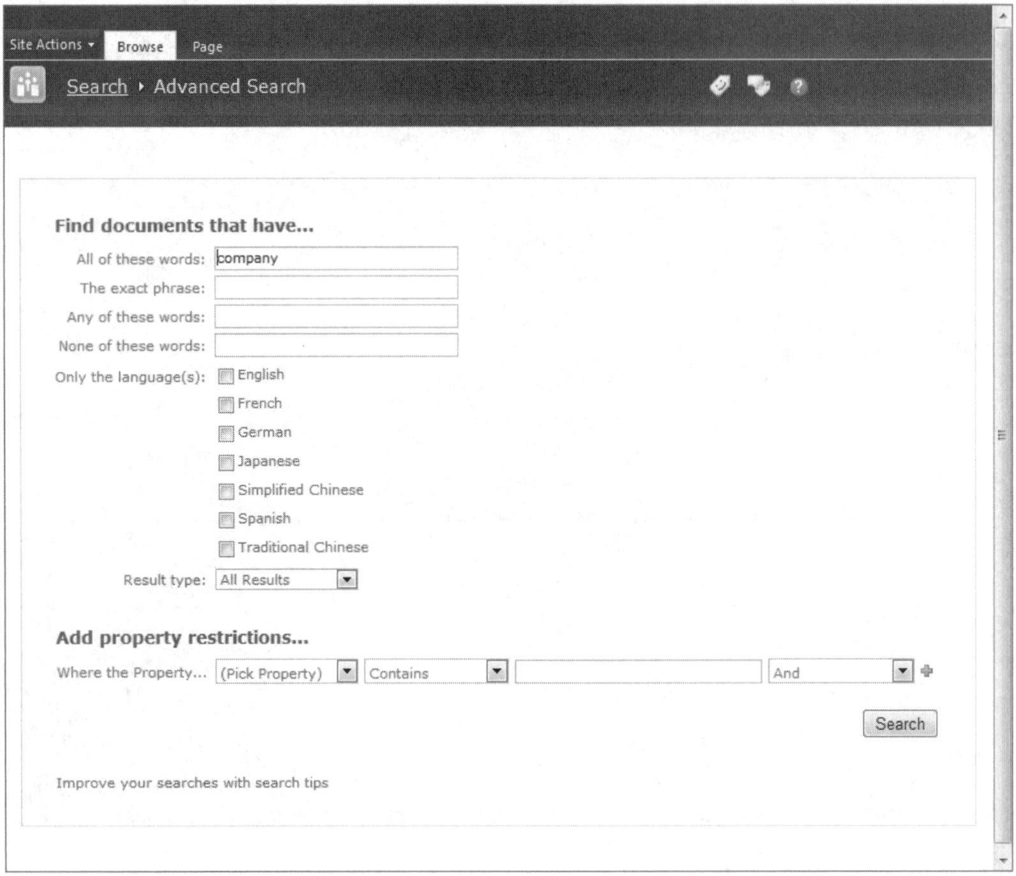

FIGURE 8-6

For example, to create an advanced search to return PowerPoint files containing the word *company*, for which the document author is Reid, you would do the following:

1. In the All These Words text box enter **company**.

2. From the Result Type drop-down select PowerPoint Presentations.

3. In the first property restriction drop-down select Author.

4. In the second drop-down select Contains.

5. Enter **Reid** into the third text box.

You can add additional rules to the property restrictions by clicking the green plus sign at the end of the first line. In that case you need to decide if the second line is an "And" or an "Or" line — whether documents must match the properties defined in both rows or only one in order for a result to be returned.

In Lesson 9 you will be looking at how you add your own search scopes to search drop-downs to help your users discover content.

 Please select Lesson 8 on the DVD or visit www.wrox.com/go/sp2010-24 *to view the video that accompanies this lesson.*

9

Search Scopes for Site Collection Administrators

A search scope enables you to allow your site collection users to carry out highly targeted searches within their site collections. However, such a search is limited to a subset of content defined as its *scope*, rather than encompassing the entire SharePoint index. For example, you can set up a search scope that looks only for Microsoft Word documents from among hundreds of different file types. In this case, the scope is defined as Word documents as opposed to the entire index.

Another example of when you can use scopes is where Sites use content categories to classify documents according to subject. Search scopes can help to narrow down search criteria and results to documents in a particular category or file type. Many users simply want see results that do not include information they are not particularly interested, and anything you can do to help reduce the number of results that they have to trawl through can be helpful and make your sites much more user friendly and efficient.

CREATING A NEW SCOPE

A search scope can be applied at the site collection level or set by a SharePoint administrator in Central Administration for the Search Service Application. If the scope is created in Central Administration, it is available in every site collection for the web application. If set at the site collection level, it is available only in that specific site collection. Setting a custom scope is a two-stage process. In stage one, you need to enable Custom Scopes (if it is not already enabled), and in stage two, you create the scope itself. To create a new scope, follow these steps:

1. Click Site Actions.

2. Click Site Settings. This opens the Site Settings page, which contains various management tools grouped into categories.

3. In the Site Settings page, click the Search Settings link located in the Site Collection Administration category. The Search Settings page enables customer scopes for the site collection. Figure 9-1 shows the Search Settings page.

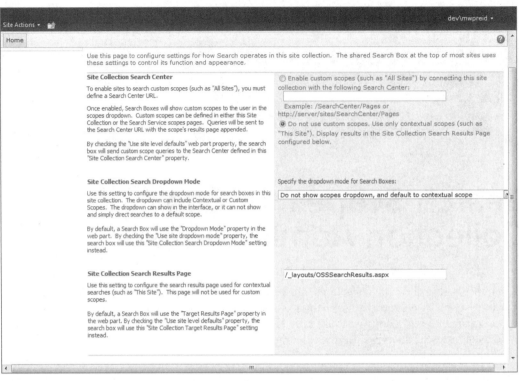

FIGURE 9-1

Several settings are available to you on the Search Settings screen related to Scopes, their presentation, and how the results are delivered to your users. You need to think about how users will search within the site collection and how scopes will be used. When a user searches for information, the results page returned is the default results page for the site collection using the search results page located at the default URL, which is `\_Layouts\OSSSearchResults.aspx`. This results page is stored on your instance of SharePoint Server and is the default search results page used by all site collections. As shown in Figure 9-1, you can redirect the results to your own search page after you enable custom scopes. However, you need to be careful because each scope could be using a different results URL, which can be confusing for the user. For example, using a custom scope may return the user to results page A. Using another scope could return the user to results page B. The options available are as follows:

➤ **Site Collection Search Center:** Rather than use the default Search Center provided out of the box, you can create your own and point your search to this area for results.

➤ **Site Collection Search Dropdown Mode:** This option enables you to control how scopes are displayed in the scopes drop-down list on your site collection. Figure 9-2 shows the options available under Specify the Dropdown Mode for Search Boxes. (I have to add that the programmers behind this list of options will never win an English award for this!)

```
Do not show scopes dropdown, and default to contextual scope
Do not show scopes dropdown, and default to target results page
Show scopes dropdown
Show, and default to 's' URL parameter
Show and default to contextual scope
Show, do not include contextual scopes
Show, do not include contextual scopes, and default to 's' URL parameter
```

FIGURE 9-2

➤ **Do Not Show Scopes Dropdown and Default to Contextual Scope:** This option simply hides the drop-down list on the site. If you look at the homepage of a new team site, you can see that a drop-down list is not available next to the search text box. Searches default to the All Sites scope. *Contextual* means that you can search within your current context. For example, if you have a list open, the drop-down displays This List, or your current context.

➤ **Do Not Show Scopes Dropdown, and Default to Target Results Page:** This defaults to the configuration of the target results page, which, if it is not set up to use custom scopes, returns all results. If the target page is configured to use a custom scope, your search results here reflect that.

➤ **Show Scopes Dropdown:** Displays the scopes drop-down list beside the search text box. The scopes available will usually default to This Site, All Sites, and All People.

➤ **Show and Default to "s" URL Parameter:** If you have carried out a search on a SharePoint site you may have noticed that the URL passed to the search results page. For example, with a custom scope, the following is passed to the results page:

```
http://dev/_layouts/OSSSearchResults.aspx/Results.aspx?k=martin%20
reid&s=My%20Documents
```

Notice s=My%20Documents, this is a key\value pair, which is part of what is often referred to as a querystring. In this case the s parameter is a custom scope (My Documents) that you will create later in the "Try It" section. Also note the use of the escape value, %20 to indicate a space in the querystring. In the absence of the s parameter the scope will be the default scope for the site.

➤ **Show and Default to Contextual Scopes:** This option will mean a default to the contextual scope, for example This Site or This List. However, all other scopes will be available in the drop-down.

➤ **Show, Do Not Include Contextual Scopes:** This setting will remove the contextual scopes (List and Library) from the drop-down.

➤ **Show, Do Not Include Contextual Scopes, and Default to "s" URL Parameter:** This setting can function as the preceding setting with the difference being that the "s" parameter will be added to the querystring.

➤ **Site collection Search results Page:** This setting may not be used for custom scopes (which can have their own results page) and will be set at the default (_Layouts/OSSSearchResults.aspx) when you open the form.

MANAGING WHERE THE SCOPE APPEARS

When you create a custom scope you can also decide where you want the scope to appear. You can display the scope in the standard search drop-down list used on the team site homepage, add it to the drop-down available within the advanced search page, or use it in both. In addition you can also create a new display group to contain your custom scopes. Of course you can also choose not to display the scope at all. In this case the only way to use the scope is through the s parameters in the query string. You will have to pass the scope within the URL to the results page.

SETTING RULES FOR THE SCOPE

In order to use a scope you must add a rule or rules that will be applied to content when the scope is populated. When you create a new scope it does not contain any rules. A scope rule can be any of the following:

➤ A web address, such as `http://www.yoursite.com`. This also includes file shares, a domain (for example `www.microsoft.com`), and sub domain.

➤ A property query (file extension = document). A scope can be restricted to a meta data property held within SharePoint for example where file extension = doc. Managed properties are available and can be used to set this rule. A default set of properties is available on the Add Scope rule screen and other properties can be added by SharePoint admins from Central Administration.

➤ All content.

A scope rule also contains instructions for how it is to be applied to content. You can include content that matches the rule, exclude content that matches the rule, or set the rule to be required, meaning that only content matching the rule will be included.

The real power of the scope rules is that you can associate multiple rules with a given scope. For example, using managed properties you can create a set of rules where:

Author = Martin Reid

AND

File extension = `.doc`

OR

File extension = `.docx`

This scope would be limited to documents authored by Martin Reid that have either a `.doc` or a `.docx` extension. These rules are created one at a time but used collectively to make up the search scope. Figure 9-3 shows the Scope Properties and Rules screen for the preceding rule.

The Settings screen will also provide information on the approximate number of items indexed by each scope rule and the total number of items within the scope. As you can also see in Figure 9-3 this screen can be used to manage the scope and the rules, and it is here that you would edit or delete a scope. You may have to wait a few minutes for your changes to a scope to take effect.

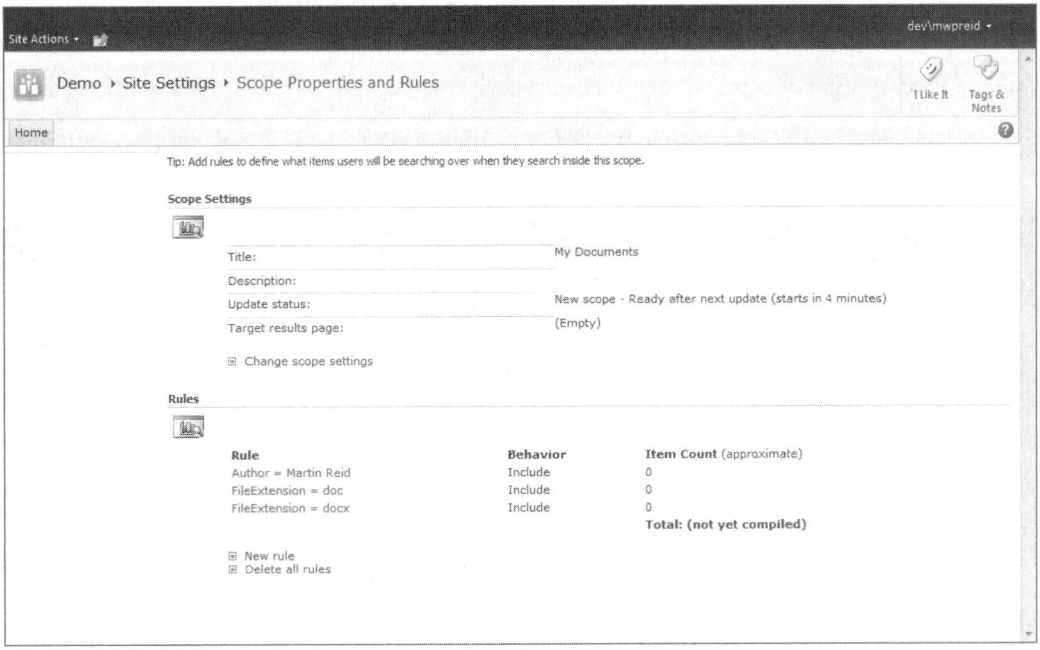

FIGURE 9-3

TRY IT

In this exercise, you create a new scope, set the scope options, and add a rule to the scope.

Lesson Requirements

To complete this Try It exercise, you need the following:

➤ A document library containing some Word files with both .doc and .docx extensions. These files are required when you carry out a search using the scope created in the exercise. If you have additional files in the library, you can extend the example to include their extensions.

Step-by-Step

To begin creating a new scope, you need to open the Search Settings page. To do this, follow these steps:

1. Click Site Actions.

2. Click Site Settings.

3. Click Search Settings (Site Collection Administration Category).

4. Click the radio button titled Enable custom scopes (such as "All Sites") by connecting this site collection with the following Search Center:

Enter `/_layouts/OSSSearchResults.aspx` into the Search Center text box. This is the default Search Center.

5. Select the Show scopes dropdown from the Site Collection Search Dropdown Mode list.

6. Click OK to save the changes and enable custom scopes. Figure 9-4 shows the Settings screen.

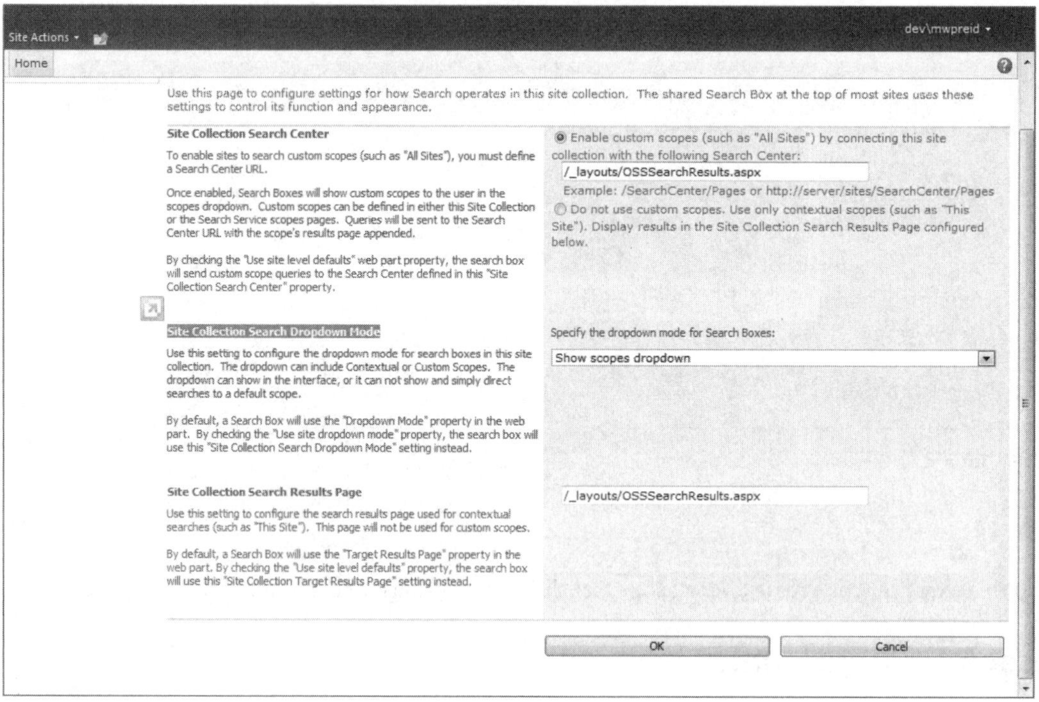

FIGURE 9-4

Now that you have enabled the use of custom scopes, create a new scope in the Site Collection Administration category by following these steps:

1. Click Search Scopes.

2. Click New Scope.

3. Enter a title for the scope (**My Documents,** for this example).

4. Enter a brief description, such as **Search scope restricted to documents authored by me.**

5. Click both the Search Dropdown and Advanced Search checkboxes to display the scope in both drop-downs.

6. Accept the default for the Target Results Page, Use the Default Search Results Page, and then click OK. Figure 9-5 shows the completed Create Scope form.

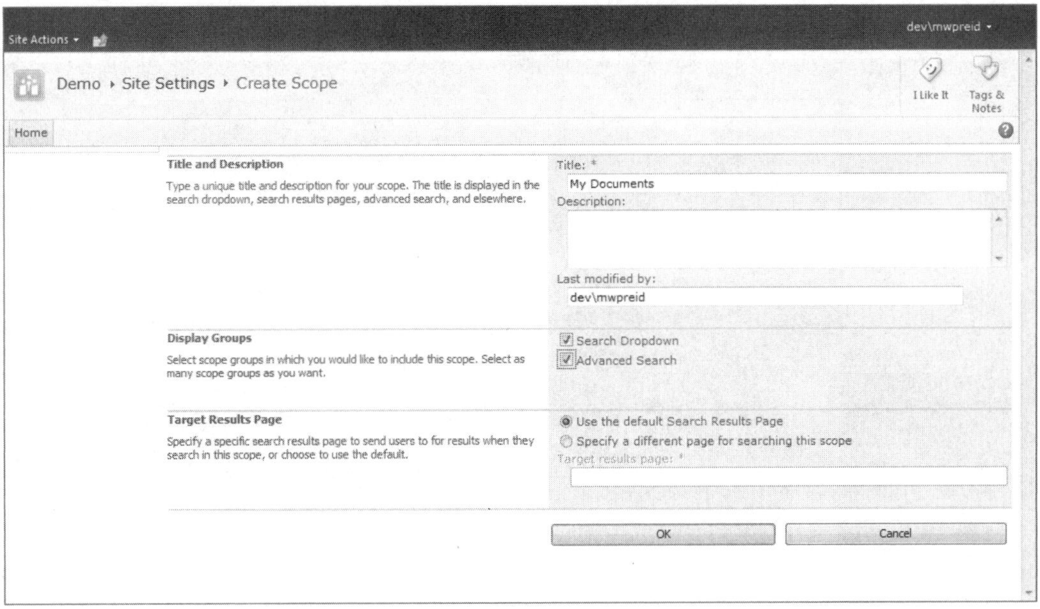

FIGURE 9-5

Now that you have enabled custom scopes and created a new scope, it's time to add rules to the scope. Follow these steps:

1. In the View Scopes page, look for your newly created scope (titled My Documents in this example).

2. On the right, click Add Rules.

3. Click the Property radio button. The screen changes, enabling you to select a property. From the Property Query drop-down, select Author.

4. Enter your own name in the text box immediately below the drop-down.

5. Accept the default behavior of Include.

6. Click OK to save the rule.

To add additional rules to the scope, click the scope name and on the Scope Properties and Rules screen click New Rule. Repeat Steps 2 through 4, selecting FileExtension from the Property Query drop-down and adding **.doc** to the text box. Repeat this process to add a rule for the `.docx` extension.

If you look at the Scope Properties and Rules screen, you will see a message telling you when the scope will be updated and available to the site. In my case, the scope will be available in four minutes. When the scope is available, you can begin to use it to search within your site.

Please select Lesson 9 on the DVD or visit www.wrox.com/go/sp2010-24 *to view the video that accompanies this lesson.*

10

Managing Search Keywords for Site Collection Administrators

SharePoint search can be a powerful aid to users in discovering and working with information. One problem with it, though, is that it can return a lot of results, leaving the user to find a needle in a haystack. SharePoint provides several features to help site collection administrators reduce the number of results and help users find the information they need. *Keywords* and *Best Bets* can help. Many different terms can be used for the same search, for example *annual leave*, *holiday*, and *time off*. Keywords and Best Bets enable you to associate several terms with a standard term producing relevant results. This process can also be used for more technical terms, again helping users to find relevant information.

Keywords and Best Bets are fairly easy to configure in SharePoint; the hard part is coming up with the right terms to use. For example, how many different terms can be used instead of *financial report*? *Workbook*, *spreadsheet*, *cost analyst*, and *project budget* are all terms someone might use when searching for company financial information. Fortunately SharePoint 2010 can help by suggesting Keywords based on your users' search habits. This feature is available as part of the Web Analytics Reports feature, and you can access it from the Manage Keywords page. Monitoring the feature will help you understand what your users are searching for and assist you in building a solid search strategy. Keywords and Best Bets can also help you surface information you want users to find, such as company policy documents or training materials. In using them you are not restricted to content within your SharePoint sites; you can create a Keyword and Best Bet that will display information from the Internet.

TRY IT

In this example you are going to add Keywords and Best Bets to help users discover financial information contained in a document library named Annual Reports. This folder contains a budget Excel Workbook and several finance-related Word documents.

Lesson Requirements

To complete this Try It exercise you need the following files, placed in a document library called Annual Reports:

➤   Annual Costs.docx

➤   Annual Report.docx

➤   Budget Policy.docx

➤   Useful Stats.xlsx

Before doing the exercise, once you have created the documents, try searching for them on your site. This will give you a before-and-after feeling for the use of Keywords and Best Bets. In the initial search you should get multiple results with a link to each individual document. Once you have enabled Keywords and Best Bets you should find that access to the full set of financial documents is a single click away as a direct link to their location will be returned.

Step-by-Step

Using Keywords and Best Bets you are going to provide a high-confidence link to the shared document folder to give users instant direct access to all financial documents. To continue, follow these steps:

1.   Click Site Actions.

2.   Click Site Settings.

3.   Click Search Keywords in the Site Collection Administration category.

This will open the Manage Keywords screen, shown in Figure 10-1.

This screen also provides access to the following:

➤   All existing Keywords.

➤   All expired Keywords.

➤   Keywords requiring review.

➤   Best Bet usage.

➤   Best Bet suggestions.

Some or all of these may not be present if this is the first time you have added Keywords or Best Bets. To add Keywords, do the following:

1.   Click the Add Keyword link to open the Add Keyword form, which contains several settings that you must complete.

2.   Enter a Keyword phrase: this is the term the search will match, returning an associated Keyword result to the user. For this example enter **Financial Information**.

3.   Enter synonyms: these are terms the user may enter when searching for the information, separated by semicolons. In this case enter **Project;Costs;Budget;Finance**.

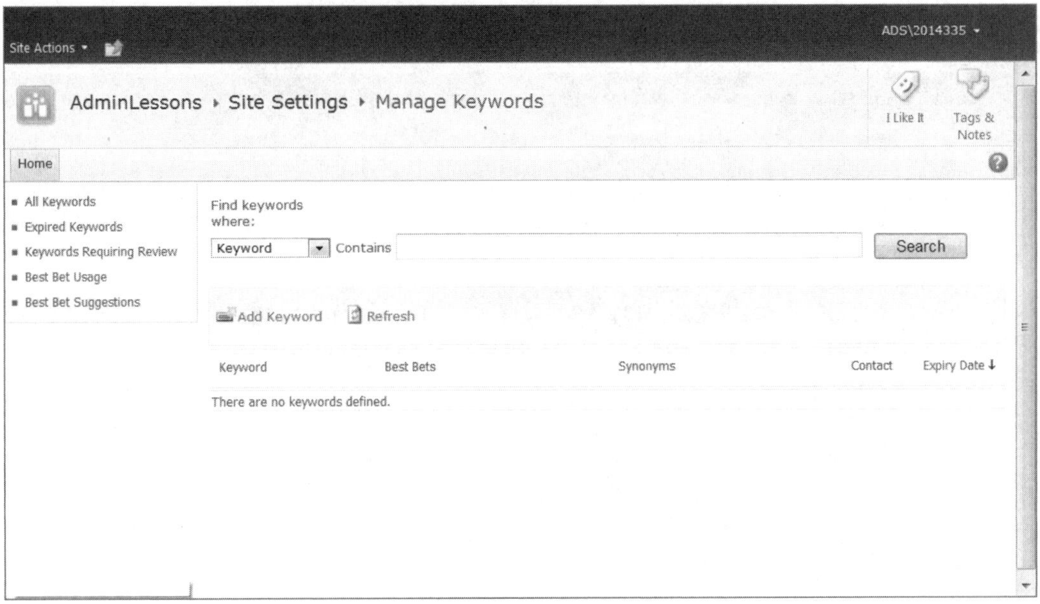

FIGURE 10-1

4. Scroll down the screen and click the Add Best Bets link. This is where you will add a link to the shared documents library containing the finance information, which you want the users to discover when searching. You can copy this link from the web browser for the shared documents library you wish to navigate to.

5. Enter a title for the Best Bet, such as **Financial Information**.

6. Enter a description, such as **Company Financial Information for Staff**.

7. Click OK to save the information and complete the additional information in the form.

8. Enter a Keyword definition: this is text presented to your user within the search results page. Enter **Company Financial Information**.

9. Enter yourself as the contact for this search. You can also enter a date to start and stop publishing or using this Keyword and Best Bet and/or enter a review date for the information. The review date provides a way for administrators to check Best Bets ensuring that they remain accurate and current. For now, accept the defaults. Figure 10-2 shows the Edit Keyword Screen at this point.

10. Click OK to save the configuration and continue.

Figure 10-3 shows the search results once the Keyword and Best Bets are added. The Best Bet link is highlighted with a star icon and clicking the hyperlink will take you directly to the Annual Reports document library. Try searching using any of the Keywords you entered (*project*, *costs*, *budget*, and *finance*) to be sure that the Best Bet link is always shown in response.

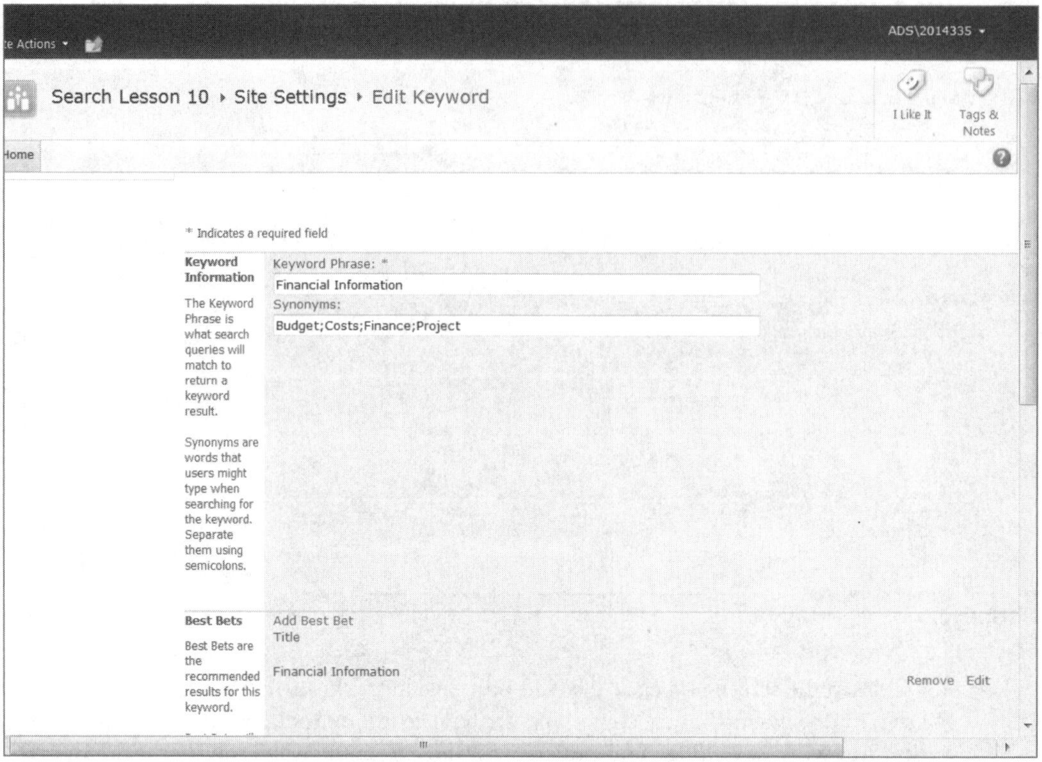

FIGURE 10-2

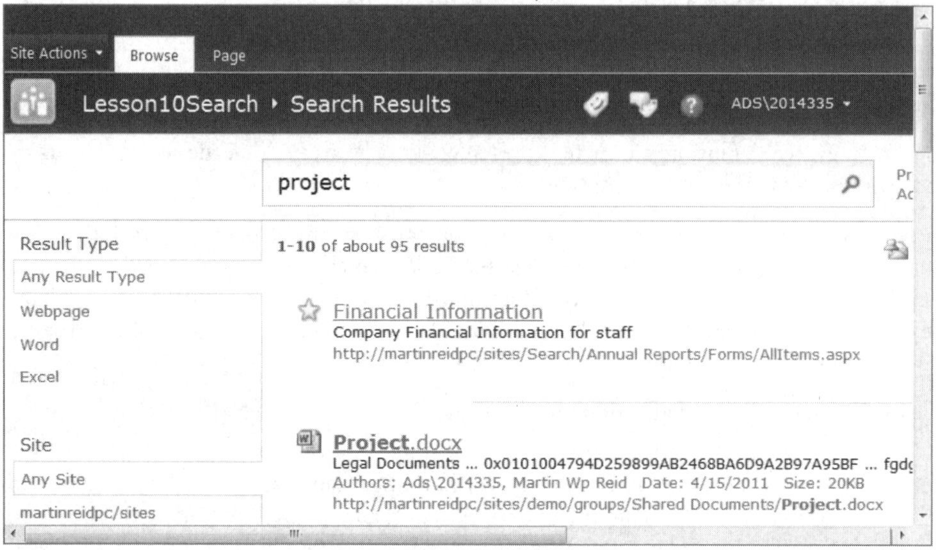

FIGURE 10-3

Your Best Bet and Keyword can also contain a link to an external website to provide the user with additional reference materials, such as (in this case) financial or technical references. To set this up, simply replace the Best Bet URL with the external URL or add an additional Best Bet URL to the external site by repeating the steps above.

> *Please select Lesson 10 on the DVD or visit* www.wrox.com/go/sp2010-24 *to view the video that accompanies this lesson.*

11

Managing Search Availability at the List and Site Level for Site Administrators

SharePoint Search has always been one of the most powerful features of the product, enabling users to find information to which they have permissions no matter which site it has been stored on. However, you might not always want them to be able to do this; at times you might want to ensure that some areas of your site collection are removed from the SharePoint index. In this lesson, we look at search settings for both your site and individual lists, and in particular at how to remove lists and even the entire site from search results. You also see how to exclude Web Part pages from appearing within the search results.

The procedure for excluding items from search results is essentially the same for libraries and lists: it is done from the Settings menu for each item. It can be a useful feature when you are using lists for things like lookup values (or the new relationships feature in SharePoint lists) and do not want to return such items using search. For example, you might have a list of ZIP codes or states that are used in several lists using a lookup column. Removing lists of value and data from search results can improve the experience of the user by making results more relevant.

You will find the Search setting in the General Settings category reached from then, Advanced Settings link in the settings for lists and document libraries. It is a simple radio button option with only a Yes or No setting. The options available are the same for both lists and libraries; Figure 11-1 shows the search setting.

In addition to showing the option for search removal, you might also notice in Figure 11-1 the option to remove Offline Client Availability. This is the option to connect the list or library to a Microsoft Office offline client, for example, SharePoint Workspace 2010. This option is briefly discussed later in the lesson, as there is little point in hiding content from search when it can be found with tools like SharePoint Workspace. When you are removing lists and libraries from SharePoint Search, it can also be appropriate to set this option to No. This is particularly useful, again, in the use of lookup values that are meaningless to users except in the context of a list or library.

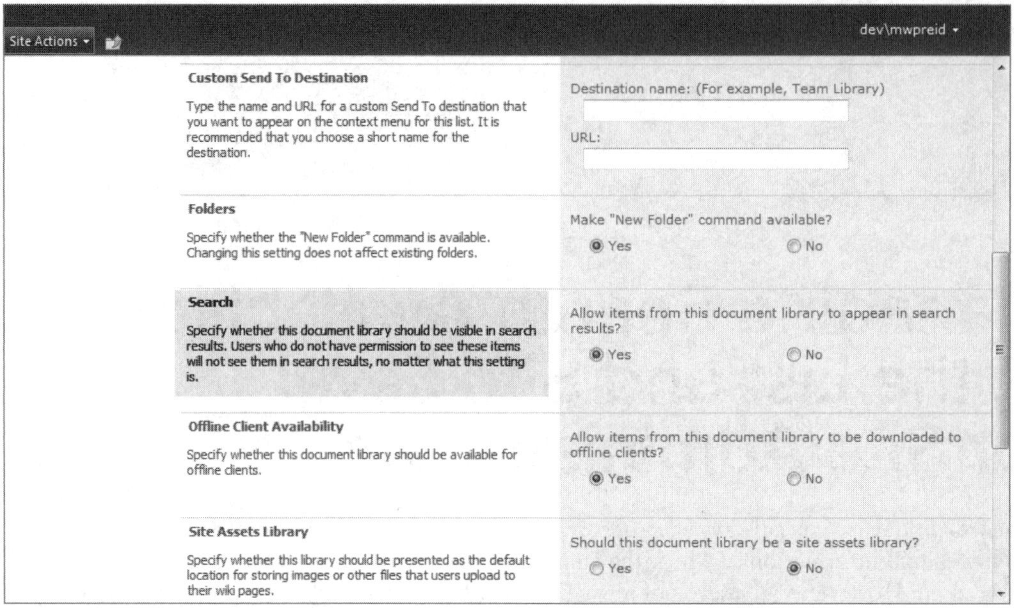

FIGURE 11-1

In addition to removing lists and libraries from search, it is also possible to remove entire sites from the Search index. When excluding a site from SharePoint search, you also have the option to remove Web Parts from the indexing process.

Figure 11-2 shows the options available to you for restricting site collection search. You can find the search removal options this way:

1. Click Site Actions.

2. Select Site Settings.

3. Within the Site Administration group, click Search and Offline Availability.

The options available for removing a site from search are:

➤ **Indexing Site Content:** This permits you to allow or disallow searching of the site and all its subsites. If you set this option to No, everything in the site collection, including subsites, will be ignored by the SharePoint Crawl and Index process. Setting this option to No removes the site collection content from search.

➤ **Indexing ASPX Page Content:** Content in an ASPX page, including content displayed within Web Parts on the page, can be indexed and returned by SharePoint Search. These options by default do not index Web Parts if the site contains fine-tuned permissions. The additional options are:

➤ Always Index All Web Parts on This Site

➤ Never Index Web Parts on the Site

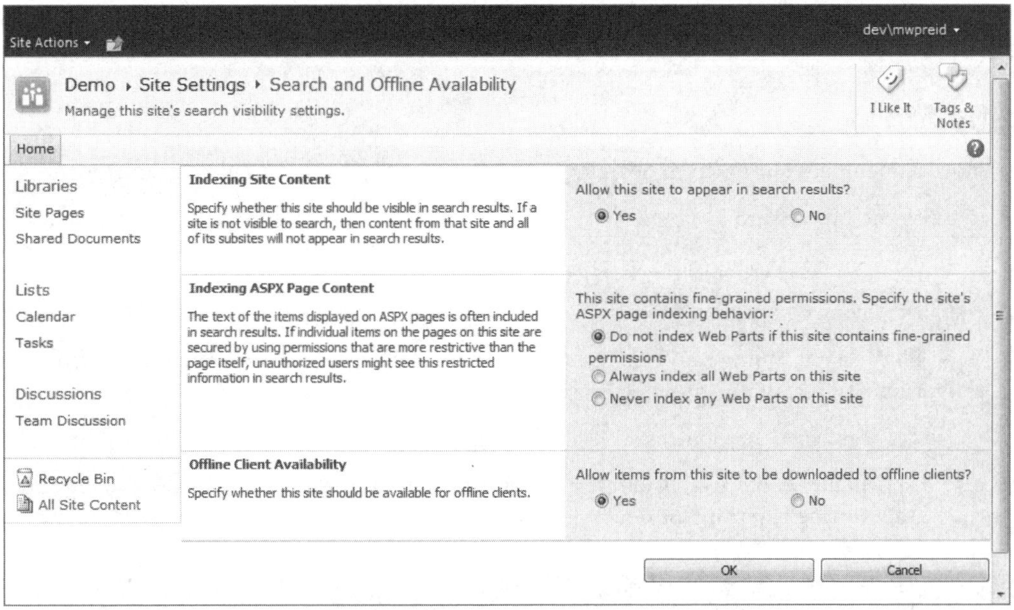

FIGURE 11-2

If the Web Parts are individually secured, users with access to the page itself may find information from the Web Parts returned by SharePoint Search. However, security trimming ensures they cannot access the Web Parts. Security trimming allows SharePoint to control who has access to objects and items based on the permissions the user has been given in the environment.

TRY IT

In this Try It exercise, you will remove several SharePoint objects from the search results, including the site itself. You might have to wait a few minutes to see the results of your actions in the search results page. If you have incremental crawl schedules, the results should be available immediately after the next crawl takes place. If you are using a development server, simply run a new incremental crawl after the Try It to see the results.

Lesson Requirements

To perform this lesson, you will need the following:

➤ A SharePoint team site containing at least one document library and at least one standard SharePoint list.

➤ A site collection administrator permission. For this example, I have created a document library called Lesson 11 Search.

Hint

To see the effect of the change in search settings, it is useful to run a search before changing any of the options. For these examples, I ran an incremental crawl immediately after changing the settings.

Hopefully you have crawls scheduled; if not, you will have to wait until your administrator runs the next crawl to see the changes.

Step-by-Step

To remove a document library from Search, you begin from within the document library:

1.   Click the Library tab.

2.   In the ribbon Settings group, select Library Settings.

3.   Click Advanced Settings.

4.   Scroll to Search Settings and change the default Search radio button (Allow Items from This Document Library to Appear in Search Results) to No.

5.   Click OK to save the changes.

Figure 11-3 shows the search results before the library is removed. Figure 11-4 shows the results after the Search setting is set to No, removing the library from the results.

FIGURE 11-3

Also note that once you turn off searching, various options become unavailable within the search drop-down list for the site. The item removed from the search scopes drop-down list will be the contextual search for the document library or list. The removal of the contextual search makes sense, of course, as you have removed this content from the SharePoint Index.

FIGURE 11-4

Figure 11-5 shows the search scopes drop-down after the option to search the library is removed.

FIGURE 11-5

If you do not see the search scopes drop-down list on your site, you might need to enable custom search scopes, as they are not enabled by default. Refer to Lesson 9 for instructions on how to do this.

To remove a SharePoint list from Search, follow these steps:

1. Click the Tasks list in Quick Launch to open it.

2. On the List Tools tab click List

3. Click the List Settings icon in the ribbon's Settings group.

4. In the General Settings group, click Advanced Settings.

5. Scroll to Search Category and change the default for Allow Items from This List to Appear in Search Results? from Yes to No.

Figures 11-6 and 11-7 show the Search Results screen before and after the preceding changes, respectively. Note that in Figure 11-7 the Tasks list result is no longer available within the search results.

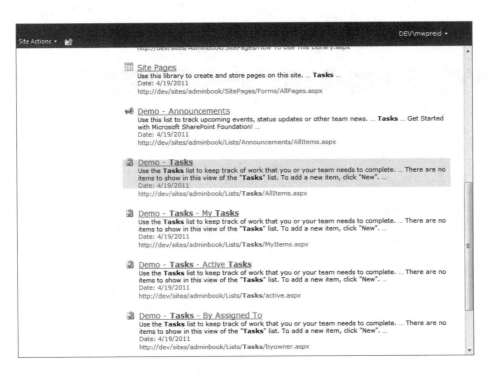

FIGURE 11-6

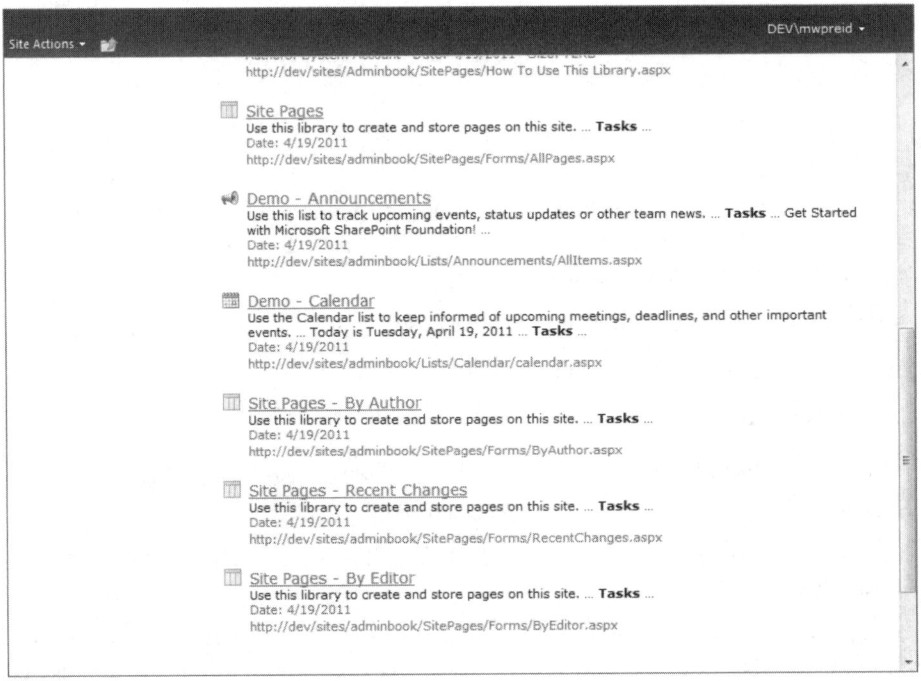

FIGURE 11-7

Just as in the previous example, the Search drop-down on the site has been changed to reflect the removal of the Tasks list.

To remove your site and its subsites from SharePoint Search, follow these steps:

1. Click Site Actions.

2. Select Site Settings.

3. Click Search and Offline Availability in the Site Administration category.

4. Change the selection of the radio button, Indexing Site Content, to No.

5. Click OK to save your changes.

Using the same screen you can also change the defaults for indexing your ASPX pages, and change the availability of your site to office clients. Figure 11-8 shows the options available on the Search and Offline Availability form.

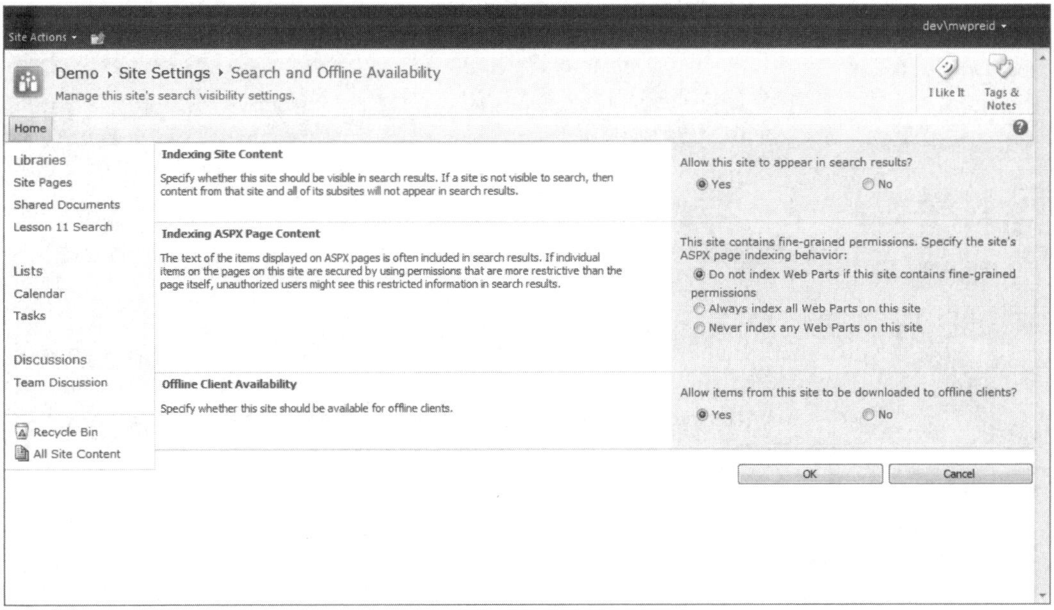

FIGURE 11-8

After you have changed the search settings for the site collection, you need to either run a crawl or wait until after the next scheduled crawl to see the effects of your changes. Figure 11-9 shows the results of turning of site collection search.

As previously mentioned, the site collection also contains an option to deny access to some areas, such as SharePoint Workspace, to offline clients. Setting this option to No can result in an error being sent to offline clients trying to connect to the list or library. Figure 11-10 shows SharePoint Workspace when trying to connect to the Shared Documents library in the Lesson 11 site when this feature is enabled.

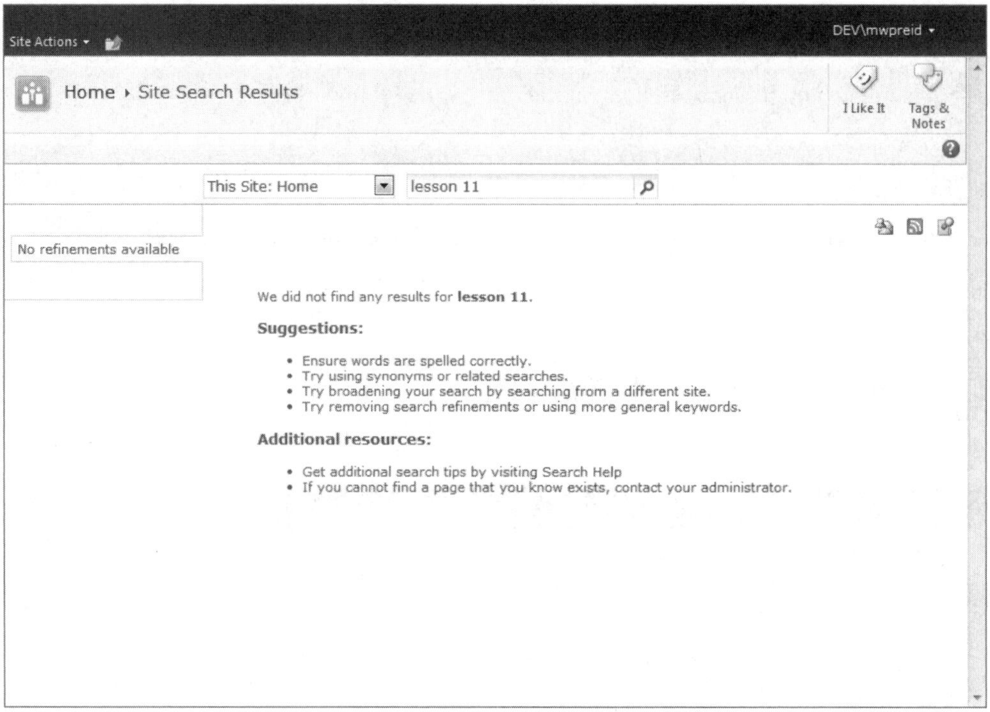

FIGURE 11-9

FIGURE 11-10

Although not directly related to Search in a strict sense, it is a useful feature to understand for working on information security and availability.

In this lesson, we examined Search and the ways in which you can use the administrative features of SharePoint to remove lists, libraries, and even entire sites from SharePoint search results. The overall objective of removing items is to improve the search experience of SharePoint users: to make information relevant and to reduce the amount of content returned. This helps to reduce clutter within the results making it easier for users to find what they need.

 Please select Lesson 11 on the DVD or visit www.wrox.com/go/sp2010-24 *to view the video that accompanies this lesson.*

SECTION IV
Setting Up Content Management Options

Setting Up Content Types

In this lesson we discuss the concept of the *content type*. Information about how to set up content types is widely available in books, on blogs, and in many other sources of information on SharePoint. Yet despite the wealth of information available on this topic, it seems that content types are rarely used. As a SharePoint administrator of a site or site collection, you should know not only how to use content types, but also why using your own content types is a better means of organizing your information than relying on the default SharePoint settings.

This lesson and the accompanying video will attempt to accomplish two objectives. They demonstrate through practical examples why content types are useful and should be used as often as possible for organizing content. Second, in the walkthrough and video example, you walk through the creation of a sophisticated example to show you the power of the content type in SharePoint.

USING CONTENT TYPES TO MANAGE CONTENT

Every organization manages a variety of content. Some obvious examples include:

➤ Documents

➤ Information kept in lists, such as employee rosters

➤ Web pages

➤ Images and multimedia

Many companies, before they consider a content management solution, attempt to organize their content by setting up a series of folders on a shared network location that everyone can access. Unfortunately people often simply duplicate the nested-folder method of data management even after installing SharePoint and do not use the powerful features that SharePoint has to offer.

A SharePoint content type is simply a structure that enables you to take a document, a list, or any of many other types of data, and attach to it descriptive columns, document templates, business processes, and other features. In this chapter, we look at the two most common types of data the average user creates: documents and list items.

Imagine for a moment that you have a particular type of document in your organization. Let's use the common example of a sales proposal. Think of the requirements that may exist for the sales proposal. As you read through this example, try to imagine some of the documents you deal with regularly. Think about how you can enhance the information concerning a sales proposal. For example, you could add a field that lists the salesperson who initiated the proposal, or you could add a field listing the total value of the sale. You could have a standard business process for reviewing and approving of the final proposal before sending it to a customer. You may want to keep an audit history of who has opened or modified the document. By using content types, you can attach data and processes to a type of information. Every time you create a new sales proposal, the data and processes will be available, without having to re-create it anew for each new document. In the example below, we will invent a fictitious document to illustrate the concepts.

Here are the requirements for a business proposal document at our fictitious company:

➤ Item #1: The sales proposal should be created from a common template so that each proposal has a standard look and outline and contains some light branding and perhaps a company logo.

➤ Item #2: There are three types of sales proposals, each for a different value of sale. The template for each type is slightly different, as is the approval level required.

➤ Item #3: Each sales proposal must go through one to three levels of approval, depending on its type. The more the sale is worth, the more the levels of management that must approve it.

➤ Item #4: Some people want to view proposals sorted by the seller's name. Others want to sort by industry, and still others by sales value.

➤ Item #5: The proposals should be designated as either "sold," "in progress," or "not sold."

➤ Item #6: The division of the company has four distinct departments. Each department manages its own proposals separately. After meeting all the previous requirements they should be repeated for each of the three other.

These requirements seem like a headache. How do companies handle this? Even when SharePoint is installed it's unfortunately common to see a plain document library with a bunch of folders separately created in each department website and the same old process of death by a thousand e-mails to ship the documents around to everyone who has to sign off on them. If a company doesn't have a document management system, the use of file folders requires everyone to categorize and aggregate the data in the same manner as determined by whoever set up the folders. If the folders are organized by company division for example, people who would rather see them listed by salesperson are out of luck. To produce other views it's not uncommon for someone to make a spreadsheet or use some other manual process to present a summary of sales proposals and e-mail it to various users.

A content type can eliminate all of these problems while at the same time giving your end users a better experience with the SharePoint interface. You can then use the Try It section and the accompanying video lesson to create an example step by step. If you take the 20 minutes to work through this material, you will be far better equipped to take advantage of one of the most powerful content management features in SharePoint.

Now, let's examine how we can use content types to address the 6 example requirements listed above.

Item #1: A Common Template

When you create a content type, you can attach a custom template to the type of content you create. In this example, the type of content is a sales proposal, so you can upload your proposal template, which is probably a preformatted word-processing document such as a Microsoft Word template. Now each time someone creates a new proposal it will open in your standard template without any need to copy and save the template with a different name.

Item #2: Three Types of Proposals in the Same Library

With content types you can add several different types of documents to the same document library. When a user goes to the document library to start a new proposal, he or she will be presented with all three types of sales proposal templates, each with a more descriptive title than the common "document" title that you see with a standard document library. The user can pick the appropriate proposal type from the list.

Item #3: A Different Business Process for Each Type of Proposal

Each content type you create can have its own individual workflow attached to it. By making a different content type for each proposal type you can assign a workflow that automatically routes documents for one, two, or three levels of approval based on the type of proposal chosen.

Item #4: Different Views of the Documents for Different People

A content type can have its own descriptive fields attached to it. When someone creates or uploads a proposal, he or she can fill out the sales value, department, and other information. Separate views can be used so that each person viewing the list of proposals can choose to see the documents sorted and filtered differently.

Item #5: A Designation of Sold, in Progress, or Not Sold

By adding a choice column to this content type, you can set the appropriate value for each proposal.

Item #6: Repeating the Process for Multiple Departments

If you attach workflows to a content type, anywhere the content type is used the workflow follows. This eliminates the need to recreate all the necessary logic for multiple sites or document libraries.

Using content types we can place all three types of sales proposals into one document library. We can activate workflows that are common to all proposals while at the same time activating separate workflows for each type of proposal. We can add descriptive fields to automatically allow for many types of views of the same data. Most of what is described here is simple to set up, as you will see in the Try It section. However, one concept requires further discussion: the creation of a hierarchy of content types.

CREATING A CONTENT TYPE HIERARCHY

Still looking at our example, you can see a couple of requirements that seem to be at cross purposes. First, common fields need to be added to every sales proposal. One field is common to all three types of proposal, which will mark its status as sold, in progress, or not sold. On the other hand, requirements vary by each proposal type, such as the number of approval levels required and the document template associated with each type of proposal.

The average SharePoint business user might be tempted to respond to this challenge, if he or she uses content types, by creating three completely separate content types and simply repeating the shared elements, such as the set of fields, in each content type. In doing so that user misses out on one of the most powerful features of content types, namely the ability of content types to inherit settings from other content types.

The proper way to create these content types is to create a hierarchy that allows each type of sales proposal to use a common set of elements while also containing elements unique to itself. You can tell if you are doing it properly if you are not repeating any elements in your content types. This type of structure uses what is known in the IT world as *inheritance*. The Try It! section clarifies the concept for the business user.

TRY IT

In this lesson we create three content types. One will be a parent in the hierarchy. Two will be child content types. The three content types together will form a content type hierarchy, with the two child content types inheriting elements from the parent type. We will add fields common to all three content types, and document templates unique to each.

Lesson Requirements

To complete this Try It exercise, you need the following:

➤ A SharePoint site and a Web browser.

➤ Three Microsoft Word documents. They should be titled Proposal A, Proposal B, and Proposal C. In a real-world application these would be three separate sales proposal templates, though their content here is not important.

➤ A pre-created SharePoint site with three document libraries. If you need to create the site, the Team Site template, provided as a default choice when creating a SharePoint site, will start you with a document library called Shared Documents. Create two other document libraries as well.

Hints

This Try It has a lot of steps and assumes that you are using a SharePoint site connected to a typical workplace network.

Step-by-Step

1. Open one of your three SharePoint sites to its home page. Use the Site Actions menu to access the site settings page.

2. In the Galleries heading, select Site Content Types (see Figure 12-1).

FIGURE 12-1

3. Click Create. Refer to Figure 12-2.

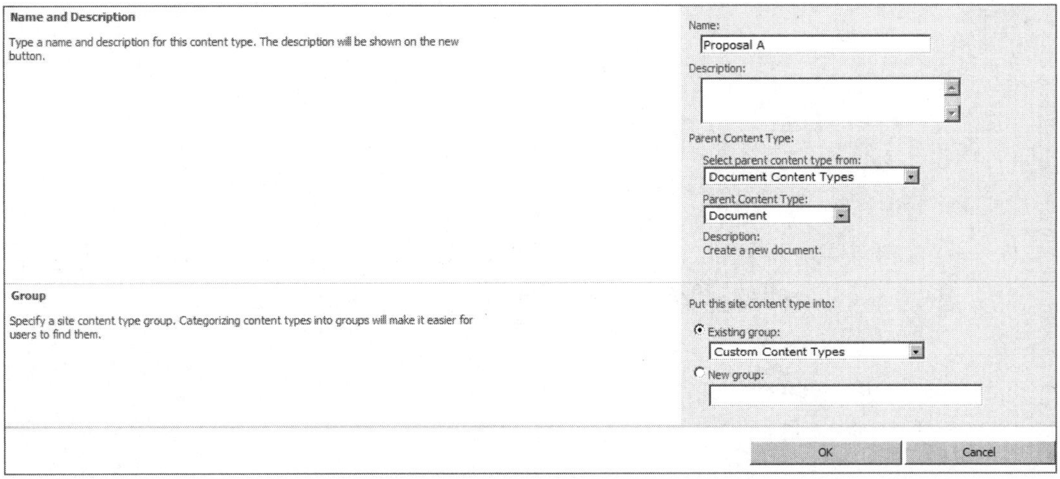

FIGURE 12-2

4. Enter the following values on the screen:

➤ Name: **Proposal A**

➤ Description: **Leave blank**

➤ Select Parent Content Type From: **Document Content Types**

➤ Parent Content Type: **Document**

➤ Put this Site Content Into: Existing group: **Custom Content Types**

Click OK. You will see a screen like the one in Figure 12-3.

A content type that you create will be available at the site where you create it and at all sub-sites. If you want the content type to be available throughout the entire site collection, create it at the top-level site in the collection. If you want the content type to be available across site collections, that is covered in the next chapter.

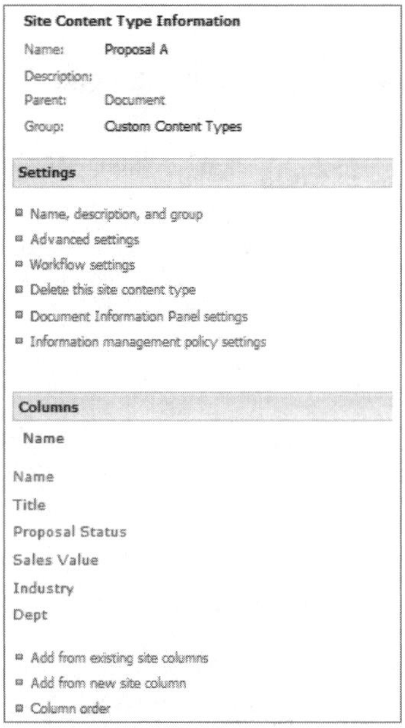

FIGURE 12-3

5. In the Columns section on this screen, click the link Add from new site Column. Create a choice column called "Proposal Status" with three choices:

➤ Sold

➤ In progress

➤ Not sold

You can leave the other default settings for the column.

6. Using the same process as in Step 5, create three more site columns. Each should be of type single line of text. Name the columns as follows:

➤ Sales Value

➤ Industry

➤ Dept

In a real-world example, it may be a better practice to use choice columns or other field types for these types of fields. For our example the purpose is to illustrate how you can take a type of document such as a sales proposal and add specific columns to it. Now you can create different views of sales proposals and use these columns to sort or filter the list of proposals. This is a more flexible solution than just using folder structures. Your site columns should look like what is shown in Figure 12-4.

7. Under the Settings tab on the Content Type page, click Advanced Settings. You will see a screen as shown in Figure 12-5 below. In the Document Template section click the radio button titled Upload a New Document Template and use the Browse... button to upload the Microsoft Word document Proposal A.

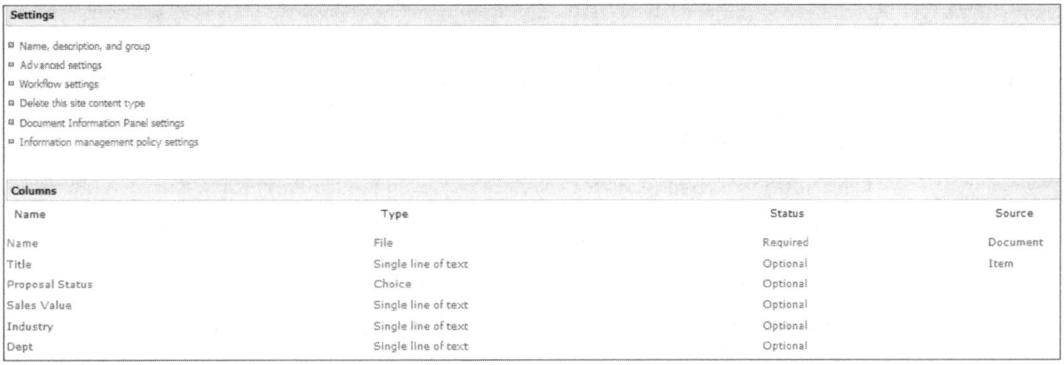

Settings
▫ Name, description, and group
▫ Advanced settings
▫ Workflow settings
▫ Delete this site content type
▫ Document Information Panel settings
▫ Information management policy settings

Columns			
Name	Type	Status	Source
Name	File	Required	Document
Title	Single line of text	Optional	Item
Proposal Status	Choice	Optional	
Sales Value	Single line of text	Optional	
Industry	Single line of text	Optional	
Dept	Single line of text	Optional	

FIGURE 12-4

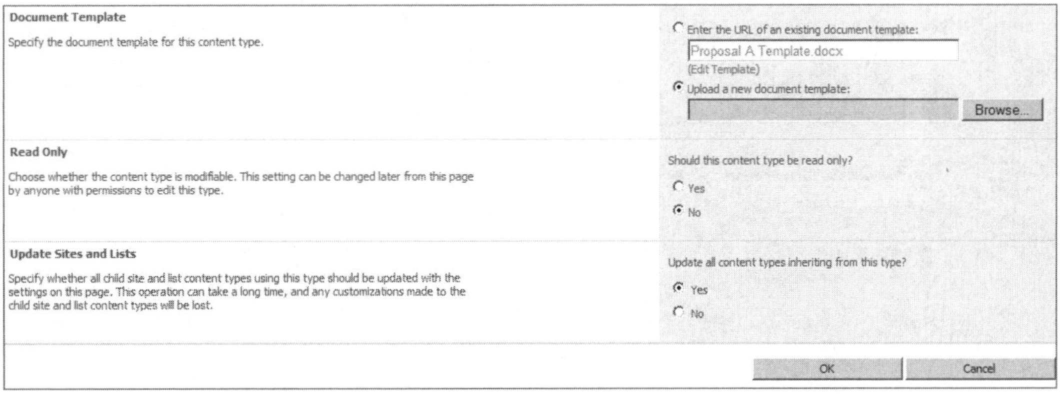

FIGURE 12-5

Now each time someone creates a new proposal Microsoft Word will open this document template, instead of the blank Word document that you would get if you just used the standard document library and its out-of-the-box "document" type.

8.   At this point the base content type has been created and the next two content types, for Proposal B and Proposal C, will be based on this one. Return to the Site Settings page (using the Site Settings link on the Site Actions menu in the upper left corner of the screen is the quickest way). On the Settings page, under the Gallery heading, click the Site Content Types link. You will see a long list of content types. The content type you just created should be under the heading Custom Content Types as shown in Figure 12-6. Notice that it should be highlighted in blue. A content type created at the site you are currently browsing will show a blue link. A content type created at a higher level will display in grey, with a blue link to its source site in the column to the right. Since the content type was created on this site, it is available to use on this site and all sites below it. Later in the example you will see how to add it to a document library.

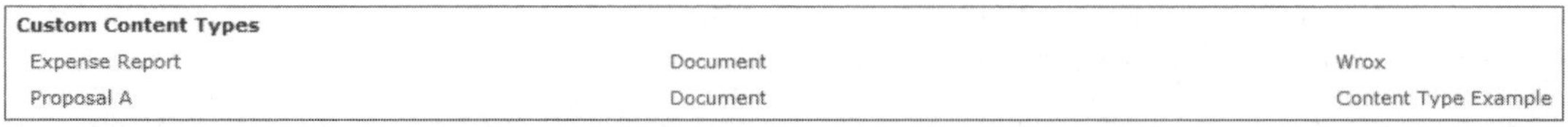

Custom Content Types		
Expense Report	Document	Wrox
Proposal A	Document	Content Type Example

FIGURE 12-6

9. Click the Create button again to make the second content type. Enter the following values:

> ➤ Name: Proposal B

> ➤ Description: [Leave blank]

> ➤ Select parent content type from: Custom Content Types

> ➤ Parent Content Type: Proposal

> ➤ Put this site content into: Existing group: Custom Content Types

Notice that for this content type, instead of selecting the document content type for the parent, you choose the proposal content type that you created earlier in the example. What this means is that all the columns you created for Proposal A are now also available for Proposal B. You don't have to recreate the same columns. A child content type inherits everything that its parent can do. In this particular case, it will include the columns and document template that you created in the previous steps. It could also include other elements such as workflows, security policies and so forth. You can see this in Figure 12-7.

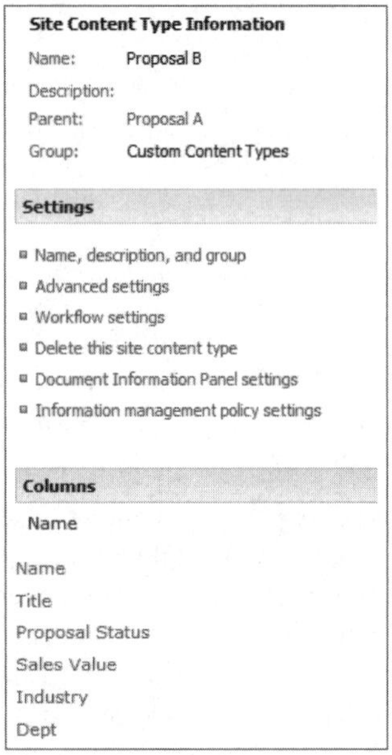

Site Content Type Information

Name: Proposal B
Description:
Parent: Proposal A
Group: Custom Content Types

Settings

▫ Name, description, and group
▫ Advanced settings
▫ Workflow settings
▫ Delete this site content type
▫ Document Information Panel settings
▫ Information management policy settings

Columns

Name

Name
Title
Proposal Status
Sales Value
Industry
Dept

FIGURE 12-7

10. Because Proposal B uses a different template from Proposal A, you want to change the template this content type uses. You can keep the things you want from Proposal A as part of Proposal B, and change the things you want to be different. Once again, choose Advanced Settings under the Settings heading and upload the Proposal B template.

11. Create Proposal C using the same process and settings as for Proposal B. Notice that when you create Proposal C we name Proposal A or Proposal B as the parent. The choice you make in setting up a hierarchy depends on your business requirements. You should put some thought into the hierarchy before creating the first content type. In our example Proposals B and C should are both "children": of Proposal A. As you did for Proposal B, upload a separate document template for Proposal C.

At this point you should have three content types, all using the same fields from Proposal A, but each using a separate document template. Note that you could also have added separate workflows for each content type to meet the requirements in the list.

12. Now let's add the content type to a document library. Open the Shared Documents library and click Library Settings on the toolbar. That will bring you to the document Library Settings page as shown in Figure 12-8. By default, libraries are not created to work with content types, so there is some configuration to do.

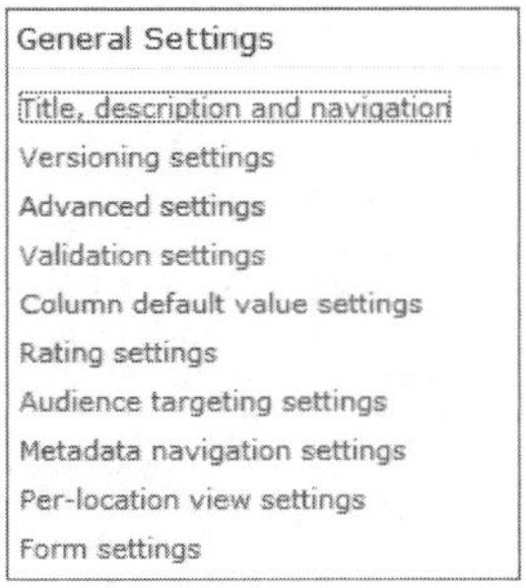

General Settings

Title, description and navigation
Versioning settings
Advanced settings
Validation settings
Column default value settings
Rating settings
Audience targeting settings
Metadata navigation settings
Per-location view settings
Form settings

FIGURE 12-8

13. On the document library settings page click Advanced Settings.

14. On the advanced settings page select Yes on the radio button labeled Allow Management of Content Types?. Click OK to return to the document Library Settings page. You will notice a previously hidden section, Content Types, below the General Settings section, as shown in Figure 12-9.

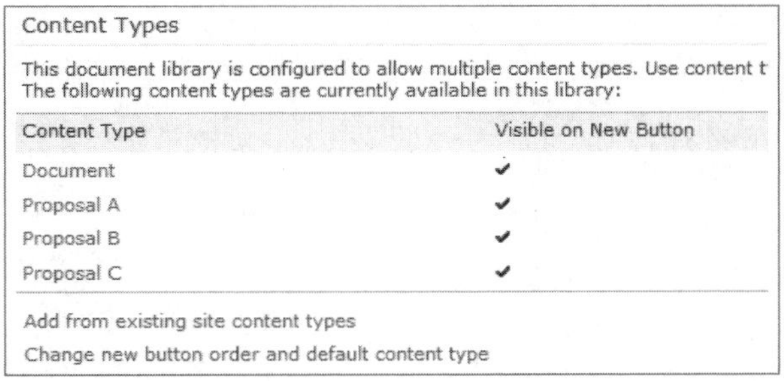

Content Types

This document library is configured to allow multiple content types. Use content t
The following content types are currently available in this library:

Content Type	Visible on New Button
Document	✓
Proposal A	✓
Proposal B	✓
Proposal C	✓

Add from existing site content types
Change new button order and default content type

FIGURE 12-9

15. Click the link Add from Existing Content Types. From the drop-down select Custom Content Types. Finally, select Proposal A, Proposal B, and Proposal C and add them to the library.

16. Go to the document library and create a new document. As shown in Figure 12-10, you are now presented with a choice of the standard documents as well as all three types of proposal. Each proposal has access to the same fields but uses a separate template when opened.

FIGURE 12-10

Please select Lesson 12 on the DVD or visit www.wrox.com/go/sp2010-24 *to view the video that accompanies this lesson.*

13

Publishing Content Types to Use Across Site Collections

In the previous lesson, we looked at creating content types and reusing them across sites in a site collection. One of the complaints from previous versions of SharePoint is how content types could not be used across site collections. A lot of the advantages of content reuse would not apply from one site collection to the next. In this lesson you are going to see how SharePoint 2010 uses content type publishing hubs to allow the reuse of content. Now it is possible to define a central location from which content types can be shared across the entire farm.

CREATING A CONTENT TYPE PUBLISHING HUB

To allow content types to be used across site collections you must first create a content type publishing hub. The requirements for doing so are as follows:

> ➤ You must have a SharePoint Standard or Enterprise license. Content type publishing requires the Managed Metadata Service, which is not available in SharePoint Foundation 2010.

> ➤ If you are not the farm administrator of your SharePoint installation you will have to enlist the administrator's help to set up the Managed Metadata Service application and perform some basic configuration.

> Once the Managed Metadata Service is running, you will be able to designate a site collection as a publishing hub for content types. Content types created in a site collection designated for publishing can be accessed from any other site collection in the farm. The Try It section contains a step-by-step example of how to configure a content type publishing hub and how to use content types across site collections.

TRY IT

In this Try It section, we walk through the entire step-by-step process of creating a content type publishing hub, including the portion to be completed by the farm administrator.

Lesson Requirements

Part of this lesson requires administrator access to the Central Administration site on your SharePoint environment. In addition, Managed Metadata Service must be running in the farm. The only other requirement is access to your SharePoint environment and enough rights to create content types.

Hints

To make sure a Metadata Service is running, open the Central Administration site. Under the Application Management heading, click the link titled Manage Service Applications. In the list of services displayed on the page, you should see one called Managed Metadata Service with a status of Started. If you do not have access to the Central Administration site ask your farm administrator to check that this service is running, especially if you do not see the elements described in the walkthrough.

Step-by-Step

1. Select a site collection that you would like to make the content type hub. The content types you create in this site collection will be the ones published to other site collections and Web Applications in the farm. Browse to the Site Settings page of the top-level site in the collection. Then select Site Collection Features under the Site Collection Administration heading, shown in Figure 13-1.

FIGURE 13-1

2. In the list of features, find the Content Type Syndication Hub feature and click Activate.

3. Open the Central Administration website. Click the Manage Service Applications link under the Application Management heading, shown in Figure 13-2.

FIGURE 13-2

4. In the list of service applications, select Managed Metadata Service (the one that is indented). Select Properties in the ribbon menu. Figure 13-3 highlights the correct choice.

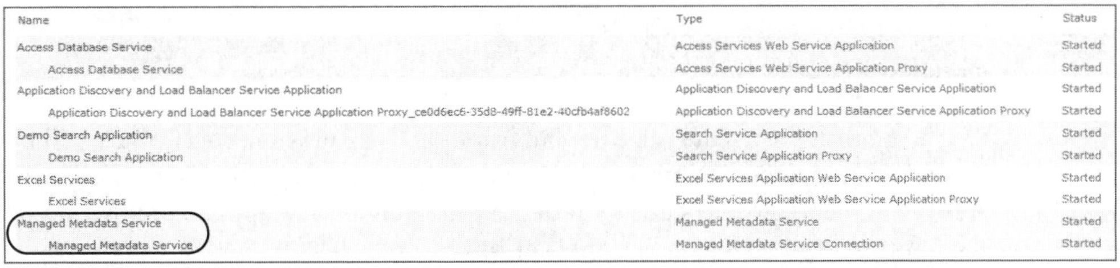

Name	Type	Status
Access Database Service	Access Services Web Service Application	Started
Access Database Service	Access Services Web Service Application Proxy	Started
Application Discovery and Load Balancer Service Application	Application Discovery and Load Balancer Service Application	Started
Application Discovery and Load Balancer Service Application Proxy_ce0d6ec6-35d8-49ff-81e2-40cfb4af8602	Application Discovery and Load Balancer Service Application Proxy	Started
Demo Search Application	Search Service Application	Started
Demo Search Application	Search Service Application Proxy	Started
Excel Services	Excel Services Application Web Service Application	Started
Excel Services	Excel Services Application Web Service Application Proxy	Started
Managed Metadata Service	Managed Metadata Service	Started
Managed Metadata Service	Managed Metadata Service Connection	Started

FIGURE 13-3

If you do not see the Managed Metadata Service, the service needs to be created. Step-by-step instructions for this are in Lesson 30.

5. Check the checkbox labeled Consumes Content Types from the Content Type Gallery at <site collection>, shown in Figure 13-4.

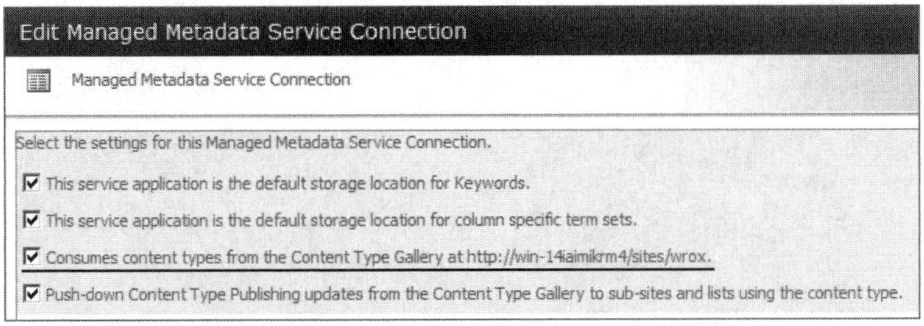

Edit Managed Metadata Service Connection

Managed Metadata Service Connection

Select the settings for this Managed Metadata Service Connection.

☑ This service application is the default storage location for Keywords.

☑ This service application is the default storage location for column specific term sets.

☑ Consumes content types from the Content Type Gallery at http://win-14iaimikrm4/sites/wrox.

☑ Push-down Content Type Publishing updates from the Content Type Gallery to sub-sites and lists using the content type.

FIGURE 13-4

6. Return to the site collection from Step 1 and create a content type. This procedure is covered in detail in Lesson 12, but here there's one difference. Now that this site collection is a content type hub, you will see an additional link, Manage Publishing for This Content Type, on the content type page, as shown in Figure 13-5. Select this link.

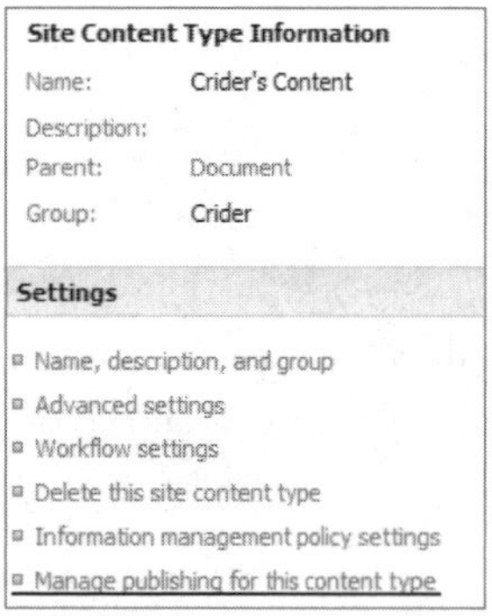

Site Content Type Information

Name:	Crider's Content
Description:	
Parent:	Document
Group:	Crider

Settings

▫ Name, description, and group
▫ Advanced settings
▫ Workflow settings
▫ Delete this site content type
▫ Information management policy settings
▫ Manage publishing for this content type

FIGURE 13-5

7. On the publish page make sure the Publish radio button is selected (which will be grayed out if you have previously published the content type) and click OK. This will make the content type available to any site collection that is part of any Web application that is connected to the Managed Metadata Service application.

8. Browse to a different site collection in your SharePoint farm. In the Content Type Gallery on the Site Settings menu you should see the content type that you created in Step 6. You will notice, however, that you range of options for the content type is reduced. Options available for published content types in a site collection are fewer than for content types created in that same site collection. Published content types can only be changed at the source and republished. See Figure 13-6 for an example of a published content type settings page with its limited options.

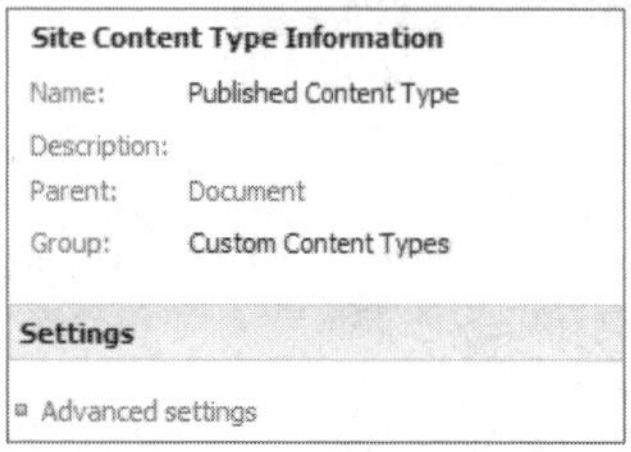

Site Content Type Information

Name:	Published Content Type
Description:	
Parent:	Document
Group:	Custom Content Types

Settings

▫ Advanced settings

FIGURE 13-6

Please select Lesson 13 on the DVD or visit www.wrox.com/go/sp2010-24 *to view the video that accompanies this lesson.*

14

Setting Up the Content Organizer

One of the challenges of setting up a content management system is creating a consistent method to categorize and store information. Even if you have a well-defined set of criteria and metadata to organize your data and documents, the users who ultimately contribute material to the system do not always understand your organization system. This leads to several undesirable results: duplicated documents, documents placed in the wrong locations, and frustration among users who cannot find the information they need.

The *content organizer* is a feature that enables users to submit documents to a central location and then uses a set of rules to automatically route the documents to locations that you specify. This takes the guesswork and inconsistency out of document storage.

This lesson will describe how to configure and use this feature to enable users to more efficiently and consistently organize their documents and data. Note that this feature does not exist in SharePoint Foundation 2010. You need at least the standard license to access this functionality.

THE CONTENT ORGANIZER'S FUNCTIONALITY

The content organizer creates a special document library called the *drop-off library* at the site where the content organizer feature is located. Users can submit documents to the Document Center using the button on the home page of a Document Center site template or simply by adding documents directly to the drop-off library as they would to any SharePoint library. Once a document is in the drop-off library, its properties and content type are checked against a series of rules that can be created to determine where the documents are routed after that. Figure 14-1 shows the Document Center home page. The Document Center is a built in site template that automatically activates content organizer functionality.

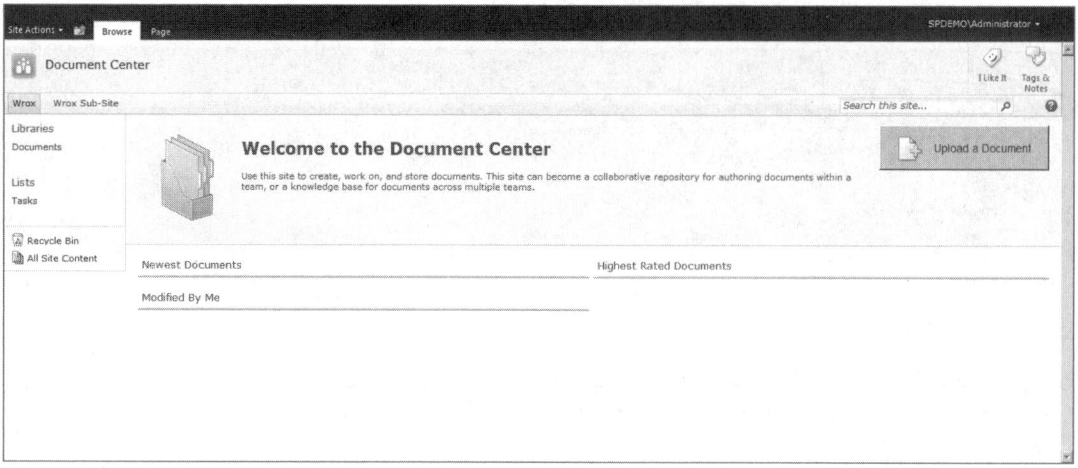

FIGURE 14-1

There are many uses for a content organizer. It is a much-underappreciated SharePoint feature, probably because it does take a few steps to configure it. But setup isn't difficult, and if you watch the video for this lesson and follow along in the Try It section, you should be able to set up a content organizer application with ease. The content organizer functionality is provided automatically when you create a new site using either the Record Center for Document Center template. One thing that is important to understand is that you do not have to use the Record Center or Document Center site template to use a content organizer. You can activate the feature on any site. The Record and Document Center site templates simply activate the necessary features for you during template creation.

This section discusses some example scenarios in which a content organizer is useful. The first usage is for a document library with a lot of folders. Each folder represents a supervisor to whom employees are to upload a status report. It takes a lot of unnecessary maintenance to create individual security for each folder so it is available only to a given supervisor's employees. In addition, you may not want employees to see what their colleagues have uploaded to their common supervisor.

In order to deal with this situation, you can create a content organizer for a status report document. The status report should have a field in which the employee can list her supervisor's name. In the content organizer you can set a rule that automatically routes a document to a library created for holding employee status reports, into a folder with the same name as a document property. Each employee submits to the drop-off library, and the document is automatically routed to the folder that is set for the supervisor. Employees do not have access to the supervisor's folder and all the supervisors get their status reports without any security maintenance or overhead.

Similar to the previous example, but with a twist, in some scenarios, you might want to set up a document library for Excel-based expense reports. Each employee sends an Excel file to the drop-off library. Based on the value of the expense report it is routed to one of two document libraries. One library runs a workflow for approval by the employee's supervisor. Reports above a certain dollar value are routed to a different library, where a different workflow sends the report to both the supervisor and a vice president. The employee does not have to be aware of the logic behind this policy. They just submit the document and note the total dollar value. This reduces errors and increases automation.

Finally, a portal site may have a variety of document libraries. By setting up a content organizer you can route everything to the proper location by content type. When users submit documents to the portal, they do not have to try to figure out your filing system. They just note the content type of a document and the content organizer routes it automatically. If an item is a vacation request form (and is associated to a vacation request content type), it is routed to one place. If the item is a company news article, it is routed somewhere else. The user doesn't need to know where these locations are, they upload both documents to the same place.

SETTING UP THE CONTENT ORGANIZER

You can activate the content organizer in a few different ways. You can activate it on any site by activating the content organizer feature on the Site Features page. (Note that the content organizer is available only with the SharePoint Standard license or higher. The feature is not included with SharePoint Foundation 2010.) It can also be activated by default when you create a site using the Document Center or Report Center template. The content organizer is the same regardless of how it is activated.

After the feature is activated, additional links become available under the Site Administration heading of the Site Administration page. The two links are:

Site Administration
Regional settings
Site libraries and lists
User alerts
RSS
Search and offline availability
Sites and workspaces
Workflows
Workflow settings
Related Links scope settings
Content Organizer Settings
Content Organizer Rules
Term store management
Content and structure
Searchable columns
Content and structure logs

➤   Content Organizer Settings

➤   Content Organizer Rules

The new Site Administration list is shown in Figure 14-2.

The Content Organizer Settings page enables you to determine a range of parameters for your sites. These elements are covered in detail in the Try It section of the lesson.

FIGURE 14-2

The Content Organizer Rules page is where you determine how to route a document that is placed into the Content Organizer drop-off library. You can make routing decisions according to content type or other properties. Content organizer rules will also be demonstrated in the Try It section of the chapter.

After you have activated the feature, determined the settings, and created the rules, your content organizer is complete.

INTEGRATING E-MAIL INTO THE CONTENT ORGANIZER

There are two different ways to integrate e-mail into the content organizer. The first is to enable the drop-off library to accept incoming e-mails as you would do with any SharePoint library. Before you do this, the following two things must happen:

➤   Incoming e-mail settings must be set by the farm administrator in the Central Administration site.

> ➤ Incoming e-mail settings must be set on the Library Settings page for the drop-off library. If the e-mail settings have not been set in Central Administration, the link to the page to set up e-mail for the library will not be visible on the E-mail Settings page under the Library Settings page.

When e-mail is set up for a document library, documents attached to e-mails sent to the document library are saved into it. The content organizer then applies rules to the documents and routes them accordingly.

The second way to integrate e-mail functionality into the content organizer is to activate a feature on the site called the E-Mail Integration with Content Organizer feature. Figure 14-3 shows the feature you need to activate on the Site Features page.

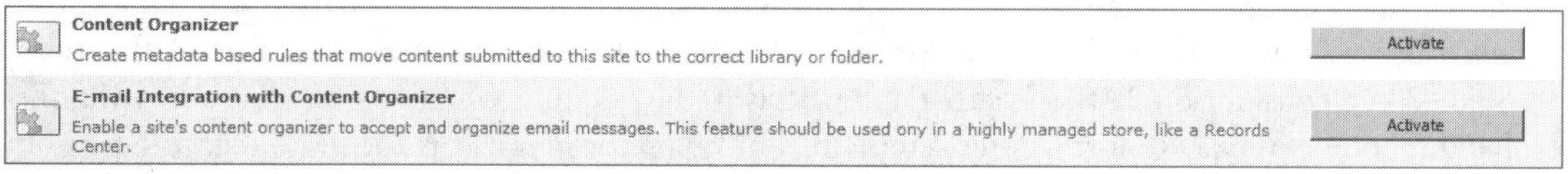

FIGURE 14-3

After the feature is activated there is an additional link on the Content Organizer Settings page, as shown in Figure 14-4, for configuring the e-mail settings. These settings are similar to those for an e-mail-enabled document library. Both types of e-mail integration are covered in the Try It section.

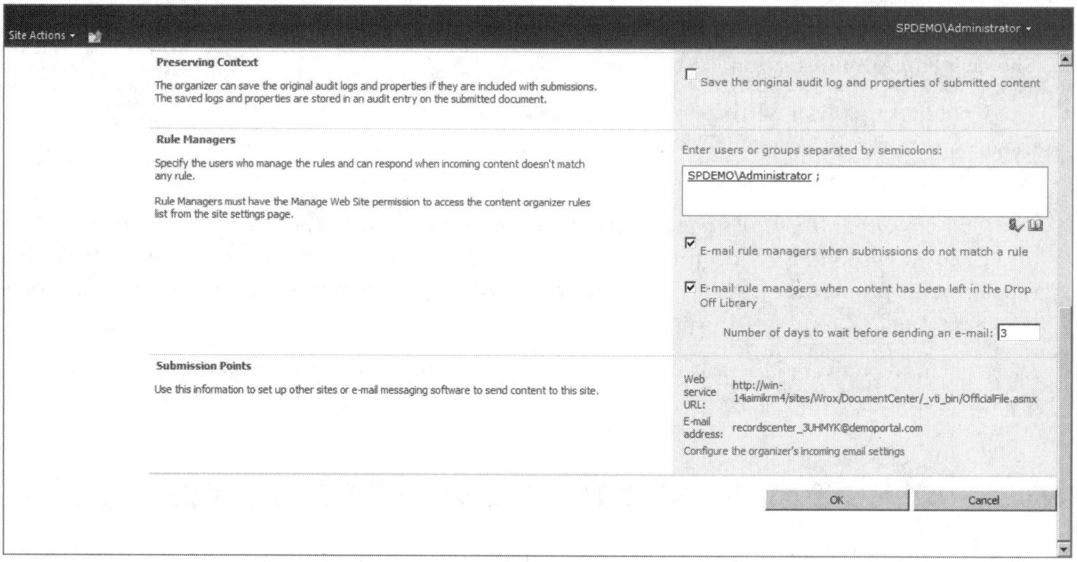

FIGURE 14-4

TRY IT

In this Try It section, we walk through the process of configuring the Content Organizer for typical use.

Lesson Requirements

To complete this Try It exercise, you need a SharePoint site with at least the Office SharePoint Service Standard license.

Step-by-Step

1. Open a SharePoint site in your environment where you would like to create a new sub-site.

2. Create a new site and use the Document Center site template. See Figure 14-5.

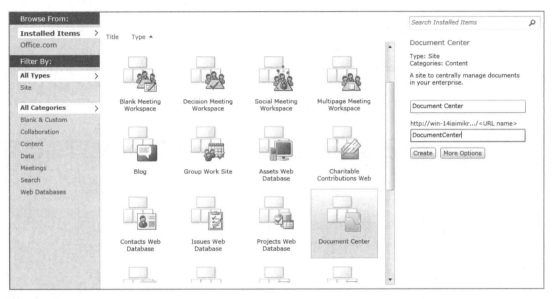

FIGURE 14-5

If you do not see this template, one possible reason is that you have not activated the SharePoint Server Standard Site Features feature. To activate this feature, go to the Manage Site Features page, located under the Site Actions heading on the Site Settings page.

3. Browse to the Site Settings page on your new site. Under the Site Administration heading, select the Content Organizer Settings link (as shown previously in Figure 14-2). This opens the page shown in Figure 14-6.

4. Set the options on the page as follows:

   ➤ **Redirect Users to the Drop-Off Library:** If you check this box, users cannot directly place documents into the target libraries where content is to be diverted. Use this option if you want to force the use of the drop-off library and not give users the discretion to place documents wherever they wish.

   ➤ **Sending to Another Site:** You can redirect content across site collection boundaries if you select this option, which is most likely to be useful for large implementations spanning a large organization.

➤ **Folder Partitioning:** SharePoint does not recommend having more than 2,500 items in one folder. You can use this setting to auto create folders to avoid having to manually add folders as this may reach this item limit. Again, this is more common for large deployments. Note that you can use the symbol %1, which will actually name the auto-created folder based on the date it was created.

➤ **Duplicate Submission:** If a document gets routed to a location where a document with the same name already exists, you can either automatically create a new file name with appended characters, or you can version the document and keep the name. Keep in mind that versioning may not be appropriate.

➤ **Role:** Here you can set who is in charge of dealing with content that doesn't match the routing rules. This allows the appointed manager(s) to follow up and place malformed documents in the correct place.

➤ **Submission Points:** There are people who cannot shake the habit of e-mailing content, and you can let them e-mail it to the document organizer as if it were any other user. The content organizer picks up the e-mail and attaches documents and route them based on their properties.

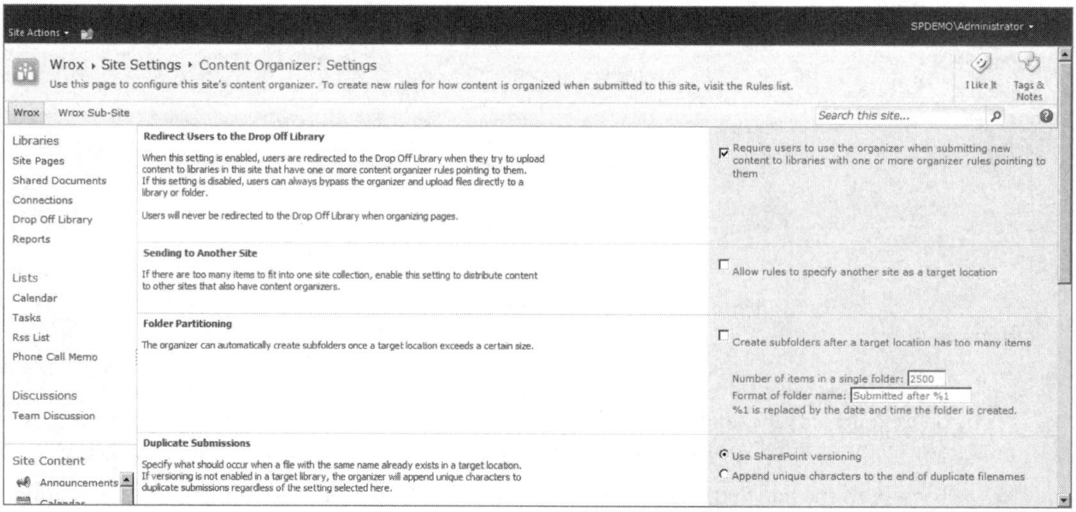

FIGURE 14-6

5. Set up incoming e-mail settings. After you have determined the content organizer settings, you should configure the e-mail settings, which you can access via the link at the bottom of the Content Organizer Settings page. Figure 14-7 shows the options available. These settings enable the content organizer and the associated lists to be used as permanent e-mail storage.

➤ **Allow this List to Receive E-mail:** This sets up the content organizer as an e-mail store and provides an e-mail address.

➤ **Save E-mail Attachments:** Documents attached to an e-mail will be saved as attachments to list items.

➤ **Save meeting invitations:** This setting allows you to save the body of the e-mail message as well as the attached document.

➤ **Save original e-mail:** Attach invites to the e-mail as a list attachment.

➤ **E-mail security policy:** Allow anyone to e-mail the list or only people set up with rights to the list.

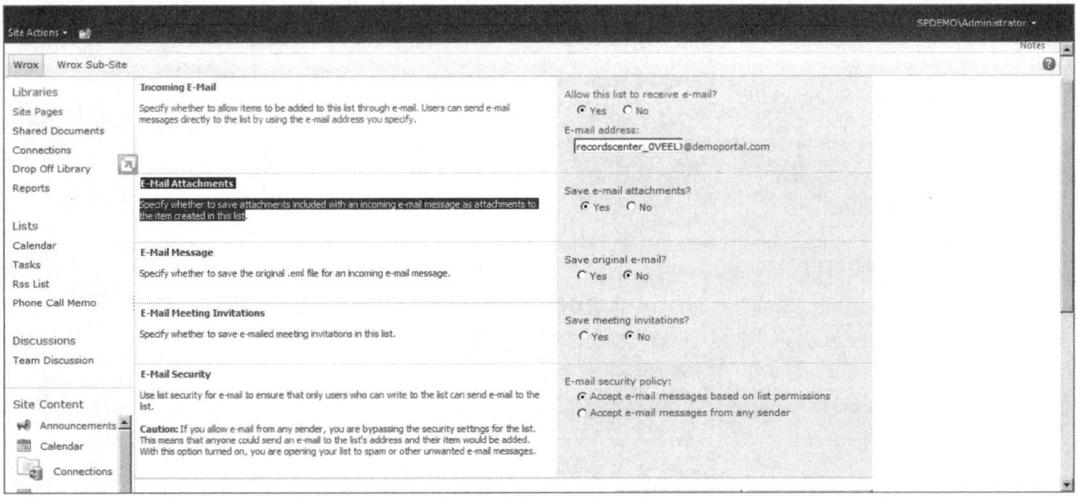

FIGURE 14-7

6. Set up the content organizer rules. In steps 4 and 5, we set up the content organizer settings. Now we will set up the content organizer rules. This is the second link, as discussed in Step 3 above, added in the Site Administration menu when you activate the content organizer feature. Content organizer rules determine how documents that find themselves in the drop-off library get routed to other locations within the site or in other sites and site collections. When you click on the Content Organizer Rules link, you are taken to an ordinary looking SharePoint list. Content organizer rules are stored in a SharePoint list. Figure 14-8 shows an example of this list.

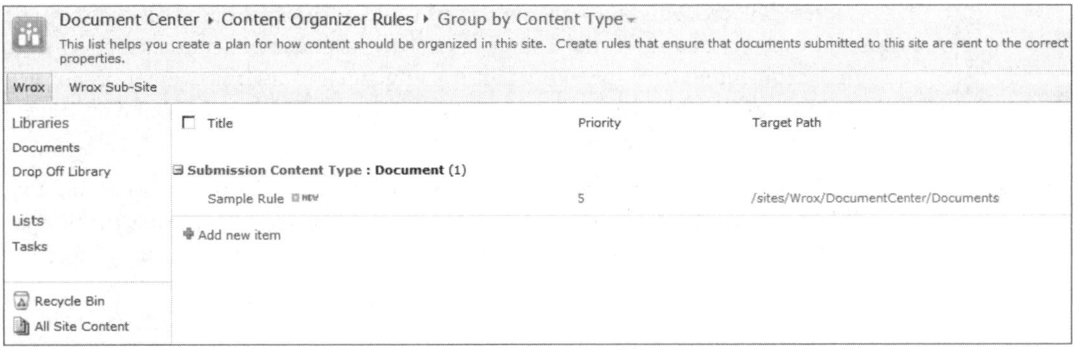

FIGURE 14-8

When you add a new item to a list, you are adding a rule that will determine how content is routed. Figure 14-9 shows the dialog box and options presented when you add a new rule to the list.

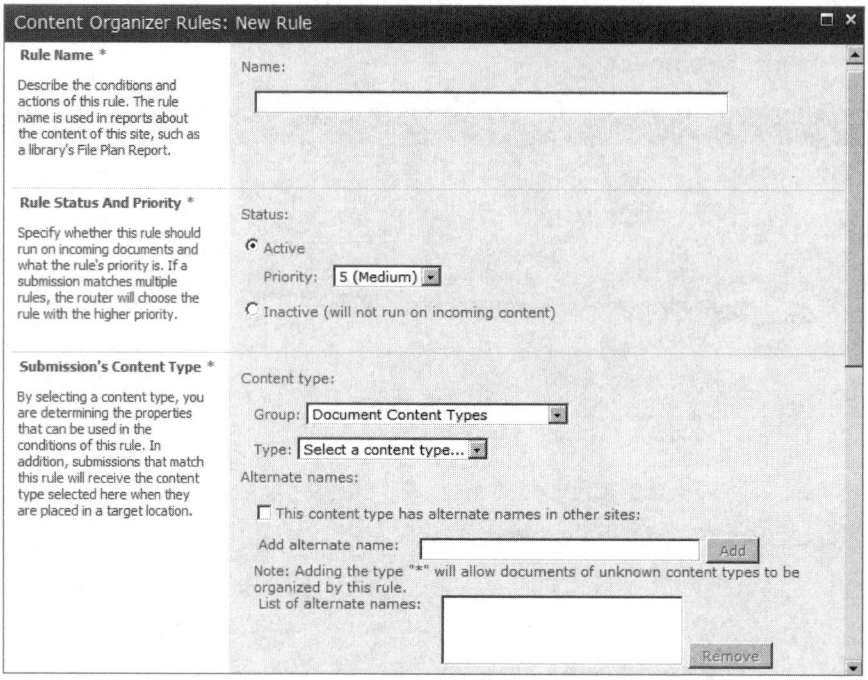

FIGURE 14-9

Here are the descriptions of the elements of a new rule, as presented in the dialog box:

➤ **Rule Name:** Each rule must have a unique name. Name this one **Sample Rule**.

➤ **Rule Status and Priority:** It is possible for rules to conflict within the same document. Set the priority to "1". Conflicting rules are resolved based on the priority setting, with higher priority rules taking precedence over lower numbered ones.

➤ **Content Type Group and Value:** You can route documents based on content types and property values. For this example, choose the document content type by selecting Document under Type. Note that if you wanted to use the content organizer for e-mails, you would select the group value of "Content Organizer Content Types" here and the type value of "E-mail Submission".

7. Go to the home page of the site where you have set up the content organizer and find the "Drop-off library". Add a document to the library and make sure the title has the words status report in it. You will be presented with a dialog box as shown in Figure 14-10.

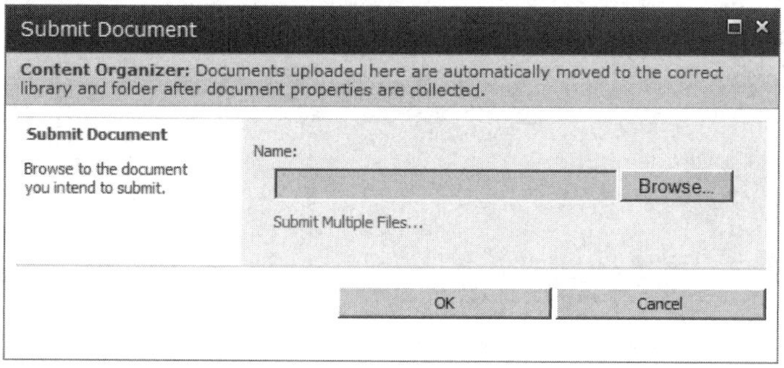

FIGURE 14-10

Figure 14-11 shows where the document properties that will determine how and if a document is routed to another location.

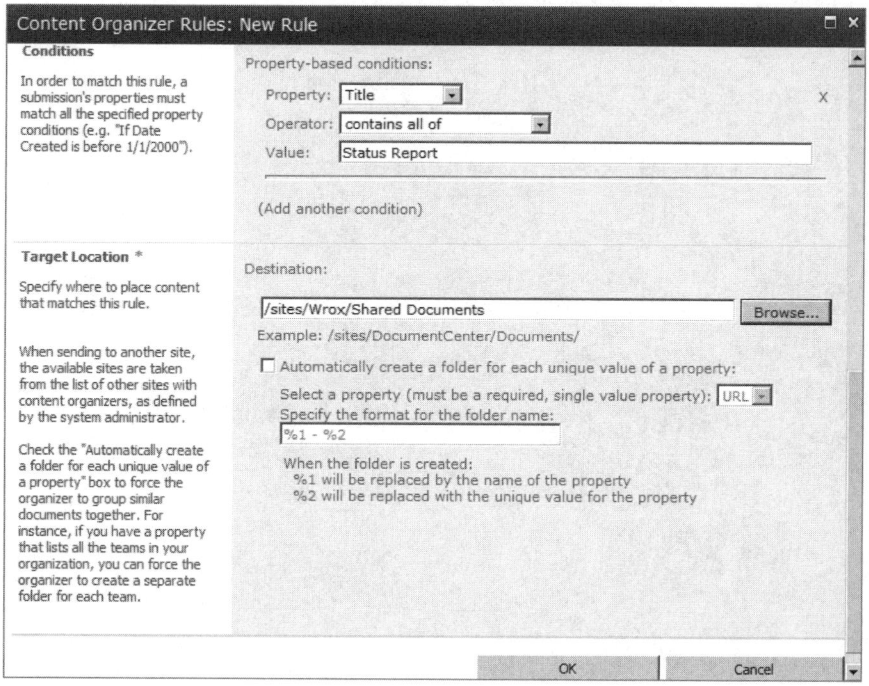

FIGURE 14-11

8. Finally, you can see the document has been successfully transferred to the Shared Documents library according to our rule, because it has the phrase "Status Report" in the title. Figure 14-12 shows the message indicating a successful routing of the document.

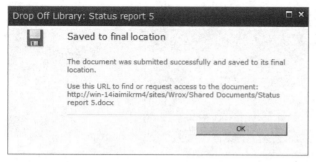

FIGURE 14-12

 Please select Lesson 14 on the DVD or visit www.wrox.com/go/sp2010-24 *to view the video that accompanies this lesson.*

15

Using Document Sets

Document Sets is a new feature offered as part of the standard version of Office SharePoint Server 2010. While it is touted as a separate feature, in fact it is just a specialized content type. Document Sets are useful when you have a group of documents that you want to treat as one item, such as in workflows and audit policies.

As an example, suppose you have a document library used to store documents for IT projects. An IT project can contain documents built at different times. Imagine that you have a PowerPoint presentation to show your idea to colleagues, a Word document for requirements, an Excel spreadsheet for budget and schedule, and so forth. You may want to apply a workflow to these documents. Perhaps the package needs management approval. You may want to apply a content expiration date so that the documents are deleted after a year. In these cases, and many others, you won't want to apply separate policies or workflows to the presentation, the requirements document, and the project plan. You will want to treat them as one unit. Enter Document Sets.

CREATE A DOCUMENT SET CONTENT TYPE

A Document Set is a feature that is scoped at the site collection level. In order to activate it you will have to be at the top-level site of a site collection. Go to the Site Settings page and under the Site Collection Administration page click the Site Collection Features link, shown in Figure 15-1.

On the Features page activate the Document Sets feature, shown in Figure 15-2.

FIGURE 15-1

FIGURE 15-2

Now you can use the Document Set content type anywhere within the site collection. The Try It section walks you through creating and adding documents to a Document Set.

TRY IT

In this walkthrough, you will be creating a Document Set. Once it is created, you will add several items to it to see the functionality.

Lesson Requirements

In order to complete this lesson you'll need a SharePoint site with at least the Office SharePoint Service Standard license.

Hints

Follow the steps given in the previous section to activate the Document Set feature before performing the walkthrough.

Step-by-Step

1. Open a document library on your SharePoint site or create a new one. In this example, our document library is called Document Set Enabled Library. (Catchy, isn't it?)

2. Browse to the Settings page of the document library. Click Advanced Settings, as shown in Figure 15-3.

3. In the Content Types section of the Advanced Settings page, Select Yes for the radio button option. Scroll to the bottom of the screen and click OK. This will return you to the Settings page. Figure 15-4 shows how this option appears on the page.

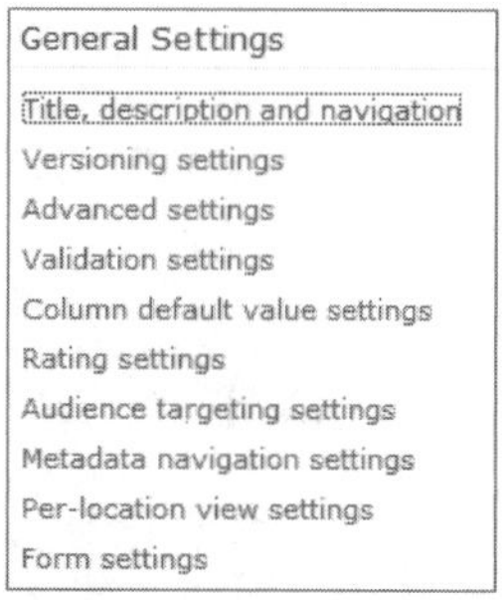

FIGURE 15-3

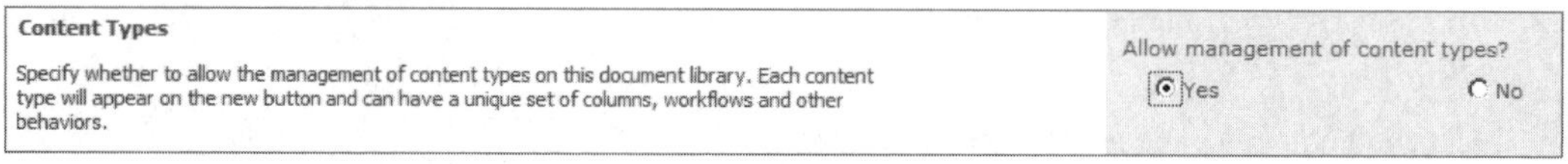

FIGURE 15-4

4. On the Settings page, in the Content Types section, click the Add from existing site content types link, as shown in Figure 15-5.

Content Types

This document library is configured to allow multiple content types. Use content types to specify
The following content types are currently available in this library:

Content Type	Visible on New Button
Document	✔

Add from existing site content types
Change new button order and default content type

FIGURE 15-5

5. On the Add Content Types page, select All Groups in the Select site content types from the drop-down control, and then select the Document Set content type from the list box and click Add to indicate you would like to add it to the available content types in the library. Click OK. Figure 15-6 shows this dialog.

Select site content types from:

All Groups

Available Site Content Types:

Allow any content type *
Article Page
Audio
Basic Page
Crider's Content
Dublin Core Columns
E-mail Submission
Enterprise Wiki Page
Expense Report
Form
Image

Add >

< Remove

Content types to add:

Document Set

Description:
Create a document set when you want to manage multiple documents as a single work product.

Group: Document Set Content Types

FIGURE 15-6

6. Browse to the document library's main page. In the Library Tools section of the ribbon, select Documents and then click the drop-down arrow from the New Document button. Select Document Set from the list of drop-down choices. When the dialog box appears, type a name and option description for the Document Set. Figure 15-7 shows how this looks in the ribbon.

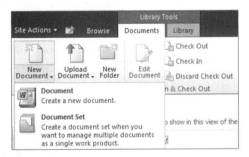

FIGURE 15-7

7. The Document Set has modified the toolbar choices slightly. To add a document to the Document Set, use the New Document or Upload Document toolbar button, as shown in Figure 15-8.

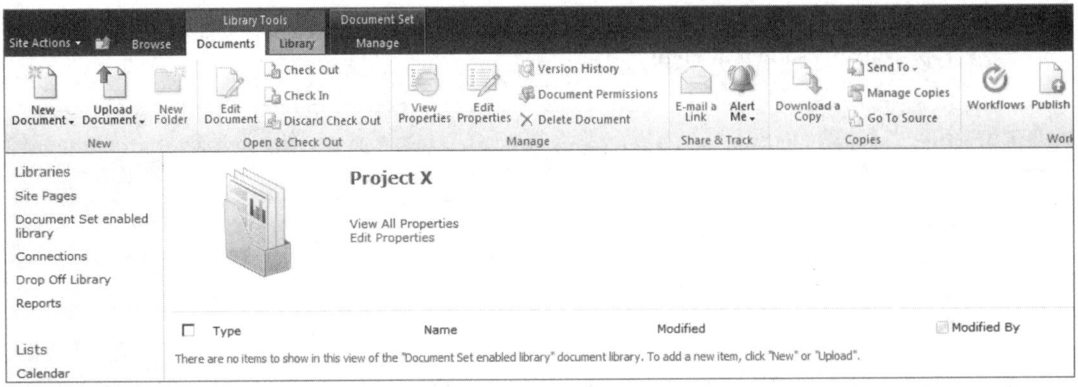

FIGURE 15-8

8. We are going to use the Upload Document button, and specifically the Upload Multiple Documents option, to upload several different types of document. In the ribbon, you should see the Library Tools section. Select the Documents tab from the Library Tools section. Both options are shown in Figure 15-9. Select any three or four items you have available of different types. Then click OK. After the files have uploaded, select Done.

FIGURE 15-9

Figure 15-10 shows the dialog after you have selected the files.

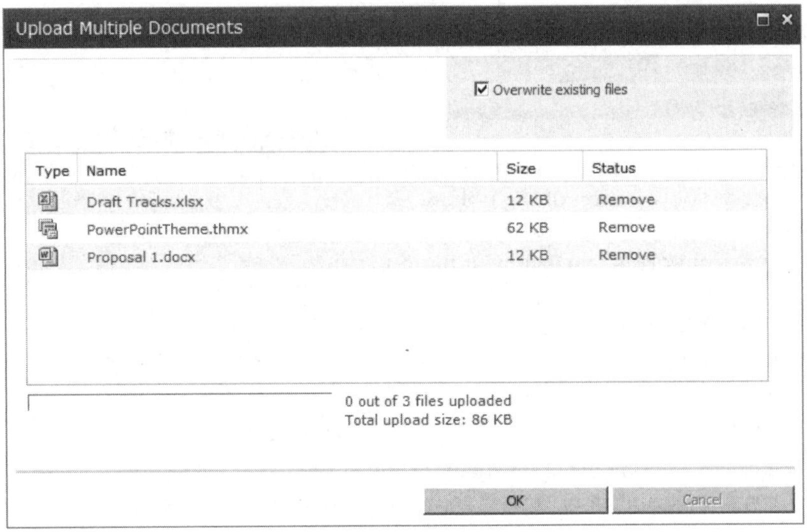

Upload Multiple Documents

☑ Overwrite existing files

Type	Name	Size	Status
	Draft Tracks.xlsx	12 KB	Remove
	PowerPointTheme.thmx	62 KB	Remove
	Proposal 1.docx	12 KB	Remove

0 out of 3 files uploaded
Total upload size: 86 KB

OK   Cancel

FIGURE 15-10

9. Click the library to see the "All Documents" view. (This is the default view of any SharePoint library or list). You will see that the item listed has the name you gave your Document Set

(Figure 15-11), not that of any of the individual items you added to it. You can manipulate this Document Set as though it were a single document. Click it and you will return to the Document Set page from Step 7, where you can individually work with your documents.

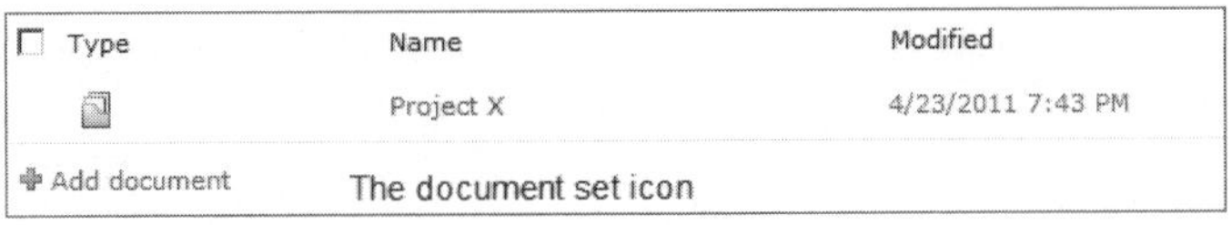

□ Type	Name	Modified
	Project X	4/23/2011 7:43 PM
✚ Add document	The document set icon	

FIGURE 15-11

Please select Lesson 15 on the DVD or visit www.wrox.com/go/sp2010-24 *to view the video that accompanies this lesson.*

16

Using Hold and Discovery

Using the Hold and Discovery (technically known as eDiscovery in the SharePoint world) allows you to find documents you don't want deleted and setting "holds" on them to ensure they won't be. A hold overrides every attempt to delete a record by any user no matter what his administrative rights.

Unlike other content management features such as retention policies and record declaration, holds and discovery are usually going to be used on an ad hoc basis rather than as part of an ongoing content management strategy. You use it when you get sued. Well, at least that's the most likely motivation. *Discovery* is a legal term meaning that a side in a legal action gets a chance to review the evidence that the other side will be using against it in court. For corporations, that translates into orders not to delete any information that might be relevant to the case, and "Oops, I didn't know those files were in that folder when I deleted it" doesn't really cut it in court.

There are other scenarios in which it is useful to find a group of related items and make sure they don't get deleted, but legal reasons are the most common.

DISCOVERY: FIND IT

In the Try It section we will discuss in detail how to activate features and work through all the settings and options. In this section we will discuss the options available for searching records and finding them. The discovery functionality uses SharePoint search-and-query syntax (rules for writing commands to help find stuff) to locate documents. Figure 16-1 shows the section of the discovery page related to searching. As you can see, it requires you to enter the name of a site to search and some keywords for finding documents. We will visit it again in more detail in the Try It section.

It is important to remember that discovery relies on a functional search service and an up-to-date crawl of the data. A crawl is a scheduled operation that finds all of the content and places it into an index to be available for searching. Content cannot be found via search (or "discovery") until it has been crawled and placed into an index.

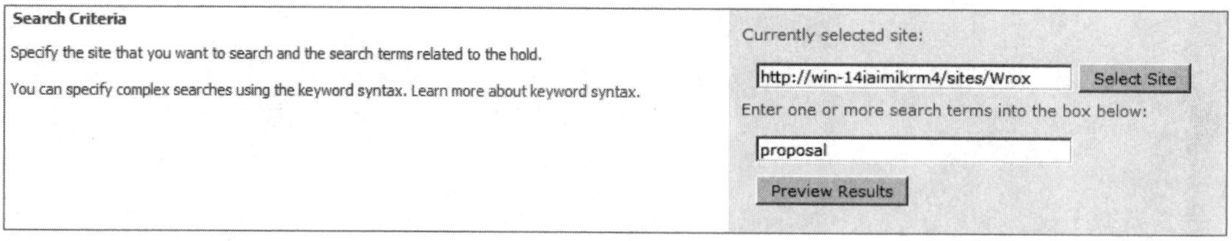

FIGURE 16-1

There are two things to remember about this search feature:

➤ The search is scoped to the site collection, but you can narrow the scope to a subsite by entering the URL of the subsite in the text box, as shown in Figure 16-1. You cannot expand the scope of the search to find items outside of the site collection, however. For that, you will have to perform searches on each site collection individually. The search functionality related to discovery is more restrictive than the Enterprise Search feature of SharePoint 2010.

➤ The search will run with elevated privileges so every document can be discovered. Enterprise Search shows you only content that you have rights to see. Your elevated privileges here don't give you the rights to open a document, just to apply holds to it.

Here are five key points that offer some examples of what you can use in the search box to help find content:

1. To find files that contain a list of ALL the words you type, type the words with spaces in between. To find files that contain both *apple* and *orange*, type: **apple orange**.

2. To find files that match exact phrases, enclose the phrase in double quotes. To find a file with the title Budget Projections type **Budget Projections**. This way you will not find files just because they contain the word *budget* or *projections*.

3. To include document properties, use the property name and a colon, like this: **Title:Sales Proposal**.

4. You can exclude keywords or properties by using a hyphen. For example, to exclude the year 2010, you would type: **-2010**.

5. Remember that attachments to list items are not included in search results.

HOLD: SAVE IT

When an item is placed into a hold, it cannot be edited or deleted for any reason, regardless of user rights.

Intuitively, one finds a document and places a "hold" on it. This is how the interface appears to work for the end user as well. However, under the covers, SharePoint handles the concept of applying holds differently. A document is not modified to be associated with a hold status. In fact, once you activate the Hold and eDiscovery feature, a list is created that you can add different holds to. The list is hidden and not visible in the normal interface. Each hold that you execute creates a new corresponding list. When you find documents as part of a discovery, you are actually applying the results to a created hold list, as opposed to marking the document directly. A document can be part of several holds at once. It is not editable until it is removed from every hold list where its name appears. By naming multiple holds you give yourself a lot of flexibility in performing discovery and putting holds on your content. The interface for the Hold and eDiscovery feature does not require you to interface with these hold lists directly. It is mentioned here just for explanation.

TRY IT

In this walkthrough, you will learn how to activate the Hold and eDiscovery feature. In addition, we will use the feature to find documents based on a criteria and place holds on them to prevent deletion.

Lesson Requirements

To complete this Try It exercise, you need the following:

➤ A SharePoint site with SharePoint Server 2010 installed. The Hold and eDiscovery feature is part of the SharePoint standard license. It is not available on SharePoint Foundation.

➤ The SharePoint search service must be installed and running for the discovery features to work.

Hints

Hold and eDiscovery is a site-level feature. Until the feature is activated, many of the links and pages displayed here will not be available. The walkthrough shows you how to activate the feature.

Step-by-Step

1. Activate the Hold and eDiscovery feature by going to the Manage Site Features section under the Site Actions heading on the Site Settings page. Activating this feature will activate the links, pages, and actions for Hold and eDiscovery. Figure 16-2 shows the Hold and eDiscovery feature listing.

Hold and eDiscovery
This feature is used to track external actions like litigations, investigations, or audits that require you to suspend the disposition of documents.

FIGURE 16-2

After activating the feature, you will see an entirely new heading in the Site Settings page, as shown in Figure 16-3.

Hold and eDiscovery
Hold Reports
Holds
Discover and hold content

FIGURE 16-3

2. On the Site Settings page, click the link in the Hold and eDiscovery section titled Discover and Hold Content. Figure 16-4 shows the Search and Add to Hold page this link opens.

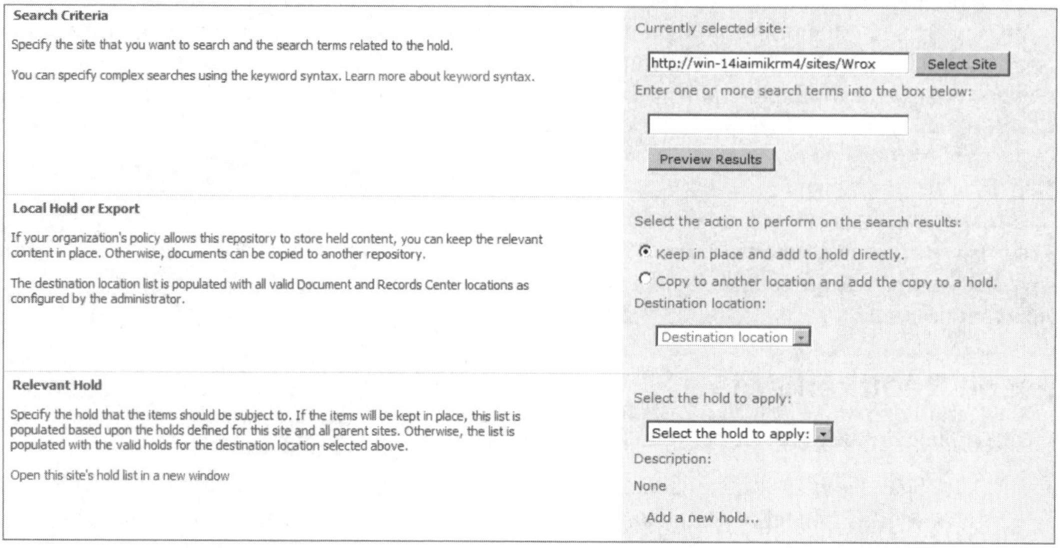

Search Criteria

Specify the site that you want to search and the search terms related to the hold.

You can specify complex searches using the keyword syntax. Learn more about keyword syntax.

Currently selected site:

http://win-14iaimikrm4/sites/Wrox   Select Site

Enter one or more search terms into the box below:

Preview Results

Local Hold or Export

If your organization's policy allows this repository to store held content, you can keep the relevant content in place. Otherwise, documents can be copied to another repository.

The destination location list is populated with all valid Document and Records Center locations as configured by the administrator.

Select the action to perform on the search results:

• Keep in place and add to hold directly.

○ Copy to another location and add the copy to a hold.

Destination location:

Destination location ▾

Relevant Hold

Specify the hold that the items should be subject to. If the items will be kept in place, this list is populated based upon the holds defined for this site and all parent sites. Otherwise, the list is populated with the valid holds for the destination location selected above.

Open this site's hold list in a new window

Select the hold to apply:

Select the hold to apply: ▾

Description:

None

Add a new hold...

FIGURE 16-4

I do not have a lot of content on my machine but I am going to look for a particular file called `draft tracks.xlsx` and place a hold on it. Find some content on your environment that you can discover via search for the example. I could just type "draft" but this would give me every document with the word *draft* in it. I am going to type the full filename inside double quotes, so that I only get the one file I want. See Figure 16-5, which shows how to fill out the search criteria section of the form. Click Preview Results and verify that you have the items you want in the result set. If you don't see any results, make sure the document is actually in your site and that the search service is operational.

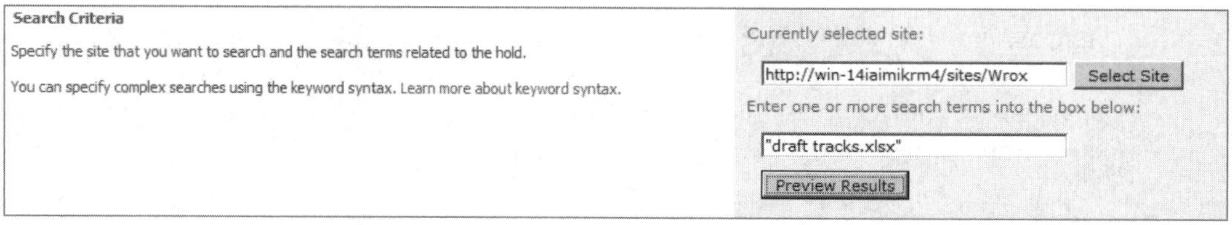

Search Criteria

Specify the site that you want to search and the search terms related to the hold.

You can specify complex searches using the keyword syntax. Learn more about keyword syntax.

Currently selected site:

http://win-14iaimikrm4/sites/Wrox   Select Site

Enter one or more search terms into the box below:

"draft tracks.xlsx"

Preview Results

FIGURE 16-5

3. In the Local Hold and Export section on the Search and Add to Hold page, you can choose whether you want the results to be held in place where they are or moved to some other pre-configured place, usually a Record Center site (Record Center sites are covered in Lesson 37). Choose to hold the records in place with the radio button titled "Keep in place and add to hold directly". This is a new feature in SharePoint 2010. Previously, your only option was to move the records somewhere else. Figure 16-6 shows this section of the page with the correct option selected.

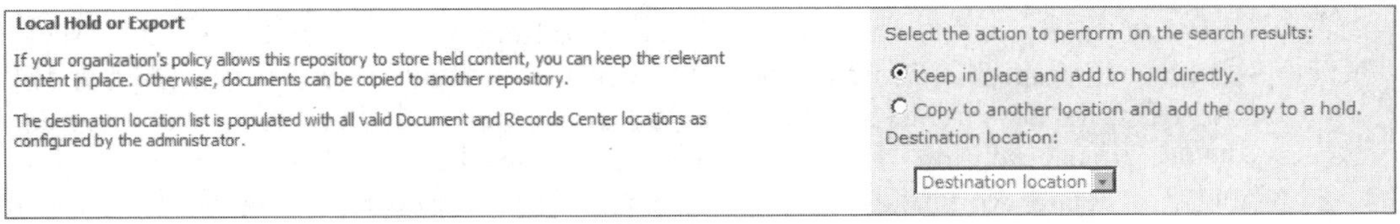

FIGURE 16-6

4. Select the hold to place these records under. You can use the link titled Add a New Hold... to add a hold on the spot if you haven't created any yet. If you have created a hold previously, the holds will be available to choose in the drop-down control. It is important to remember that the hold does not exert any special power. It is merely a container that links the results of any given discovery under one banner and prevents the items added to the hold from being deleted. Figure 16-7 shows this section of the page.

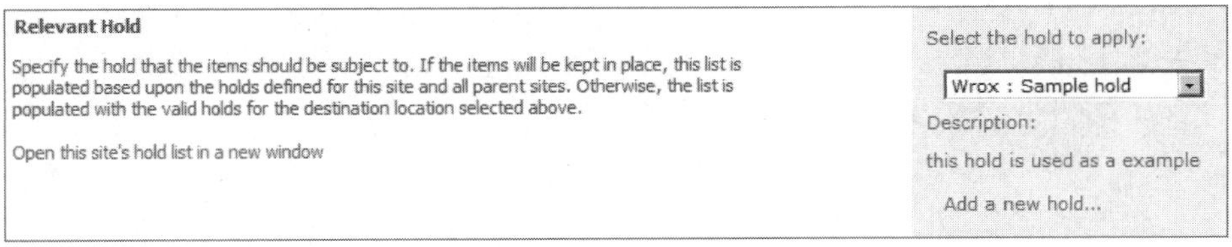

FIGURE 16-7

5. Finally, click the Add Results to Hold button. This is the button that actually takes the files and applies holds to them. You will see the dialog box shown in Figure 16-8. Notice it says the holds have been scheduled. Holds are applied not instantly, but rather as part of a timer job. A timer job is an operation that runs in the background on a schedule and performs various operations. In this case, the holds will only apply after the timer job completes.

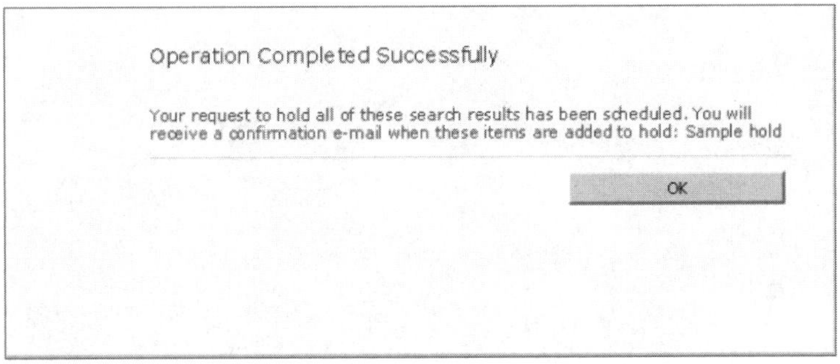

FIGURE 16-8

6. When you return to the Site Settings page, click the Holds link in the Hold and eDiscovery section of the page shows the holds you have created. This is the source for the drop-down control you saw in Step 4 if you created a hold.

7. Return to the Site Settings page and click the Hold Reports link in the Hold and eDiscovery section of the page. The Hold Reports library is the other link created by the Hold and eDiscovery feature. This library will be populated from a timer job that runs in the background. The report is in the form of an Excel library and shows the items that exist under a given hold. The default for this job is daily, so do not expect to see a report right away if you are testing this functionality.

Please select Lesson 16 on the DVD or visit www.wrox.com/go/sp2010-24 *to view the video that accompanies this lesson.*

17

Setting Up Records Management

Records management is a somewhat vague term, but in the SharePoint world it usually refers to a specific set of functionalities, and the concept of a "record" in this case is fairly specific. A record in SharePoint is a document or other element marked for special treatment (usually long-term, read-only storage) or redirected to a special site for long-term storage.

The Record Center site template, used to create sites to which items can be redirected, is covered in Lesson 37. In this lesson we examine how to declare items as records without moving them, and some of the special options that are available once an item has been declared a record.

RECORDS IN SHAREPOINT 2010

Following are examples of reasons to declare items as records in SharePoint.

➤ The item should permanently retain its current status and be stored for the long term, so that even people with editing rights to a document cannot modify or delete it. A good example would be an invoice document that you would not want to change once the transaction is completed, even by accounting staff who would normally have edit rights on the item.

➤ The item should kick off a business process after some amount of time. For example, users may upload a request form to a library that another user is supposed to approve. If the document sits there for more than a week, you may want it automatically routed to someone for final approval.

➤ You want the item to eventually automatically delete. In addition to storing data for the long term, you can use records to help you "clean out the attic." For example, you may want to retain the company newsletter articles for six months, after which no one will read them. Instead of leaving them to clutter up your site, you can have them declared as a record after six months and then set up a date after that to be removed automatically.

➤ You want to move a document to another location, usually to a long term archive site. Items marked as records can be transferred to Record Center sites, as described in Lesson 37.

As noted earlier, there are two ways to handle records. One is to ship it off to a special long-term storage site (the Record Center). The other is to leave it where it is and give it special "record" status. Assigning this status is called *in-place* record declaration and is new for SharePoint 2010. To enable in-place record declaration you must first activate the feature. It is a site collection–scoped feature, so you have to go to the Site Collection Features link on the Site Settings page of the top level site in your site collection. Once you activate the feature you can perform the tasks in this lesson.

In addition, at the site collection level you can define the sort of treatment a file will get when it is declared as a record. This is demonstrated in the Try It exercise.

DECLARING AN ITEM A RECORD

The following list identifies different ways to declare an item as a record. We cover them all in the Try It exercise.

➤ You can individually and manually declare an item a record by using the Compliance Actions option from the drop-down action menu for a list or library item.

➤ You can declare a record as part of a retention policy attached to a content type. A retention policy determines how long the record should remain in its current location and what should happen when that time expires.

➤ You can declare a record as part of a retention policy attached to a document library or list. Declaring a record in a content type affects that item everywhere the content type is used. Declaring in a single library or list only affect items in that library or list.

TRY IT

In this Try It exercise, you will declare some items as records and examine the various options that exist for documents designated as records.

Lesson Requirements

To complete this lesson you will need a SharePoint site with SharePoint Server 2010 installed. This feature is part of the SharePoint standard version. It is not available on SharePoint Foundation.

Hints

These features all require activation. Until the features are activated, many of the links and pages displayed on the screenshots in this walkthrough are not available. There are two required features, the in-place records definition feature and the SharePoint Server standard site collection feature. You will activate them in step 1 of the walkthrough.

Step-by-Step

1. Activate the records management features by going to the Site Collection Administration heading on the Site Settings page. Make sure the SharePoint Server Standard Site Collection Features and the In Place Records Management, shown in Figure 17-1 and 17-2, are both activated. Activating these will activate the links, pages, and actions for in-place records management.

SharePoint Server Standard Site Collection features
Features such as user profiles and search, included in the SharePoint Server Standard License.

FIGURE 17-1

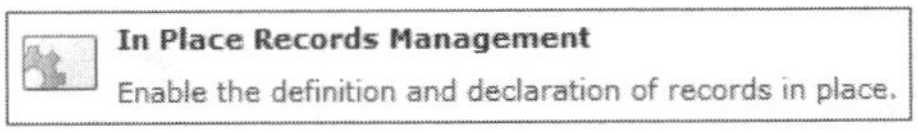

In Place Records Management
Enable the definition and declaration of records in place.

FIGURE 17-2

2. To view or change the default record settings for a site collection, click the Record Declaration Settings link in the Site Collection Administration settings. You should see the Record Declaration Settings page as shown in Figure 17-3.

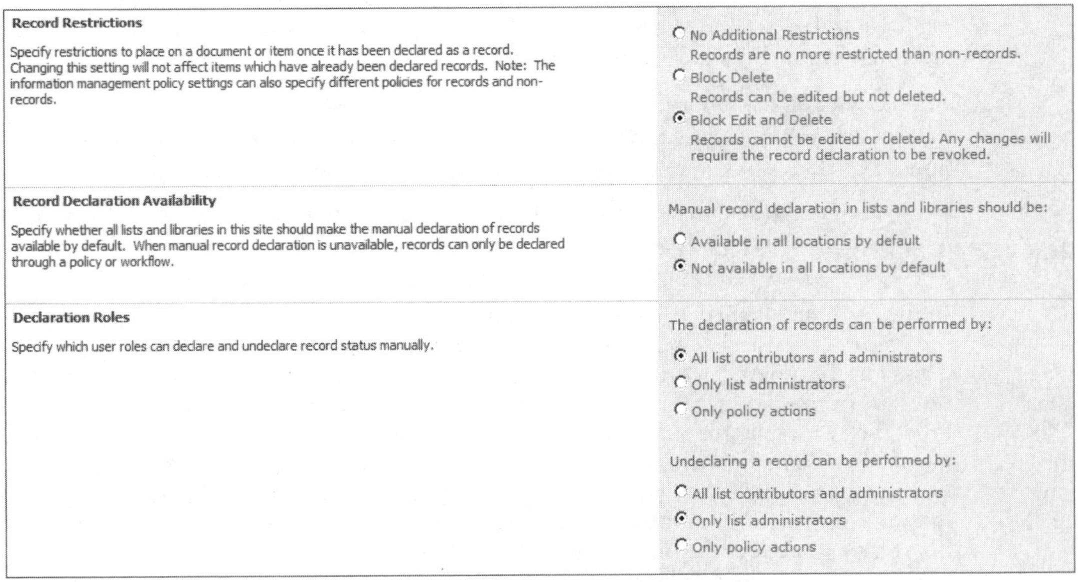

Record Restrictions
 	
Specify restrictions to place on a document or item once it has been declared as a record. Changing this setting will not affect items which have already been declared records. Note: The information management policy settings can also specify different policies for records and non-records.
	○ No Additional Restrictions
	   Records are no more restricted than non-records.
	○ Block Delete
	   Records can be edited but not deleted.
	◉ Block Edit and Delete
	   Records cannot be edited or deleted. Any changes will require the record declaration to be revoked.

Record Declaration Availability Specify whether all lists and libraries in this site should make the manual declaration of records available by default. When manual record declaration is unavailable, records can only be declared through a policy or workflow.	Manual record declaration in lists and libraries should be: ○ Available in all locations by default ◉ Not available in all locations by default
Declaration Roles Specify which user roles can declare and undeclare record status manually.	The declaration of records can be performed by: ◉ All list contributors and administrators ○ Only list administrators ○ Only policy actions Undeclaring a record can be performed by: ○ All list contributors and administrators ◉ Only list administrators ○ Only policy actions

FIGURE 17-3

Here you can set the records policy for the entire site collection. The first section, Record Restrictions, defines the editing policy for any file declared as a record.

The Record Declaration Availability section defines the default status for manual record declaration. As shown previously, this can be changed for each library. Manual record declaration means the user will select an item to be marked as a record as opposed to it occurring as part of an automatic retention policy or a workflow.

Finally, the Declaration Roles setting determines who can mark an item as a record or return it as a regular document. This setting also determines who can see the menu items in the examples that follow. If you select All List Contributors and Administrators, then anyone with rights to add items to a list can declare items in that list as a record. If you select Only List Administrators, then only users with administrator rights on a list can declare items in that list as records. Finally, Only Policy Actions refers to the process of setting a policy either for an individual content type, or setting a policy at the site collection level. A policy refers to a security policy which can be applied to a content type. If you select this option, you will not be able to manually mark an item as a record. It can only be done by a policy declaration.

3. Browse to a library on your SharePoint site. In the toolbar, select Library under the Library Tools section on the toolbar. On the right side of the toolbar, select Library Settings to open the Document Library Settings page. In the right column you should see a couple of new links, as shown in Figure 17-4.

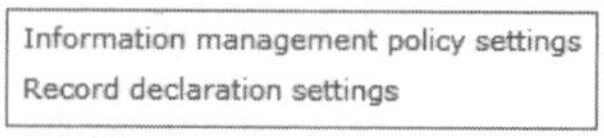

> Information management policy settings
> Record declaration settings

FIGURE 17-4

4. Click the Record Declaration Settings link. This page gives you two options. The first set of radio buttons enable you to override the settings for the site collection for just this document library. (We look at how to set the site collection default settings in just a moment.)

The second option enables you to declare that any record added to this library will automatically be declared a record, so that you can create a record repository without the manual effort of declaring documents to be records.

5. Another link on the Library Settings page is Information Management Policy Settings. This link enables you to change how a retention schedule affects the setting of records for this library. Click this link to open the Information Management Policy Settings page.

Every content type can have a retention schedule applied to it. This schedule determines how long a file sits around before another action is taken on it. (Usually it is deleted or moved to another area for long-term storage.)

In the first part of this page you can specify whether the content types of the items in the library will use the retention schedules of their content types or of the library itself. This is useful if you have a special-purpose library and wish to override the content type settings. In most cases you will want to use the settings you established for the content types. For example, for a content type of Tax Return, you might have set a retention policy of seven years before auto-deletion. This is the period beyond which a return cannot be audited. But perhaps you have also created a document library to permanently store tax returns. You don't want the seven-year rule to apply to tax returns placed in this library, so you select the library instead of the documents' content types as the source of the retention schedule. You can do this by clicking the Change Source link, shown in Figure 17-5. In addition, this page gives you a rundown of the content types this library uses and their retention schedules, if any.

6. Click the Change Source link, shown in Figure 17-5. On the following page, select Library and Folders. This reveals more options. (If you select Content Types, these same options exist, but you would have to go to the Content Type Gallery and change the settings there). See Figure 17-6.

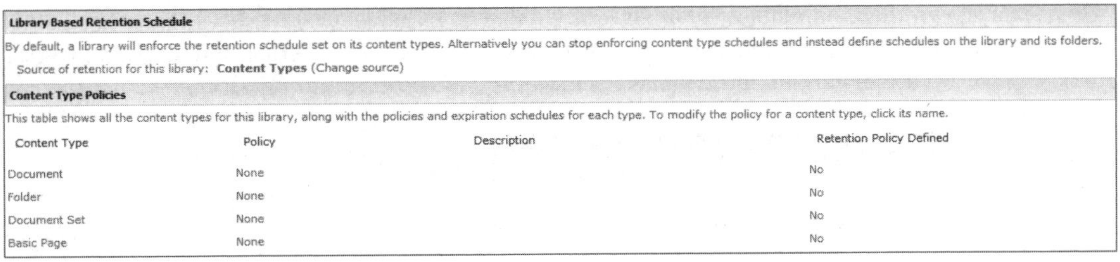

Library Based Retention Schedule			
By default, a library will enforce the retention schedule set on its content types. Alternatively you can stop enforcing content type schedules and instead define schedules on the library and its folders.			
Source of retention for this library: **Content Types** (Change source)			
Content Type Policies			
This table shows all the content types for this library, along with the policies and expiration schedules for each type. To modify the policy for a content type, click its name.			
Content Type	Policy	Description	Retention Policy Defined
Document	None		No
Folder	None		No
Document Set	None		No
Basic Page	None		No

FIGURE 17-5

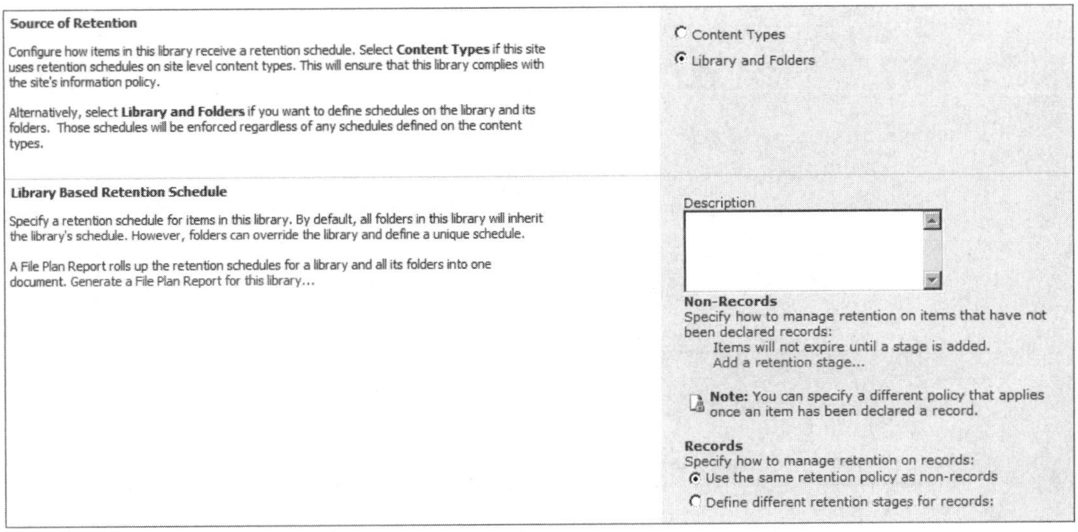

FIGURE 17-6

7. You can set two types of retention schedule: one for records and one for non-records. Using the Site Collection Settings page and the retention options shown here, you essentially create the options that separate "records" from "non-records." Usually the purpose of record retention is to put certain types of documents in long-term storage or delete them as obsolete after a time. As you will see, however, the actions you can take on items declared as records are practically limitless because you can fire off any sort of workflow as part of a record retention schedule.

For this example you will not add any retention policy to non-records, but you will add one to records. Click the radio button near the bottom of the screen titled Define Different Retention Stages for Records. A retention stage is one step in a multi-step process that you can define for what happens to records after the previous stage is complete. In other words, you can define several actions that apply to a record that will execute in order. Each retention stage represents one such action.

8. Add a retention stage for records. Note that you can add multiple stages. In this example you will add only one for demonstration. A common retention policy is to move something to the Recycle Bin after a certain period of time has passed. Click on the Add a Retention Stage... link to open the dialog as shown in Figure 17-7.

As you can see in Figure 17-7, retention policy always begins with an event, either a period since a file was last touched, or its being declared a record — either manually, via workflow, or via a previous retention stage.

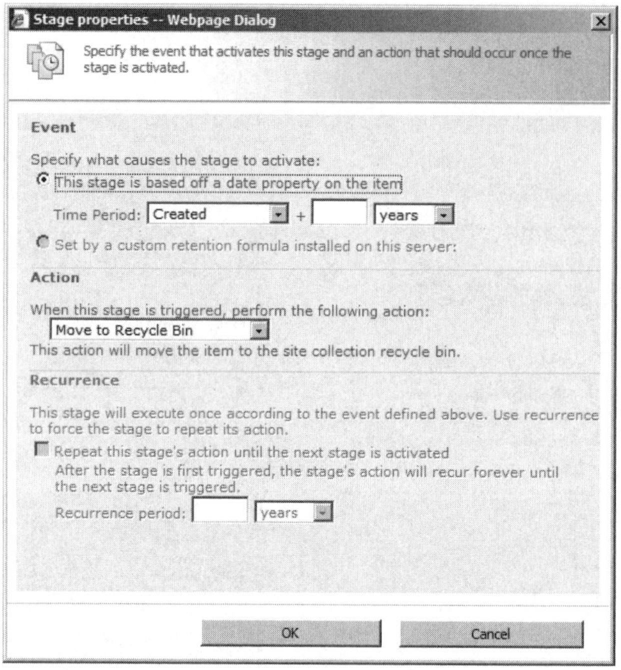

FIGURE 17-7

9. Select Declared Record. (This will make testing the event later easy.) Select +0 days, so the retention stage will start right away. Notice the grayed-out button labeled Set by a Custom Retention Formula Installed on this Server. Clicking this button makes it possible via custom coding to create your own events here. This option is beyond the scope of this book.

10. Select an action to take (Figure 17-8). Notice that most options involve moving the item or deleting it. However, you can also start a workflow or move to another stage. For this simple example, select Move to Recycle Bin. You can see in the drop-down control there are several other options as well.

Finally, you can determine under Recurrence if this action will recur regularly. Not every action features this setting so it might be grayed out at times.

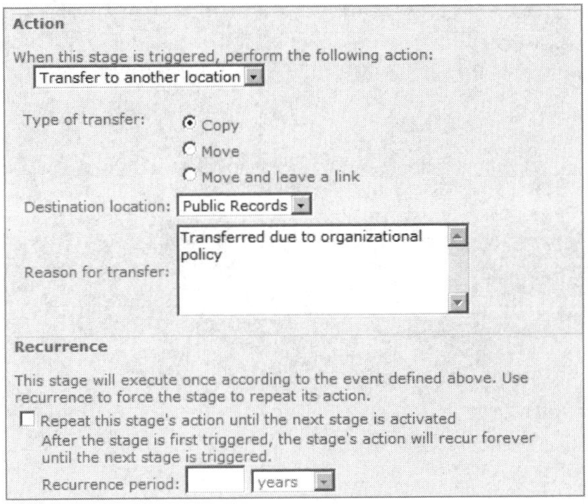

FIGURE 17-8

11. You will see the retention policy. Click OK to return to the Information Policy Settings. You have created a policy that will execute for any item in this library that is declared as a record. The policy will run immediately and will cause the file in question to be moved to the Recycle Bin.

12. Return to the library itself to examine how to mark an item as a record manually. Use the drop-down menu for an item in the document library and you will see another drop-down menu, similar to the one in Figure 17-9. Select the Compliance Details option.

13. The dialog box that opens shows several options and pieces of information. Note the one called Record Status. Here you can toggle on and off the status of this item as a record. Figure 17-10 shows the dialog box.

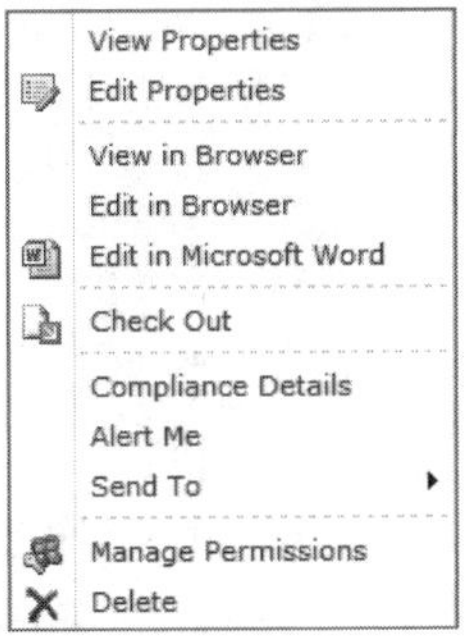

FIGURE 17-9

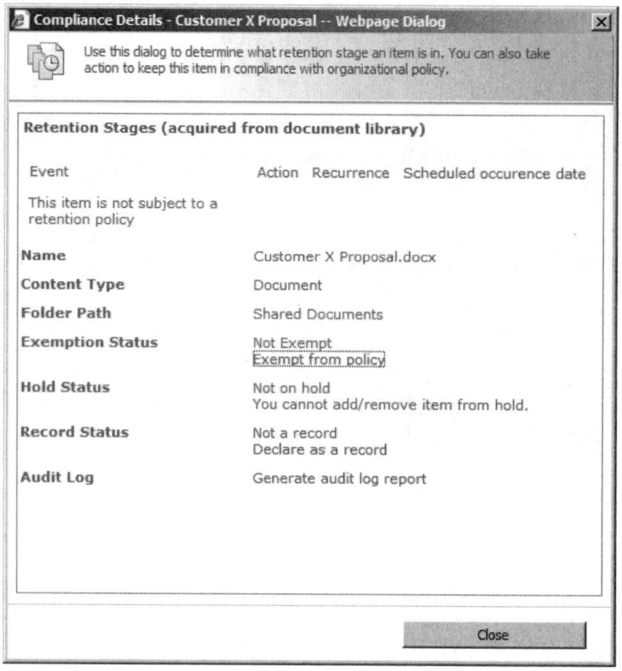

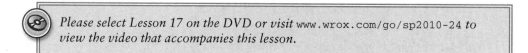

FIGURE 17-10

14. Select Declare as a Record and note how the retention policy moves the item to the Recycle Bin. This might not happen right away because even though we selected "move in 0 days," the actual move will not occur until the completion of a *timer job*, which runs on its own schedule behind the scenes. A timer job is a procedure that runs behind the scenes on a schedule. It is a source of confusion for SharePoint administrators when results of an action do not appear instantly as they might expect.

Finally, note how the icon for the document has changed to denote its status as a record with a small yellow lock. See Figure 17-11.

FIGURE 17-11

In this lesson, we looked at the many options available for declaring items in a SharePoint site as records. In addition, we experimented with several options for manipulating items declared as records.

> *Please select Lesson 17 on the DVD or visit* www.wrox.com/go/sp2010-24 *to view the video that accompanies this lesson.*

18

Setting Up Related Lists

Relational data structures are a feature that SharePoint users have requested for years, but have not yet been fully implemented. A simpler solution known as related lists does however exist, where the items in one list provide the detail for items in another list, with the two lists related to one another by a field such as an ID or other column. SharePoint 2010 adds some features to make modeling list relationships easier and provides some new functionality for maintaining the lists.

Using related lists makes it easy to create sophisticated views with a master-detail type of presentation. For example, one list may contain sales orders, while another list may contain detail about the customer that made the purchase. Related lists enable you to create a view showing the orders from one list, combined with the customer's address from the other list.

The main element used to create related lists is the *lookup column*. You need at least two lists, though it is possible to create relationships that span multiple lists. Each list provides detail for and refers back to a column in the list above it. In this chapter you will learn how to connect two lists.

A lookup column enables you to draw values from other lists on the same SharePoint site and use their values in the current list. Using a lookup list and a column from the parent list, you can create a relationship to the *child list*, also known as the *detail list*.

In this lesson we are going to examine the pieces that go into creating related lists and walk through the steps to create two lists and display the related records as Web Parts on a page.

TRY IT

Once you have placed a list view Web Part on a page, if the list represented in the view contains a lookup field that refers to a parent list, you will have the option to automatically connect it to its parent list and create the master-detail view immediately on the page. In this walkthrough, we will connect two related lists that share a common field and display of view that combines data from both lists.

Lesson Requirements

To perform this lesson, you need a SharePoint site with SharePoint Foundation or SharePoint Server.

Hints

Prior to completing the walkthrough, create the following lists:

➤ List 1: Orders, derived from the custom list type.

    ➤ Rename the Title field to **Order Name**.

    ➤ Create a new record. Enter **My first order** for the Order Name field.

    ➤ Create another new record. Enter **My second order** for the Order Name field.

➤ List 2: Order Details, derived from the custom list type.

    ➤ Rename the Title field to **Items**.

    ➤ Create a new record. Enter **Some wine** for the Items column and select 1 for the Order ID column.

    ➤ Create a new record. Enter **Some cheese** for the Items column and select 1 for the Order ID column.

    ➤ Create a new record. Enter **Some music** for the Items column and select 2 for the Order ID column.

Step-by-Step

1. Go to the list settings for the Order Details list.

2. Create a new column of type lookup. Name it **Order ID**.

3. In the Additional Column Settings section, select Orders from the Get Information From drop-down. Figure 18-1 shows the interface.

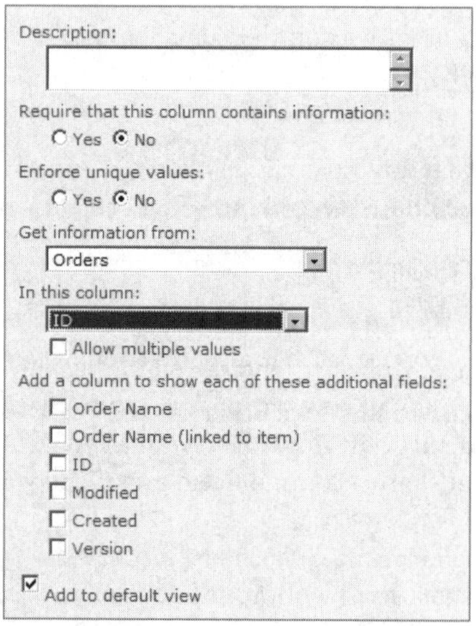

FIGURE 18-1

4. In the Relationship Settings section, select Enforce Relationship Behavior. If you choose Restrict Delete, you will not be allowed to delete rows in the Order list if records exist in the Order Details list. If you select Cascade Delete, deleting a row in the Orders list will delete every associated row in the Order Details list. Select Cascade Delete. Figure 18-2 shows this option.

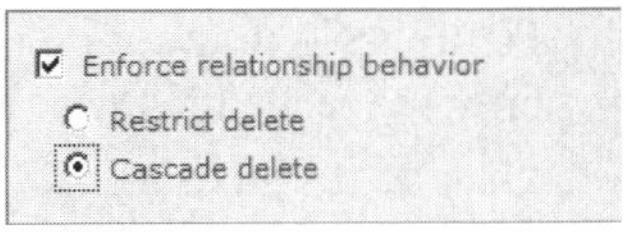

FIGURE 18-2

5. Browse to any web page and add a list view Web Part of the Orders list to the page. To add the Web Part, you will need to place the page into edit mode. Select the Edit Page option from the Site Action drop down menu. Then you can select the Insert Web Part option from the toolbar. Once you have placed the Orders Web Part on the page, assuming you are still in edit mode, you should see the toolbar option called Web Part Tools. Select Options below it. Make sure the Orders Web Part is still your selected Web Part. You should see an Insert Related List command, as in 18-3.

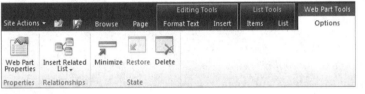

FIGURE 18-3

6. When you click Insert Related List, you will see an option for Order Details. Select the list and the Web Part will be automatically added to the page and connected to its parent list, the Orders list view Web Part above it. Figure 18-4 shows the detail.

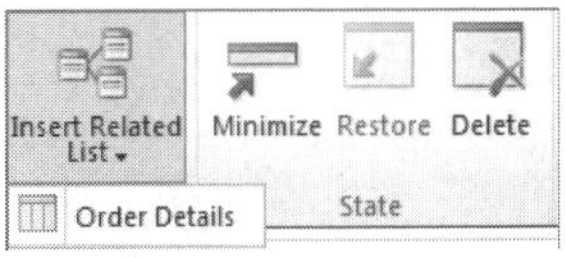

FIGURE 18-4

7. Notice the Select column in the Orders list. Clicking the double-arrow image for a given record in the Orders list will show the associated orders in the Order Details list below it. Figure 18-5 shows the double-arrow image you should click.

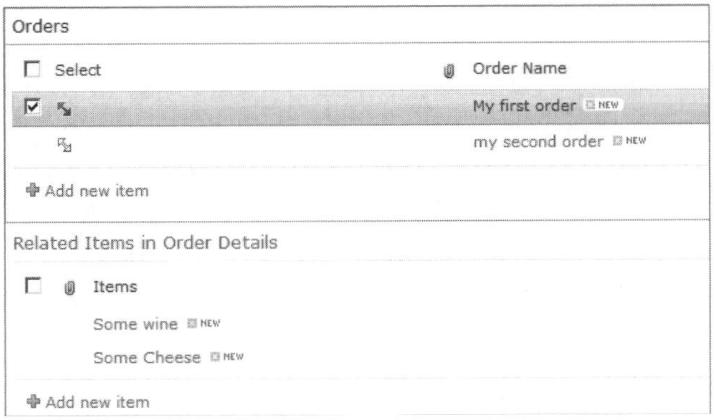

Orders	
☐ Select	📎 Order Name
☑ ↘	My first order ☐ NEW
↖	my second order ☐ NEW
➕ Add new item	
Related Items in Order Details	
☐ 📎 Items	
Some wine ☐ NEW	
Some Cheese ☐ NEW	
➕ Add new item	

FIGURE 18-5

Figure 18-6 shows the effect of selecting a particular item in the master list. The detail list shows only the related items.

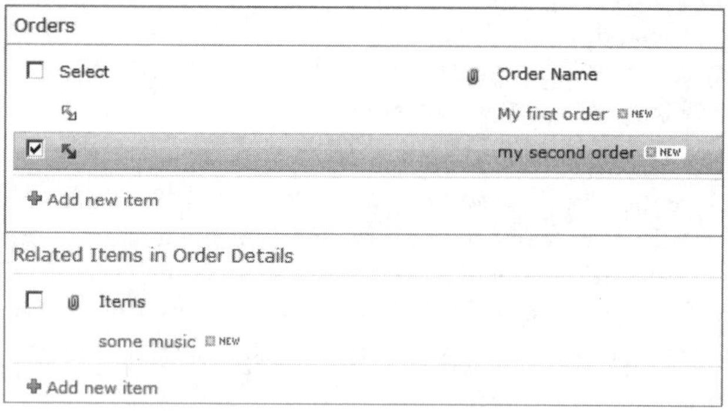

Orders		
☐ Select	🔖	Order Name
⌐		My first order ⊡ NEW
☑ ⌐		my second order ⊡ NEW
✚ Add new item		
Related Items in Order Details		
☐ 🔖 Items		
some music ⊡ NEW		
✚ Add new item		

FIGURE 18-6

 Please select Lesson 18 on the DVD or visit www.wrox.com/go/sp2010-24 *to view the video that accompanies this lesson.*

SECTION V
Managing Publishing Sites

19

Setting Up a Publishing Site

SharePoint 2010 is a multifunctional product. Among its many features is its capability to be used as a fully fledged web content management system when you enable the publishing infrastructure at the site collection level for existing sites, or create a Publishing Portal After you create a publishing portal or enabled the publishing features, you can find many differences from a standard SharePoint team site.

Figure 19-1 shows an out-of-the-box SharePoint publishing site. A site has two core perquisites enabled: the publishing infrastructure and additional specific publishing features. The publishing infrastructure provides publishing ability to the site collection as a whole, whereas the publishing features can be enabled for the site collection and subsites as required. Both must be enabled before you can take advantage of SharePoint publishing.

PUBLISHING SITES

The publishing infrastructure and features also provide you with several useful tools to aid in content management.

After a publishing portal has been created, several additional document and system libraries, user groups, and Web Parts are available within the site structure, including the following:

> **Site Content and Structure Reports:** Reports that will provide information on aspects of the publishing process, for example all pages due to be published within the next seven days.

> **Site Collection Documents:** Documents to be used throughout the site collection.

> **Site Collection Images:** Images to be used throughout the site collection.

> **Content Query Web Part:** Allows you to publish information from your publishing portal by using a query. For example, if you have information in a subsite list you can use this Web Part to display that information on the portal homepage.

➤ **Media Web Part:** Used to add video and other multimedia content to your web page.

➤ **Summary Links Web Part:** Used to group related links and present them to the user in a much more friendly way than the standard links Web Part.

➤ **Table of Contents Web Part:** Used to generate a site map for the publishing portal.

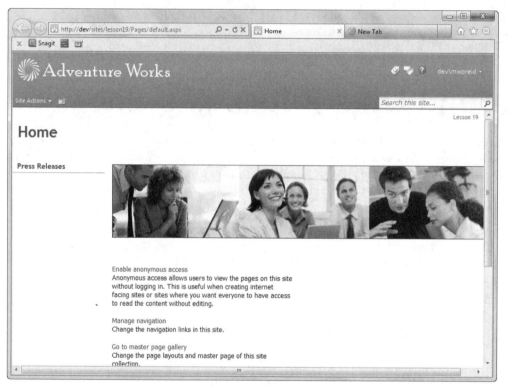

FIGURE 19-1

One of the other major changes you can find within publishing sites as opposed to standard SharePoint team sites, is your ability to change the look and feel of the site completely. For example, `http://sharepoint.microsoft.com/en-us/pages/default.aspx` is a SharePoint-based site that has been completely changed from the default look and feel usually associated with SharePoint.

> *Another nice place to view custom SharePoint 2010 site designs is* `http://www.wssdemo.com/livepivot/` *— this site is worth a look! Changes to the look and feel of the site are achieved by using a combination of Master pages and Cascading Style Sheets, both of which are discussed in Lesson 21, "Setting Branding Options in Publishing Sites."*

Pages

When you add a new page to the publishing site, things change. Before your page is published, it will have to be created, submitted for approval, and approved. SharePoint helps with this process by enabling you to begin an approval workflow.

Pages can also be scheduled for publication and you can include a start and end date for publication and a requirement that you be notified before publication ends. To prevent stale content, you can also set up a notification schedule for page review; the schedule can last for days, weeks, months, or even years. When the review date is reached SharePoint sends an email to a reviewer requesting that he or she check the page content.

Navigation

One of the major differences from SharePoint team sites you will find when working with a publishing site is the difference in control you will have over navigation. With a standard team site, you have a limited range of navigation options available to you. With a publishing site, you have much more control over how the navigation works and, in fact, you can customize it to meet your own specific needs. Once the publishing features have been enabled (they are enabled out of the box for a publishing portal), you have access to a range of new navigational features. A non-publishing site enables you to customize the Quick Launch menu, add a tree view for navigation, and add and reposition items on the top link bar. Beyond these options you will find that you are limited in how much you can customize the navigation. Figure 19-2 shows the navigation screen in a publishing site. Lesson 20, "Setting Navigation Options in Publishing Sites," examines navigation in more detail and provides some examples of customization.

Site Administration

You will also find many additional options available to you in terms of site administration aimed at web content management and page publishing. These administration options are not available when you do not have the publishing features activated. For example, navigation management and customization can be managed within the Site Administration menus.

When creating a publishing site you have several options. From SharePoint 2010 Central Administration, you can use the default publishing template to create site collections with the publishing infrastructure and features already enabled. From an existing site, you can create a publishing site with a Workflow or you can enable the publishing features on an existing site. In the Try It section, you will create a publishing site with a Workflow and enable publishing on an existing team site.

> *When you have a publishing site with a workflow and you want to create subsites, the choice of site templates is limited. However, from your publishing portal site settings page, you can make other templates available. Under the Look and Feel section, click the Page Layouts and Site Templates link. Using the subsite list box on the left, you can pick those site templates that you want to make available. This is also a good way to hide templates you may not want your site owners using.*

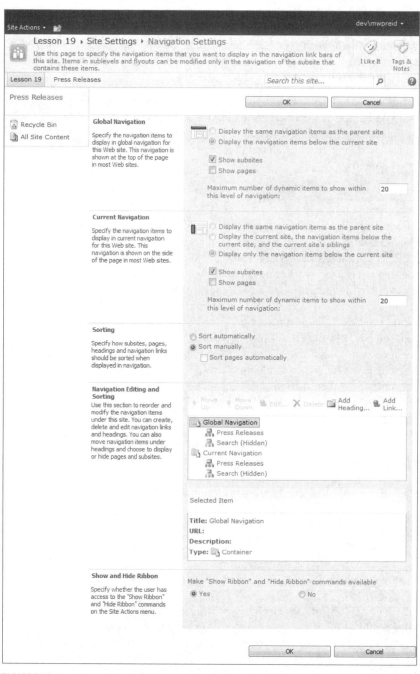

FIGURE 19-2

TRY IT

In this exercise, you will create a publishing site with a Workflow and enable publishing features on a team site. After each site is enabled, you will look at some of the new features available to you, including the approval workflow.

Lesson Requirements

To complete this Try It exercise, you need the following:

➤ Site collection administrator permissions.

➤ Existing SharePoint team site.

➤ Access to SharePoint Central Administration to create a site collection.

Hints

➤ Add your username to the security group Approvers.

Step-by-Step

To create a publishing portal from Central Administration, perform the following steps:

1. Click Application Management.

2. Click Create Site Collections.

3. Enter **Example Publishing Site** as the title.

4. If required, change the website URL to /sites/ and enter **demopub** as the rest of the example URL.

5. Click the Publishing tab in the Template section.

6. Select Publishing Portal.

7. Enter your username as the Primary Site Collection Administrator

8. Leave the Secondary Site Collection Administrator field blank.

9. Click OK to confirm and save the publishing portal.

10. Click the new site URL to open the site after it has been processed. Figure 19-3 shows the newly created publishing site in the browser.

To examine some of the features and objects in the new site, click Site Actions and select View All Site Content. This will give you some appreciation of the range of new objects available to you.

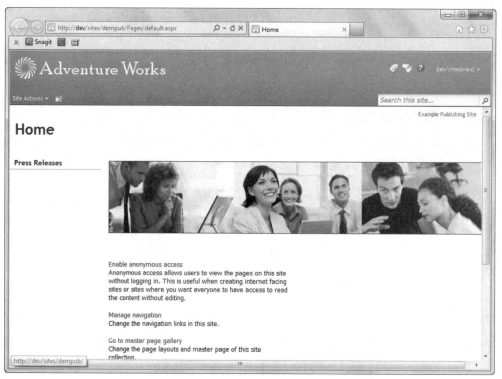

FIGURE 19-3

The next example takes a standard team site and enables the publishing features. To continue with this exercise, it is useful to have a new team site to see the full effect of the new objects and functionality. To continue, perform the following steps:

1. Click Site Actions.

2. Click Site Settings.

3. Select Manage Site Features in the Site Actions category.

4. Scroll down through the list of features until you get to SharePoint Server Publishing. Click the Activate button to enable publishing.

At this point you may get an error message, part of which is shown here:

> "...The feature being activated is a scoped feature, which has a dependency on a Site Collection scoped feature, which has not been activated. Please activate the following feature before trying again: PerformancePoint Services Site Collection Features a1cb5b7f-e5e9-421b-915f-bf519b0760ef."

We missed one important thing: Publishing features depend on the publishing infrastructure's being enabled for the site collection first, and this has to be done at the site collection level. To continue, do the following:

1. On the error page, click the Go Back to Site hyperlink.

2. Click Site Actions.

3. Click Site Settings.

4. Click Site Collection Features in the Site Collection Administration category.

5. Scroll down to and activate SharePoint Server Publishing Infrastructure by clicking the Activate button.

6. Return to your team site's homepage and click the All Site Content link to view the additional objects now available on your site.

Notice that there is another publishing feature that you can enable, the publishing approval workflow. To enable the workflow, return to the Manage Features form and click the Activate button. You have now enabled the publishing infrastructure for the site collection and enabled the publishing workflows. Now you can return to the Manage site Features screen for the site to enable publishing features. Repeat Steps 1 through 3 of the preceding list to perform this action. After the features are activated, publishing will be enabled on your team site.

The publishing process includes a workflow that can handle the approval process. To see this workflow in action, return to the publishing portal you created in the first example and do the following:

1. Click Site Actions.

2. Click New Page.

3. Enter **DemoPage** as the new page title.

4. Click Create.

5. Enter **This is an example of a publishing page for Lesson 19** as the page content.

6. Click the Publish tab.

7. Click the Submit icon on the Ribbon to submit the page for publishing approval.

8. Enter **First Publishing Page** as the comment.

9. Click Continue.

Figure 19-4 shows the page approval workflow form that should immediately open. The workflow is automatically assigned to members of the SharePoint security group Approvers, so you are not required to enter the information it asks for.

When creating the workflow, you are required to complete the following:

➤ **Request:** The message you want to post to those who are responsible for approval.

➤ **Due Date for All Tasks:** The date the task is due for completion.

➤ **Duration Per Task:** Enter a number in Days, Weeks, Months.

➤ **Duration Units:** Applied to the preceding number, for example, days, weeks, or months.

After the workflow is complete, as a member of the Approvers group, you should receive an email requesting that you approve the content. Figure 19-5 shows the form you will be required to complete as part of this process.

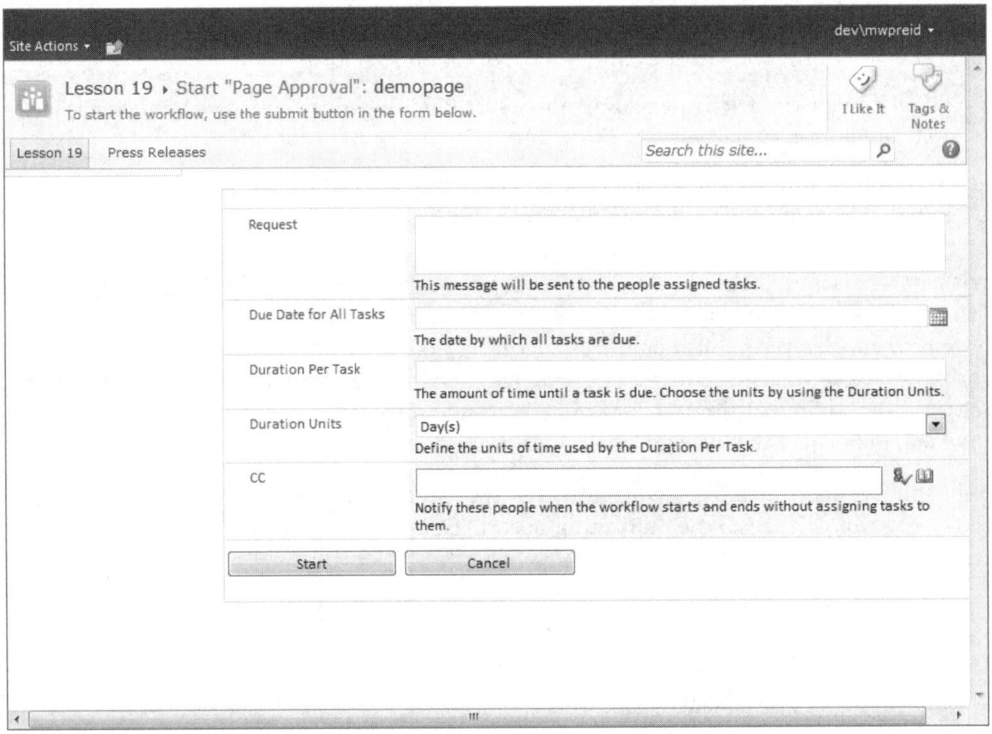

FIGURE 19-4

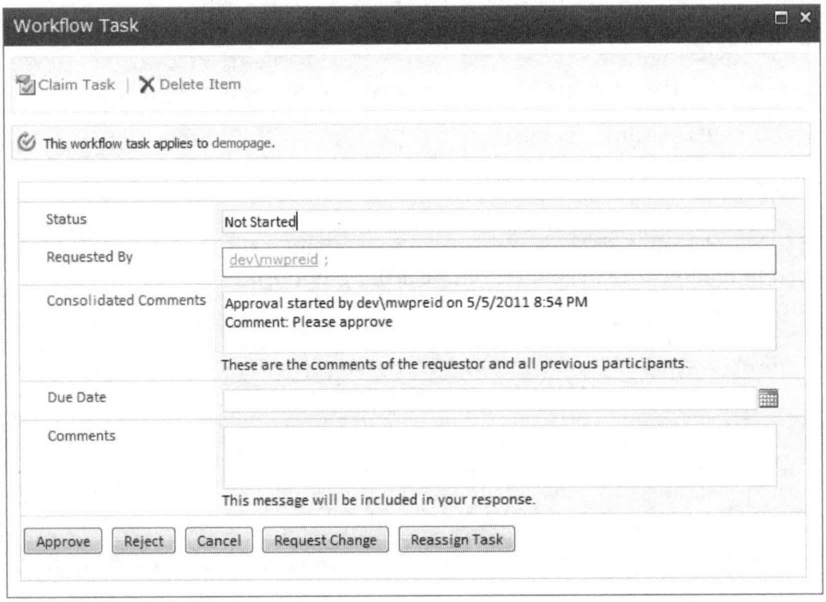

FIGURE 19-5

The first thing you should do is click the Claim Task link at the top left of the form; this will let the other members of the approval groups know you are working on the approval.

The status of the task should change to In Progress, and you will have five options:

➤ **Approve:** Approve the publication of the page.

➤ **Reject:** Reject the page and return the form with comments.

➤ **Cancel:** Cancel the current progress.

➤ **Request Change:** Send a request for change back to the author.

➤ **Reassign Task:** Reassign the task to another approver for approval.

To approve the page, simply click Approve; this changes the page status from Pending to Approved. The page can now be published to the Internet site.

 Please select Lesson 19 on the DVD or visit www.wrox.com/go/sp2010-24 *to view the video that accompanies this lesson.*

20

Setting Navigation Options in Publishing Sites

As you saw in Lesson 19, "Setting Up a Publishing Site," one of the major site management changes from team sites you'll encounter when working with publishing sites is in navigation. There are many changes awaiting you and much more control over how SharePoint navigation is controlled within a publishing site. In this lesson, we look at a SharePoint site with publishing features enabled.

NAVIGATIONAL OPTIONS

The navigation options when publishing features are enabled on the Site Settings screen for a publishing site are as follows:

➤ **Global Navigation:** Navigation links available to all sites within the site collection. You can choose to display subsites and pages within the site collection global navigation.

➤ **Maximum Number of Dynamic Items to Show Within This Level of Navigation:** This is used to display a drop-down submenu showing subsites within a site on the global navigation. The number defines how many levels of information to make available on the drop-down.

➤ **Current Navigation:** Navigation links for the current site which are located on the Quick Launch–type menu on the left side of the web page. In the current navigation, you can also choose to show subsites and pages within the menu.

➤ **Sorting:** You can choose automatic sorting of navigation subsites, pages, headings, and individual navigations links, or have SharePoint sort these items automatically. If you choose automatic sorting, you can choose the column under which you would like to sort using a drop-down list that is made available. You can choose to sort by title, created date, or last modified data.

➤ **Navigation Editing and Sorting:** In this section, you have almost total control over how navigation is presented. This section also provides you with the opportunity to edit existing links, add new links, group links together under standard or custom headers, and hide links you may not want to appear within navigation. You can edit both global and current navigation menus using this area.

Figure 20-1 shows the global navigation settings available to you within a site collection.

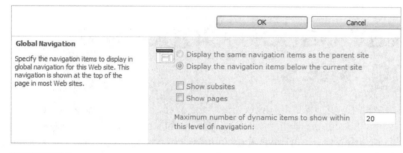

FIGURE 20-1

GLOBAL NAVIGATION OPTIONS

Global navigation is the navigational links that display on the top of every page within your SharePoint site. Figure 20-2 shows the global menu items on a team site with publishing features enabled. In this case the global links, Reporting and Training, take you to the appropriate subsite. If a user is in either of the subsites, the global navigation remains the same and includes a link back to the home site.

The Navigation option used in the subsite was Display the Same Navigation Items as the Parent. This was set within the navigation options for each of the two subsites. That's one of the problems with this approach: You need to set the same global navigation settings on each of the subsites in the site collection. Although this is not a complex task, it can be annoying when you have a lot of subsites in a site collection.

Instead of automatically picking up subsites and pages for global navigation, you can manually enter this data directly into the navigation options within the site. This gives you almost total control over what is actually displayed. Figure 20-3 shows the main Global Navigation menu with another feature, a fly-out menu, displaying two subsites within the Reporting site.

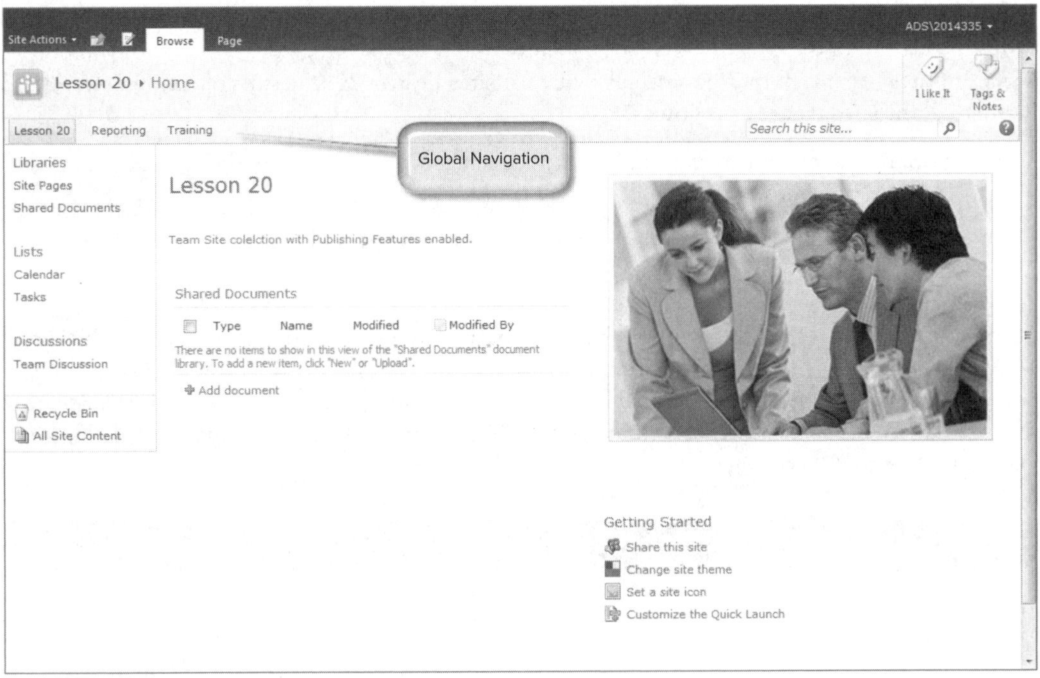

FIGURE 20-2

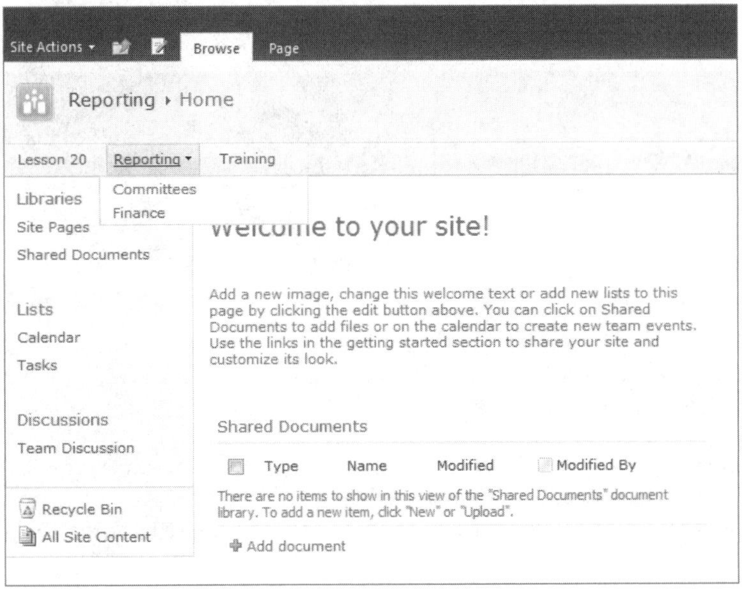

FIGURE 20-3

This is achieved by using the navigations settings in the Reporting site to display its subsites. If you want this feature in the Global Navigation menus, you need to change the settings for the subsite to Show Subsites. At this point, the settings made for sites Lesson 20 (the site collection home site) and Reporting (the subsite) are as follows:

➤ **Lesson 20:** Global Navigation; Display the navigation items below the current site, Show subsites, and Show pages.

➤ **Reporting:** Global Navigation; Display the same navigation items as the parent site, Show subsites.

The settings for the third site, Training, have not been changed from the default Global Navigation settings which are Display the navigation items below the current site and do not show subsites or pages. Figure 20-4 shows the global navigation on the Training site homepage with these default settings. Figure 20-5 shows the same menu once the settings for Global Navigation are changed to match those of the Reporting site.

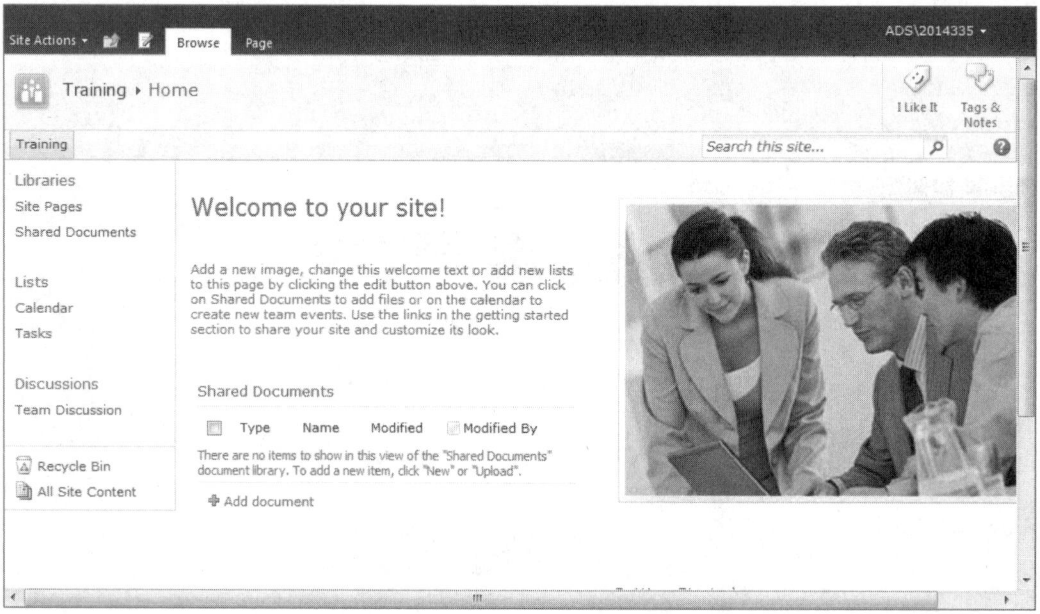

FIGURE 20-4

As you can see, the settings shown in Figure 20-5 provide a much more consistent navigational structure across the site collection. Consistent and obvious global navigation is important to site users to help them find their way around SharePoint sites, and becomes even more important when site structure is complex.

In addition to the automatic inclusion of sites and pages on the Global Navigation menu you can add links manually. For example, Figure 20-6 shows the site collection global navigation with an external link, which in this case goes to SharePoint training materials on `www.microsoft.com`. We will be looking at how the external link is created in the Try It section later in the lesson.

FIGURE 20-5

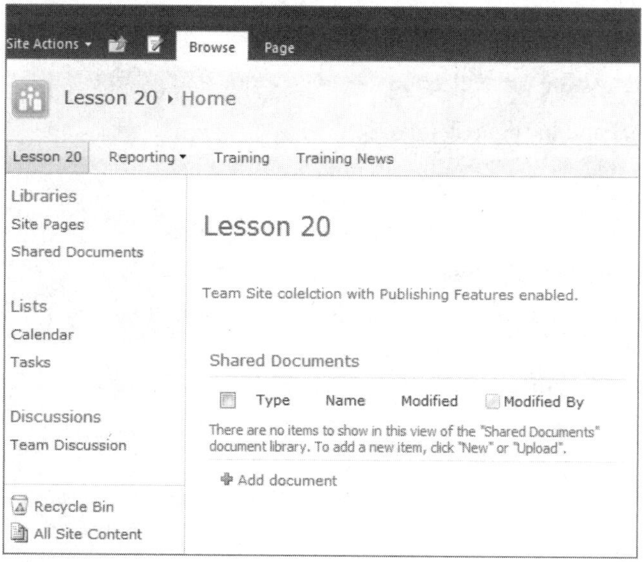

FIGURE 20-6

Local Navigation

In addition to global navigation, you also have to give some consideration to local navigation within the site itself. Local navigation is normally navigation relevant to where the person is in the site collection. In addition to using the standard features of a team site, such as the ability to add an item to the Quick Launch when you create it, you are able to work directly with navigation once publishing features are activated. The following section of the navigation form offers the following options:

➤ Display the same navigation items as the parent site

➤ Display the current site, the navigation items below the current site, and the current site's siblings

➤ Display only the navigation items below the current site

➤ Show subsites

➤ Show pages

Figure 20-7 shows the current navigation set to Show Subsites. In this case, the links simply duplicate those shown on the global navigation and do not serve any useful purpose.

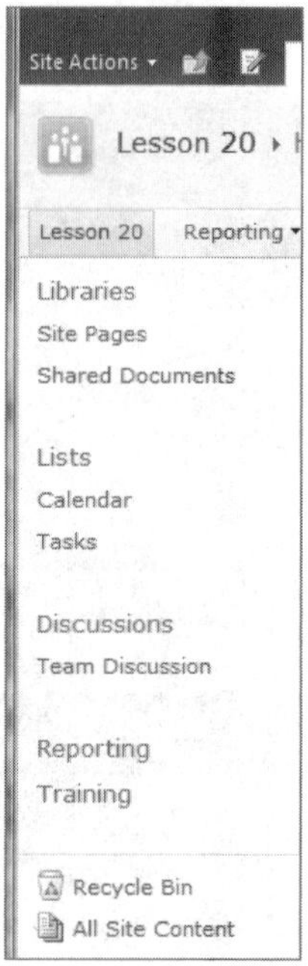

TRY IT

In this exercise, you create a site collection containing three subsites. After the sites have been created, you will do the following:

➤ Enable publishing infrastructure

➤ Enable publishing features

➤ Implement global navigation across the site collection

➤ Add manual links to both global and local navigation

Lesson Requirements

To complete this Try It exercise, you need the following:

➤ A site collection that contains three subsites, which you can create as part of the Try It (Reporting, Training, and Committees)

➤ SharePoint Publishing features activated at the site collection and individual site level

Step-by-Step

From the homepage of the site collection, you need to enable the publishing infrastructure and publishing features. To do this, follow these steps:

1. Click Site Actions.

2. Click Site Settings.

3. Click Site Collection Features in the Site Collection Administration category.

FIGURE 20-7

4. Click the Activate button for the SharePoint Server Publishing Infrastructure feature.

5. Click the Site Collection Administration breadcrumb to return to the Site Settings page.

6. Click Manage Site Features in the Site Actions category.

7. Click the Activate button for the SharePoint Server Publishing feature.

To continue with the example, create the three team sites within your site collection:

➤ Reporting

➤ Training

➤ Committees

When this is done, ensure you are on the homepage of the site collection before continuing. At this point, global navigation is not set up. To begin the process, do the following:

1. Click Site Actions.

2. Click Site Settings.

3. Click Navigation in the Look and Feel category.

4. Click Show Subsites in the Global Navigation section of the screen.

5. Click OK.

You should now have three subsites showing in the global navigation of the site collection parent site. Figure 20-8 shows the navigation at this point.

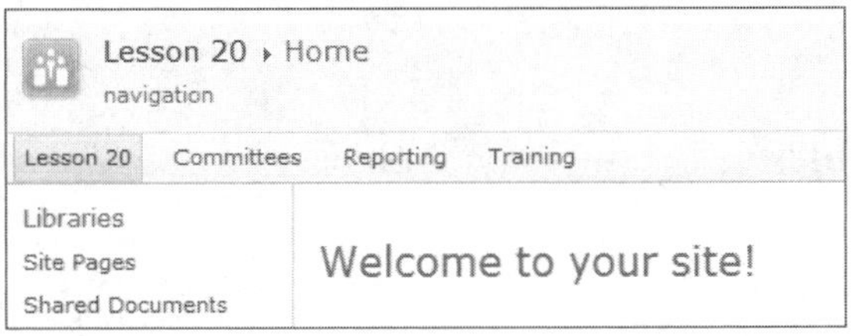

Lesson 20 ▸ Home
navigation

| Lesson 20 | Committees | Reporting | Training |

Libraries
Site Pages   **Welcome to your site!**
Shared Documents

FIGURE 20-8

6. Click Committees to open the Committee subsite. Note that the global navigation is not available.

7. Click Site Actions.

8. Click Site Settings.

9. Click Navigation in the Look and Feel category.

10. Click the Display the Same Navigation Items as the Parent Site radio button.

11. Click OK to save the changes and create the global navigation.

12. Repeat Steps 6 through 11 for the Reporting and Training sites.

It is also possible to add manual links to the SharePoint navigational system. To proceed, open your training subsite, and then follow these steps:

1. Click Site Actions.

2. Click Site Settings.

3. Click Navigation in the Look and Feel category.

4. Scroll to the bottom of the Navigation screen to the section entitled Navigation Editing and Sorting (see Figure 20-9).

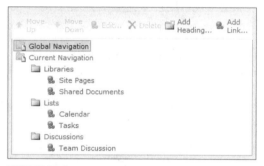

FIGURE 20-9

Look at the section heading Current Navigation. This is the menu to which you are going to manually add a heading and a link. Follow these steps:

1. Click Current Navigation to select it.

2. Click the Add Heading link.

3. Enter **Microsoft Training** as the title.

4. Enter # (the hash symbol) in the URL field.

5. Click OK to save and create the new heading.

6. Click the new heading to ensure it is selected.

7. Click Add Link.

8. Enter **Microsoft Resources** as the title.

9. Enter the following URL into the URL field: `http://sharepoint.microsoft.com/en-us/resources/Pages/End-User-Training-Guide.aspx`

10. In the description box, enter **Microsoft SharePoint 2010 end user materials**.

11. Click OK to save the changes.

12. Click OK to save the navigation changes and return to your Site Settings page.

You should now have a new section on the Quick Launch, Microsoft Training, containing a single link to an external website, Microsoft Resources. You can reposition the Microsoft Training heading on your Quick Launch by returning to the Navigation screen, clicking the heading to select it, and then selecting Move Up in the Screen to move the heading and link up one place in the current navigation structure.

 Please select Lesson 20 on the DVD or visit www.wrox.com/go/sp2010-24 *to view the video that accompanies this lesson.*

21

Setting Branding Options in Publishing Sites

People either love or hate the branding and look-and-feel of SharePoint out-of-the-box. Many people, particularly those who are using SharePoint for public-facing Internet sites, extensively redesign the interface; others don't change the interface. I don't recommend extensive changes to SharePoint sites for internal use. In my experience, intranet users are happy with the out-of-the-box styling. However, SharePoint does provide you with many ways to brand sites to meet the highest standards on the Web, and many SharePoint sites have been rebranded so much you cannot recognize them as SharePoint.

MASTER PAGES

Core to the development of branding a SharePoint site is the *master page*. A master page looks after things like navigation (global and context) and the general look and feel of your sites. Master pages are used with page layouts, which manage the content of your pages. Master pages and page layouts are combined to produce most SharePoint pages on your site.

The actual content on your page, together with its look and feel, is controlled by another web authoring technology, Cascading Style Sheets (CSS). In SharePoint, a major CSS sheet is the `corev4.css` file, which is applied to almost every site you create — unless of course you override it with your own CSS file or override individual CSS styles! SharePoint CSS files can range in size from thousands of lines to only a few styles.

When branding SharePoint, it is important that you do not edit or change the supplied master pages or style sheets. Always make a copy of a file and work using the copy. When working with master pages do not remove any of the existing placeholders. Placeholders are blocks of code that are replaced at run time with content (for example, the title of your site). If you remove placeholders the master page may break; it is best practice to hide the placeholders you do not require. A full list of the default placeholders is available from `http://msdn.microsoft.com/en-us/library/ee539981.aspx`.

Master Page Gallery

You can view the master pages in a site collection by looking in the master page gallery within the site settings, where you will also find the page layouts. Figure 21-1 shows the master page gallery for a publishing portal.

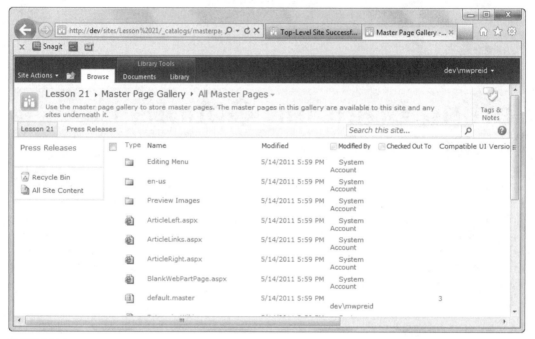

FIGURE 21-1

You can check which master page a publishing site is using by checking the site settings. Publishing portals use the `nightandday.master` and most other SharePoint sites use a master page called `v4master.master`. Another master page used on search pages is `minimal.master`. The odd thing about this master page is that it has no navigation.

Those familiar with SharePoint 2007 should know that this minimal master page is not the same as the one used as a starting point for branding. Figure 21-2 shows a custom page in SharePoint Designer 2010 with a master page attached. Everything except the center of the page is controlled by the master page, in this case `v4master.master`.

The following master pages are available with SharePoint 2010:

➤ **default.master:** Used by SharePoint sites that are still running in MOSS 2007 interface mode, meaning sites that have not been visually upgraded to the SharePoint 2010 user interface.

➤ **v4master.master:** Default master page for SharePoint 2010 team sites.

➤ **minimal.master:** Master page used by the search pages in SharePoint. It is also used by Office web applications. This master page contains no navigation.

➤ **simple.master:** Used by log-in and error pages in SharePoint. This page cannot be customized but you can replace it with a custom page of your own.

➤ **nightandday.master:** Master page used by publishing portals.

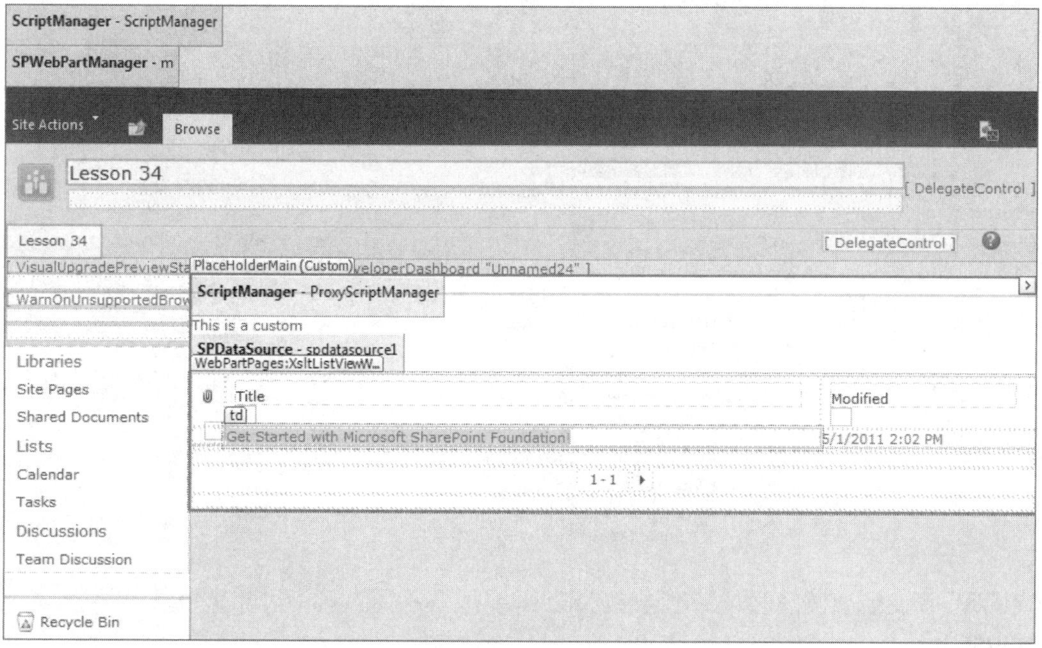

FIGURE 21-2

There are a number of additional master pages, such as `application.master` that you do not use when customizing a SharePoint site. The master page gallery is a little like a publishing site in that content must be checked out before it can be edited, checked back in when edits are complete, and then published and approved.

Setting Master Pages

You can of course change the master page for your site in the SharePoint interface using the Site Settings menu. This gives you limited options for changing the master page used by the site and its subsites. Site Settings also enable you to change the CSS file used by the site and the subsites. For example, within a publishing site the site collection will use `nightandday.master` while the system pages and views use `v4master.master`. Figure 21-3 shows the same publishing site using two different out-of-the-box master pages to demonstrate the changes that can be made. Even this simple example demonstrates the power of a master page to change the entire look and feel of a SharePoint site.

When you set the master page you also have the option of using the same page for all subsites within the site collection. For example, in a publishing portal the top-level site uses `nightandday.master`. Subsites use `v4master.master`. In the master page settings under the Site Settings menu, it is possible to simply click a check box labeled Reset All Sub Sites To Inherit This Site Master Page Setting to make subsites use the same master page as opposed to `v4master.master`, which is used by default.

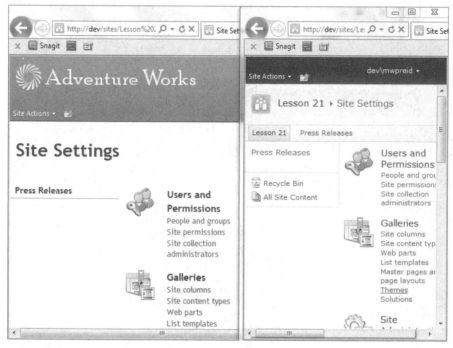

FIGURE 21-3

SETTING STYLE SHEETS

Just as you can switch master pages at the site and subsite levels, you can also make changes to the style sheets used on your sites. In the site settings, you can control the following:

➤ **Alternate CSS URL:** Enter the URL to your own alternative CSS file.

➤ **Use Default CSS:** Use the site's default CSS file.

➤ **Inherit Alternative URL:** Use the same alternative CSS file as the site's parent.

After you have created a new CSS file, you can use the settings to associate your master page with the site and subsites if required. In a publishing site, the normal practice is to store the CSS file in the site collection style library. The CSS settings enable you to browse your site structure to locate any files required. SharePoint Designer makes it fairly easy to work with SharePoint CSS and gives you direct access to the styles used on every element of a SharePoint page. Two more useful tools for working with CSS and SharePoint are the IE Developer Toolbar and, for Firefox users, Firebug. Firebug tends to be the tool of choice for identifying CSS elements used on a web page. A good resource for learning about the various CSS styles on a SharePoint page is `http://erikswenson`

`.blogspot.com/2010/01/sharepoint-2010-base-css-classes.html`. This site provides a breakdown of each style and tells you where in the interface it is applied.

When you are going to work with CSS on your sites, it is best practice to enable publishing features if they are not already enabled. This way, you have a ready-made directory structure for saving files. For example, you will have a style library where you can create additional folders to meet your requirements.

Branding System Pages

Just as you can change the appearance of SharePoint site pages, you can also change the look of the pages used by the system. The option to view and change the CSS used by the system and applications is also available within the master page settings for the site in the System Master Page section. You are offered the same options as for the site master.

Themes

A discussion of branding would not be complete without a few words about SharePoint themes, which also enable you to change the look and feel of a site. You may have already noticed the Change Site Theme link on the team site homepage, which will open the Theme Settings page. Themes are generally an end-user tool, and with SharePoint 2010 a fair amount of customization can be achieved by site owners using the built-in themes.

Themes are available in the Look and Feel category of your Site Settings and here you can inherit the theme used by the parent site, select an existing theme, or create your own custom theme. You create custom themes using an Office client, either Microsoft Word or PowerPoint. You can apply your custom theme to the site you are currently working on and include the subsites if you want. Themes differ from master pages in that they mainly deal with cosmetic options like link color. Master pages, on the other hand, give you total control over virtually everything on the page. Changing a theme is straightforward thanks to the Site Settings menu. To view themes, perform these steps:

1. Click Site Actions.
2. Click Site Settings.
3. In the Look and Feel section, click Site Theme.

In the Site Theme form you can view the current theme being used and select any of the other themes supplied. A nice feature is the ability to preview the selected theme before applying it to the site. Simply click the Preview button at the bottom of the screen to see how your changes would look within the site. You can also create new themes using Microsoft PowerPoint 2010 and upload them to the Themes Gallery. A new tool for creating themes that is still in beta is available at `http://connect.microsoft.com/themebuilder`.

TRY IT

In this exercise, you apply a custom master page and style sheet, set inheritance options, and set master pages for system pages.

Lesson Requirements

To complete this Try It exercise, you need the following:

➤ Custom master page

➤ Custom style sheet

➤ SharePoint Designer 2010

➤ Site collection administrator permissions

➤ SharePoint publishing site

➤ Starter master pages downloaded from `http://startermasterpages.codeplex.com/` (This set of pages can be used to replace the minimal master pages available with SharePoint 2007, and has been made available by Randy Drisgill. Save the extracted master pages to a local folder on your PC.)

Step-by-Step

To begin the process you need to add the downloaded starter master pages to the master page gallery. To upload the files, follow these steps:

1. Click Site Actions.

2. Click Site Settings.

3. In the Galleries category click Master Pages and Page Layouts.

4. Click Documents tab on the Ribbon.

5. Click Upload Document.

6. Select the first starter master page you would like to upload.

7. Click OK to upload.

At this point, you are required to complete some details before the upload can complete. This is because the master page gallery is under source control and you will have to check in, publish, and approve any files placed into this area. Figure 21-4 shows the Upload dialog.

8. Use the drop-down menu to change the content type to Publishing Master Page.

9. Remove the underscores from the master page name so that it is `starterpublishing` `.master`.

10. Accept the remaining defaults and click the Check In button.

11. Locate the new master page in the gallery and open its context menu.

12. Select Publish a Major Version.

13. Click OK.

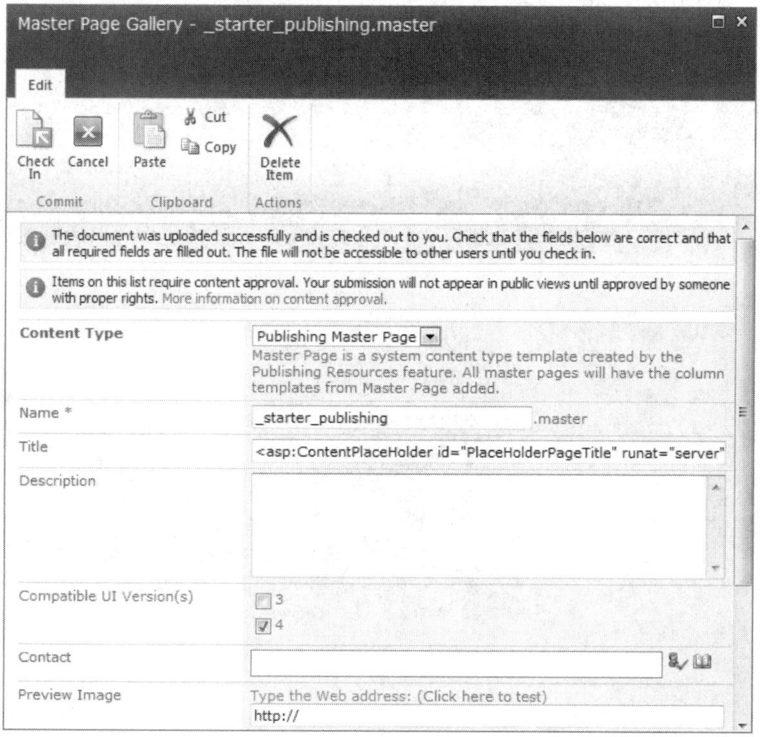

FIGURE 21-4

14. Return to the file and reopen the context menu.

15. Select Approve/Reject.

16. Click the Approved radio button.

17. Click OK to approve the master page.

After the master page has been uploaded, checked in, and approved, it is ready for use on the site. To use the master page on the site, continue as follows:

1. Click Site Actions.

2. Click Site Settings.

3. Click Master Page in the Look and Feel category.

4. Use the drop-down list to change the site master page to `starterpublishing.master`.

5. Scroll to the bottom of the screen and click OK.

Figure 21-5 shows the effect of this change on the homepage of your publishing site. The same site is displayed in the background using the original master page; notice the broken image displayed in the upper left-hand corner of the new page.

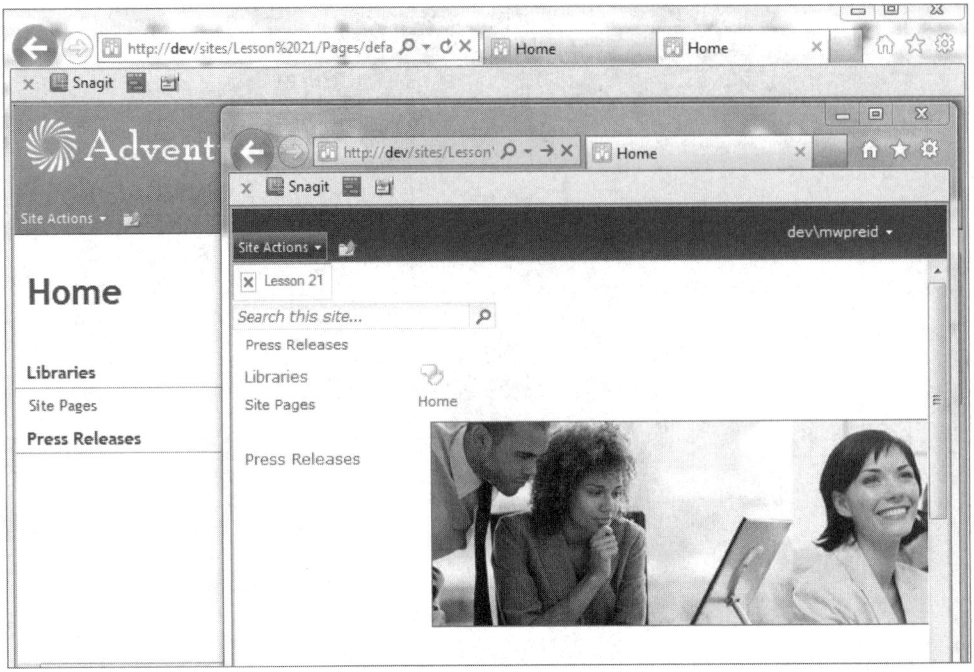

FIGURE 21-5

To edit the master page, return to the master page gallery and do the following:

1. Select the `starterpublishing.master` file.

2. Select Edit in Microsoft SharePoint Designer from the context menu.

3. Click OK to check the file out.

4. Click OK in response to the Open Document dialog. The master page should now open within SharePoint Designer for editing.

5. Click the missing logo placeholder. In the page code, view the following fragment of code should be highlighted:

```
<SharePoint:SPLinkButton runat="server"
NavigateUrl="~sitecollection/">
<SharePoint:SiteLogoImage
LogoImageUrl="/Style Library/sitename/logo.png" runat="server"/>
</SharePoint:SPLinkButton>
```

Note the line `LogoImageUrl="/Style Library/sitename/logo.png" runat="server"/>`. This is a placeholder for an image named `logo.png` located within the style library of your site. At the moment this image doesn't exist.

6. Select any image file and upload it to your site's style library. For this example I downloaded the cover image for this book from `wrox.com` and renamed it `trainer.jpg`. Replace the preceding line with the following line, replacing the image file name with your own image's name:

```
LogoImageUrl="/Sites/Lesson 21/Style Library/Images/trainer.jpg"
```

7. Save the changes to the master page and return to the master page gallery, where you will find the master page marked as a draft.

8. Use the file's context menu to check the file in as a major version (publish).

9. Use the context menu again to approve the file for use. This will change the file status from Draft to Approved.

10. Click Site Actions.

11. Click Site Settings.

12. Click Master Page.

13. Change the site's master page to `starterpublishing.master`.

14. Click OK to save the changes.

Figure 21-6 shows the site's homepage using the new custom master page.

FIGURE 21-6

Bear in mind that this is a very crude example used to demonstrate a single change. Branding a full SharePoint site is complex and involves a number of different web authoring skills including SharePoint administration. On a large scale it is not something to be undertaken lightly. The next CSS example makes use of the ability to use an alternate CSS file, and again makes a major change to the SharePoint site. Again this is to demonstrate the ability of CSS to change the site, so it is a simple example. You are going to change the background color of the title bar on the page, or rather you are going to add the CSS instruction that will do it for you.

This is a simple change of background color to reset the title bar to orange. Before continuing, you need to make a few changes to SharePoint Designer to enable yourself to look at a master page and see which CSS styles are applied to any given element. Changes to SharePoint Designer 2010 make this process fairly easy. To continue with the `v4master.master` page open, do the following:

1. Click the View tab.

2. Click the task panes.

3. Select CSS Properties, and close all other task panes.

4. In the CSS Properties task pane click the Summary button. This shows all active CSS properties.

5. To check the CSS applied to a particular element on the screen, click the element on the page. CSS properties will dynamically change to show the individual CSS code for each of the elements you select.

6. Click the blue header on the master page. The control name appears in the top-left corner of the element: `SharePoint:SPRibbon`. To get the correct element that has been styled, click the solid line at the top of the blue title row.

7. In the CSS Property task pane, note the CSS properties displayed, including the background color, `#21374c`. Click in the background color cell, and use the drop-down list to select a new color.

Your title background row should reflect the new color chosen. Behind the scenes, SharePoint Designer 2010 has rewritten the CSS style for you. The new style is shown in the following code; in this case, the background color is yellow:

```
body #s4-ribbonrow{
      min-height: 43px;
/* [ReplaceColor(themeColor:"Dark2",themeShade:"0.9")] */;
      background-color: #FFFF00;
      overflow-y: hidden;
}
```

There are also some fairly simple ways to change areas of your site without using master pages or CSS. For example, in Site Settings you can change the title, icon, and description used in your site. This is a common approach for sites that require their own logos; the main drawback is that you have to make the changes on all your sites if you are storing the image file locally in the site structure. In the earlier example in which you added an image to the master page, you could also have uploaded it to the style library for your site and referenced it in the Site Settings area if a logo is required for a single site. However, it is possible to save the image to each of your front-end web servers — in the `_Layouts` folder, for example. It is then available to each site using the correct image file URL.

Please select Lesson 21 on the DVD or visit www.wrox.com/go/sp2010-24 *to view the video that accompanies this lesson.*

Using Content Approval in Publishing Sites

In many cases you will not want every page on your SharePoint site to be immediately available to your users. For example, a page outlining your company's absence policy would need to be checked and approved before you make it visible to staff. Fortunately SharePoint provides you with several tools to help you keep pages hidden until they're ready. A Pages Library within SharePoint can be used to create additional SharePoint pages for use within your site, or used as part of a publishing portal for external access. Each page created can of course be immediately published to the site, but they can also be "held up" while waiting on approval for publishing. In order to create a Pages Library you must have publishing enabled both at the site collection and individual site level or create a new site collection using the Publishing template. It's worth noting that you can only have one Pages Library within the publishing site. To view the Pages Library in a publishing site, follow these steps:

1. Click Site Settings.
2. Click View all site content.
3. Click the Pages link to open the Pages Library.

To continue to the actual settings screen for the versioning options, do the following:

1. Click the Library tab.
2. Click Library Settings.
3. Select the Versioning Settings link.

Figure 22-1 shows the versioning settings page for the library.

The settings found in Figure 22-1 are discussed next:

➤ **Content Approval:** This is the main setting for content approval. In this case the default setting for the publishing portal is Content Approval is enabled by default.

➤ **Document Version History:** Enable version history for your pages. This can be a useful setting if you need to roll back to earlier versions of pages. Just be aware that version history can have a high storage overhead if you are saving multiple versions of every page.

➤ **Draft Item Security:** This is an important section when you are enabling approval of content. If you leave it at the default setting, any user who can read items will be able to view all content within the library, including content that has not been approved. This is not what you want; just think of a draft security policy placed into the library being read by all staff before its approval! When you set Require Content Approval for Submitted Items to Yes, the default for this option will automatically change to Only Users Who Can Approve Items will be able to see documents pending approval.

➤ **Require Check Out:** Checkout can be enforced for those working with pages (and other documents) in SharePoint. The default is No, but for Pages it is perhaps useful to change this to Yes: this should help to ensure documents are not overwritten while they are being worked on.

Content Approval

Specify whether new items or changes to existing items should remain in a draft state until they have been approved.   Learn about requiring approval.

Require content approval for submitted items?
○ Yes   ◉ No

Document Version History

Specify whether a version is created each time you edit a file in this document library.   Learn about versions.

Create a version each time you edit a file in this document library?
○ No versioning
◉ Create major versions
   Example: 1, 2, 3, 4
○ Create major and minor (draft) versions
   Example: 1.0, 1.1, 1.2, 2.0

Optionally limit the number of versions to retain:
☐ Keep the following number of major versions:

☐ Keep drafts for the following number of major versions:

Draft Item Security

Drafts are minor versions or items which have not been approved. Specify which users should be able to view drafts in this document library.   Learn about specifying who can view and edit drafts.

Who should see draft items in this document library?
◉ Any user who can read items
○ Only users who can edit items
○ Only users who can approve items (and the author of the item)

Require Check Out

Specify whether users must check out documents before making changes in this document library.   Learn about requiring check out.

Require documents to be checked out before they can be edited?
◉ Yes   ○ No

[OK]   [Cancel]

FIGURE 22-1

SharePoint also provides workflows to assist you with the management of the approval process. Many of us who spend all day in SharePoint tend to think that everyone else does as well. This is not the case, and workflows will be very useful in managing the approval process. A workflow will automate and track the approval process for content by tracing its progress in the SharePoint Tasks lists and by using e-mail to manage communication to approvers. Setting up an approval workflow requires you to adjust the setting for the Pages Library. From within the Pages Library, do the following:

1. Click the Library Tools tab.

2. Click Library.

3. Click Library Settings.

4. Click Workflow Settings in the Permissions and Management category.

This will open the Add a Workflow screen, where you can choose and configure the appropriate workflow for the library. There is also another, quicker way to reach this screen. Figure 22-2 shows the Workflow icon on the Library ribbon group. This gives you quick access to the workflow management forms. Using the management form you can do any of the following:

➤ Go to Workflow Settings for existing workflows.

➤ Add a workflow.

➤ Create a workflow in SharePoint Designer.

➤ Create a reusable workflow in SharePoint Designer.

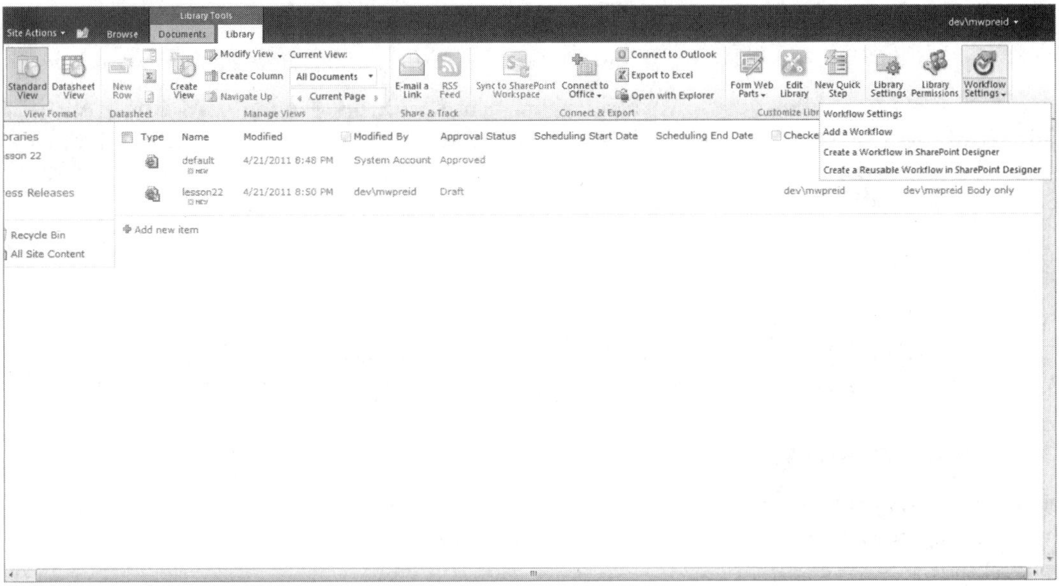

FIGURE 22-2

> *When you create a workflow within a list or library using the SharePoint interface, the interface is bound to that list or library and is not available to others. A reusable workflow, on the other hand, can be associated with other lists and libraries within the site collection.*

When a workflow is used to approve content you must of course identify the person or people who will do the approval. SharePoint 2010 also enables you to create a serial workflow, for example by entering multiple approvers. In this case the approval will be routed to each approver in the in the order in which the user name is added to the workflow. When a workflow is created it is assigned to those who can approve it, and a task is created either in the default Workflow Tasks list or in a new task list you create for the workflow. As the person creating the workflow, you will receive an e-mail once it starts, and the first potential approver will also receive an e-mail. If this person approves the content the second potential approver, if there is one, will then be assigned his or her task. This process is repeated for each person who can approve the serial workflow. An approver can also reassign his or her workflow task, for example to a more knowledgeable staff member.

SharePoint contains several workflows out of the box and depending on your site you may find there are additional workflows available:

➤ **Disposition Workflow:** Used to manage document expiration and retention; users can also decide whether to keep or delete expired documents.

➤ **Collect Feedback:** Enables you to collect feedback on documents from others. The feedback is compiled and returned to the workflow creator.

➤ **Collect Signatures:** Collects signatures used for Office documents.

➤ **Approval Workflow:** Used to approve content. This is one of the more popular workflows.

You can also create workflows using Microsoft Office SharePoint Designer 2010, Microsoft Visual Studio 2010, and Microsoft Visio 2010. Each of these packages enables you to extend workflows to enhance even the most complex business process. SharePoint Designer can also be used to extend workflows you create within your lists and libraries.

TRY IT

In this section you will be setting up an approval workflow for a Pages Library. You will enter an approver for a page to see the operation of the approval process from an administrator's point of view.

Lesson Requirements

You will need a Pages Library in a publishing site and of course some sample pages. To see the full effect of the approval workflow you should have a test user or colleague to whom you can assign the approval.

Hint

Ensure you have created a publishing portal containing a Pages Library before beginning the step-by-step.

Step-by-Step

To begin the workflow process you need to enable content approval within the Pages library. From within the Pages Library, do the following:

1. Click the Page tab within the Page Library.

2. Click the Library Settings icon.

3. In the General Settings category click the Versioning Settings link.

4. Change the Content Approval setting to Yes. The Draft Item Security setting should change to Only Users Who Can Approve Items (and the Author of the Item).

5. Set Require Check Out to Yes.

6. Click OK to save the changes.

This process enables content approval for the library and enables check-in and checkout. In addition you have ensured that only potential approvers and the content authors can see content that has not been approved. Also note the addition of new metadata columns to the library including, Approval Status and Checked Out To. To continue you will of course need some content within the library, so add a new page:

1. Click the Library tab within the Library Tools group on the ribbon.

2. Click the Library Settings icon.

3. Click Workflow Settings and select Add a Workflow to open the Add a Workflow form. This form requires you to make several choices.

4. Select Page from the Content Type drop-down list. We want our approval workflow to execute only for pages.

5. Select Approval SharePoint 2010 from the Select a Workflow drop-down list.

6. Enter a meaningful name for the workflow in the Name field, such as **Content Page Approval**.

7. Accept the Task List default of Workflow Tasks. You can also select New History List, in which case a new list will be created.

8. You want the workflow to start automatically, so under Start Options choose Start This Workflow When a New Item Is Created. However, you also want edits approved, so also check the box labeled Start This Workflow When an Item is Changed.

9. Click OK to save the initial configuration and go to the second stage of the process, the actual assignment of the workflow task.

10. In the Assign To text box enter the name or names of your potential approvers. You can add multiple approvers by clicking the Add a New Stage link immediately below the Assign text box.

11. In the Request text box enter a message for them, for example **Please approve the page content**.

12. Enter today's date in the Due Date field.

13.   Enter **1** as the value for Duration of Task. This number can represent days, weeks, or months.

14.   Leave the CC field blank.

15.   Check Enable Content Approval.

16.   Click Save.

Step 15 will automatically change the status of the content to Approved if the workflow receives approval by the individuals responsible. To check out the workflow add a new page to the library. This should automatically trigger the approval workflow created and your approvers should receive an immediate e-mail notifying them of the approval task. You can check that the workflow is actually running by:

1.   Click the library settings icon.

2.   Clicking Workflow settings.

3.   You can then see the Workflow in Progress notification to the right of the workflow name.

More detailed information about the workflow and its progress is also available from the properties of the page within the library itself. To view the properties of the page from the Pages Library:

1.   Click the page name to select it.

2.   On the Ribbon click View Properties.

3.   On the View table in the properties form click Workflows.

4.   Click a workflow name to review detailed information about the workflow.

Once the page or document is approved its Approval Status within the library will be changed from Pending to Approved and the document will then be available to your users. Figure 22-3 shows this screen with details of a simple test workflow available. Also note that in this case the workflow was canceled before completion and this information is also provided in this form.

In addition to an approval workflow you can also manually approve pages within the library. To manually approve a page form within the library the page must be checked in before it can be approved or indeed rejected.

1.   Select the page required

2.   Open the page context menu

3.   Click the Approve/Reject link

Figure 22-4 shows the Approve/Reject form where you can approve the page, reject the page, or set the page to continue to be pending.

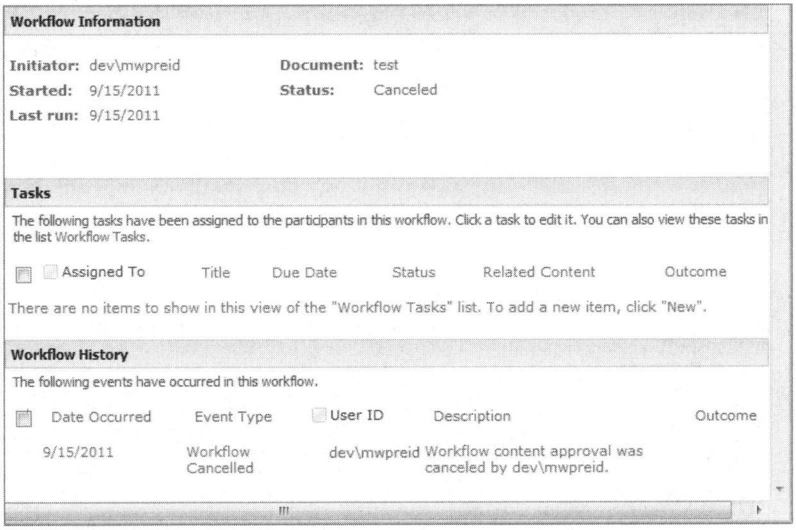

Workflow Information

Initiator: dev\mwpreid   Document: test
Started: 9/15/2011   Status: Canceled
Last run: 9/15/2011

Tasks

The following tasks have been assigned to the participants in this workflow. Click a task to edit it. You can also view these tasks in the list Workflow Tasks.

	Assigned To	Title	Due Date	Status	Related Content	Outcome

There are no items to show in this view of the "Workflow Tasks" list. To add a new item, click "New".

Workflow History

The following events have occurred in this workflow.

	Date Occurred	Event Type	User ID	Description	Outcome
	9/15/2011	Workflow Cancelled	dev\mwpreid	Workflow content approval was canceled by dev\mwpreid.	

FIGURE 22-3

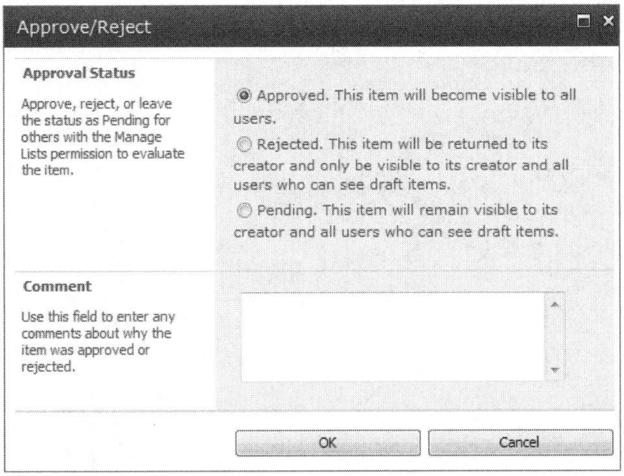

Approve/Reject

Approval Status

Approve, reject, or leave the status as Pending for others with the Manage Lists permission to evaluate the item.

- ◉ Approved. This item will become visible to all users.
- ○ Rejected. This item will be returned to its creator and only be visible to its creator and all users who can see draft items.
- ○ Pending. This item will remain visible to its creator and all users who can see draft items.

Comment

Use this field to enter any comments about why the item was approved or rejected.

[OK]   [Cancel]

FIGURE 22-4

Please select Lesson 22 on the DVD or visit www.wrox.com/go/sp2010-24 *to view the video that accompanies this lesson.*

Using Variations in Publishing Sites

In some cases you may want to publish pages or indeed entire sites in multiple languages. Or perhaps you want to give your users the option to view a site in a particular language. With SharePoint 2010 you can do these things using *variations*. SharePoint of course cannot translate content for you; what it can do is help you organize the content to allow your users to choose the language they prefer once the content has been translated. For completeness, the variations process is not restricted to different languages. It can be used to provide many different types of content to a variety of audiences or, for that matter, to different devices such as different types of smartphones.

VARIATIONS

Variations enable you to configure multiple sites within a SharePoint publishing portal, specifying one as the core content site and automatically or manually copying content to other specified sites, where it can be translated into the language or languages required. In order to use variations, you must enable the SharePoint publishing features for the site collection.

Variations are not available with standard SharePoint 2010 Team Sites. You can, however, use another feature of SharePoint 2010 to give users access to content in other languages: this is the Multilingual User Interface (MUI), which was introduced with SharePoint 2010. The MUI will enable you to change the display language used by sites, but it has no effect on content. You can change the display language for the following:

➤ Site title and description

➤ SharePoint standard menus

➤ Standard SharePoint columns

➤ Custom columns (list or site)

➤ Navigation bar links

➤ Managed Metadata services

Figure 23-1 shows a SharePoint site that has been changed from the default language of English to French within the browser. The language picker is also shown. You can of course use the MUI for the user interface and variations for the actual content.

FIGURE 23-1

In order to use the MUI you are required to download the specific language packs available for SharePoint. Language packs can be downloaded for both SharePoint Server and SharePoint Foundation. Language packs can be downloaded from `http://www.microsoft.com/download/en/details.aspx?displaylang=en&id=3411`. After downloading you must run the language pack executable and then run the SharePoint Products Configuration wizard to complete the process. Once the pack is installed and configured you will find a language setting has been added to the Site Settings category under Site Administration. Language Settings enable you to select the additional languages you require for the site collection. The selected languages are in addition to the default language used when the site was created. For example, if your install language is US English and you add the French Language Pack the end result is the ability to switch between US English, the default language used when installing SharePoint, and French.

Variation Settings

Once you have created a publishing site or publishing portal you will find the variations features located within the Site Collection Administration category of the Site Settings at the top level of your site collection. The settings available are as follows:

➤ **Variation Home:** This is the URL to the core variation site from which content will be copied down into the variation subsite.

➤ **Automatic Creation:** In this section you can choose to publish variations either manually or automatically to the target site or sites.

➤ **Recreate Deleted Target Page:** If a source page is republished and the copy has been deleted this option will let you recreate it. This could happen, for example, if an end user deleted a page in the target site. You can also choose not to recreate deleted content.

➤ **Update Target Page Web Parts:** Specify how to update target Web Parts when the source is updated.

➤ **Notification:** Choose whether or not to be notified by email when a new page is created or updated by the variation system.

➤ **Resources:** Resources used by the source page can be copied into the target site or left in the main site. If left in the main site links to them would be used in the target site content.

Setting Variation Labels

Variation labels are used to identify each language you would like to use within a given variation hierarchy. For each language you would like to use you are required to create a variation label. A specific SharePoint site will then be created for each of the variation labels defined. The options available are:

➤ **Label name and description:** Text describing the label

➤ **Display Name:** The name for the navigation menu. For example, if the secondary site is using German you would create a display name of German.

➤ **Language:** The language that will be used for the user interface for the variation site.

➤ **Locale:** The location determining date, time, and currency data within the site.

➤ **Hierarchy Creation:** Allows you to select what area of the SharePoint site you would like to publish to other sites.

➤ **Source Variation:** This sets up the source variation for your variations and cannot be changed once created.

Setting Translatable Columns

The Translatable Columns option enables you to specify which columns in your site collection will require translation. This is a setting available at the top level of the site collection within the Site Collection Administration category. Once chosen this option you will be able to pick which of the available site collection columns are allowed to be translated into the target language.

Set Variation Logs

Variations are managed and organized by SharePoint timer jobs. Variation logs enable you to view the jobs that have been executed and any associated errors. Again this option is available from the root of the site collection in the Site Collection Administration category. Logs are limited and are read-only on screen. For example, unlike many of the SharePoint system logs they cannot be exported to Excel for analysis. You can view the timer jobs used from Central Administration by clicking the Monitoring link and then selecting Check job status. From the status page you can review all timer jobs on the server including those related to variations.

TRY IT

In this Try It exercise you are going to configure your SharePoint site for multiple languages, in this case French and English. You will do the following:

➤ Enable the MUI for SharePoint 2010

➤ Configure variation settings for a multilingual interface

➤ Set labels for a second language

➤ View sites in browser

Lesson Requirements

To complete this exercise, you need the following:

➤ The SharePoint 2010 Server language packs, which can be downloaded from http://www.microsoft.com/. Simply search for the language pack you require. You will also require a site collection with the publishing infrastructure activated.

➤ The Step-by-Step section that follows assumes that a language pack has been installed and is fully functioning.

Step-by-Step

From the home page of your site collection you will first enable the MUI, which will allow your users to change the language used by the site menus and other SharePoint features. This will have no effect on the site content. To allow a user to select a language, follow these steps:

1. Click the Site Actions button

2. Click Site Settings

3. Click Language Settings in the Site Administration category.

4. Click the checkbox in the Alternative Language section to choose the alternative language for the site. In my case, because I installed only the French language pack, the only option is French.

5. Click OK to save the changes.

6. Click Home to return to the home page of the site collection

7. Click your username, located at the top right of the screen, to open the context menu.

8. Click Select Display Language.

9. From the resulting submenu select the alternative language (in this case French).

Your page should now refresh in the browser and your SharePoint menus and other system items should be displayed in your chosen language. Refer to Figure 23-1, which shows the effect of the change from the sites default language. To return to the site's default language simply repeat Steps 7 through 9. Remember, the MUI deals only with the interface to SharePoint. If you require content in multiple languages you will have to use variations.

Configuring Variation Settings for a Multilingual Interface

To configure your site for variations, make sure that the publishing infrastructure has been activated for the site collection and that the publishing features have been activated for the individual site. Once the publishing infrastructure has been enabled the following options will become available:

➤ Variations

➤ Variation labels

➤ Translatable columns

➤ Variation logs

To continue with the example follow these steps:

1. Click Site Actions.

2. Click Site Settings.

3. Click Variations in the Site Collection Administration category.

4. Type "/" in the Variation Home text box.

Accept the following default settings, which will be set to Available:

➤ Automatically create site and page variations

➤ Recreate a new target page when the source page is republished

➤ Update Web Part changes to target pages when variation source page update is propagated

➤ Send email notification to site and page contacts when a new site or page is created or a page is updated by the variation system

➤ Reference existing resources

5. Click OK to save the changes.

The next step is to create the variation labels, one for each language you will be using. Here we are using English (default language) and French, and we will create a label for each language. To proceed from your Site Settings page and the Site Collection Administration category, do the following:

1. Click Variation Labels.

2. Click New Label.

3. Enter "English" as the Label Name.

4. Enter "English language site" as the Description.

5. Enter "English" as the Display Name.

6. Select English as the site template language using the Site Template drop-down list.

7. Select English (United States) as the locale using the Locale drop-down list.

8. Accept the default of Publishing Sites and All Pages in the Hierarchy Creation section.

9. Check the box labeled Set This Variation to be the Source Variation.

10. Select Publishing as the site template you would like to use.

11. Click OK to create the first label. We have set this as the source variation, and this setting cannot be changed once you click OK.

12. Repeat this process to create a label for the second language, in this case French. Make the following changes and click OK to create the additional variation label.

   ➤ Label Name: French

   ➤ Display Name: French

   ➤ Site Template Language: French

   ➤ Locale: French (France)

13. Click the Create Hierarchies on the Variation Labels Page link to trigger the creation of your variation timer job. The following message will be displayed: "A variation hierarchy will be created. The timer job 'Variations Create Hierarchies Job Definition' will be run based on the following schedule: 'daily between 00:00:00 and 03:00:00'."

14. Click OK to complete the process.

At this point in the process you will have to wait until the variation hierarchy is created by the timer job. (You could, of course, ask your SharePoint administrator to run the job for you immediately from SharePoint Central Administration.) Once the timer job has been executed and completed, the status of the hierarchy will be displayed on the Label Management page. Figure 23-2 shows the screen once a successful timer job has completed.

If you return to the home page of your site collection you should see the effect. In my case I have enabled the display of subsites in the site collection navigation (Site Actions, Site Settings, Navigation) to see the effect of the previous series of steps. In this case there are two subsites, English and French. The English site is the source site, from which content is copied into the French site for translation. In the case of the French site we have set the locale to French so that the user interface is already in that language. When you edit or add a page to your English site it will be copied into the French site by a timer job running on the server. Figure 23-3 shows the results when a page is edited within the English site. The same page can be seen in the corresponding French site and all that is required is its translation to the source language.

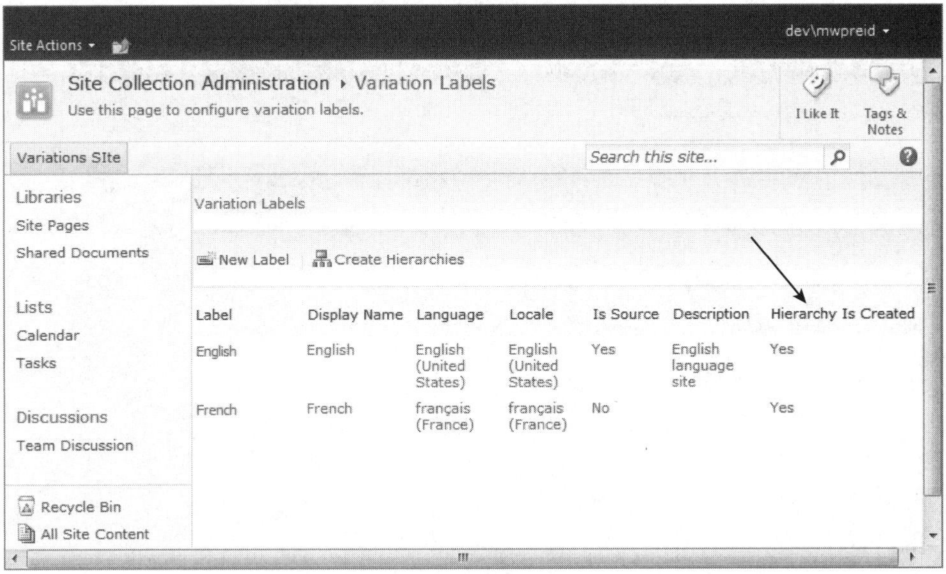

FIGURE 23-2

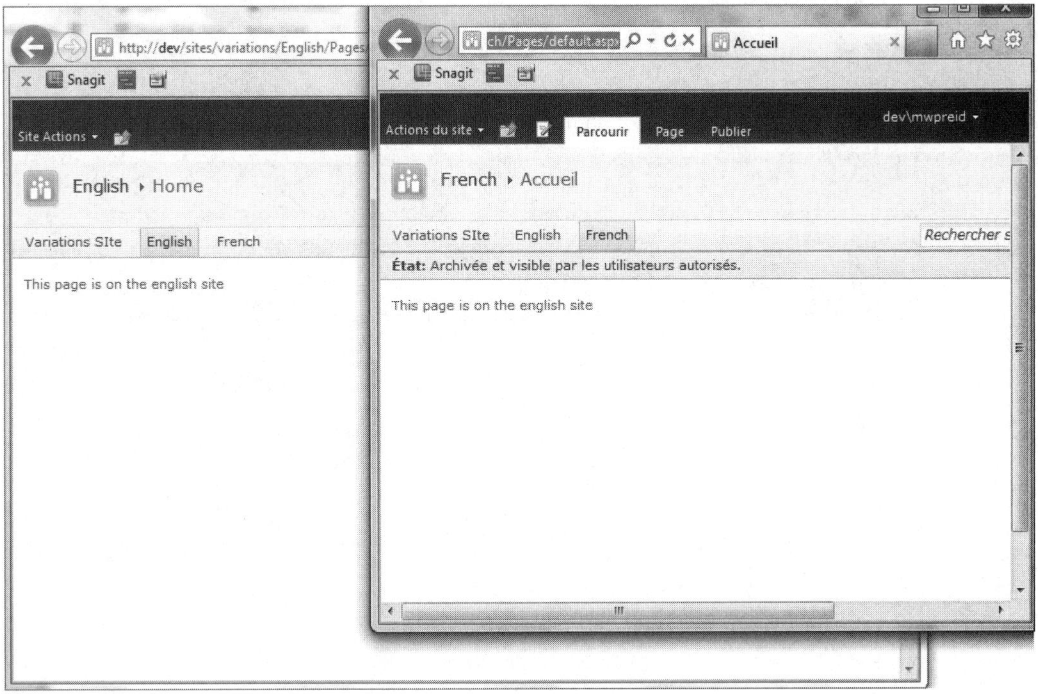

FIGURE 23-3

It is important when working with multiple sites and languages that you have some sort of idea of what has been copied into your target (French) site. Within the French site it is possible to view the edits that have taken place on a given page: Figure 23-4 shows our example page, which has been edited to contain a small amount of French (thanks Grace).

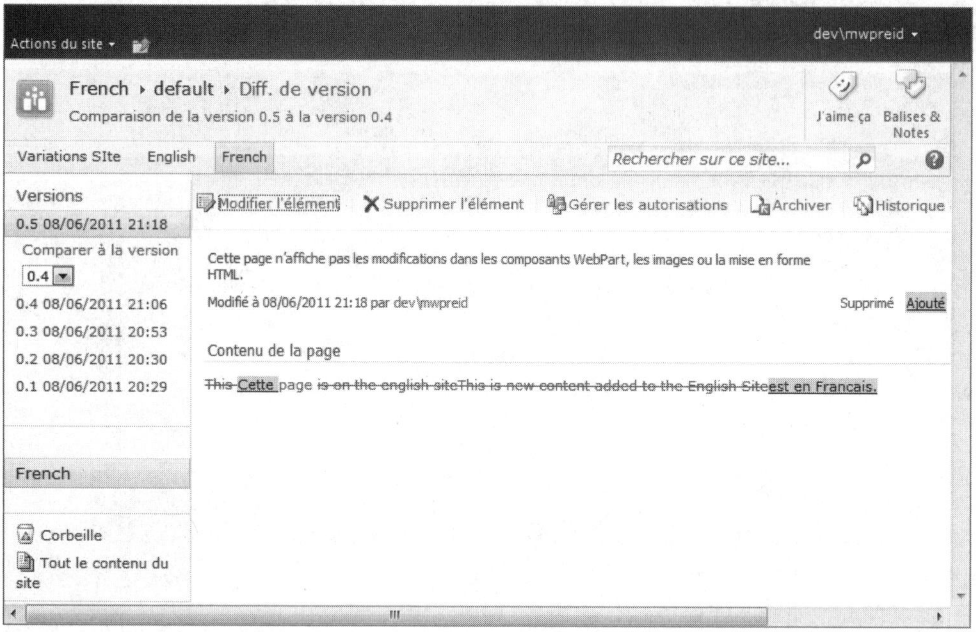

FIGURE 23-4

You can see the page history by clicking the Page tab when editing a page and selecting Page History. From the History page you can view all edits that have taken place within the page over specific time periods.

Please select Lesson 23 on the DVD or visit www.wrox.com/go/sp2010-24 *to view the video that accompanies this lesson.*

SECTION VI
Configuring Users and Permissions

24

SharePoint Security Groups

Security in SharePoint is something that many people new to the software can find confusing, especially those who are not used to managing sites and security. At a basic level SharePoint security is fairly straightforward to set up and manage; at a more complex level it has broken the heart of many a SharePoint administrator as security and users got out of control. One of the major problems with SharePoint is that it does not enable you to quickly see who has access to what within your site collection. SharePoint 2010 addresses this problem, but not completely, as you will see in this lesson.

Out of the box SharePoint security is based on permission inheritance when you create a site. Initially your users will have access to all objects based on their permissions to the site itself, including for example the Shared Documents library and calendar. Users who have access to the site will have access to these libraries and lists.

INHERITANCE

People and groups are given access to a SharePoint site; as a result they will have access to document libraries, individual documents, and lists. When you create new objects, those objects also inherit the permissions of the site and users of your site have access to them. This process also applies to subsites. When you create a subsite, users with permissions to the main site collection (the parent site) will also by default have access to the subsite and its objects. In many cases this is not what you want. Fortunately, SharePoint provides you with a way to break this inheritance, enabling individual permissions to be set for objects down to the individual document level. This is where new problems can begin, however, as the more you break inheritance the more you have to manage, and the fewer tools you have to manage security with.

SharePoint and Active Directory Groups

Groups are the basic tools used to organize and manage user security within your site collection. SharePoint will create groups, you can create groups, and you can reuse Active Directory groups if they are available. A group within SharePoint is assigned a permission level that controls how the group and thus its users interact with the environment. (Permission levels are discussed in Lesson 25.) Groups provide you with a basic tool for managing security on your site collection.

Active Directory groups are usually managed outside the SharePoint environment and populated from business systems for example, for example human resources data. In addition, AD groups are normally based on business groups. For example, you could have AD groups called Finance, Purchasing, and IT. Each of the preceding groups contains employees working in the designated area. This should make managing SharePoint security easy.

However, many organizations simply use AD as an authentication tool and do not use it to its full potential by creating and managing users in groups. In such cases you are left with no alternative but to use both built-in and custom SharePoint groups for site and content management. In this lesson you will look at AD groups, built-in SharePoint groups, and creating custom groups.

As previously stated, a group is assigned a permission level that specifies the rights it has to SharePoint objects and functionality. This gives you an easy way to manage users and their access to business areas and sites. Once a user is added to a group and the group is given permission to a site or object, the user immediately receives the same permissions. Similarly, when you revoke permission for a group, all members of that group will have their permissions revoked. This is a much easier system than managing the permissions of individual users. However, on occasion this is exactly what you need to do, as at times fine-grained user permissions are required to meet business needs.

An AD group is treated like a built-in SharePoint group in that it is given a permission level within the site environment. One difference is that you have no direct control over the membership of the AD group. Membership is normally handled by your system's management team and is generally automatic that is, populated into the AD based on employment role or business area. Another difference between AD groups and built-in SharePoint groups is that you cannot see inside AD groups — that is, you cannot view the individual memberships from within SharePoint. With SharePoint groups you have total control and can view, add, edit, and delete memberships as required. Unfortunately, you cannot add a SharePoint group to an AD group; you can, however, add an AD group to a SharePoint group, which can be useful.

Default SharePoint Groups

What happens when you create a new team site depends on the options you choose. By default the new site will automatically inherit its permissions from its parent site. If you need to break this inheritance you can do so later using the Site Actions menu. It is also possible to break inheritance at the point of site creation and create unique SharePoint groups to manage security. In this case your subsite will have its own unique set of users and associated permissions. Figure 24-1 shows the security options available: Use Unique Permissions and Use Same Permissions as Parent Site.

In general, when you are using SharePoint groups three groups are created for you by the system. They are normally named after the site in which they are created, as follows:

➤   **Sitename Owners:** This group has all permissions on the site. It contains the site owners and administrators.

➤   **Sitename Members:** This group normally contains all other members of the site's user community who have contribute permissions.

➤   **Sitename Visitors:** This site contains visitors to your site who do not require extensive permissions.

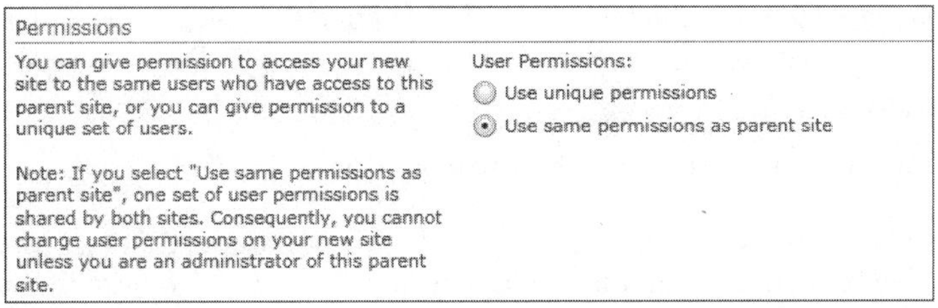

FIGURE 24-1

In addition to these groups you could use an AD group within, for example, your site's Owners or Members group. This AD group will already contain members who automatically have access to the site.

A useful practice is to include all your users in the site's Members group. This is to ensure that the membership Web Part in SharePoint My Site picks up all site memberships. If you are in the Owners group but not in the Members group the site will not be listed in your site memberships.

TRY IT

In this exercise you are going to do the following:

➤ Create a new team site and break permission inheritance.

➤ Add a SharePoint group to an existing site.

➤ Add an Active Directory group to a SharePoint group.

➤ Create a new group.

Lesson Requirements

➤ Site collection administrator permissions.

➤ Access to an Active Directory account.

➤ A test user account.

Step-by-Step

To begin the process you will create a new team site, break permission inheritance, and create custom security groups. To continue from the home page of your site collection, follow these steps:

1. Click Site Actions.

2. Select New Site.

3. Select Team Site from the options.

4. Enter **Lesson 24 Groups** as the site's title.

5. Enter **Lesson 24 Groups** as the URL.

6. Click the More Options button to open the Detailed Options form. It is from here that you will break security inheritance.

7. In the Permissions section click the radio button labeled Use Unique Permissions. This will result in the screen's changing to allow you to create the custom groups. The existing group's drop-down list will be removed.

8. Accept the remaining default selections and click the Create button.

Figure 24-2 shows the Set Up Groups for This Site screen. At this point note that two custom groups for the site have been made available: Members and Owners. Also note that the default visitors group has been used.

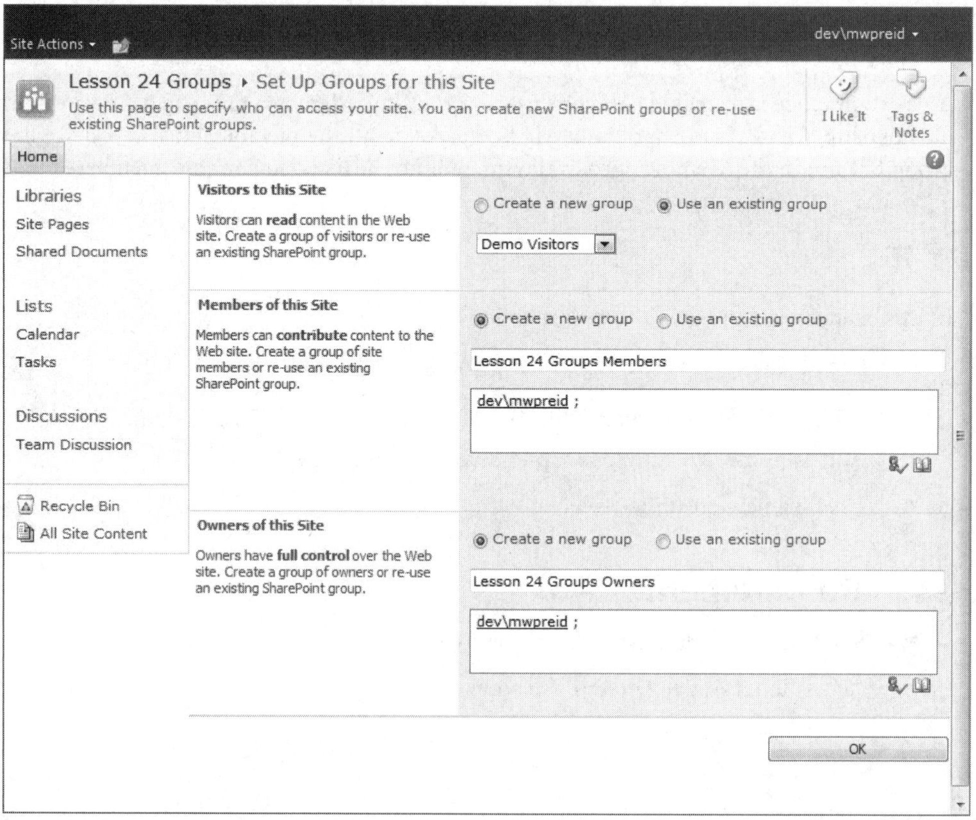

FIGURE 24-2

9. Change the default visitors group to a custom group by clicking the radio button labeled Create a New Group. The name will default to Lesson 24 Visitors and have no members. You can if you wish overwrite the group names. You do not need to add a member to this group at the moment.

10. Accept the two additional new groups, Members and Owners (in which you will automatically be given membership to both groups), and click OK to create the site using the custom security groups.

Figure 24-3 shows the Site Permissions screen once the site with the unique groups has been created. The ribbon contains a message confirming that the site is using unique permissions.

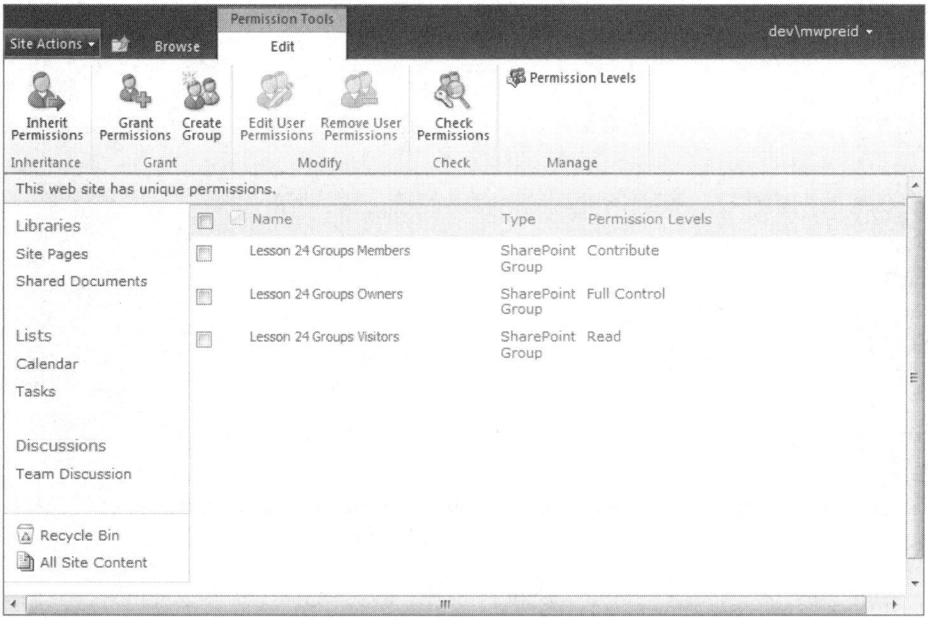

FIGURE 24-3

If you find that you have made an error you can at any time reset the site to inherit permissions from the parent by clicking the Inherit Permissions icon on the ribbon.

Of course at this point you are the only user in the groups. The next stage is usually adding another user. To add a user to the group called Lesson 24 Groups Members, from the Site Actions menu select Site Permissions.

1. Click the Grant Permissions icon on the ribbon to open the Grant Permissions form. Figure 24-4 shows the Grant Permissions form before user selection. The Browse (book) icon enables you to search for users while the Check Names (person) icon will check that a user entered directly into the User/Groups box is valid.

2. Enter the name of the user or group (remember you can place an AD group within a SharePoint Group) you wish to add, or click the Browse icon to begin searching for users and groups.

3. Once you have entered or selected a user or group, the name will appear in the Users/Groups box. If a user or group is not valid, a red wavy line will be placed below the name to indicate there is an problem. You can remove the name and enter the correct information.

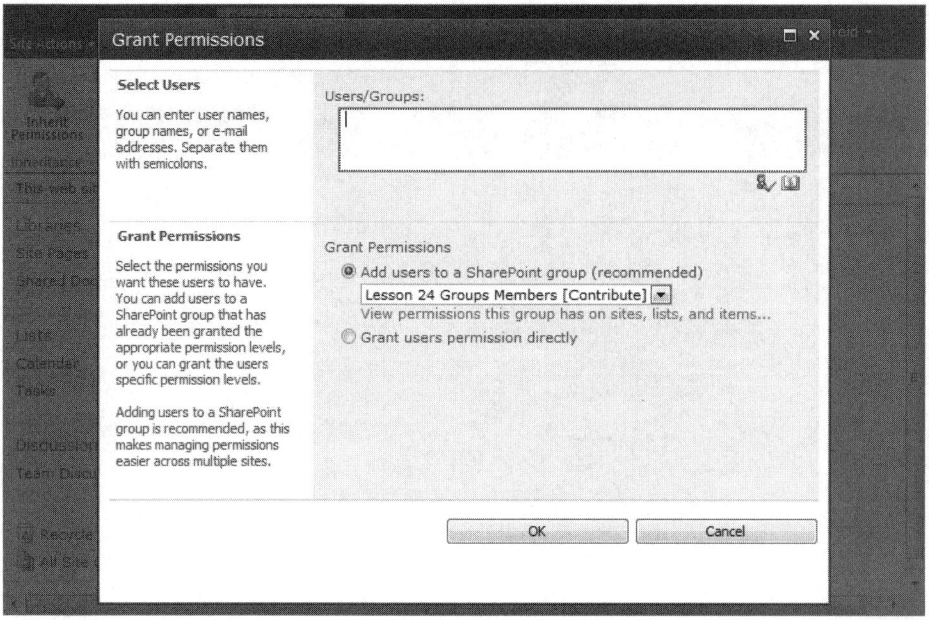

FIGURE 24-4

The Grant Permissions form enables you to assign permissions directly to individual users or groups. If, for example, you want to grant an AD group direct permissions on your team either search for or enter the name of the group. You add an AD group just as you would a standard SharePoint group. To enter an Active Directory group by searching the directory, proceed as follows:

1. Click the Grant Permissions icon.

2. Click the Browse (book) icon to search for an AD group.

3. Enter the name of an AD group. In this case I entered **Finance Department**.

You may be required to add the AD domain if you are using Active Directory. For example, in the preceding case I would have entered **dev\Finance Group** using **dev** to indicate the AD domain. Figure 24-5 shows the Grant Permissions dialog.

4. The Finance Department AD group will be added to the site's default Members group with contribute permissions. To continue click OK. This will add the AD group to the Members group. As a result the members of the AD group Finance Department will now have access to the SharePoint site.

As previously stated, you can create your own groups to help with site permissions. To create a custom group, from the Site Permissions screen proceed as follows:

1. Click Create Group.

2. Enter a name for the group into the Name text box, for example **Personnel Managers**.

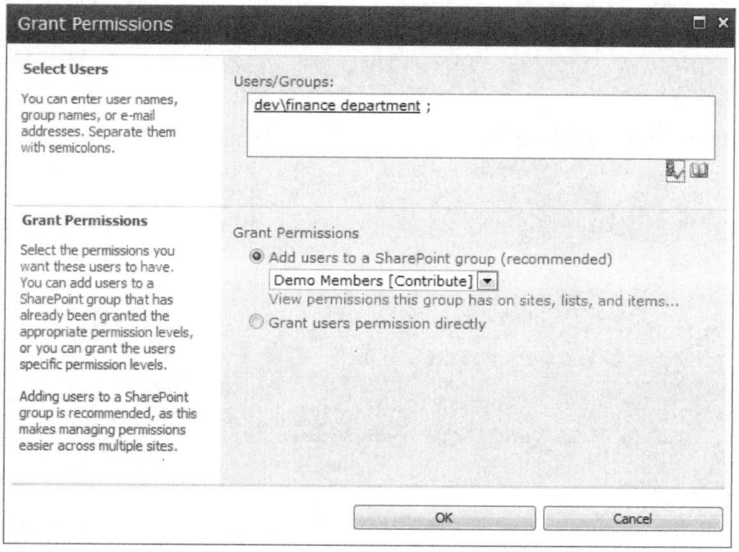

FIGURE 24-5

3. Enter a short description for the group into the About Me Description text box such as, **Managers from HR who will manage areas of the site.**

4. You own username will be added as the default site owner. You may change this if required for example if you are handing a site over to someone else and they become the site owner.

5. In the Group Settings section accept the default settings.

Group Settings enable you to manage who can view the membership of the group, group members only, or everyone, and who can edit the membership of the group, the group owner, or all members. It is usually better to allow only the owner to manage membership, as this simplifies things.

6. Accept the default for membership requests. The Membership Request section enables you to manage how people request access to the group. You can permit requests to join or leave the group, or have requests automatically sent to the e-mail address entered in the Email Address text box. The group owner's e-mail address should probably be the one entered here; e-mail must be configured on your SharePoint server if you want to use this feature.

7. Click the Full Control checkbox in the Give Group Permission to this Site section. This section enables you to set the explicit permissions this group has on your site.

8. Click the Create button to finish the process and create the group. You will be taken to the People and Groups page for the new group, where you can then add new members as required.

Figure 24-6 shows the People and Groups screen for the new group, which has a single member.

FIGURE 24-6

Please select Lesson 24 on the DVD or visit www.wrox.com/go/sp2010-24 to view the video that accompanies this lesson.

Permission Levels

One of the most important areas you will manage as a SharePoint site administrator is that of permissions. In many companies and businesses the use of file shares usually means that permissions to data and information are controlled centrally by the IT team. With SharePoint this central control is delegated to site collection administrators and site owners. Site collection administrators manage the security for the site collection as a whole, while site owners usually manage security for a team site or collection of subsites.

As you saw in Lesson 24, SharePoint security is built around security groups, both SharePoint and Active Directory groups. When you use a security group you assign a permission level to that group, such as *contributor* or *owner*. The group can then interact with SharePoint according to the permission level assigned to the group and the rights available within that level.

However, SharePoint is also flexible enough to enable you to edit the permission levels and in fact create your own. (Remember that permissions can be given only as part of a level; individual permissions contained within a permission level cannot be assigned individually to one user.) This ability to create your own permission levels and associated rights can be useful when you find certain permissions do not meet your requirements. The core permission levels provided out of the box for a team site include the following:

> **Full Control:** All available rights are granted to this level.

> **Design:** All permissions on lists and restricted rights on the site itself. This permission is usually restricted to design rights, for example the ability to change themes and styles.

> **Contribute:** Standard permission containing rights given to the majority of site users.

> **Read:** Read-only rights to the site and its content.

> **Limited Access:** Permission to access certain lists and libraries within the site structure.

> **View Only:** Rights to view list and library content.

Additional permission levels can be available depending on the features that your sites may have, for example with a publishing site additional levels related to publishing will be available.

Permission level defaults are usually broken down into three categories, each covering a particular area of SharePoint object management. Each category contains a specific set of rights that are made available to users via their permission levels.

➤ **List Permissions:** Permissions relating to SharePoint lists and libraries, such as permission to add, edit, view and delete list items.

➤ **Site Permissions:** Permissions relating to the site itself, for example the ability to create subsites or change a site's theme or style.

➤ **Personal Permissions:** Permissions that enable users you to personalize areas of SharePoint, for example by creating personal views of lists and working with personal Web Parts.

Figure 25-1 shows the list management permissions available for the full control permission level within a team site collection.

List Permissions

☑ Manage Lists - Create and delete lists, add or remove columns in a list, and add or remove public views of a list.

☑ Override Check Out - Discard or check in a document which is checked out to another user.

☑ Add Items - Add items to lists and add documents to document libraries.

☑ Edit Items - Edit items in lists, edit documents in document libraries, and customize Web Part Pages in document libraries.

☑ Delete Items - Delete items from a list and documents from a document library.

☑ View Items - View items in lists and documents in document libraries.

☑ Approve Items - Approve a minor version of a list item or document.

☑ Open Items - View the source of documents with server-side file handlers.

☑ View Versions - View past versions of a list item or document.

☑ Delete Versions - Delete past versions of a list item or document.

☑ Create Alerts - Create alerts.

☑ View Application Pages - View forms, views, and application pages. Enumerate lists.

FIGURE 25-1

It is also possible to create your own permission levels as required: for example, you may want a user to have a limited subset of permissions rather than all permissions for a particular level. On one large SharePoint site, I manage a specific group of high-level users who need very specific permissions. None of the built-in permission levels contained what was needed, so I created a specific level just for this group. This new custom level granted a subset of the permissions for an existing level.

Permissions and permission levels can also be managed at the web application level. For example, if there is a specific permission level right that you do not want users to have, you can remove it at the web application level as opposed to manually within each site collection. However, remember that your changes will apply to all site collections created for that web application.

SETTING NEW PERMISSION LEVELS

New permission levels can be based on existing categories or created from scratch. You should never change the out-of-the-box levels. Doing so can cause problems: if you do change a default permission level, every group using that level will find its permissions changed. It can also make your site difficult to manage, especially for others, who will expect the default permission levels to remain unchanged. When creating permission levels, either copy an existing permission that gets you up and running or create a completely new level yourself. Once you have created a new custom level it will be available within your site and can be used to give permissions to groups and users.

Adding Rights Levels to a Permission Level

When a permission level is created it is assigned rights to carry out actions on SharePoint objects. If you choose to copy a permission level it will contain the existing permission rights for that level and you can then add or remove rights as required.

You will also find that certain rights can be dependent: that is, when you assign one right to a level, other rights are enabled as a consequence. For example, if you assign the right to add list items, the right to view list items will also be enabled. If you enable the right to approve content, the view and edit item rights will also be enabled. Always be careful because dependency does not work in reverse: removing the approve right will not automatically remove the view and edit items right. Double-check all permission rights before saving, to ensure that you are giving only those you wish to give.

Best Practice

There are some things you can do to make working with custom permission levels easier for yourself as a site administrator, including:

➤ Do not customize existing permission levels. Create new levels either by copying an existing permission level or by creating your own.

➤ Always double-check before saving the level to make sure that the rights you are assigning are correct.

➤ Don't get carried away and create multiple custom levels. This only makes security harder to manage and (of course) to document.

➤ Document all changes to permission levels and custom levels.

➤ Create permission levels infrequently. Out-of-the-box permissions should meet most of your requirements.

➤ Always test a new level by logging in as a user with that level, to ensure that it behaves as expected.

TRY IT

In this exercise you are going to create a new SharePoint permission level that will allow users to edit list content. You will then save the new permission level and assign it to a SharePoint user group called Lesson 25 Users.

You will then copy an existing permission level, add the right to create subsites, and make the new custom level available for use within your site collection.

Requirements

➤ SharePoint site collection administrator permissions.

➤ A site group named Lesson 25 Users, or an equivalent group.

Step-by-Step

You are going to create a new permission level to allow users to view and edit lists. As this is a site collection configuration, to begin the process you must be on the home page of your site collection. The permission levels of a subsite that inherits permissions from its parent are managed at the site collection level. If you are using a subsite with its own unique permissions, the process is just the same as in the following steps, but you can work from within the subsite itself.

1. Click Site Actions.

2. Click Site Settings.

3. In the Users and Permissions category, click Site Permissions.

Figure 25-2 shows the Site Permissions screen and the Permissions ribbon. Note that the default groups and users with permission to the site are displayed.

4. Click the Permission Levels icon on the ribbon to open the Permission Levels screen, where you can add, edit, and delete existing permission levels.

5. Click the Add a Permission Level hyperlink to open the Add Permission Level screen.

6. Enter a name for your permission level, in this case enter **Lesson 25**.

7. Check the box entitled Edit Items — Edit Items in Lists, Edit Documents in Document Libraries, and Customize Web Part Pages in Document Libraries. Checking this option will also enable the view right, and if you scroll down through the form you'll see that the view pages and open rights are also checked.

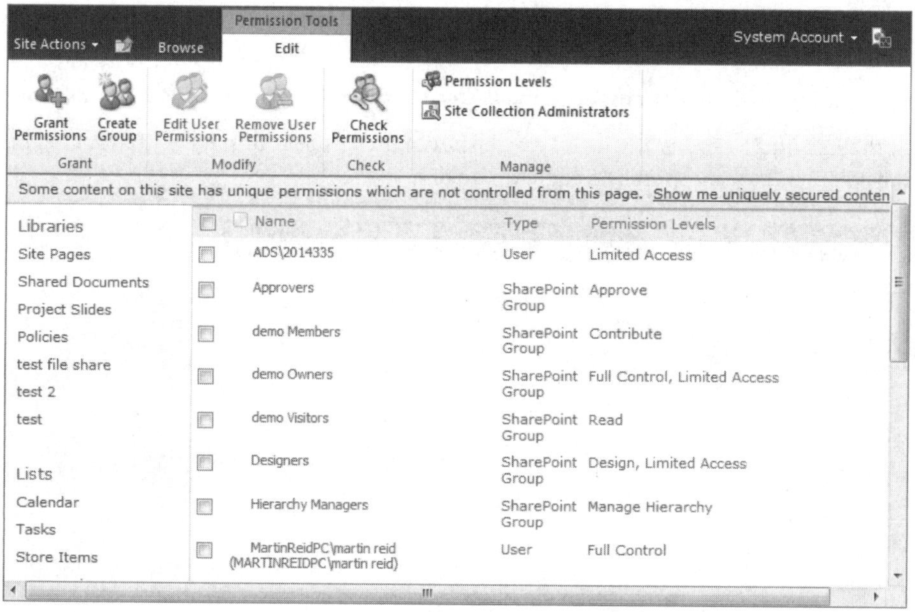

FIGURE 25-2

8. Leave all the other options blank and click Create to save the new permission level.

Figure 25-3 shows the newly created permission level in the Permission Level screen.

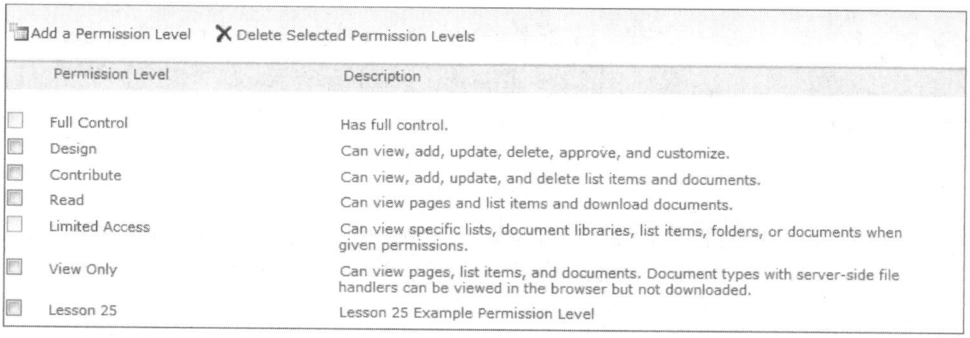

FIGURE 25-3

Now that the permission is available, you can assign it to a user group or to individual users. To grant a group permissions to your site collection and use the new Lesson 25 permission level from the home page of the site collection, do the following:

1. Click Site Actions.

2. Click Site Permissions.

3. Click the Grant Permissions icon on the ribbon.

4. Enter the user group name **Lesson 25 Users** into the Users/Groups text box.

5. Click the Check Names icon (which looks like a disembodied head) to confirm that the group is valid.

6. In the Grant Permissions settings, click the Grant User Permissions Directly radio button.

7. Check the Lesson 25 permission level, which should now appear in the list of available permissions. Figure 25-4 shows the screen at this point.

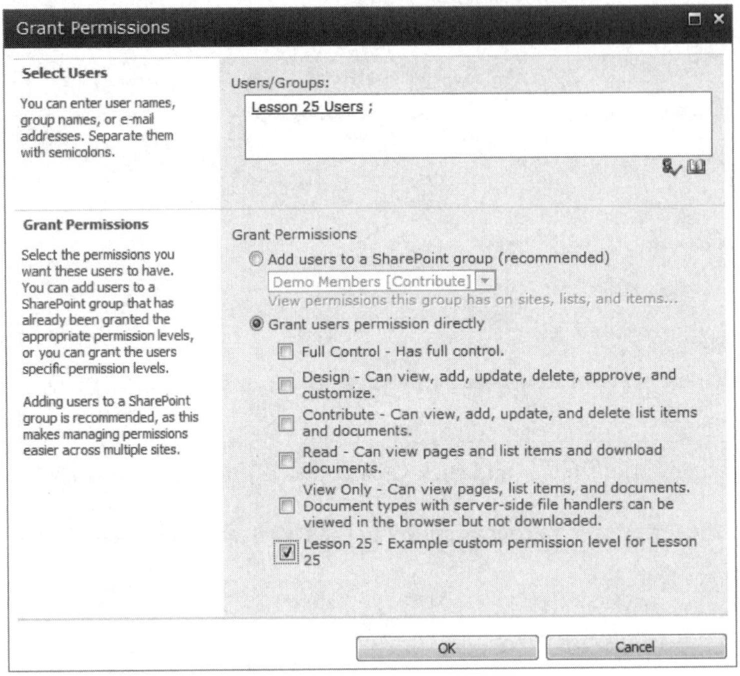

FIGURE 25-4

8. Click OK to save the changes.

Your new permission level has been created and you have assigned it to a group within SharePoint. You can try out the effect of the permission level by logging in as a member of the group to see how it works.

The process for copying and customizing a permission level is very similar. The main difference on this occasion is that you will be working with the full set of rights already available and copied into the new level for your use. For example, to copy and change the contributor permission level and add the right to create subsites, do the following:

1. Click Site Settings.

2. Click Site Permissions.

3. Click Permission Levels.

4. Click the Contribute permission level to open the Edit Permission screen. This screen shows all the rights associated with the selected permissions.

5. Scroll to the bottom of the screen and click the Copy Permission button shown in Figure 25-5. This will copy all the current rights associated with the permission into your new custom level.

FIGURE 25-5

6. Enter a name for the permission level. In this case use the name **Lesson 25 Contributor — Add Sites**.

7. Enter a description, in this case **Customized contribute permission level with add subsite rights**.

8. Scroll to the Site Permissions section and check the Create Subsites permission level.

9. Scroll to the bottom of the screen and click Create to copy and create your custom permission level.

Your new custom permission level will now be available for use within the site collection. You can use the new level as you did in the previous example, by assigning it to groups or individual users.

Please select Lesson 25 on the DVD or visit www.wrox.com/go/sp2010-24 *to view the video that accompanies this lesson.*

SECTION VII
Configuring Service Applications

26

Configuring Access Services

Microsoft Access is without rival when it comes to working with desktop databases and is a favorite development tool for millions of database developers the world over. But one feature has long been missing from this popular solution: the ability to manage an Access database from a web browser. Many attempts have been made to do this over the years, and Microsoft Access 2010 with SharePoint is perhaps the best solution for many of the less complex Access databases in use today.

ACCESS SERVICES

SharePoint contains a service application to manage the process of converting and running your Access database in browser. Access Services is created and maintained at the SharePoint server level. However, as a site collection administrator, you will also be involved in working with Access on the Web or, in the world of SharePoint and Access, with Access *web databases*. Figure 26-1 shows an Access web database.

The combination of SharePoint and Access is one of the nicest new features available, and it can all be set up with a couple of mouse clicks. Access Services still has some limitations, but if you are careful when creating web databases you won't go wrong. Databases can be created whether templates are available in SharePoint or offline in the Access client. You can also create web databases yourself using the Access client and move existing databases to SharePoint. However, not all databases are suitable to move to the Web; databases that use a lot of Visual Basic code or are complex in structure will not convert to the web format without a lot of rewriting.

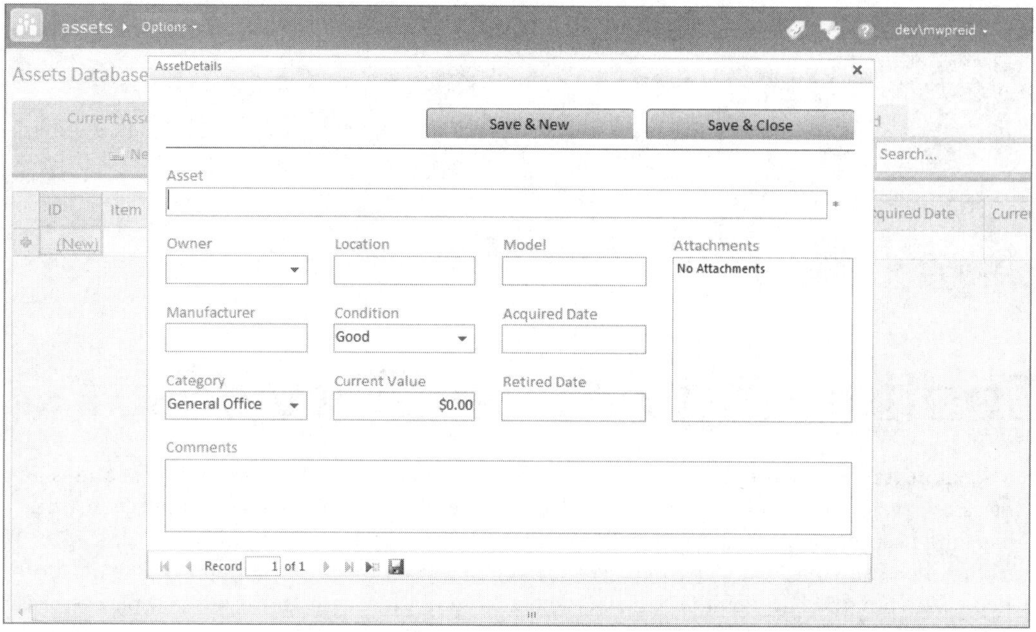

FIGURE 26-1

Sometimes when running Access Services, the reports don't work in your web database. This is because Access Services relies on SQL Server Reporting tools, which must be installed and configured for reporting to work with Access. You will also need to speak to your server administrator to ensure that session state is configured and available. You can download the Reporting Services add-in for SharePoint from `http://www.microsoft.com/` and install it on your server.

Figure 26-2 shows the reporting screen on SharePoint for the Charitable Contributions web database.

Once you create web database sites you will lose all the familiar SharePoint site management tools; in fact, the Site Actions and Site Settings menus will totally disappear, to be replaced with screens that enable you to manage the Access web database lists. Permissions to the web database site itself are the only remaining management tool that is directly related to SharePoint. But once you access the permissions screen, you will find links back to all the familiar SharePoint site settings, proving that this is actually a SharePoint site hosting an Access web database.

In addition to creating web databases from within the Access 2010 client, you can create them using the site templates available within SharePoint. The following web database site templates are available:

➤ **Assets Web Database:** For managing company assets.

➤ **Charitable Contributions:** For managing financial contributions received.

➤ **Contacts Web Database:** For managing company contacts.

➤ **Issues Web Database:** For tracking issues (problems) and tasks.

➤ **Projects Web Database:** For managing company projects.

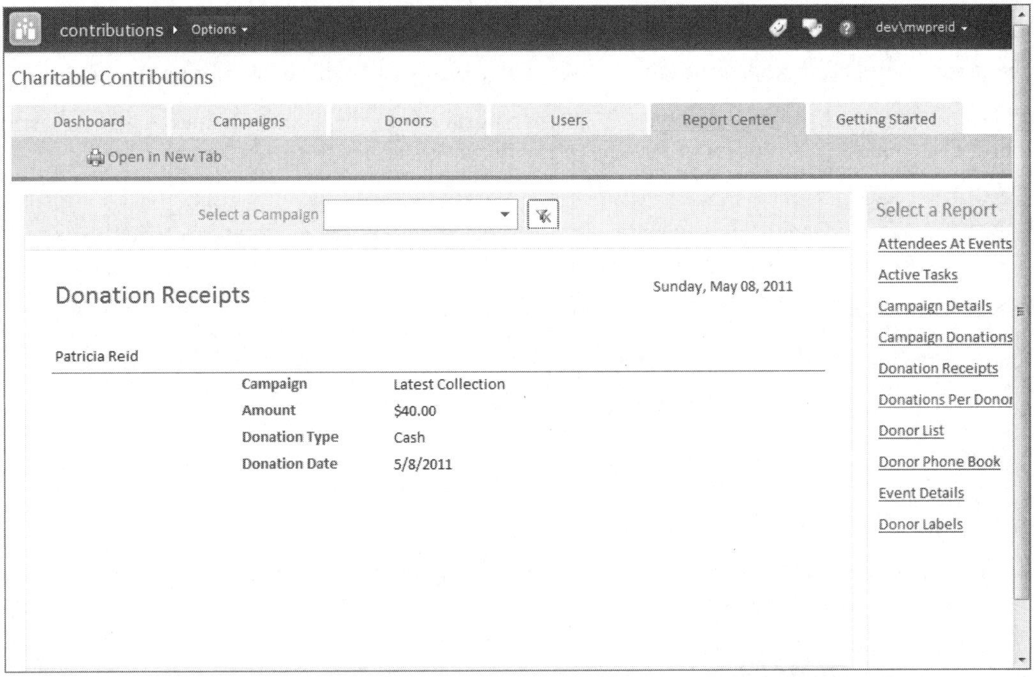

FIGURE 26-2

Using a template within SharePoint does not create the client application in Access 2010. You need to do that yourself using the Options menu for the Web Database once it has opened. This menu offers you the following choices:

➤ **Open in Access:** Opens the current web database in the client program.

➤ **Manage Site Permissions:** Opens the standard SharePoint site permissions form. Also gives you access to the standard SharePoint site settings menus.

➤ **Settings:** Gives you access to all the database objects in the web database: tables, queries, forms, reports, and macros. Selecting an object will open a new Access client database containing all objects with the selected object open for editing.

You need to be careful with databases: for example, your users could execute queries that return large numbers of records, and this in turn can affect your servers' performance. For this reason, several options can be set at the Access Services level related to the performance of your web database, including:

➤ **Maximum Columns Per Query:** The maximum number of columns one can reference in a database query. The value can range from 1 to 255. The default value on my install was 40, while the published default is 32.

➤ **Maximum Rows Per Query:** The number of rows a list based on a query can have. The value can range from 1 to 200000. The default on my install was 25000. The published default is 5000.

➤ **Maximum Sources Per Query:** The maximum number of lists a query can reference. The value can range from 1 to 20. The default on my install was 12. The published default is 8.

➤ **Templates:** The maximum size of database templates in megabytes. The value can range from -1 to any positive integer. The default is 30.

There are a number of other configuration settings which will be discussed in this lesson's video.

When you are creating a web database there are a number of things you can do to assist Access and SharePoint to make the process of moving to the browser that much easier. Some of the things you need to do include:

➤ Use Access Data Macros when possible to automatic processes instead of Visual Basic code to provide logic in your Access forms.

➤ Create table relationships using Lookups columns.

➤ Use single field primary keys for your tables adding an Autonumber Primary to each table.

➤ Save Access files using the ACCDB database format.

TRY IT

In this exercise, you will create a new Access Service, configure the Access Services options, and create an Access Services-based site.

Lesson Requirements

➤ To complete this Try It exercise, you need the following: Access to SharePoint 2010 Central Administration and permissions to create the Access Service.

➤ Site collection permissions.

➤ A Microsoft Access 2010 client to create the web database.

➤ A managed account to run the Access Services.

Step-by-Step

The first part of the process of getting your Access 2010 databases to the Web is creating and configuring the Access Services. In Central Administration, follow these steps:

1. Click Manage Service Applications in the Application Management category.

2. On the ribbon, click New.

3. Click Access Services.

4. Enter **Lesson26** as the service name.

5. Click the Create New Application Pool radio button and enter **Less26AppPool** as the new application pool name.

6. Select the managed account to use for the service. In this case, it is **Lesson26AccessAcc**.

7. Accept the Add to Default Proxy List setting to make the service available to all web applications. You can also configure the service to be associated with individual web applications if you like.

8. Click OK to save the initial configuration.

9. Click the Access Services name Lesson26 to review the options available. In this case, accept the defaults, as they meet the requirements for this exercise. The options are discussed earlier in the lesson and are also further examined in the Lesson 26 video.

It is worthwhile reviewing any existing Access applications you may be considering moving to Access Services to ensure that the settings will enable the most efficient use of the database.

At this point, you have configured the Access Services and accepted the default configurations. The next step in the process is to create a web database using the Access 2010 client. Follow these steps:

1. Open the client and click File.

2. Select New.

3. Click Sample Templates.

4. Click the Projects Web Database to select it.

5. Leave the default name and click Create.

At this point you may be informed that there are no users in the database. If that is the case, do the following:

1. Click New User in the Users dialog.

2. Enter a user's full name. In this case I entered **Martin Reid**.

3. Enter an e-mail address for the user.

4. Enter a domain account. In this case I entered my own account, **dev\mwpreid**.

5. Click Save & Close to continue.

6. Select a user and click Login.

7. Click the Enable Content button on the ribbon if required (you may also be required to log in again)

Now that the database is created, you can publish it to Access Services. Follow these steps:

1. Click File.

2. Click Publish to Access Services.

Figure 26-3 shows the Publish screen.

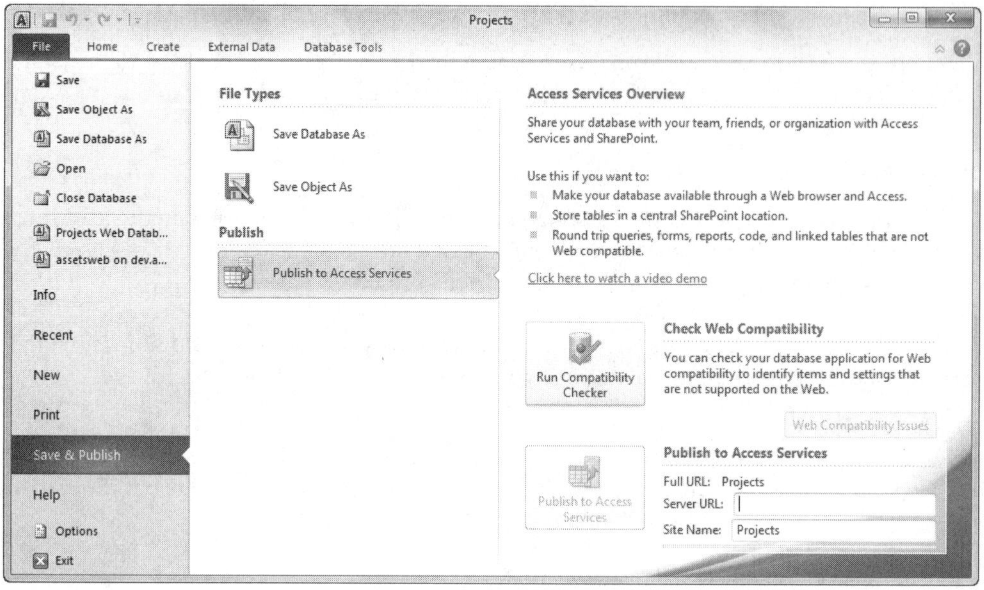

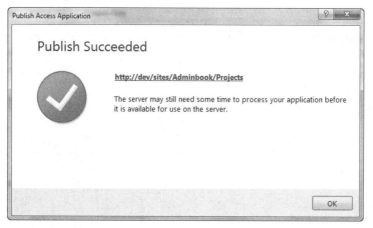

FIGURE 26-3

At this point, you can also check the database for compatibility with Access Services. This is a good idea if you are not using a template and want to ensure your database will publish with no problems. In the Publish to Access Services section, follow these steps:

1. Enter the URL of your SharePoint site.

2. Accept the default site name of Projects.

3. Click the Publish to Access Services button.

   A synchronization dialog opens and keeps you informed of the process. Figure 26-4 shows the confirmation screen that opens when the move is complete.

FIGURE 26-4

6. Click OK to finish the process.

In this case, the database tables will be moved to a new SharePoint site called Projects as SharePoint lists, and a link will be created back to the Access client database, which remains open on screen. Figure 26-5 shows the Access backend application and the SharePoint web database open in the browser. It is important to remember that the data will not be held in Access but inside SharePoint as list data.

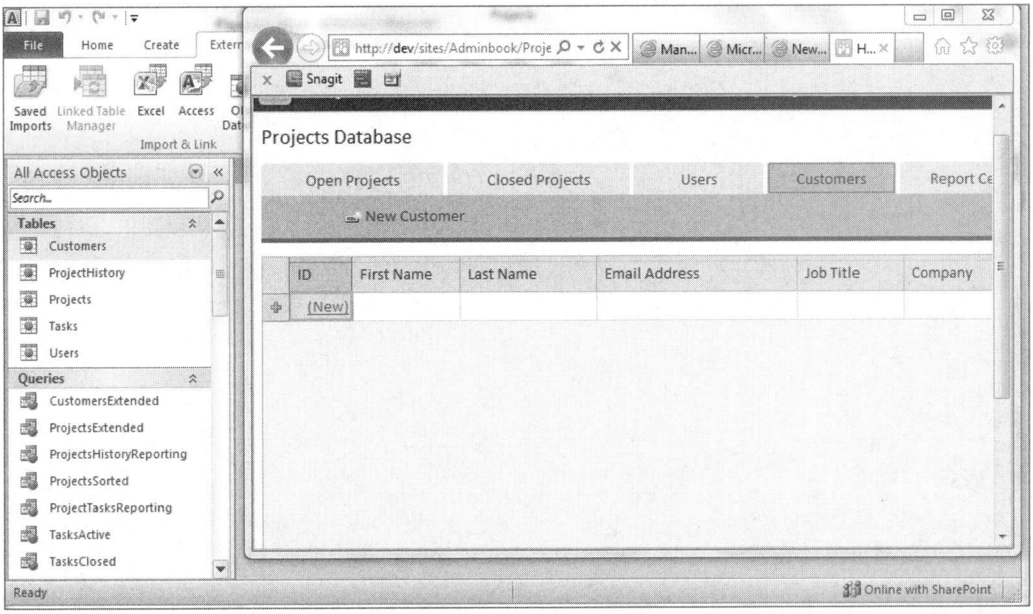

FIGURE 26-5

Please select Lesson 26 on the DVD or visit www.wrox.com/go/sp2010-24 *to view the video that accompanies this lesson.*

Configuring Excel Services

Excel Services is an application service configured at the farm level and then made available to sites in the SharePoint environment. Excel Services enables you to interact with Excel workbooks in the browser. There are three main components to Excel Services:

➤ **Excel Calculation Services:** Responsible for carrying out calculations on the workbook.

➤ **Excel Web Access:** Displays your Excel workbooks within the browser.

➤ **Excel Web Services:** Provides access to the Excel Services application via code and web services.

> *Note that even if you are using Excel Services, your workbook will not be fully editable nor will you be able to create new workbooks using the browser. If you require these features, you have to install Office Web Applications in addition to SharePoint.*

Before you can take advantage of Excel Services, you need to get your Excel documents to the SharePoint server. Publishing to Excel Services is as simple as saving your workbook to a document library and then opening it in the browser. Generally, with documents like this, you should set the default behavior for opening documents in the library to open web-enabled applications in the browser using the document context menu. The user can then, if required, continue working on the document by opening it in the Excel client.

One of the differences between SharePoint 2007 and SharePoint 2010 is that in order to publish a workbook to SharePoint 2007, you have to define a trusted location in SharePoint Server Central Administration; while you can still define trusted locations in SharePoint 2010, it is made easier as, out of the box, every site is trusted for Excel Services.

CONFIGURING A TRUSTED LOCATION

In SharePoint Central Administration, the default trusted location for Excel Services workbooks is set to all SharePoint Foundation site locations. Figure 27-1 shows the default settings for Excel Services. Here you'll want to identify the SharePoint Foundation trusted location, set the location type to SharePoint Foundation, and declare that child locations should be trusted. This is every location on your SharePoint farm, which might not be what you require and this can be changed to enable Excel Services for locations specific to your requirements.

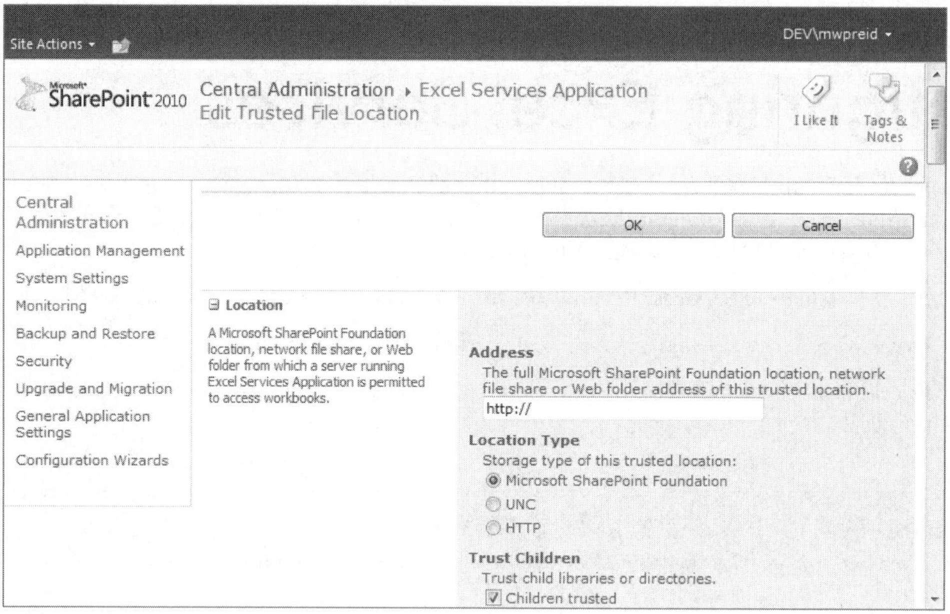

FIGURE 27-1

Although you might not have access to Central Administration, it is always useful to understand the options available. The following settings are available in Central Administration when configuring a trusted location (the details are beyond the scope of this lesson):

➤ **Location:** The location for a workbook can be a SharePoint document library, a network file share, or a web folder. The server running the Excel Services application must have access to the location. For the location the additional settings are available:

➤ **Location Type:** SharePoint, UNC (file share), or HTTP (web folder).

➤ **Trust Children:** Allow workbooks in child sites or, in the case of a file server, subfolders.

➤ **Session Management:** This section deals with Excel Services calculations services and timing for different aspects of the service. For example, it determines the length of time before a user session is ended by inactivity.

➤ **Workbook Properties:** Sets the maximum size of workbooks and chart images allowed.

➤ **Calculation Behavior:** Manages the behavior of functions that change frequently.

> ➤ **External Data:** Manages the interaction of the service with any external data used in your workbooks. You can use this setting to prohibit the use of any external data on the servers.

> ➤ **User-Defined Functions:** Turn on or off the ability to use user-defined functions.

As you can see, the server administrator has a lot of control over how your Excel workbooks interact with the SharePoint environment, and a little knowledge of what is available will benefit you if you use Excel in your site collections. Later in this lesson, you create a new Excel Services application and configure it for use.

USING YOUR WORKBOOK

After you have the Excel Services application created and configured, you can begin to save your workbooks to SharePoint and work with them within the browser. The easy way to get your workbooks to SharePoint is to use the Office backstage view and simply publish the workbooks to SharePoint Server. Figure 27-2 shows the backstage view of Excel 2010 when a workbook is being published.

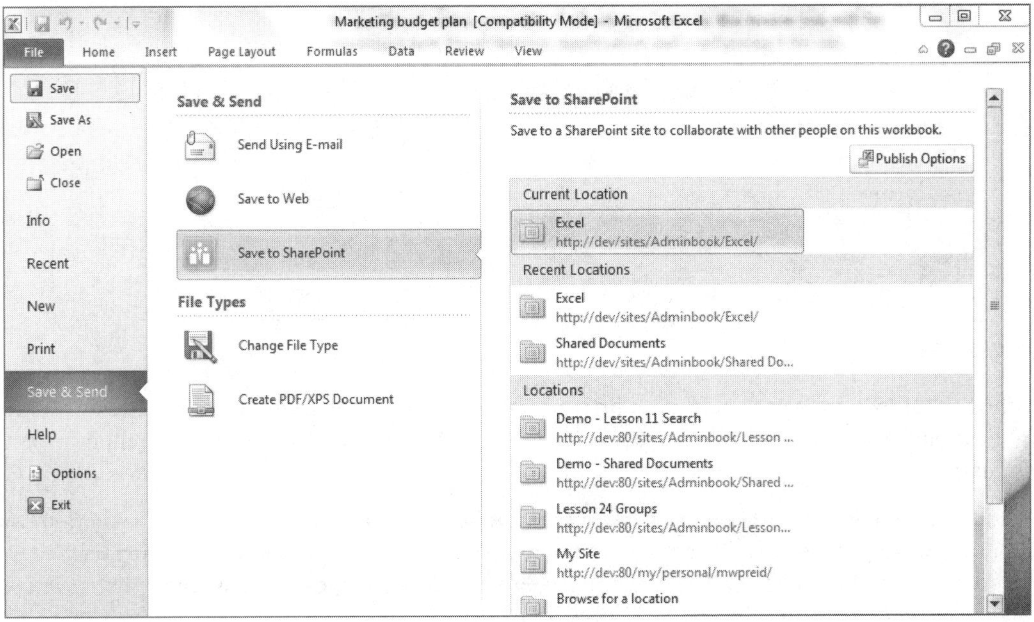

FIGURE 27-2

When saving to a SharePoint document library from within Excel 2010, you also have the following options:

> ➤ Publish entire workbooks, selected sheets, or individual items (*named ranges*). If you are publishing named ranges, please note that the workbook is saved to SharePoint; only the named range is viewable in the browser.

> ➤ **Set Parameters:** Parameters enable you to pass values to a workbook when it is displayed in the browser. For example, you can create a What If analysis workbook that you can change

based on values entered into named parameter cells. To use parameters, you must name the parameter cells in the workbook before saving to SharePoint.

Figure 27-3 shows an Excel 2010 workbook using a single parameter in the browser. In this case, a parameter is entered into the Branding text box displayed in the Parameters pane. Branding is a named cell in the displayed workbook and the parameter entered would appear in this specific cell. If the parameter cell is used in a calculation, it too would be updated to reflect the new value.

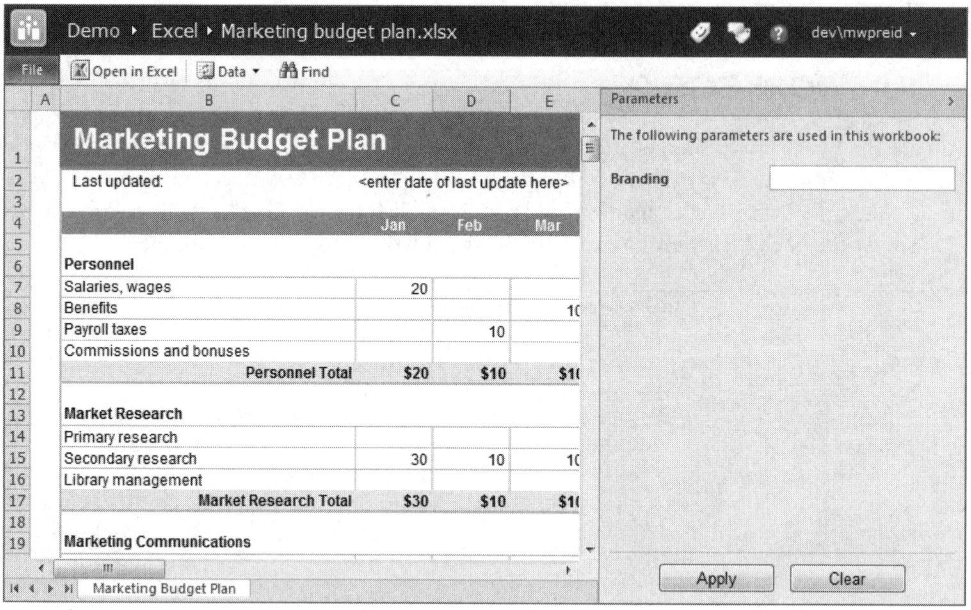

FIGURE 27-3

Although the examples used here are a little trivial, they do demonstrate the power of the Services application, particularly for workbooks that need to carry out calculations based on input from the end user.

In addition to working with a workbook in the browser, you can also display the information using the Excel Services Web Part. This is one of the first steps you can take toward building dashboards and business intelligence Web Parts. Figure 27-4 shows the same workbook as the previous figure, this time displayed within the Excel Services Web Part.

Many people use Excel to display and manipulate data held in corporate systems, for example data cubes in SQL Server 2008. Excel Services and SharePoint have features that enable you to view workbooks connected to external systems. If you need to do this, you need to work with both Excel Services and external data connections. Your SharePoint server administrators and database managers will control access and security for such files on SharePoint. Figure 27-5 shows an Excel workbook displaying data contained within SQL Server. This is a simple example to demonstrate the concept. In this case, data is stored on an SQL Server running on the SharePoint system, which is an unlikely setup in the real world. A real deployment would have more complex requirements for security and performance.

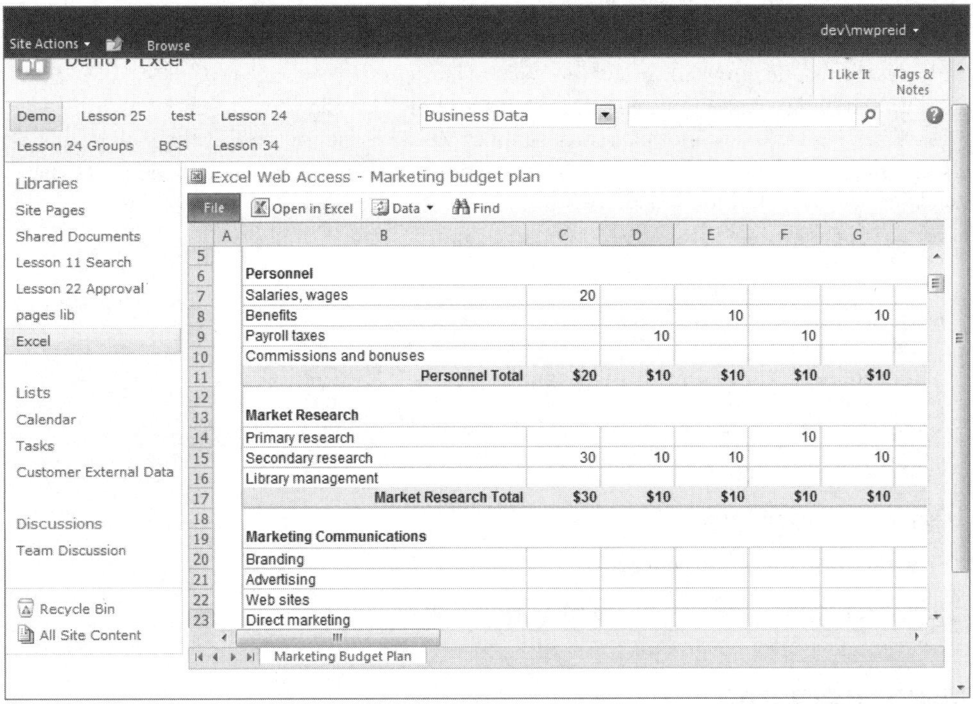

FIGURE 27-4

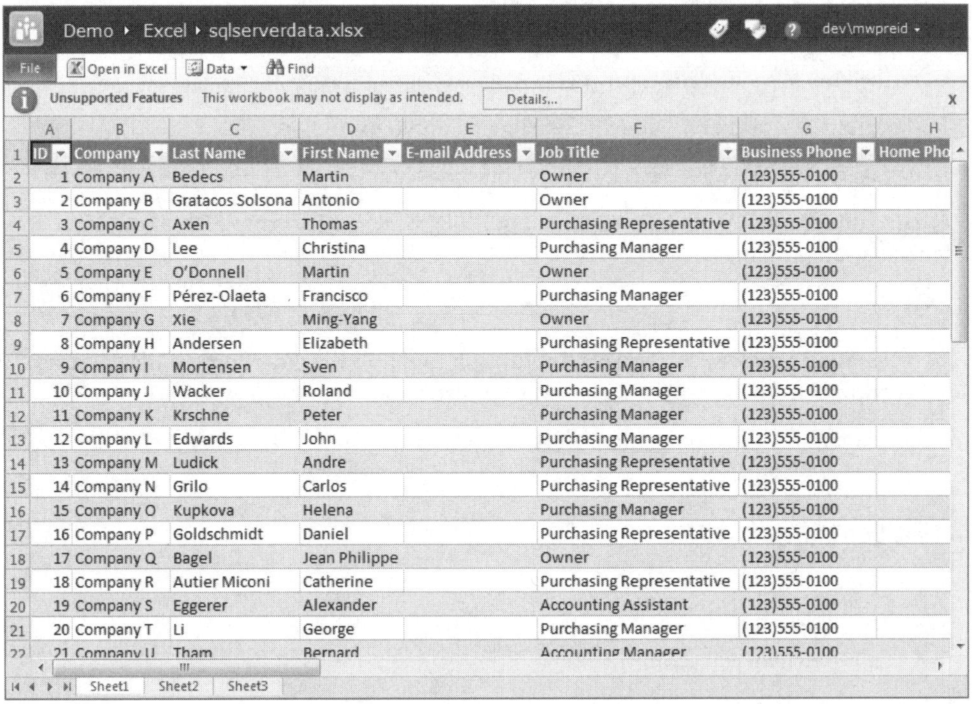

FIGURE 27-5

You might have noticed the warning in Figure 27-5 about unsupported features within the workbook. While Excel Services does display many features of the Excel client software, some Excel functionality remains unsupported. However, rather than not display the workbook, Excel Services in SharePoint 2010 will try and ignore such features and provide the warning showing in Figure 27-5. Excel Services does not currently support Visual Basic for Applications code, chart visual effects supported by the client, and of course you will be unable to create a new workbook using Excel Services. The following Microsoft blog covers feature support in some detail: `http://msdn.microsoft.com/en-us/library/ms496823.aspx`.

TRY IT

In this Try It exercise, you will do the following:

➤ Create a new Excel Services application.

➤ Set the global settings.

➤ Define a trusted file location.

➤ View the trusted data providers.

➤ Publish an Excel workbook to SharePoint.

Lesson Requirements

To perform this lesson, you need the following:

➤ Access to SharePoint Central Administration to create the Excel Services application.

➤ Site collection administration permissions.

➤ An Excel 2010 workbook (we will create an example for this section).

➤ A managed account called ExcelServicesAcc.

➤ A data connection library called excelconnections which connects to a an SQL Server containing a sample data set.

Step-by-Step

We'll start by creating a new Excel Services application to set up the environment for the rest of the example. To continue from SharePoint Central Administration, do the following:

1. Click Manage Service Applications in the Application group.

2. Click the New icon.

3. Select Excel Services Application.

4. Enter **Lesson27App** as the Excel Services application name.

5. Enter **ExcelServicesAppPool** as the new Application Pool name. For this example I created this as a new managed account.

6. Select excelservicesacc as the security account for the application pool.

Figure 27-6 shows the screen at this point in the process.

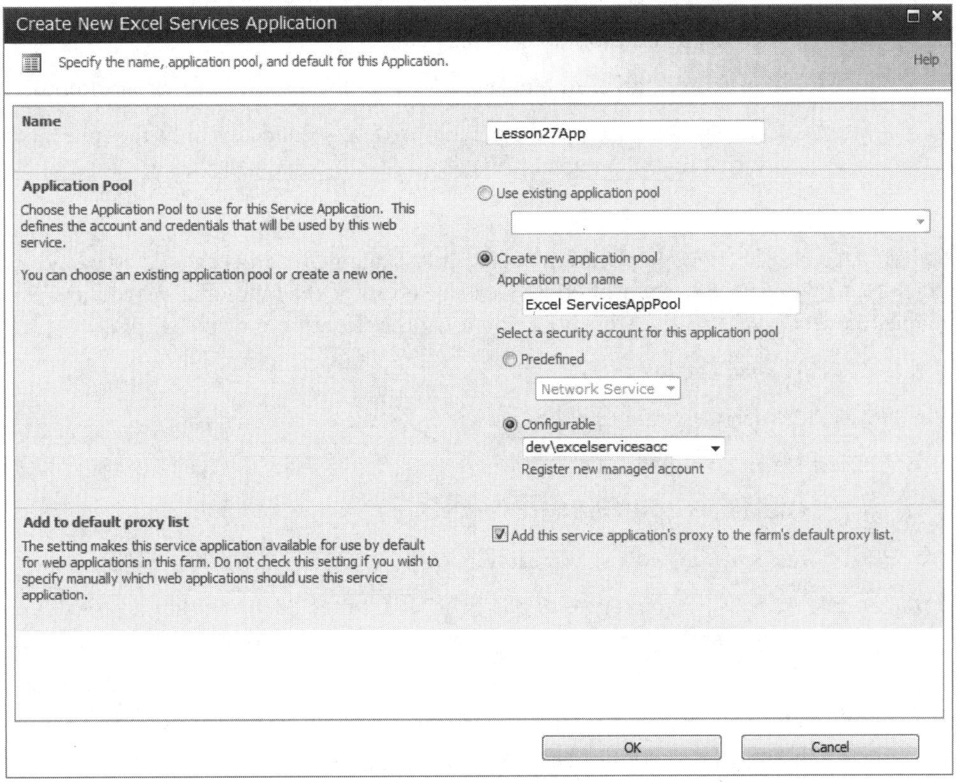

FIGURE 27-6

7. Click OK to save the changes.

Once the services application has been set up it must be configured. To configure the service do the following:

1. Click the Excel Services application you just created, Lesson27App. This will open the Manage Excel Services Application screen to enable you to configure the service. To continue and configure the global settings:

2. Click the Global Settings link which provides options related to the general performance and security context of the service.

➤ **Security:** File access method. How will Excel Services get the actual workbooks from SharePoint locations? You can choose either Impersonation or Process Account. This setting has no effect on workbooks that are stored within SharePoint itself. Accept the default here as you will be accessing workbooks only on SharePoint.

➤ **Connection Encryption:** Accept the default, Not Required. If you require encryption you will have to configure SSL.

➤ **Allow Cross Domain Access:** Again, accept the default which prohibits the options.

➤ **Load Balancing:** Accept the default of Workbook URL.

➤ **Session Management:** Accept the default of 25 sessions per user.

➤ **Memory Utilization:** Accept the defaults.

➤ **Workbook Cache:** Accept the default of 40960 MB for your workbook cache.

➤ **External Data:** Accept the default of 1800 seconds which is the time a connection is allowed to remain open.

3. Click OK to save the changes.

The Manage Excel Service Application page displays again. To proceed, add a trusted location in which to display your Excel workbooks. As a side effect of the following instructions you will be unable to open Excel Services workbooks on any other location on your server.

1. Click Trusted File Locations.

2. Click the default location, `http://`, and open the drop-down list.

3. Select Delete to remove this location.

4. Click OK in response to the warning.

5. Click the Add Trusted File Location link.

6. In the Address text box, type or paste the URL to the document library for this example. In this case, it is `http://dev/sites/Adminbook/Excel/`. Please amend the URL to match your own development server URL.

7. Accept the default location type, Microsoft SharePoint Foundation.

8. Click the Trust Child Libraries or Directories checkbox. You will add as trusted locations for Excel Services all locations below the SharePoint site you enter as the location address.

9. Accept the remaining defaults and scroll to the end of the screen and click OK to close the form and save the changes.

Up to this point, you have created and configured the Excel Services application and set up your trusted locations. You could save a workbook to SharePoint and view it in the browser. Before doing that, you need to configure the other settings available to you for the service application.

Trusted data connection libraries are libraries in SharePoint in which you can save the connection files for your external connections. For example, to add a document connection library called excel-connections, do the following:

1. Click Manage Service Applications in Central Administration.

2. Click the Excel Services application Lesson27App.

3. Click Trusted Data Connection Libraries.

4. Click the Add Trusted Data Connection Library link.

5. Enter the URL to your data connection library. In this case, it is `http://dev/sites/Adminbook/excelconnections/`.

6. Click OK to save and close the form.

You can now view the data connection link in Central Administration. Any existing connections are also displayed on the page. The final area of configuration for the Excel Services application is the most technical-sounding: *user-defined function assemblies* register managed code assemblies that can be used by spreadsheets which can write customer functions that can be called and used by Excel Services. In this case, we will not be looking at this area!

So that's it! Excel Services are configured for the example. Now the big moment has arrived: putting a workbook onto SharePoint and viewing it in the browser. For this final exercise, begin in Microsoft Excel 2010 and then follow these steps:

1. Click File.
2. Click New.
3. From the Office.com templates, select Budgets.
4. Double-click Business Budgets to open the folder.
5. Select the Small Business Expenses Budget template to open the file.
6. Click the File menu and select Save & Send.
7. Click Save to SharePoint.
8. Click the link to your site. In this case, the URL is `http://dev/sites/Adminbook/Excel/`.
9. Accept the default file names and click Save.

Figure 27-7 shows the workbook as viewed in the browser.

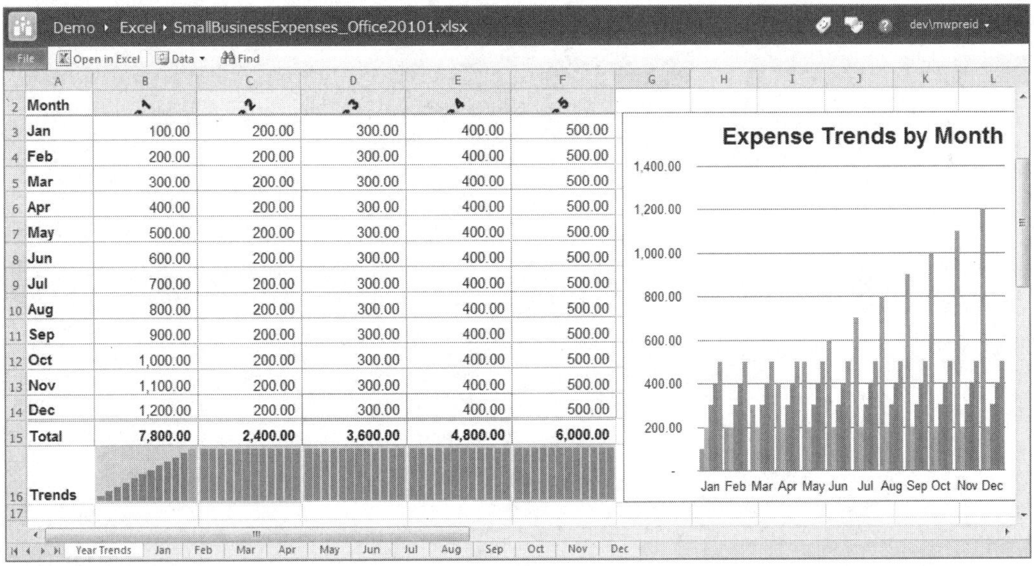

FIGURE 27-7

Please select Lesson 27 on the DVD or visit `www.wrox.com/go/sp2010-24` *to view the video that accompanies this lesson.*

Configuring Visio Services

Microsoft Visio 2010 is not available as part of Microsoft Office and must be purchased separately if you want to use the diagramming tool. Visio Premium or Professional 2010 enables you to create interactive data-driven diagrams and can also be used to visualize SharePoint workflows. Integration between SharePoint and Visio 2010 has been improved with the release of the 2010 product versions and SharePoint can now work directly with Visio using the browser and the Visio Graphics Service. If you are going to create a workflow, you will eventually need SharePoint Designer, but a picture is worth a thousand words and Visio is a great tool for visualizing workflows for many non-SharePoint users.

This lesson provides a broad overview of the Visio service and how you can enable it and begin to use its features to work with SharePoint and in particular SharePoint Workflows.

THE VISIO GRAPHICS SERVICE

For existing Visio users, the Visio Graphics Service offers a way to expose diagrams in the browser without having to worry if the user has the client or viewer installed. Figure 28-1 shows a sample Visio 2010 web diagram in a SharePoint document library.

When you simply store a Visio file in SharePoint, it is saved as a web drawing which is the file that you actually view in the browser. It is rendered using the Visio Graphics Service. In addition to displaying the web drawings directly in the browser, Visio can also show them using the Visio Web Part. Figure 28-2 shows this Web Part in action. Web drawings are supported by Visio Graphics Service and SharePoint 2010, and the end user does not need to have the Visio client or viewer to see them.

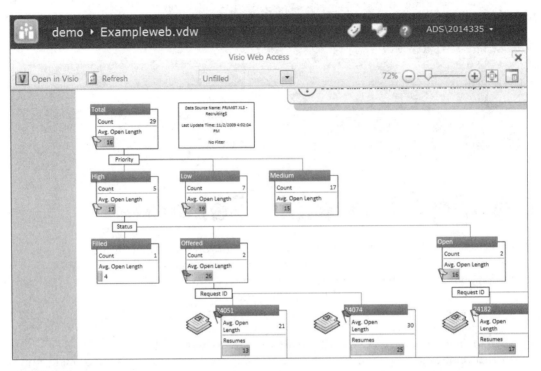

FIGURE 28-1

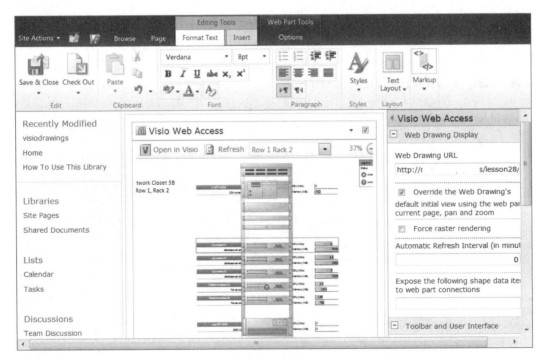

FIGURE 28-2

Many features of Visio are available to you when you view the document in the browser, and working with the Visio Web Part does give you some control over how the document is presented and the functionality available. Using the Web Part properties, you can do the following:

➤ Enable or disable data refresh

➤ Allow the user to open the diagram in Visio

➤ Display page navigation

➤ Show shape information

➤ Show a diagram's background

Visio Process Repository

A specific document library for storing Visio process documents is available in SharePoint. This library contains all the standard document library features in SharePoint, and some Visio-specific columns and content types. The process used to create a Visio Process Repository library is exactly the same as creating a standard Document Library, and you can give it any meaningful name. Figure 28-3 shows the document templates available in the document library that can be used to create documents in Visio 2010.

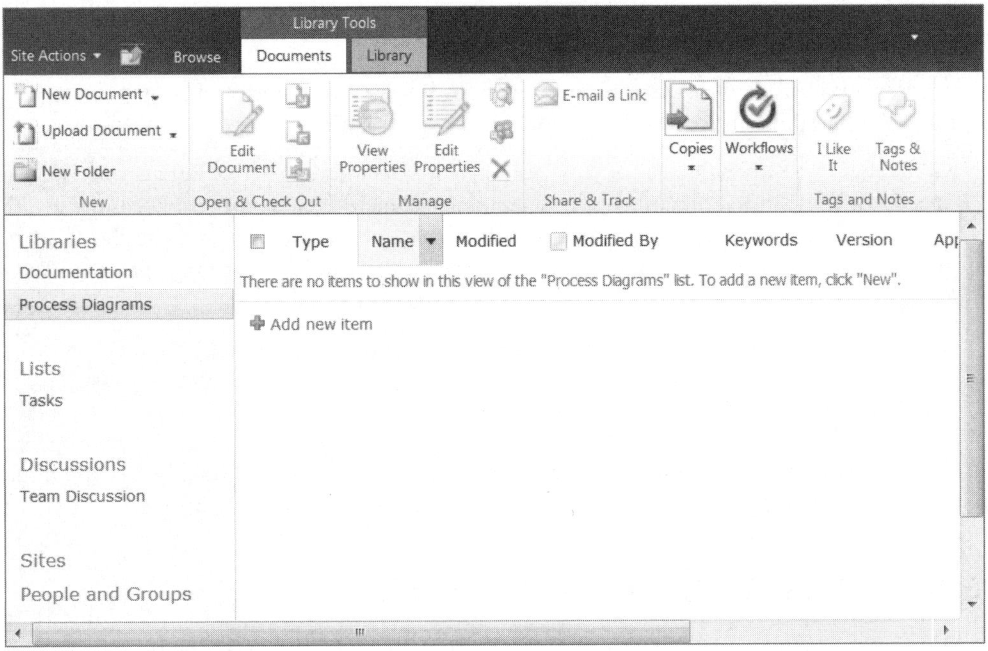

FIGURE 28-3

The following document templates are available within the Visio library:

➤ Basic Flowchart (metric)

➤ BPMN Diagram (metric)

➤ Cross Functional Flowchart (metric)

➤ BPMN Diagram (US Units)

➤ Cross Functional Flowchart (US units)

Selecting a template can open the particular file in Microsoft Visio 2010, and make it ready for you to begin the design process.

DATA-DRIVEN DIAGRAMS

In addition to static Visio drawings, data-driven drawings are also supported by the Graphics Service. The following data sources are supported on SharePoint:

➤ Excel (the workbook must also be stored in the same site)

➤ SQL Server tables and views

➤ SharePoint lists

➤ Recent OLE DB/ODBC drivers

Visio Graphics Application

The graphics application is configured within Central Administration under Manage Service Applications. A limited number of configuration settings are required:

➤ **Global Setting:** Settings that deal with performance, security, and how data connections are refreshed. Within this category you can set the maximum drawing size allowed, the length of time a web drawing is cached in memory, and the length of time before the cache is cleared. In terms of controlling data connections you can set the number of seconds before a data refresh times out and set an unattended service account for the service.

➤ **Trusted Data Providers:** Provides a listing of all data providers trusted by default and enables you to add providers to this list. You will find SQL Server, Oracle, SharePoint Lists, and Excel Web Services already listed.

As you can see, not many configuration options are available to you at this time, but as you might guess, more will become available as developments in SharePoint and Visio continue.

SHAREPOINT DESIGNER AND VISIO 2010

Visio 2010 enables you to visualize a SharePoint workflow and take that visualization into SharePoint designer to add the "smarts" to it. Visio 2010 Premium now contains a set of SharePoint workflow templates that can be used to create visualizations of workflows. In addition, three sets of SharePoint-related shapes are available, which you can drag onto the design surface to create workflows. Once created, the workflow visualization can be exported from Visio and opened for more work within SharePoint Designer 2010.

TRY IT

In this exercise, you will create a new Visio Graphics Service, configure the service, and view a visual workflow status page in the browser.

Lesson Requirements

To complete this Try It exercise, you need the following:

➤ Access to SharePoint Central Administration to create the Visio Graphic Application

➤ Access to a SharePoint site collection

➤ Microsoft Visio Premium 2010

Step-by-Step

From within SharePoint Central Administration you are going to create a new Visio Graphics Service. To continue do the following:

1. In the Application Management category, click Manage Service Applications.

2. Click New.

3. Select Visio Graphics Service.

4. Enter **Visio Graphics Service Lesson 28** in the Visio Graphics Service Application Name text box.

5. Enter **VisioAppPool** in the Application Pool text box Create a New Application Pool.

6. Select the account to be used for the Application Pool.

7. Click OK to create the service.

8. In the Manage the Visio Graphics Service page, click Global Settings.

The global settings enable you to configure the Visio Graphics Service to your own specific business and system requirements, and for the purposes of this example, you can accept the available default settings. In the real world, the Visio Service global settings are specific to your environment and infrastructure. The same is true for the trusted data providers. The more common providers are already listed, and additions to this list will depend on the systems you need to access within your own environment. The default settings are as follows:

➤ **Maximum Web Drawing Size:** 5 MB.

➤ **Minimum Cache Age:** 5 minutes.

➤ **Maximum Cache Age:** 60 minutes.

➤ **Maximum Recalc Duration:** 60 seconds.

➤ **External Data:** This value is blank by default, but you must set it to access external data.

After the service has been configured, Visio web drawings can be rendered in the browser from SharePoint 2010. To continue with the exercise, start Microsoft Visio Premium or Professional 2010. Then, follow these steps to render the drawings:

1. Click File in the Visio menu.

2. Click the Sample Diagrams icon at the bottom of the screen.

3. Select the Project Management diagram.

4. Click Open to open the diagram in Visio.

5. Click File.

6. Click Save and Send.

7. Click Save to SharePoint.

8. Select your SharePoint site from the Available Sites listing.

9. Enter **Project Management** as the filename.

10. Select Web Drawing from the Save as Type drop-down.

11. Click Save.

Your diagram opens in the SharePoint document library in the web browser. Figure 28-4 shows the controls available in the browser view of the Visio drawing.

➤ Open in Visio link, which enables you to open the drawing for edit directly in Microsoft Visio 2010.

➤ Refresh Data Sources link. This enables you refresh the data used by Visio diagrams connected to external data stores for example Excel or SQL Server.

➤ Drop-down list to choose the page for viewing in multipage documents.

➤ Slider to increase and decrease the scale of documents in the browser.

➤ Zoom tool which allows you to quickly zoom the page to fit the available screen resolution.

➤ Icon to open data shapes data details which can enable you to view the data points associated with a particular Visio Shape if they are available. For example, a sales image may have underlying data associated with it, and clicking this icon displays the underlying data.

FIGURE 28-4

Please select Lesson 28 on the DVD or visit www.wrox.com/go/sp2010-24 *to view the video that accompanies this lesson.*

Configuring PowerPoint Services

PowerPoint 2010 has a new feature called Broadcast Slideshow. This feature enables you, with SharePoint's and Office Web Apps' help, to push your Microsoft Office 2010 PowerPoint presentations out to invited users (50 or fewer simultaneous users for best results) via a SharePoint 2010 site collection. If you don't have SharePoint or Office Web Apps, you can still use this feature with Windows Live ID and Microsoft broadcast servers. It removes the need for third-party providers when remote access to PowerPoint presentations is required.

POWERPOINT SERVICE APPLICATION

To run the PowerPoint broadcast operation on your own SharePoint servers, you need to install Office Web Apps. After this software is installed, the PowerPoint Service Application is started on the SharePoint server. A new site collection template and a default PowerPoint broadcast site collection are also installed. Figure 29-1 shows the PowerPoint Service Application configuration screen in SharePoint Central Administration, following an installation of Office Web Apps. The PowerPoint Service Application configuration enables you to do the following:

➤ **Specify the File Formats Supported:** You can choose the newer PowerPoint file format of PPTX and/or PowerPoint 97-2003 file format using the PPT extension.

➤ **Broadcast Site:** You specify the default PowerPoint broadcast site or create a new broadcast site collection.

➤ **PowerPoint 97-2003 Presentation Scanning:** SharePoint scans older format files for malicious content. You can disable the behavior in this section.

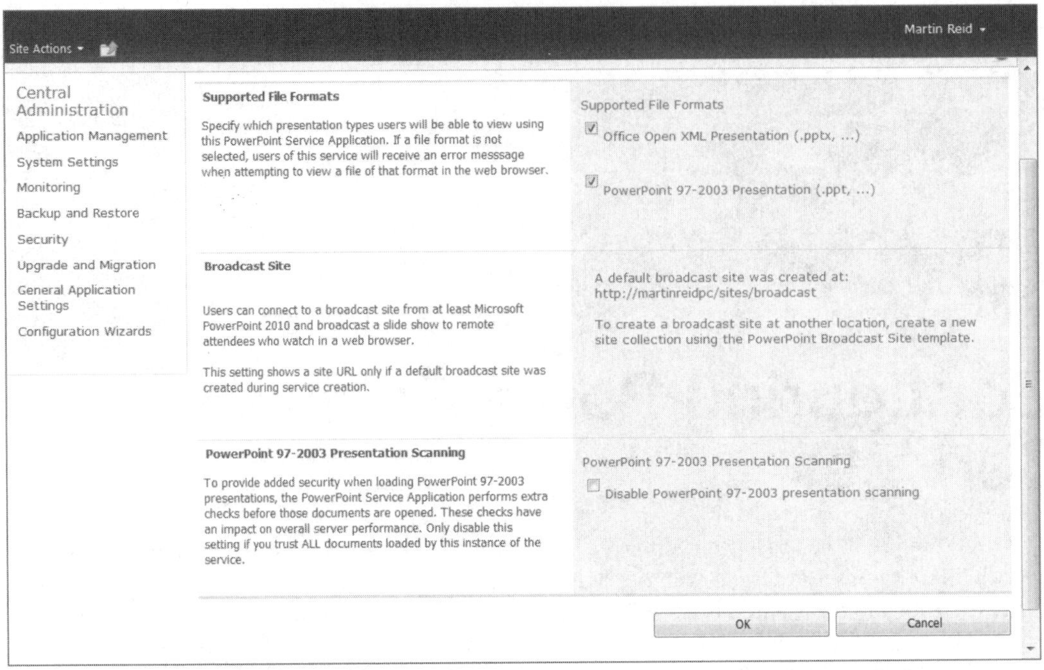

FIGURE 29-1

When the PowerPoint service application has been configured on SharePoint, you can use PowerPoint broadcasting. You will use the default server broadcast site or create a specific site collection to host the broadcast.

TRY IT

In this exercise, you will set up a broadcast site collection and broadcast a PowerPoint slideshow.

Lesson Requirements

To complete this Try It exercise, you need the following:

➤ PowerPoint presentation saved as a PPTX file.

➤ If you do not have Office Web Apps installed, you also need a Windows Live ID (required to use the Microsoft broadcast service).

➤ Office Web Apps and a default broadcast site created.

Step-by-Step

To begin the exercise, you need to create a new broadcast site collection from SharePoint Central Administration. To do this, follow these steps:

1. Click Application Management.

2. Click Create Site Collections.

3. Enter a title for the site collection, and name it **Lesson 29**.

4. Enter a URL: **/sites/lesson29**.

5. Click the Enterprise tab in Template Selection.

6. Select PowerPoint Broadcast Site.

7. Enter your user details as the site collection administrator.

8. Click OK to save the changes and create the broadcast site collection.

Figure 29-2 shows the new site collection in the browser. As you can see, it is slightly different from other site collections, because its sole purpose is to host PowerPoint broadcasts and not to store content.

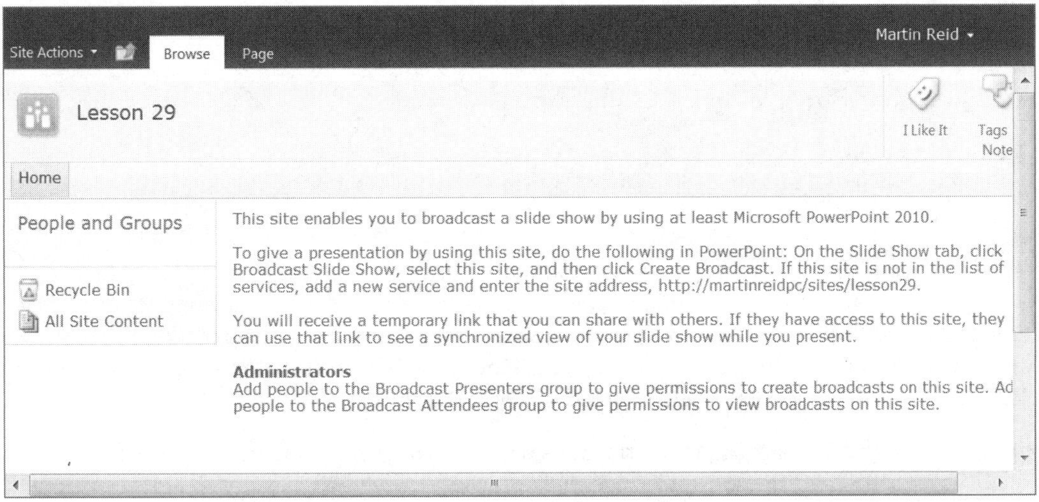

FIGURE 29-2

Permissions are the same. People and Groups in the site collection provides your users permissions to create or to attend PowerPoint broadcasts. Three default groups are available:

➤ **Broadcast Administrators:** Full control on the site.

➤ **Broadcast Presenters:** Broadcast permissions on the site collection; these users can only add items.

➤ **Broadcast Attendees:** Ability to attend PowerPoint broadcasts; read-only permissions.

To continue the exercise, follow these steps:

1. Open Microsoft PowerPoint 2010 (keep the new site collection open).

2. Click File.

3. Select New.

4. Click Sample Templates.

5. Select the Project Status report template.

6. Click Create.

7. Return to the File menu.

8. Click Save and Send.

9. Click Broadcast Slide Show in the Save and Send category.

10. Click the Broadcast Slide Show icon to open the Broadcast Slide Show dialog.

At this point, the Broadcast Slide Show dialog opens. If you already have a site set up, you might have to substitute the new site you just created. If this is the first time you have used this option, proceed as follows:

11. Click Change Broadcast Service.

12. Click Add a New Service.

13. Enter the URL of the site collection you just created.

14. Click Add.

15. Click Start Broadcast.

The service connects to your SharePoint site and provides a URL to use in your invitations to the broadcast. You can copy the link and paste it into an email, or create an email to invite users directly from within PowerPoint by clicking Send in Email to open Microsoft Outlook. When you are ready to begin the broadcast, click the Start Slide Show button. To end the broadcast, you can click the End Broadcast button below the PowerPoint Ribbon.

Figure 29-3 shows a broadcast in an attendee's browser before the presentation begins.

If you do not install Office Web Apps, you can still make use of the PowerPoint 2010 broadcast feature by using a Microsoft server to host the broadcast. You do this by choosing PowerPoint Broadcast Service in the Broadcast Slide Show dialog. To use this service, you must have a Windows Live ID. The running of a broadcast and the process of inviting attendees is the same as with using your own SharePoint server and the Office web apps.

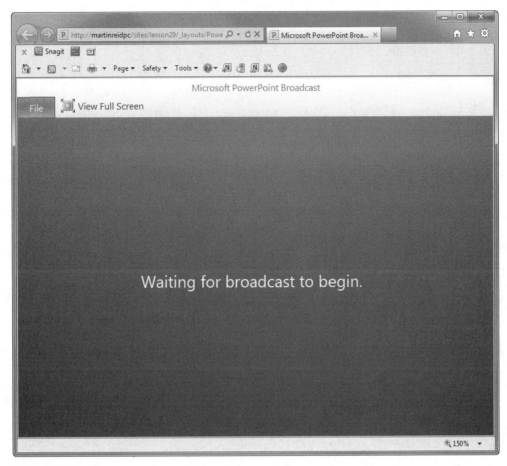

FIGURE 29-3

 Please select Lesson 29 on the DVD or visit www.wrox.com/go/sp2010-24 *to view the video that accompanies this lesson.*

30

Creating Metadata Services

The Metadata Service enables you to tag content with notes, keywords, or brief canned phrases such as "I like it." It also enables you to apply ratings to items in lists or libraries according to a five-star system. And it enables you to create content types that span site collections. (See Lesson 12 for more details.) Most people associate this service with the ability to create hierarchies of tags made up of things like sales division names or product line titles and then apply those tags to categorize data. You can use the data to enable better search and navigation.

This lesson departs slightly from the overall theme of this book. Most of the lessons deal with administrative elements of SharePoint that do not involve the Central Administration site or anything that requires farm level access. Because of the nature of the Metadata Service, we are making an exception for this lesson. SharePoint 2010 is a series of services. If you want to perform a search, you activate a service. If you want My Sites, you activate a service. And if you want to be able to tag your content, you activate the Metadata Service.

With all these services, it is possible to make an individual user an administrator for just one. Practically speaking, the average business user who is not a SharePoint expert or farm administrator isn't going to be put in charge of configuring search or the business intelligence features, for example. With the Metadata Service, however, it is generally much more appropriate for an everyday user to be an administrator. This is because the role of the administrator (and of some other permission levels as well) is to manage the collection of terms used for tagging content. This is an activity more suited to the people creating the content than to the IT people running the SharePoint farm. For this reason, it is not uncommon to see non-IT types with administrative control of this service.

ACTIVATING THE SERVICE

This is an activity that needs to be performed by a farm-level administrator. We have included a brief discussion of it here only because if you are a business user or a site collection administrator you might want to use a Metadata Service. This section tells you what needs to be done to make that happen. If you go to the Central Administration main page you will see a link called Manage Service Applications under the Application Management heading, as shown in Figure 30-1.

FIGURE 30-1

On the following page you can start a new managed Metadata Service by clicking the New toolbar button and selecting the Managed Metadata Service option. It is possible to create more than one, so make sure one hasn't been created already (unless you want a second one). See Figure 30-2.

You will be asked to name the service when you create it. (Usually it is named something like Managed Metadata Service.) After it has been created, you will see it in the list on the right of the screen. There are usually two items for each service: the service itself and its connection. In the case of this service, you can click either one and the Term Store Management Tool page will open.

Make sure the service has been started on the Services on Server page. This link is located on the Central Administration main page under the System Settings heading. See Figure 30-3, which shows the line item on the Services on Server page indicating that the service is stopped or started.

FIGURE 30-2

FIGURE 30-3

Now the service has been created and you can set up *groups*, *term sets*, and *terms*. Setting these up will be the focus of the Try It exercise and video lesson. In the next lesson you will see how to use the metadata on the site.

GROUPS, SETS, AND TERMS

Metadata is organized in terms of groups, term sets, and terms. Here is the difference at each level:

➤ **Groups:** This is the highest level of organization for creating a structure for tagging. There are two levels of permissions for groups: administrator and contributor. Administrators and contributors in groups have the same privileges, except that administrators can add contributors to the group. Contributors can only add new term sets. Both administrators and contributors can create new term sets. Think of a term group as a division or department within a company. Within that department, perhaps there are an administrator and a couple of contributors. They can add new term sets. A term set is used to create a logical category under which to place terms used to tag documents.

➤ **Term set:** This is another abstract layer of organization. These are used for logical groupings of actual terms to be used for tagging documents and other items. For example, an HR department may create a term set for benefit documents. The terms in that set may be words like "401K," "paid time off," "insurance," and so forth. These terms are then used to tag items in the SharePoint portal that relate to these terms. If you find a useful link on company 401K plans, you may tag it with the term "401K." This makes it easier for other people to find this article later. Therefore, it is important for people in control of term sets to create a compelling and comprehensive list of terms for everyday uses such as this. Continuing with our HR example, imagine the group contributors creating a term set for benefit documents, another for legal compliance, and a third for company policies. Each term set has an owner who has full rights to modify that list of terms in that set. It has a contact e-mail for suggestions for items to be added to the term set. Finally, it has a stakeholder list of people who should be notified if the terms change.

➤ **Metadata terms:** These are the actual terms, arranged in a hierarchy, that will be used in the application for tagging, search, navigation, and so on. They can be added, deleted, and edited by term group contributors, admins, and term set owners.

TRY IT

In this exercise, you will create a term group, a term set, and some terms, and you will set some users with permissions.

Lesson Requirements

To complete this Try It exercise, you need the following:

➤ A SharePoint site with SharePoint Server and access to the Central Administration application on the server.

Hints

This exercise assumes the Metadata Service application has already been created, as detailed earlier.

Step-by-Step

1. Go to the Central Administration page. Click the Manage Service Applications link under the Application Management heading.

2. Click the link for the managed metadata service application. The actual name of this link is the name given to the service when it was created. This opens the Term Store Management Tool page.

3. On the left side of the screen, the top-level item in the hierarchy is the name of the service: it will have a "home" icon. By clicking it you will get a drop-down option to create a new group. See Figure 30-4.

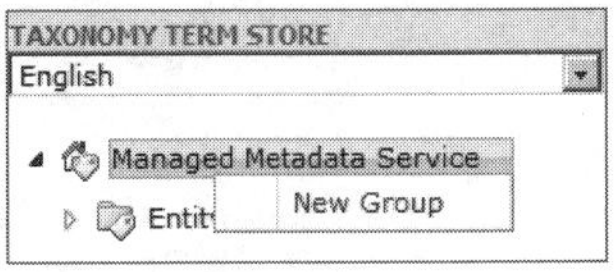

FIGURE 30-4

4. Set the settings for the term group:

➤ **Group Name:** The name as it will appear in the User Interface.

➤ **Description:** A description to help users understand the purpose of this term set.

➤ **Group Managers:** Users who can add term sets and contributors.

➤ **Contributors:** Users who can add term sets.

Figure 30-5 shows this page and options.

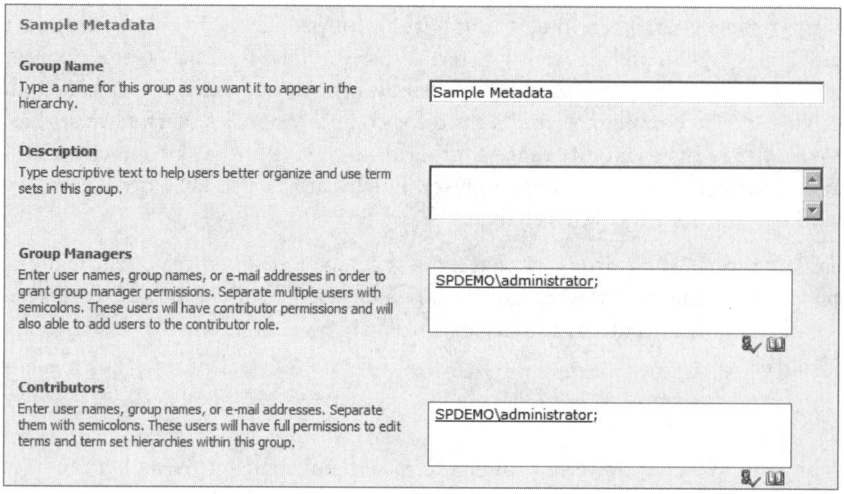
Sample Metadata
Group Name
Type a name for this group as you want it to appear in the hierarchy.
Sample Metadata
Description
Type descriptive text to help users better organize and use term sets in this group.
Group Managers
Enter user names, group names, or e-mail addresses in order to grant group manager permissions. Separate multiple users with semicolons. These users will have contributor permissions and will also able to add users to the contributor role.
SPDEMO\administrator;
Contributors
Enter user names, group names, or e-mail addresses. Separate them with semicolons. These users will have full permissions to edit terms and term set hierarchies within this group.
SPDEMO\administrator;

FIGURE 30-5

5. Click on the new term group. The drop-down menu gives you several options. You can create a term group, the option we will select. You can also import a term set from a specially formatted Excel file. Finally, you can delete a term group. Figure 30-6 shows the drop down interface. Select the option to add a new term set. A blank text box will appear with an orange background. Enter the name of the term set here. Notice the different icon for the term set as well.

Sample Metadata
New Term Set
Import Term Set
Delete Group

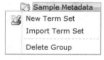

FIGURE 30-6

6. After you name your new term set, the term set options page displays. Figure 30-7 and Figure 30-8 show the term set user interface.

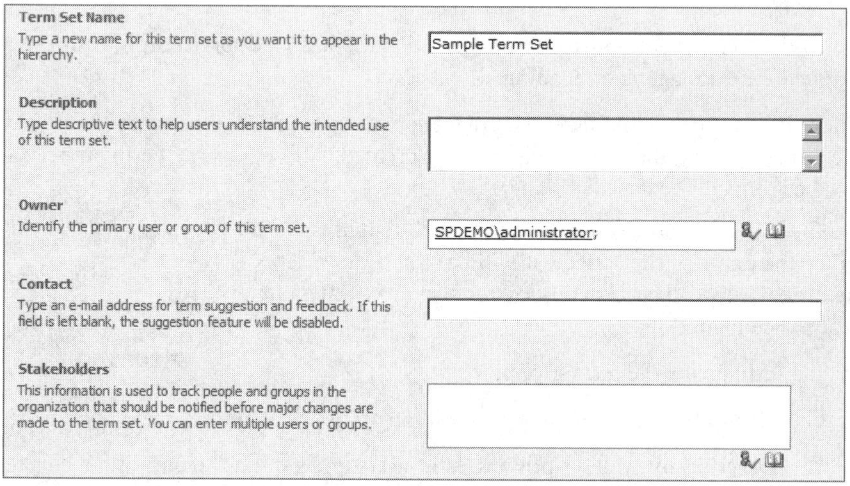
Term Set Name
Type a new name for this term set as you want it to appear in the hierarchy.
Sample Term Set
Description
Type descriptive text to help users understand the intended use of this term set.
Owner
Identify the primary user or group of this term set.
SPDEMO\administrator;
Contact
Type an e-mail address for term suggestion and feedback. If this field is left blank, the suggestion feature will be disabled.
Stakeholders
This information is used to track people and groups in the organization that should be notified before major changes are made to the term set. You can enter multiple users or groups.

FIGURE 30-7

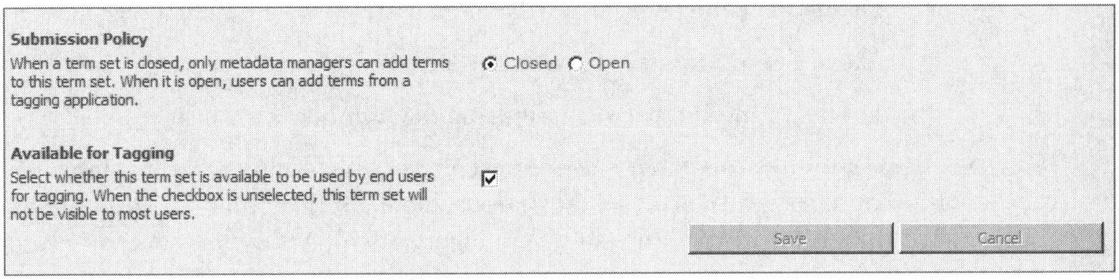

FIGURE 30-8

7. Set the options for the term set as follows:

➤ **Term Set Name:** The name as it will appear in the User Interface.

➤ **Term Set Description:** A description of the term set.

➤ **Term Set Owner:** The user with administrative rights over the term set.

➤ **Contact:** Enter an e-mail address to which users can send suggestions about content of the term set.

➤ **Stakeholders:** Users who should be notified before major changes are made to the term set.

➤ **Submission Policy:** When adding metadata columns to lists or libraries, you can assign an option for users to add terms ad hoc. If you select a closed policy here, that option is not available at the list/library level and only terms already in the list can be used.

➤ **Available for Tagging:** If this box is selected, only administrators can use the term set for tagging.

Click the Save button when finished.

8. Once you have configured the term set, right click on the term set name and choose Create Term from the drop-down menu. This will let you create the actual terms used for tagging items in SharePoint. After adding the first term, you can either use the right click drop-down menu (Figure 30-9) from the term set each time to add a new term or simply hit enter after each term to automatically begin a new term. Set a few metadata terms.

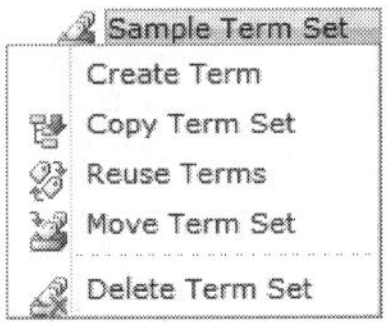

FIGURE 30-9

9. You can create terms quickly by typing them and pressing Enter. There is one more drop-down menu for each individual term as well, offering you the following options:

➤ **Create Term:** Add a new term to the term set.

➤ **Copy Term:** Copy a term to use somewhere else in another term set.

➤ **Reuse Terms:** This will open a browser of all other terms that you can place into this term set to avoid retyping.

➤ **Merge Terms:** This will open a browser of all other terms and allow you to select any of them, which will be removed from their current locations and be replaced by the currently highlighted term.

> ➤ **Deprecate Term:** The term will still be visible, but additional tags may not use it.

> ➤ **Move Term:** Move the term to another set.

> ➤ **Delete Term:** Remove the term from the term set.

10. In addition to the drop down menu for each term, other options are available on the main portion of the page. To access these options, highlight the term in the term set by clicking on it. The options on the page are shown in Figure 30-10, and defined in the list which follows.

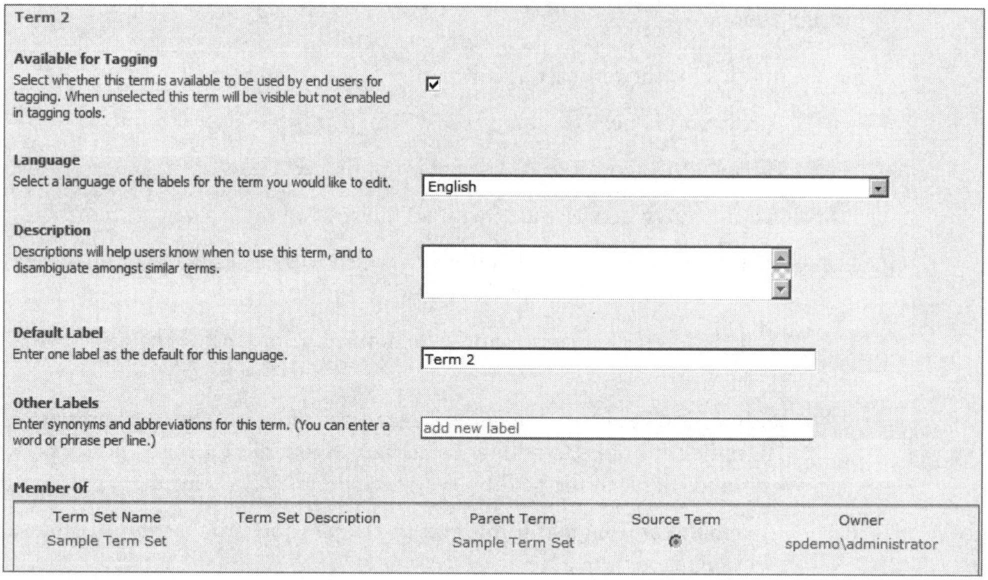

Term 2

Available for Tagging
Select whether this term is available to be used by end users for tagging. When unselected this term will be visible but not enabled in tagging tools.   ☑

Language
Select a language of the labels for the term you would like to edit.   English

Description
Descriptions will help users know when to use this term, and to disambiguate amongst similar terms.

Default Label
Enter one label as the default for this language.   Term 2

Other Labels
Enter synonyms and abbreviations for this term. (You can enter a word or phrase per line.)   add new label

Member Of

Term Set Name	Term Set Description	Parent Term	Source Term	Owner
Sample Term Set		Sample Term Set	⦿	spdemo\administrator

FIGURE 30-10

> ➤ **Available for Tagging:** When checked, this checkbox makes individual terms available for tagging by general users. If the box is unchecked, these terms are available only to administrators.

> ➤ **Language:** Select a language for this term from all language packs that have been installed on the server.

> ➤ **Description:** Describes the use of the term.

> ➤ **Default Label:** This is the label you set when you initially created the term. You can modify it here.

> ➤ **Other Labels:** Synonyms for the term. This is where other names are placed when you do a merge terms operation. You can also manually set your own synonyms. Synonyms are useful for anticipating other terms that users may want use to tag items in the portal which are similar to the term suggested in the term set. You may think of the term "helpdesk" for example, and add synonyms such as "desktop support" so that either term is related to the same tag. This helps to avoid redundancy in terms used for tagging.

➤ **Member Of:** An informational table that describes where the term is located in the term set hierarchy and who is the owner of the term set.

 Please select Lesson 30 on the DVD or visit www.wrox.com/go/sp2010-24 *to view the video that accompanies this lesson.*

31

Using Metadata

In Lesson 30 you learned how to create a Metadata Service. In this lesson we will examine the various places in SharePoint where metadata is useful and how it is used in SharePoint.

➤ **Metadata in Lists:** To use metadata and enable tagging of content in a SharePoint list or library, you can create a Metadata field type as a list column. This is a new column type in SharePoint 2010. You can assign this column type directly to a list or library or to a content type that is used in the list or library. Figure 31-1 shows an edit screen for a list that contains a metadata column.

Refiners to limit
search results
based on tag
column values

FIGURE 31-1

➤ **Metadata in Search:** When you use SharePoint search or FAST search (an upgraded version of search) in 2010, you will be presented with a series of refiners that can be based on metadata fields. In other words, you can limit the results you want to see from the search to only those items tagged with a metadata value that you select from the list of metadata values presented. FAST search gives you more advanced refiner functionality than the SharePoint Enterprise Search product that is part of a Standard or Enterprise License. Refiners are not included in SharePoint Foundation search. Figure 31-2 shows a list of results from a search query on an announcement list. On the left-hand side you can see the refiners, which you can use to limit the results of the search. By selecting one of the refiners, you will further limit the set of search results to only those items whose properties contain the selected refiner.

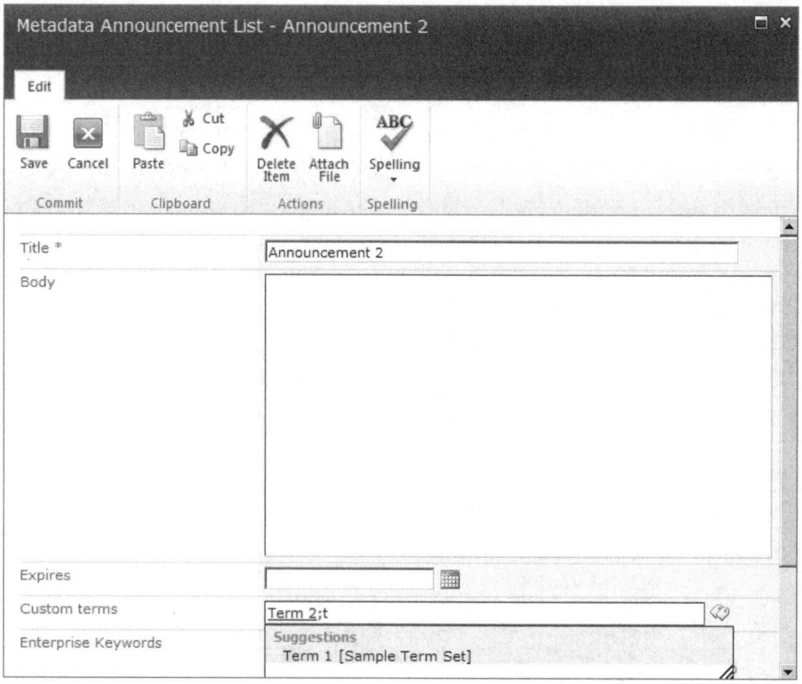

FIGURE 31-2

➤ **Metadata in Navigation:** When looking at a list or a view of a list (or library), you can use metadata values in order to drill down into lists based on the values of metadata columns. Figure 31-3 shows the navigation options available to a list using values from a metadata field.

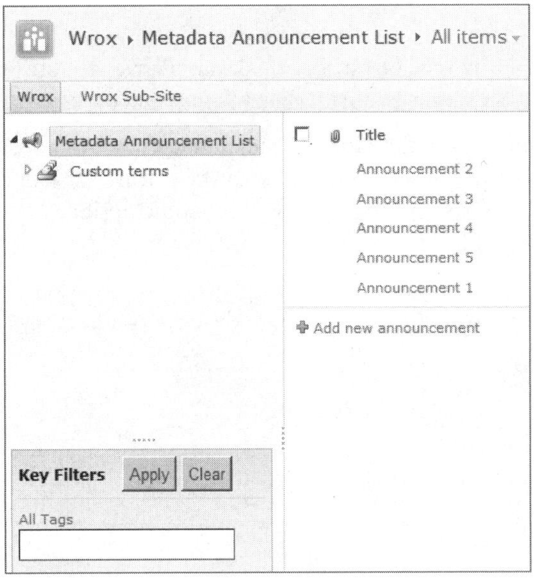

FIGURE 31-3

TRY IT

In this lesson, you will create a new list, and add a metadata column to the list. In addition, you will see how to use the column to tag a document with keywords. This lesson does not cover the administrative task of setting up a Metadata Service, which is a prerequisite step discussed in Chapter 30.

Lesson Requirements

To complete this Try It exercise, you need the following:

➤ A SharePoint site with SharePoint Server.

Hints

This Try It assumes the Metadata Service application has already been created and some term sets created, as covered in Lesson 30. It also assumes you can perform some minor tasks such as creating lists and libraries.

Step-by-Step

1. Create a list on a SharePoint site. It can be any type of list. For this example we will use an announcements list.

2. In the List Settings for the list, add a column of type Managed Metadata. If you do not see this type listed, make sure you have started the service and activated the features as demonstrated in Lesson 30. Once you have selected this column, you will see some options specific to this field type.

3. In the Display Format section (see Figure 31-4) you can choose to display the tag alone in the column or the entire hierarchy and path from the top-level term down to the term you have selected.

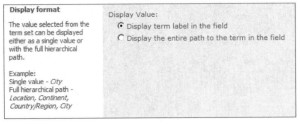

FIGURE 31-4

4. In the Term Set Settings section (see Figure 31-5) you can select one term set that will be the basis for the values you can use in this column. The search box allows you to easily find the terms you need if you are dealing with a large term store with many term sets.

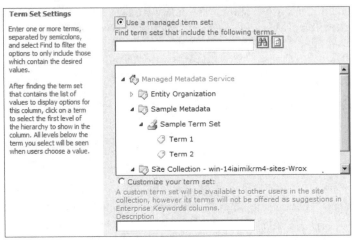

FIGURE 31-5

5. You can also customize your term set. This allows you to make a term set on the fly that will be useable only within the current site collection. Such a term set will not offer suggestions in other columns based on typing, as term sets with managed keywords do.

6. Optionally, opt to allow additions to the term set to be made by letting users add their own terms if they cannot find the one they need in the list.

> *Allowing users to add their own terms is useful if you want to be able to capture the terms people actually use in their day-to-day work, which can differ from the official terms set by some faraway IT committee. On the downside, it may lead to more inconsistent tagging of information, which can frustrate attempts to create easier navigation and search strategies. Note that according to the options you chose when creating the term set in the Metadata Service, this option may not be available for users.*

7. Finally, choose a default tag value for the column. Click OK when finished.

8. Back at the List Items View page, you can edit an item and add terms to the column you just created. Notice how it will give you type-ahead suggestions. You can hit the Tab key at any time, click the suggestions with your mouse, or continue typing to place a value in the field.

9. In the list settings you can opt to add an enterprise keyword column to the list. The two options, as shown in Figure 31-6, enable you to add a field to a list or library to tag content with keywords, and to report on the use of and display the tags onto a user's individual MySite if they are activated.

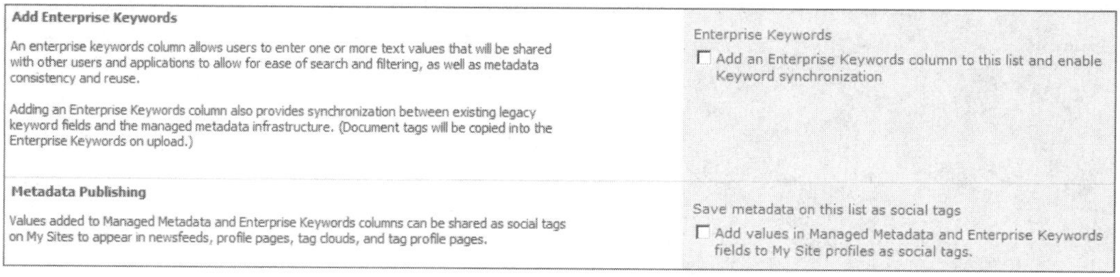

Add Enterprise Keywords

An enterprise keywords column allows users to enter one or more text values that will be shared with other users and applications to allow for ease of search and filtering, as well as metadata consistency and reuse.

Adding an Enterprise Keywords column also provides synchronization between existing legacy keyword fields and the managed metadata infrastructure. (Document tags will be copied into the Enterprise Keywords on upload.)

Enterprise Keywords

☐ Add an Enterprise Keywords column to this list and enable Keyword synchronization

Metadata Publishing

Values added to Managed Metadata and Enterprise Keywords columns can be shared as social tags on My Sites to appear in newsfeeds, profile pages, tag clouds, and tag profile pages.

Save metadata on this list as social tags

☐ Add values in Managed Metadata and Enterprise Keywords fields to My Site profiles as social tags.

FIGURE 31-6

After selecting this option, edit one of the list items and you will see the keyword field has been added. The options for this field derive from the Enterprise keyword list that you set up as part of the Managed Metadata Service. (Refer to lesson 30 for more details on this feature.)

10. Optionally, you can select the Metadata Navigation Settings link, shown in Figure 31-7, to set up the options for this navigation. The list settings page enables you to set up a special navigation option for your list or library that enables you to filter your view of the list based on a variety of items such as metadata fields, content types, and choice columns.

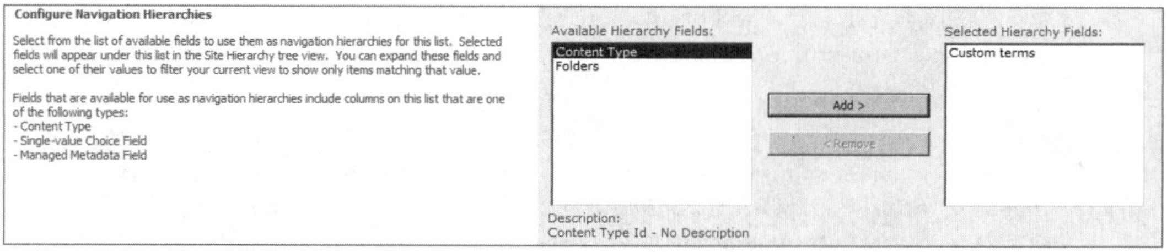

FIGURE 31-7

On this same page you can also use manually typed filter values based on selected columns, as shown in Figure 31-8. The navigation options at the beginning of this lesson (refer to Figure 31-3) result from the selections you make here on the List Settings page.

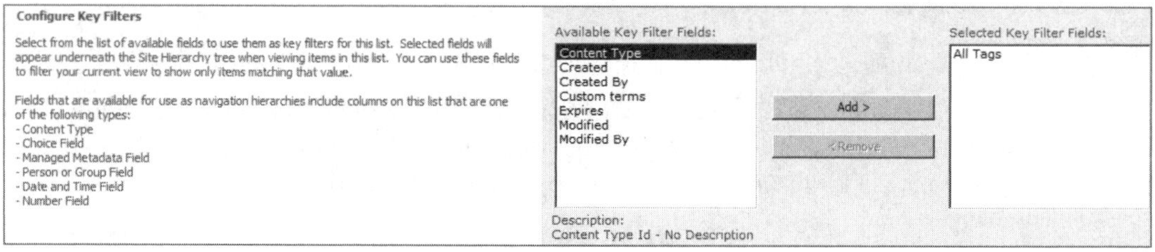

FIGURE 31-8

Please select Lesson 31 on the DVD or visit www.wrox.com/go/sp2010-24 to view the video that accompanies this lesson.

Configuring PerformancePoint Services

In Lesson 33 you will get an introduction to how PerformancePoint works from a SharePoint perspective. In this lesson you learn how to set up and configure the PerformancePoint Services application. At one time PerformancePoint was a distinct product, but with this new version it is an integral part of SharePoint 2010 and enables you to build highly informative and interactive Business Intelligence (BI) SharePoint sites.

ACTIVATING BUSINESS INTELLIGENCE FEATURES

Before you can use PerformancePoint there are several configuration steps that must be completed:

➤ Set up and configure the Secure Store Service if you haven't already done so.

➤ Create the PerformancePoint Services application.

➤ Start PerformancePoint Services on the application server that will host the service.

➤ Enable PerformancePoint on your site collection.

You will find that this lesson is mostly "hands-on," as several stages of the configuration are easier to understand with a demonstration.

Secure Store and Unattended Service Account

The unattended service account is an Active Directory domain account used by PerformancePoint to access external data sources such as SQL Server 2008. This account works in conjunction with the Secure Store Service, which must also be configured in order for PerformancePoint to use the unattended service account. In fact, if you add an account and the store is not configured you will be notified that it needs to be set up.

The Secure Store Service (like the single sign-on service in SharePoint 2007) is used to store credentials for systems and users. For example, if you log into SharePoint with one account but access another system using a different account, the second account can be placed into the Secure Store and matched with your SharePoint credentials. When you require access to the second system from SharePoint, your Secure Store credentials are used. This gives you the seamless access to external systems that you had with SharePoint 2007 Single Sign-On. The Secure Store credentials can then be used to allow external content types to access external data.

When setting up the Secure Store Service in Central Administration you will be required to enter a passphrase, which is used to create the encryption key for the stored credentials. Once this is done you can configure a target application, for example an SQL Server that maps the Secure Store credentials to the external system. When creating a Secure Store Service you are required to provide the following:

➤ Name for the Secure Store Service.

➤ Database details, including authentication method.

➤ Failover server name (if applicable).

➤ Application pool details.

➤ Name of an existing managed account (you can also create a new account for this service).

PerformancePoint Services Application

Once the Secure Store Service has been created and configured you can then proceed to create the PerformancePoint Services application and complete the configuration. As part of the configuration process you will be required to select the Unattended Service Account and associate the application with the Secure Store Service.

In the Try It example that follows we will look at many of the detailed features required to get PerformancePoint up and running.

TRY IT

In this exercise you will do the following:

➤ Create the Secure Store Service application.

➤ Add a passphrase.

➤ Create a target application.

➤ Create a new PerformancePoint application.

➤ Enable the PerformancePoint service for the farm.

➤ Set the unattended service account.

- ➤ Set miscellaneous settings.
- ➤ Associate the new service with a web application.
- ➤ Enable PerformancePoint on a site collection.
- ➤ Create a Business intelligence site.

Lesson Requirements

To complete this Try It exercise, you need the following:

- ➤ Access to Central Administration with appropriate permissions to create the required services.
- ➤ Site collection administration permissions.

Step-by-Step

To create the Secure Store Service application you need to open SharePoint Central Administration. To proceed from Central Administration, do the following:

1. Click Manage Service Applications in the Application Management category.

2. Click New.

3. Click Secure Store Service.

4. Enter **PerformancePointSecureStore** as the Service Application Name.

5. Accept the default Database Server and Database Name.

6. Accept the default database authentication of Windows.

7. Click the Create New Application Pool radio button and enter **perpointapppool** as the application pool name.

8. Select the account to use for the application pool.

9. Accept the defaults for audit logs (30 Days and Enabled).

10. Click OK.

11. Click OK in response to the dialog box.

12. Locate the new Secure Store Service application and click to highlight the name.

13. Click Manage on the ribbon.

14. Click the Generate New Key icon on the ribbon in response to the onscreen message, *before* creating a new Secure Store target application, you must generate a new key for this Secure Store Service application from the ribbon.

15. Enter a passphrase of **MARTIN123!%$** (make sure you write this down and store it safely). The passphrase must be a combination of letters in both uppercase and lowercase, digits, and symbols or it will be rejected.

16. Reenter the passphrase as confirmation.

17. Click OK to generate the encryption key.

Figure 32-1 shows the Create New Secure Store Service Application form.

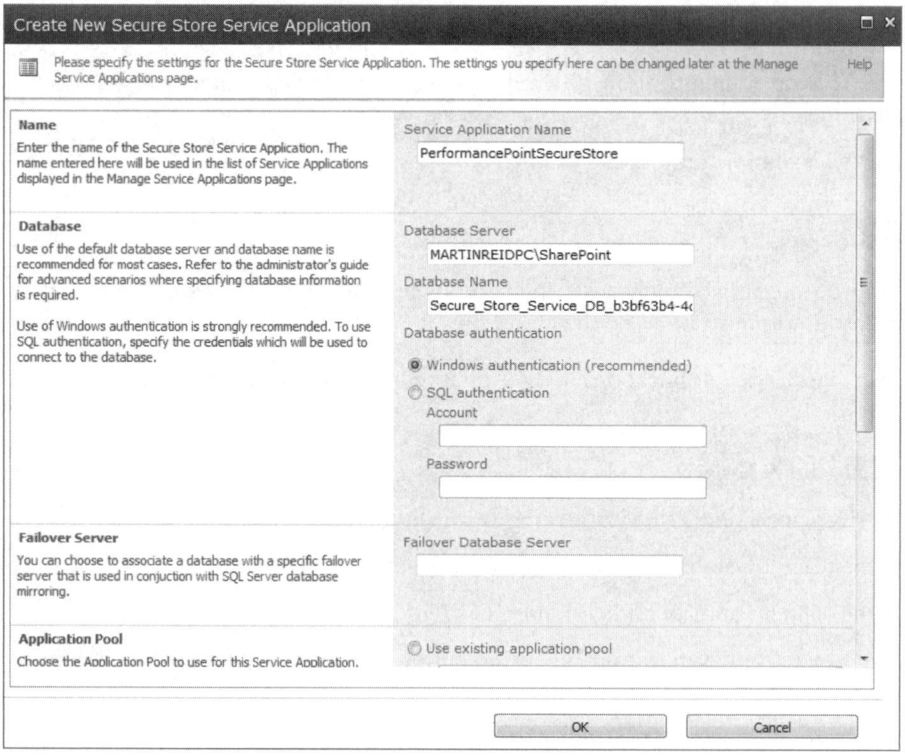

FIGURE 32-1

Once the Secure Store Service and encryption key have been created you can proceed to create the target application and select the authentication method. To continue, follow these steps:

1. Click New.

2. Enter a Target Application ID, such as **CompanySQL**. This cannot be changed once the application has been created.

3. Enter a Display Name, for example **Company Data**.

4. Enter a Contact E-mail address. This is the primary contact for the target application.

5. Select the target application type using the drop-down. There are two basic options, Group and Individual. Choose Individual here: this option is for mapping individual user credentials to distinct credentials on the data. Choose Group when you want to associate a group or groups with a single credential on the external data. For both Group and Individual you can choose Restricted or Ticket. Choosing Restricted and Ticket, respectively, allows you to work with data stores that support claims-based authentication. Choosing neither (selecting Individual or Group) enables standard authentication communication.

6. Select the Target Application Page URL: accept the default of Use Default Page.

7. Click Next.

8. Enter the name of the Windows user for the SQL Server database.

9. Enter the Windows password for the user entered in the previous step.

10. Click Next.

11. Enter your own credentials as the application administrator.

12. Click OK.

Figure 32-2 shows the Target Application Settings form.

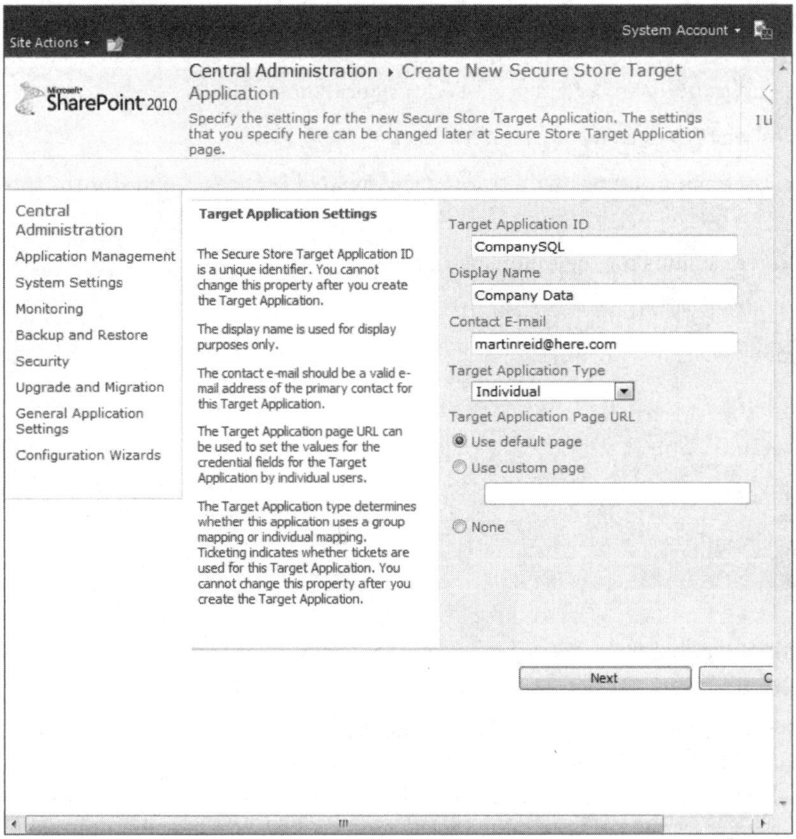

FIGURE 32-2

Once we have the Secure Store and target application created we can proceed to create the service application itself. To create the service application from within Central Administration, do the following:

1. Click Manage Service Applications in the Application Management group.

2. Click New.

3. Click PerformancePoint Service Application.

4. Type **Lesson 32 PerformancePoint** as the name.

5. Check the box entitled Add This Service Application's Proxy to the Farm's Default Proxy List. This will associate the service with existing web applications. If you do not check this box you will be required to manually associate the service with specific web applications.

6. Enter **PerformPointApppool** as the application pool name.

7. Select the managed account for the application pool using the drop-down.

8. Click Create.

Now that the PerformancePoint Services application has been created it must be configured. To proceed:

1. Click the service application name, Lesson 32 PerformancePoint.

2. Click PerformancePoint Services Application Settings.

3. Enter the domain user name and password for the Unattended Service account for the service application.

4. Accept the remaining defaults for the following options:

   ➤ Cache

   ➤ Data Sources

   ➤ Filters

   ➤ Select Measure Control

   ➤ Show Details

   ➤ Decomposition Tree

5. Click OK.

Figure 32-3 shows the initial section of the PerformancePoint Settings form at this stage in the process.

You can now specify the trusted locations used by SharePoint to store data sources. These trusted locations can be every site within SharePoint, or you can choose to allow only particular sites. To configure this setting click Trusted Data Source Locations. If you select Specific Locations the screen will refresh and you can then enter the URLs of your preferred sites. The default is All SharePoint

Locations, which may not be appropriate for your circumstances. For this example accept the default of All SharePoint Locations.

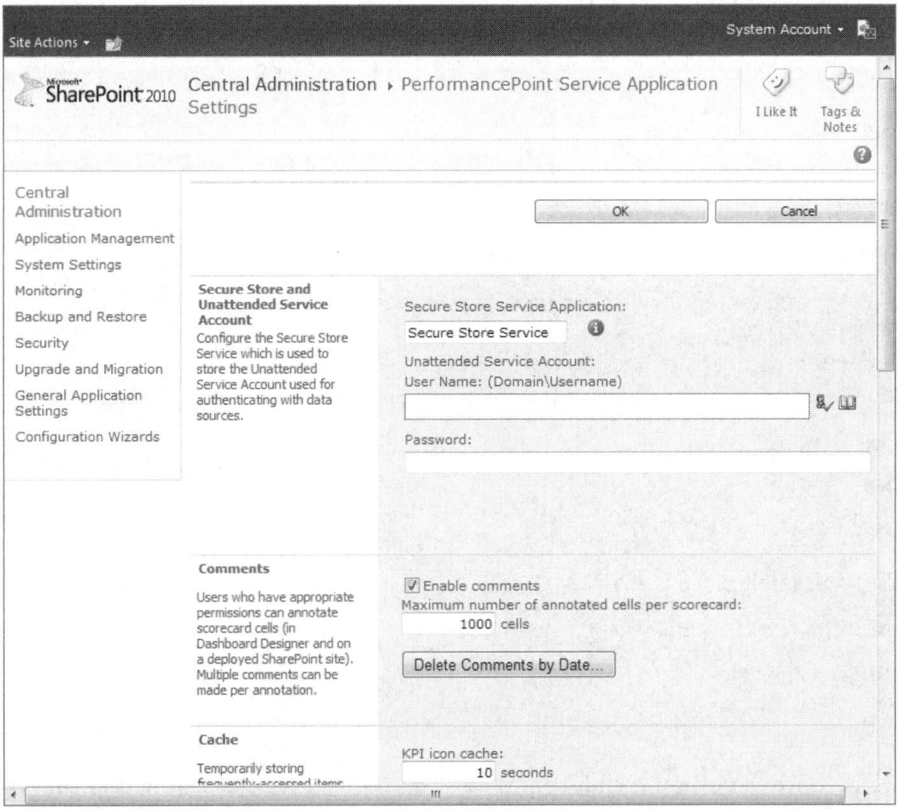

FIGURE 32-3

Trusted Content Locations

The options for trusted locations for your PerformancePoint content are the same as for SharePoint data sources: all SharePoint locations or specific SharePoint sites. For this example follow these steps:

1. Click Only Specific Locations.

2. Click Apply.

3. Click Add Trusted Content Location.

4. Enter the full URL of your SharePoint site collection. This should be the URL of the site collection home and not of an individual document library.

5. Accept the default location type of Site Collection (and subtree).

6. Click OK. The new trusted location will now be listed on the screen.

Now that you have configured the PerformancePoint Services application you are required to enable the PerformancePoint features on your site collection. To continue from the home page of your site collection do the following:

1. Click Site Actions.
2. Click Site Settings.
3. Click Site Collection Features.
4. Click the Activate button for PerformancePoint Services Site Collection Features. This will also activate the publishing infrastructure if it is not already activated.
5. Return to the settings page and click Manage Site Features.
6. Click the Activate button for PerformancePoint Services Site Features.

At this point you are ready to create your first BI SharePoint site and make use of its PerformancePoint features. From the home page of your site collection do the following:

1. Click Site Actions.
2. Click New Site.
3. Click Data.
4. Click Business Intelligence Center.
5. Enter **My BI Site** as the title.
6. Enter **BISite** as the URL.
7. Click Create.

Lesson 33 continues with this example and focuses on using the features of PerformancePoint.

 Please select Lesson 32 on the DVD or visit www.wrox.com/go/sp2010-24 *to view the video that accompanies this lesson.*

33

Creating a PerformancePoint Site

With SharePoint 2007, PerformancePoint was a distinct product used to provide business intelligence (BI) features and reporting dashboards. PerformancePoint is now an integral feature of SharePoint 2010 and is built into the product as a service application. The PerformancePoint service application is configured at the server level and can be consumed by site collections. Your SharePoint administrative team will need to configure the service application for you, as there are several levels of settings that must be specified before it is functional.

BI SITES AND FEATURES

Given the breadth of PerformancePoint and BI tools in general, one lesson can only skim the surface. This lesson shows you how to use the PerformancePoint template, activate PerformancePoint features, and create a basic dashboard using the design tools. Each of these topics could make up a book on its own and a lot of what you will do with PerformancePoint depends on your business need. This lesson looks at a new site collection based on the BI template. Figure 33-1 shows a BI site.

To use PerformancePoint you create a business intelligence site collection using Central Administration, create a BI site from the homepage of a site collection that has the PerformancePoint features activated, or activate the features for an existing team site. For an existing site, you first activate the publishing infrastructure and then activate PerformancePoint features at the site-collection level. You can then activate PerformancePoint features at the individual site level. If you already have PerformancePoint data from SharePoint 2007, it can be imported into the SharePoint 2010 version using the tools provided as part of the PerformancePoint Service Application in Central Administration.

The PerformancePoint site shown in Figure 33-1 shows many of the features of BI in SharePoint and contains multiple links to help you get started. It also includes tips and instructions to help you build BI sites based on PerformancePoint. Areas of the screen are dynamic and if you move the mouse over the text "Monitor Key Performance" they will change, displaying additional information about the chosen topic. Notice the link on the homepage to View SharePoint Samples, which, if clicked, will open a new page to demonstrate some of the features in PerformancePoint. The examples are shown in Figure 33-2.

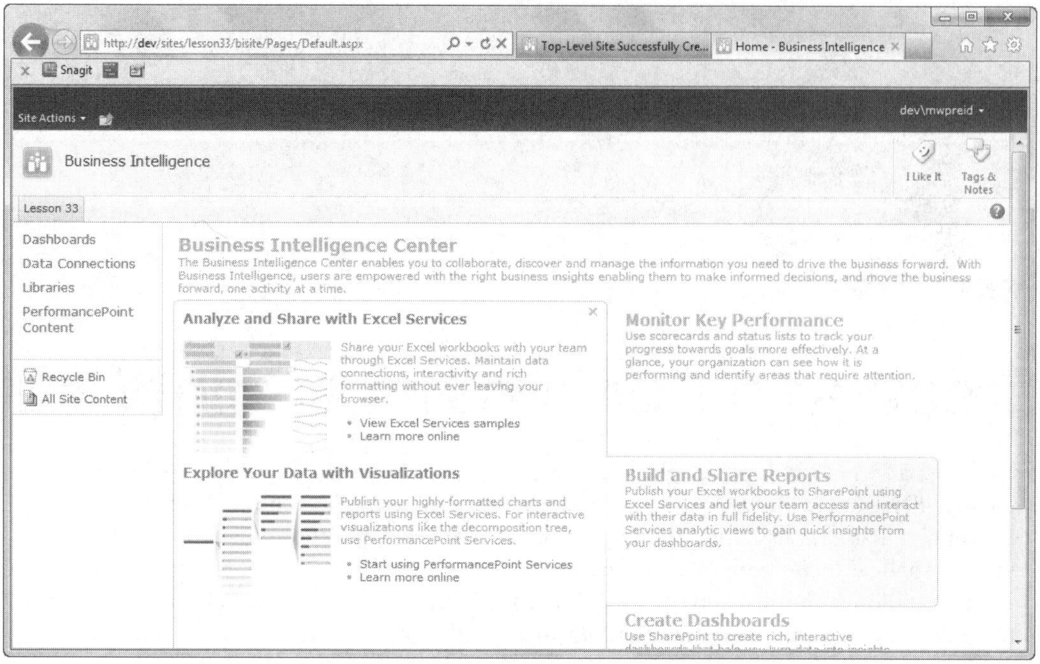

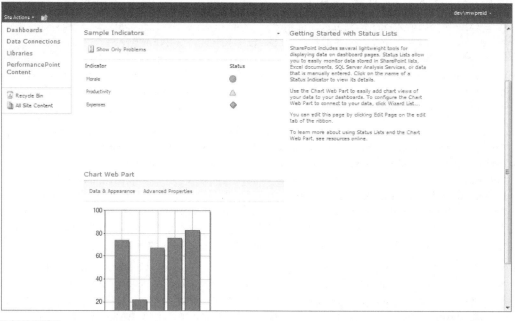

FIGURE 33-1

FIGURE 33-2

In this case, a status list and SharePoint chart are displayed. Several other examples are included in the site, including Excel Services demonstrations; you will also find links to useful websites for more information. The BI site contains several objects used by SharePoint that are not usually available in a standard team site, including libraries for the following:

➤ **PerformancePoint Content:** PerformancePoint items, including scorecards, KPIs, reports, filters, indicators, and dashboards.

➤ **Sample Indicators:** Some sample indicator data for the site.

➤ **Dashboards:** Web Part pages, Web Part pages with status lists and PerformancePoint-deployed dashboards.

➤ **Data Connections:** Connections used by PerformancePoint to access external data.

One of the other major changes from team Sites, you will find when using the PerformancePoint site template, is the Dashboard Designer. Figure 33-3 shows the Designer when opened. The Designer is, as you probably have already guessed, used to build dashboards. It is available in your PerformancePoint site. This is a powerful tool and it enables you to gather data from various sources to build BI dashboards and publish them to your SharePoint site. Using the Dashboard Designer, you can connect and return data from the following:

➤ SQL Server database tables

➤ Analysis Services

➤ Excel Services

➤ Data imported from Excel workbooks

➤ SharePoint lists

This gives you a wide range of information to choose from when working with BI and PerformancePoint in your site.

A basic component of a PerformancePoint site is the status list. An example status indicator list is provided with the site template. A sample status indicators list enables you to set a goal and measure your progress toward it. A set of icons is used to highlight targets and issues, for example, targets that are not currently being met. At this stage, you can simply enter the information manually. For example, you can set a goal for travel expenses in a department of $500 per month. You can then manually enter a monthly value of $600. The status indicator list reflects this by using a "danger" icon to show that you are over budget. Of course, at another level, this data can be pulled out of a financial system and automatically populate your list. Figure 33-4 shows the travel expenses example in a status indicator list. You can see that the value for expenses exceeds the goal; this is indicated by the red diamond-shaped icon.

The status list can also be populated from values held within another SharePoint list, which can be centrally maintained or created using the Dashboard Designer. You do of course need permissions to use different aspects of the Dashboard Designer. The following permissions are required:

➤ **To open the Designer:** Any authenticated user can open the designer.

➤ **To create dashboard items:** Contribute permissions are required.

➤ **To view and use dashboard items:** Read permissions are required.

➤ **To add or edit permissions:** Full control permissions are required.

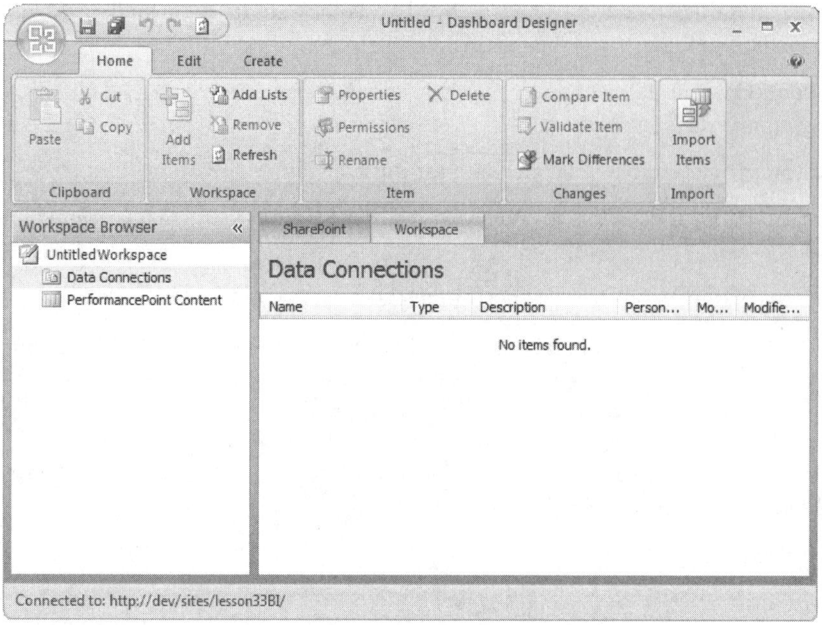

FIGURE 33-3

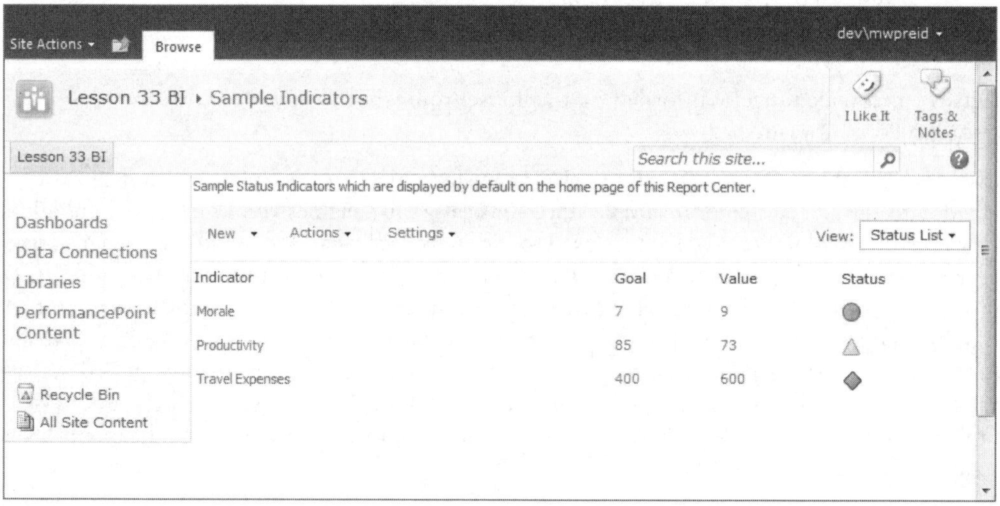

FIGURE 33-4

Keep in mind that if you access external data sources, you need at least read permissions on those sources. These are in addition to whatever permissions you have in SharePoint.

Running the Dashboard Designer requires only a simple button click within the BI site and it is downloaded and opened, ready for you to start. The Designer can also be opened to add specific content to PerformancePoint lists using the list Ribbon. If you take this approach, the following items can be added once the Designer opens:

➤ PerformancePoint KPI

➤ PerformancePoint Score Card

➤ PerformancePoint Indicator

➤ PerformancePoint Report

➤ PerformancePoint Filter

➤ PerformancePoint Dashboard

After the Designer is open, you can begin to add data sources and other objects to your site and amaze your users with interactive dashboards.

> *Microsoft's website* technet.microsoft.com *provides you with more information on PerformancePoint, SharePoint, and instructions for their use.*

TRY IT

In this exercise, you will do the following:

➤ Activate the publishing infrastructure at the site collection level.

➤ Activate the PerformancePoint features on a standard team site.

➤ Create a business intelligence site.

➤ Open the Dashboard Designer and add a data connection to SQL Server and an Excel Services workbook stored in SharePoint.

Lesson Requirements

To complete this Try It exercise, you need the following:

➤ A sample data set in SQL Server. You can download sample SQL Server 2008 data from codeplex.com if you would like to create the same data connection used in this example.

➤ A new team site collection in which to enable the various features.

➤ A workbook stored in a SharePoint document library.

Step-by-Step

To start, you activate the PerformancePoint features on a SharePoint team site. To proceed from within a team site, do the following:

1. Click Site Actions.

2. Click Site Settings.

3. Click Site Collection Features within the site collection administration group.

4. Scroll down through the Features screen and click the Activate button for the SharePoint Server publishing infrastructure.

5. Scroll down through the Features screen and click the Activate button for the PerformancePoint Services site collection features.

6. Return to Site Settings and click Manage Site Features under the Site Actions category.

7. Click Activate for the PerformancePoint Services site features.

You configured the SharePoint environment to support PerformancePoint features and sites. To continue with the process, do the following:

8. Click Site Actions.

9. Click New Site.

10. In the Data category select Data.

11. Click the Business Intelligence Center to select it.

12. Enter **Business Intelligence** as the title.

13. Enter **bisite** as the URL.

14. Click Create.

The BI site should open. Figure 33-5 shows the new site open in the browser. Click around to examine the various examples and tutorial links available in the new site.

You can also open the Dashboard Designer to begin learning how this additional tool works. To continue and open the Designer, do the following:

1. Click Monitor Key Performance.

2. Click the Start Using PerformancePoint Service link that appears.

3. Click the Run Dashboard Designer button to download and open the Designer.

4. In the Designer windows, right-click Data Connections.

5. Select New Data Source from the menu.

6. Select SQL Server Table.

7. Click OK.

Figure 33-6 shows the new window that opens to enable you to configure the SQL Server connection.

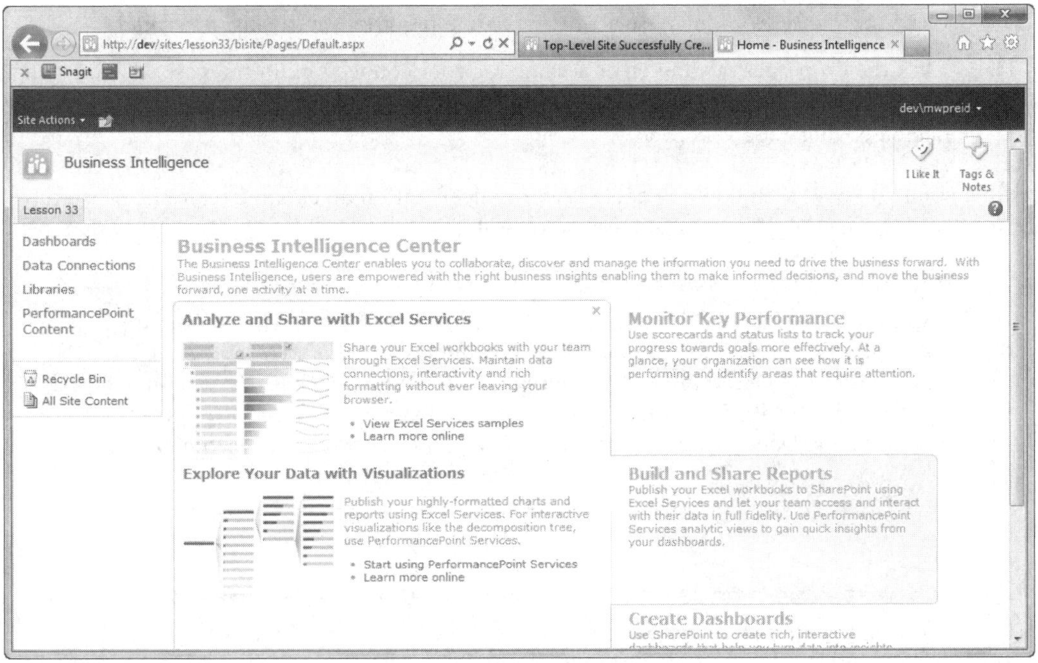

FIGURE 33-5

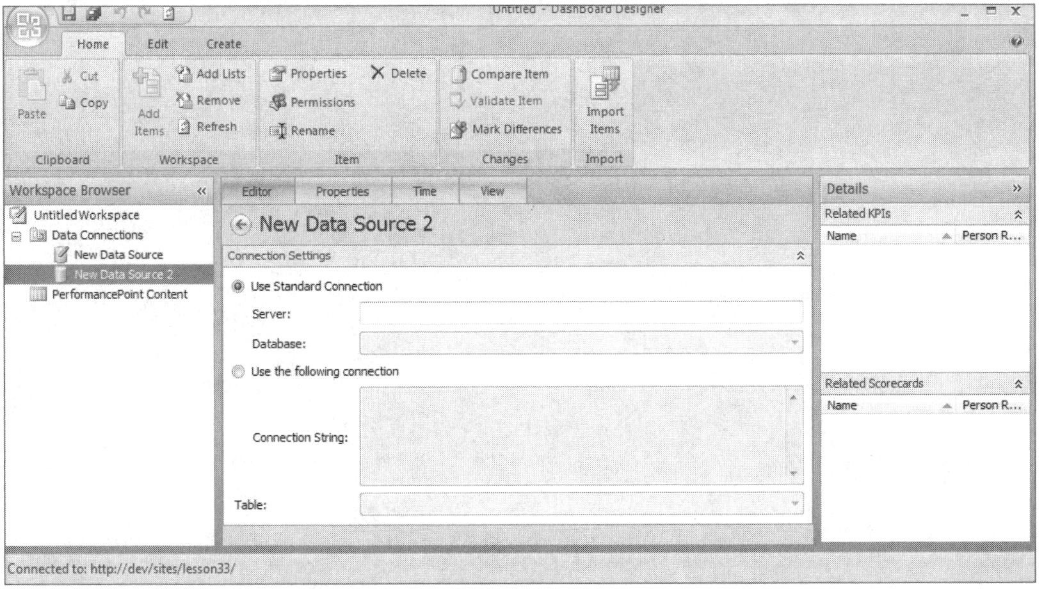

FIGURE 33-6

8. Enter the name of your SQL Server into the Server text box.

9. Using the Database drop-down, select the database required.

10. Using the Table drop-down, select the table you require from the list presented.

11. Click the Properties tab and enter a name for your connection. In this case, as I am using the AdventureWorks example database, I entered **AdventureWorksDW**. You can download the database from `codeplex.com`.

At this point you have seen how to enable PerformancePoint on an existing team site, open the Dashboard Designer, and create a connection to SQL Server.

As I said at the start of this lesson, PerformancePoint is a topic for a book of its own, and it is impossible to cover in any detail here. For further information on this complex tool and to continue your training with BI, I recommend SharePoint 2010 Business Intelligence 24-Hour Trainer *by Adam Jorgensen, Mark Stacey, Devin Knight, Patrick LeBlanc, and Brad Schacht, also published by Wiley.*

Please select Lesson 33 on the DVD or visit www.wrox.com/go/sp2010-24 *to view the video that accompanies this lesson.*

34

Creating a Business Connectivity Service

The Business Connectivity Service (BCS) is one of the features in SharePoint that can take business-centric data out of the hands of the IT professional and put it into the hands of the user. BCS enables you to connect to business data stores, for example SQL Server and Oracle databases, in a secure manner. For the first time, SharePoint 2010 puts features in the reach of non-IT users through the *external content type*.

BCS is a server-level service that needs to be made available on your SharePoint farm by being enabled and configured by your SharePoint Administrators. It is normally set up and configured by a server administrator and it provides all the services required to connect with and use line-of-business data. A similar service was available with SharePoint 2007 but was complex and confusing to use and normally required a programmer to make any sense of it at all. Several third-party tools became available to simplify its use but with SharePoint 2010, these are no longer needed. If you find you are unable to use external content types, notify your SharePoint administrator to ensure that BCS has been enabled on the farm.

EXTERNAL CONTENT TYPES

External content types (ECTs) are used to work with and expose data held outside the SharePoint system, such as SQL Server or Microsoft Access 2010 data stores. An external list enables you to expose that data within SharePoint. For this lesson, you work with both SharePoint Designer 2010 and a *team site*. SharePoint Designer 2010 is required to create the ECTs and for the examples in this lesson, data held within an SQL Server 2008 database system is used. External lists are discussed in Lesson 35, where we extend the example ECT used here.

ECTs are likely to be provided for you by your SharePoint administrators, and you can use them to expose company data in team sites as SharePoint lists. If you are using another data source, such as a SQL Server database, remember to change the options to suit your information. However, you as a site collection administrator may be required to create your own ECTs, and even if that's not the case, an understanding of how they are constructed can prove useful.

ECTs are created and managed using SharePoint Designer 2010. It's a tool that creates dread for administrators, as in the hands of a user it can create chaos in SharePoint. SharePoint Designer 2010 is available as a free download from the Microsoft Download Center located at Microsoft.com.

ECTs are a powerful feature of SharePoint 2010, and in this lesson, we take only an introductory look at their configuration. It is possible to connect ECTs based on relationships in the database. A basic understanding of databases, particularly of how relationships are created and enforced, is required. For example, provided access to data held in a corporate database, you could display a list of customers and, when a customer name is clicked, show the orders he or she has placed. You set all of this up within a secure SharePoint site and build using SharePoint Designer 2010, including help from its configuration wizards. The one major drawback to the use of Designer in this scenario is that if two or more tables are required for the relationship then it is not supported, and Visual Studio 2010 is required. In the preceding example, if you wanted to display product data in addition to orders you would need to use Visual Studio 2010 to create the associations. In database-speak this particular relationship is normally referred to as *many-to-many relationships*.

TRY IT

In this exercise, you use SharePoint Designer 2010 to create the external content type connected to a Microsoft SQL Server database.

Lesson Requirements

To complete this Try It exercise, you need the following:

➤ SharePoint Designer 2010.

➤ Access to your site collection enabled for SharePoint Designer 2010.

➤ A SQL Server database containing at a minimum a Customer table. I simply copied the table from the Northwind Microsoft Access 2010 example database.

➤ SharePoint team site.

Hint

If you have access to an instance of SQL Server, in either a test or a development environment, you can create a simple database quickly by upsizing the Northwind Access 2010 database to SQL Server. In the following exercise, that's exactly the tool used to move the Access Northwind Customer table to SQL Server.

Step-by-Step

To begin the process you will need to use Microsoft SharePoint Designer 2010.

1. Open SharePoint Designer 2010.

2. Click Open Site.

3. Enter the URL to your team site.

4. Click Open.

   If you have not used Designer before you can carry out a quick search for SharePoint Designer 2010 tutorials to reach the designer portal containing tutorials and overviews of the software.

   Figure 34-1 shows the initial screen of Designer. If ECTs are already available in your site collection, they will be displayed in SharePoint Designer when you click External Content Types in the Navigation tab.

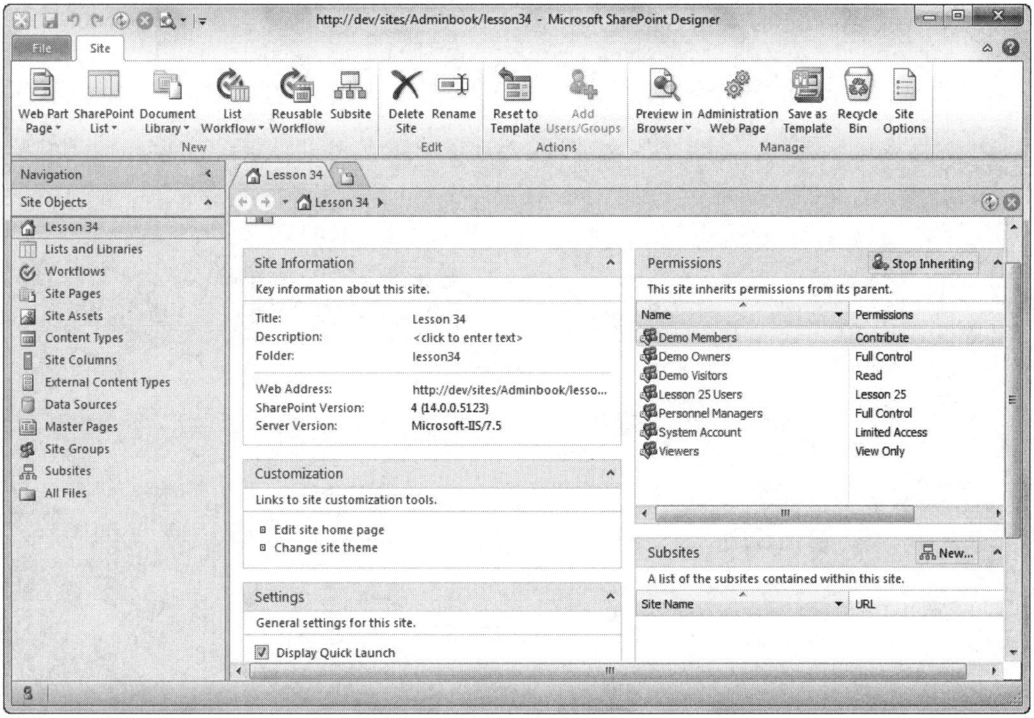

FIGURE 34-1

5. Click External Content Types in the site navigation. If ECTs are already defined, SharePoint Designer will return them from the BCS as defined on the server.

6. On the Ribbon, click External Content Type to open the configuration page. Figure 34-2 shows the ECT design window.

You must set multiple configuration settings when defining the ECT. This section assumes you are using an SQL Server customer table. If you are not, please adjust the lesson instructions to match your server and database names. The configuration settings available include:

➤ **Name:** Click the Name hyperlink and enter a name for the new ECT. In this case, use **Customers**.

➤ **Display Name:** Enter **Customers** as the Display Name by clicking the hyperlink Display Name.

➤ **Identifiers:** These are used to uniquely identify items returned by the ECT. For this example, they are not required.

➤ **Office Item Type:** This drop-down list enables you to select how your ECT will interact with offline clients, for example Microsoft Outlook 2010 and SharePoint Workspace. For this example, accept the default of generic list. However, you can map your ECT to an Outlook appointment, contact, task, or post.

➤ **Offline Sync for External List:** Enables you to synchronize the list with offline clients. The default is enabled; leave it there for this example. If you disable it you will be unable to sync the list with Outlook or SharePoint Workspace. The ability to take line-of-business data offline and sync later is a powerful feature of external content types.

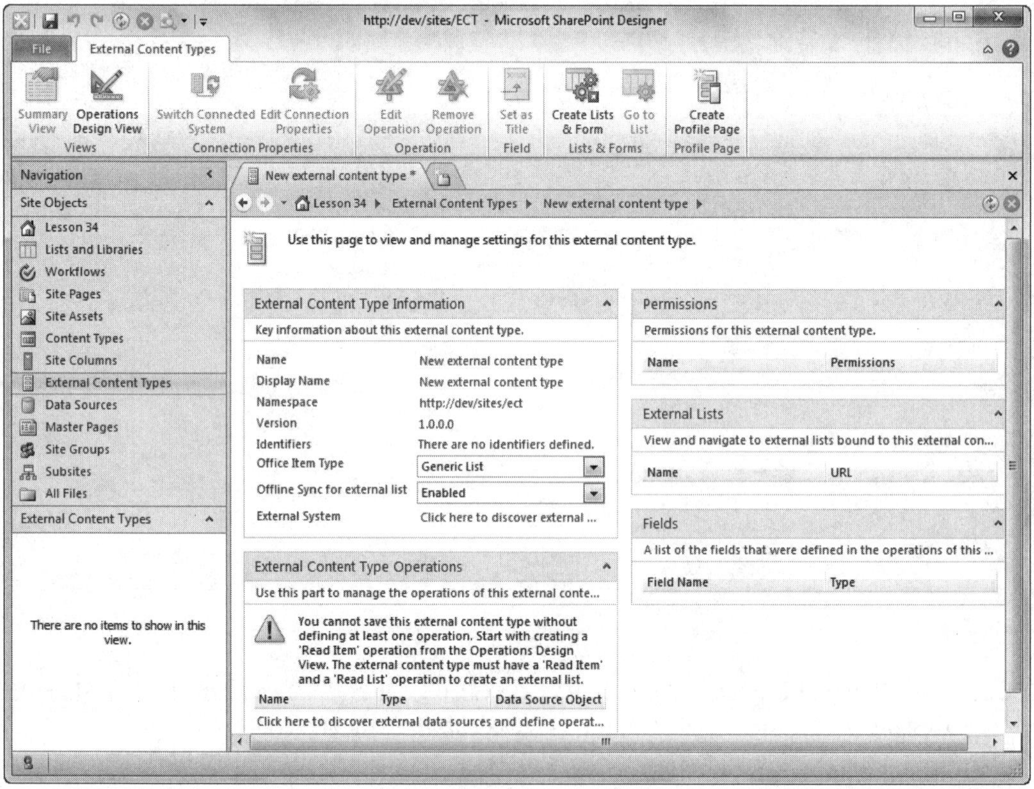

FIGURE 34-2

At this point, you have set up some of the minor features of the content type. Next, you need to either connect it to an existing data source or create a new data source to a corporate system, for example SQL Server databases. You will do one or the other depending on the permissions you have for such systems and how the BCS application is made available to you. For this example, assume you have access to the data held on SQL Server and can go ahead and create the data source to return the required information. To create a new connection, proceed as follows:

External Content Type Operations: This area will enable you to reuse an existing data source, create a new data source, and define how the user will interact with the data set returned. You can define standard data operations using the ECT, add, edit, delete, and of course read. Click the hyperlink Click Here to Discover External Data Sources and Define Operations. This will open the Operations Designer shown in Figure 34-3. The main options in the designer are as follows:

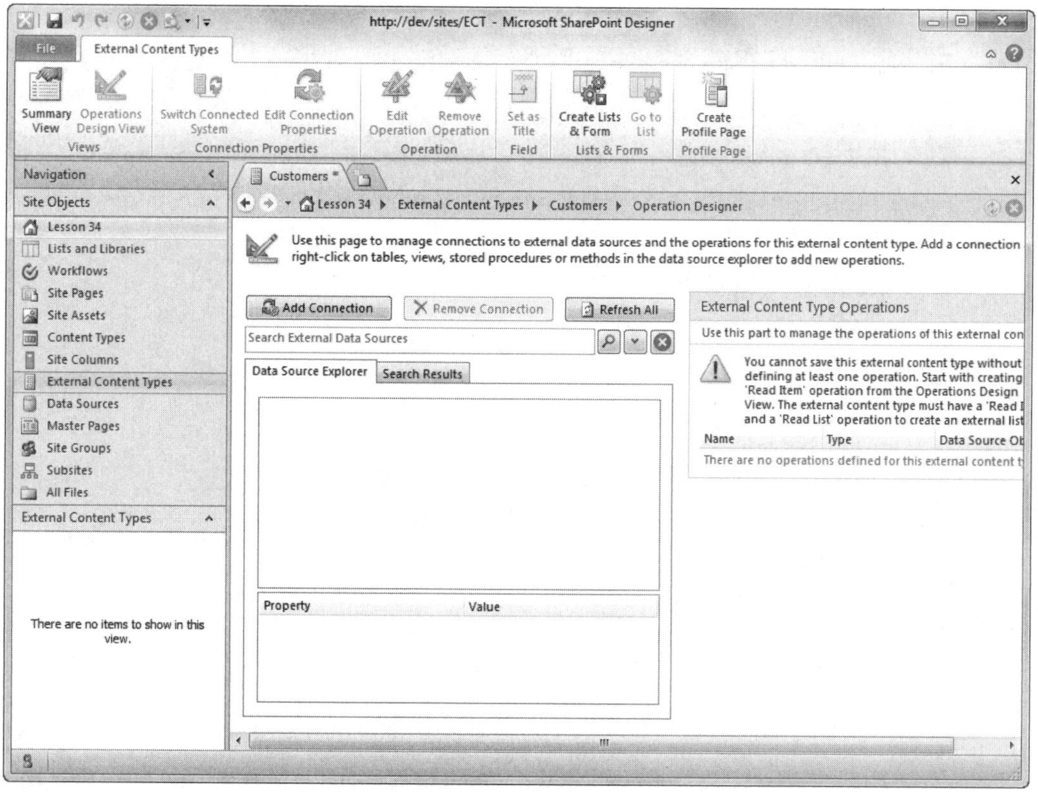

FIGURE 34-3

➤ **Add Connection:** This button enables you to create a new connection to a data store.

➤ **Refresh All:** Refreshes all existing data connections.

➤ **Remove Connection:** Deletes the selected connection.

➤ **Data Source Explorer:** This tab displays existing connections that can be used when available.

➤ **Search Results:** This tab displays the results of data source searches.

➤ **External Content Type Operations:** Displays the allowed operations (read, write, update, delete) for the ECT which you have created, or will display operations set on an already existing ECT. Note that initially it will contain a warning message that you must define at least one operation, which will be a read operation.

7.   Define a data source by following these steps:

   1.   Click the Add Connection button.

   2.   Select SQL Server from the External Data Source Type Connection drop-down list.

   3.   Click OK.

   4.   Enter the name of your SQL Server instance into the Database Server text box.

   5.   Enter the database name into the Database Name text box.

   6.   Accept the default security account. Connect with the user's identity.

   7.   Click OK to validate the accounts and create the connection to your database.

Figure 34-4 shows the Data Source Explorer tab after a valid connection has been added to the ECT.

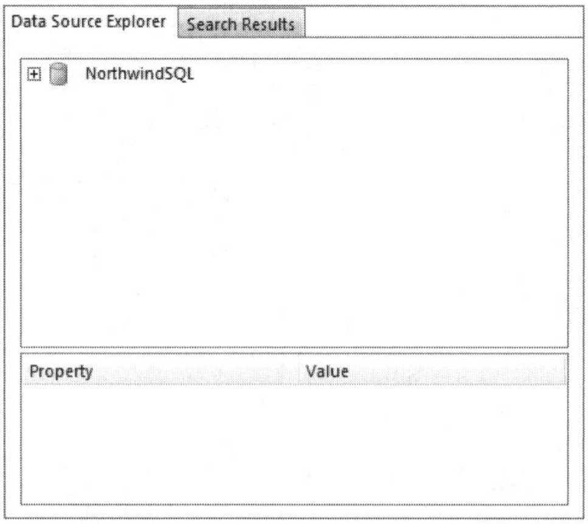

FIGURE 34-4

8.   To view the tables and views in the connection, click the plus symbol beside the database name. This expands the view to display tables, views, and routines.

9.   Expand the Tables sub-folder by clicking its plus symbol. In this case I have a single table called Customers. If you have multiple tables they will be shown in the Designer window.

10.   Expand the Columns item by clicking the plus symbol. This will display the individual columns available within the database table.

11.   Click on the table named Customers.

12.   Right-click Customers to open the Operations shortcut menu. This menu is used to define the database operations that are allowed on the Customers table. For this example you are going to allow all operations (read, add, edit, and delete records) on the external content type. Figure 34-5 shows the menu for the Customers table.

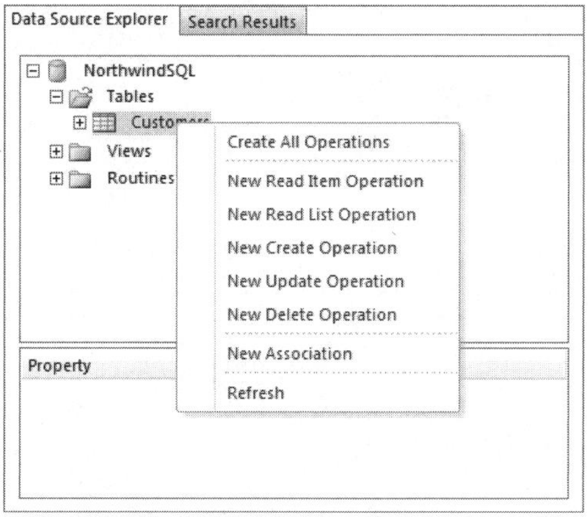

Data Source Explorer   Search Results

- NorthwindSQL
  - Tables
    - Customers

      | Create All Operations |
      | New Read Item Operation |
      | New Read List Operation |
      | New Create Operation |
      | New Update Operation |
      | New Delete Operation |
      | New Association |
      | Refresh |
    - Views
    - Routines

Property

FIGURE 34-5

13. Select Create All Operations from the shortcut menu to open the wizard, which will walk you through the process of creating an operation.

14. Click Next on the first page of the wizard.

15. Deselect all fields other than ID, Company, LastName, FirstName, and EmailAddress. For this example, you do not need all fields available in the Customers table.

16. Click Next.

17. We do not require a filter, so simply click Finish to move ahead. However, it is worth remembering that when you are working with large data sets a filter may be required to restrict the number of records retrieved from the database to SharePoint.

18. Select File ⇨ Save All to save all changes, including the new content type.

In Lesson 35, you use the external content type to display data within SharePoint.

Please select Lesson 34 on the DVD or visit www.wrox.com/go/sp2010-24 *to view the video that accompanies this lesson.*

Creating an External List

In Lesson 34 we looked at creating an external content type that connected to an SQL Server customer table and returned a small set of data. In this lesson we are going to expose that data within SharePoint as a list and have a look at creating a custom Web Part page, again exposing the data to users. Creating the external list is perhaps one of the easier exercises you will do in this book.

This ability to allow users access to external content within SharePoint cannot be underestimated, as among other advantages it gives you a way to expose data held outside the main SharePoint system. In this way some of the pressure is removed from IT staff to provide information from central systems. Many users welcome such access and with this release of SharePoint and SharePoint Designer 2010 it is now possible for such access to be given in a secure controlled way.

There are currently a couple of limitations when using External Lists in SharePoint including:

1. Workflows cannot be associated with the External List.
2. No versioning or version history exists for list items.
3. Users cannot export list data to client programs, including Excel.
4. Unable to add attachments to list items.
5. Dataview features are not available.

This appearance of external data as a standard Sharepoint list can be confusing to users who expect the full range of list functionality to be available. Perhaps the best way to view the External List is as a version one technology whose use and integration with SharePoint will improve over time.

TRY IT

In this exercise you are going to do the following:

➤ Create an external list.

➤ Configure the list to use external data.

➤ View the list in the browser.

➤ Modify the list data.

Lesson Requirements

To complete this Try It exercise, you need the following:

➤ An external content type called Customers, as was created in Lesson 34.

Step-by-Step

To create an external list and configure it to expose SQL Server data, do the following from within a SharePoint team site:

1. Click Site Actions.

2. Click More Options.

3. Click the Data category.

4. Click External List.

5. Click Create.

6. Enter **Customer External Data** as the name.

7. In the Description field enter **Data from external SQL Server.**

8. Accept the default navigation, Display This List on the Quick Launch? (This option is set to Yes.)

9. In the Data Source Configuration section click the second data source icon, which is high-lighted in Figure 35-1.

10. The External Data Type Picker will open, enabling you to search for or select external con-tent types. Select the content type created in Lesson 34 and click OK.

11. Click Create to save the configuration and create the external list. The list will open within SharePoint, as shown in Figure 35-2.

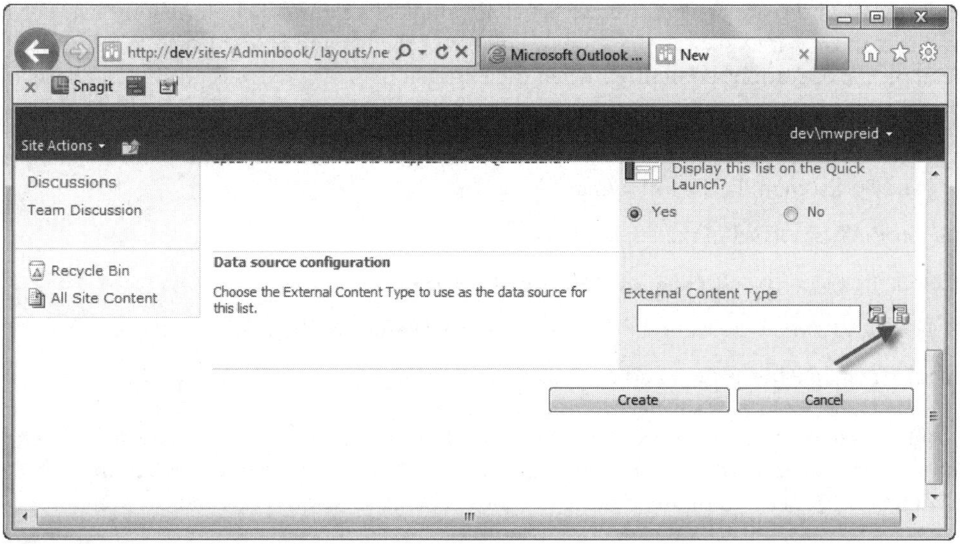

FIGURE 35-1

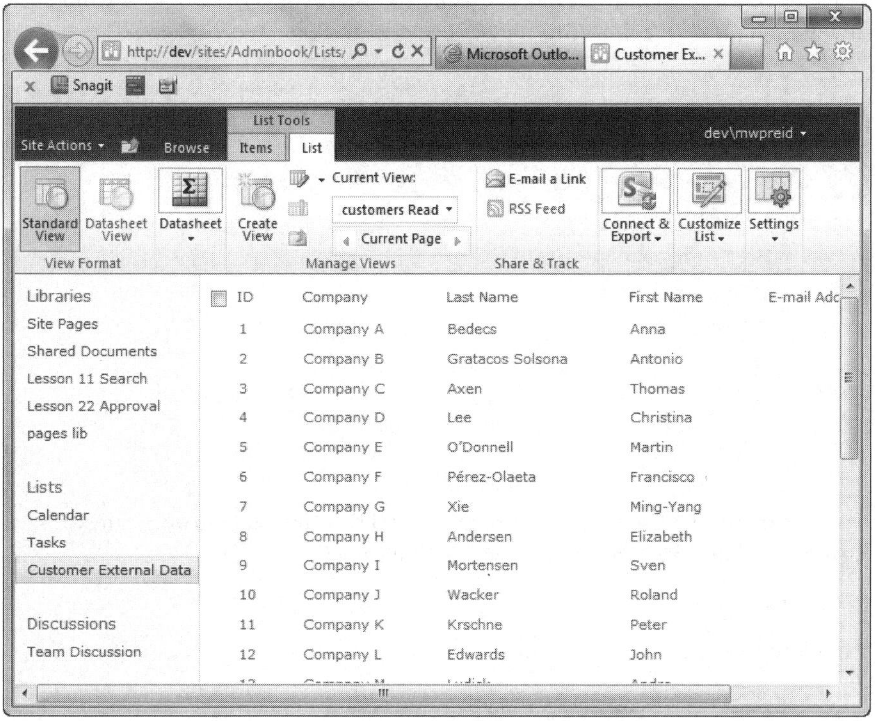

FIGURE 35-2

As you can see, from the site perspective the list simply looks like any other SharePoint list. For most situations you can treat it as such. Operations available of the list and its data such as editing items will depend on the operations configured when the external content type was created in SharePoint Designer 2010.

Working directly with the data in the external list is just like working with a standard list. For example, to edit a list item do the following:

1. Select the first record in the external list.

2. Select the record by checking the Selector checkbox.

3. Click Edit Item on the ribbon. The standard SharePoint Edit Item form will open.

4. Make a change to the item and click the Save button.

You have just edited a database record and saved it back to the database via the external content type and list. Depending on the permissions you have you should be able to carry out any of the standard functions on the external list and write those changes back to the database system.

Recall that in Lesson 34 you disabled the ability to connect this data to offline clients such as Outlook, by setting the external content type to be a generic list. Figure 35-3 shows the error that appears when you try to connect the list to Outlook using the SharePoint ribbon. You would get a similar message if you attempted to connect to the list using SharePoint Workspace 2010.

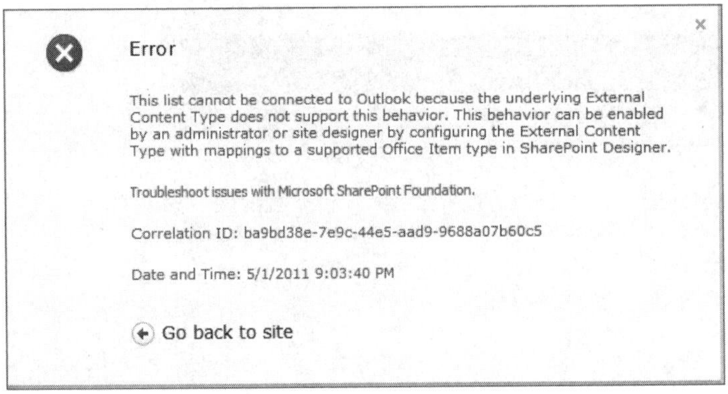

Error

This list cannot be connected to Outlook because the underlying External Content Type does not support this behavior. This behavior can be enabled by an administrator or site designer by configuring the External Content Type with mappings to a supported Office Item type in SharePoint Designer.

Troubleshoot issues with Microsoft SharePoint Foundation.

Correlation ID: ba9bd38e-7e9c-44e5-aad9-9688a07b60c5

Date and Time: 5/1/2011 9:03:40 PM

⊕ Go back to site

FIGURE 35-3

External content types can also be used within the BDC Web Parts available in your site. To see how this works you must first create a new Web Part page. To continue:

1. Click Site Actions.

2. Click More Options.

3. Click the Page link.

4. Click the Web Part Page icon in the page types.

5. Click Create.

6. Enter **ECT** as the page name.

7. Select the default layout template for the page: a header, a footer, and three columns.

8. Accept the default save location, the Site Assets library.

9. Click Create. You will be returned to the Web Part page in edit mode.

10. Click the Add a Web Part link in the middle column.

11. Click Business Data in the Web Part Category section.

12. Click the Business Data list in the list of available of Web Parts in this category.

13. Click the Add button to add the selected Web Part to the page.

14. Click the Open the Tool Pane link in the Web Part. This will open the tools used to configure this Web Part. Figure 35-4 shows the screen at this point.

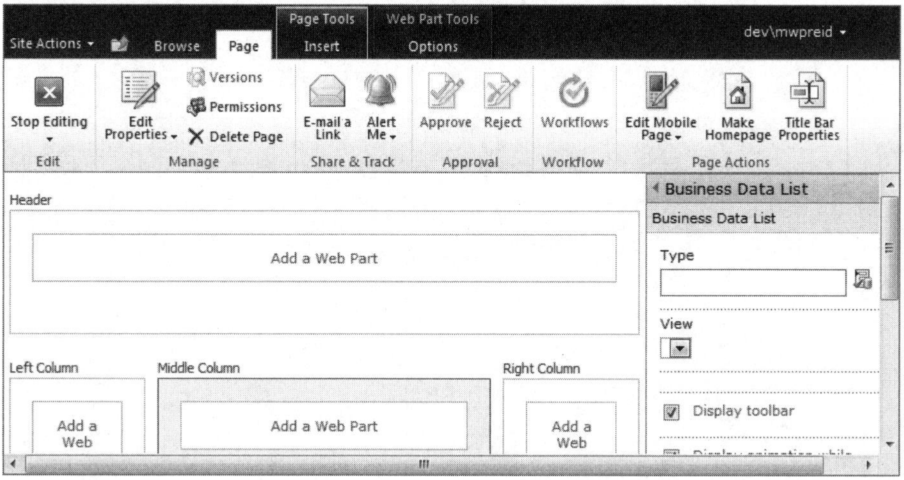

FIGURE 35-4

15. Click the Select External Content Type icon in the Tool pane, next to the Type text box.

16. In the External Type Picker select the External Content Type created in Lesson 34.

17. Click OK.

18. At the bottom of the Tool pane click OK to save the changes and view the data within the Web Part.

This simple process gives you a quick convenient way to display corporate data using either a standard SharePoint list or Web Parts. If you are using multiple external content types with associations between them, Web Parts are the way to go.

> *Please select Lesson 35 on the DVD or visit* www.wrox.com/go/sp2010-24 *to view the video that accompanies this lesson.*

SECTION VIII
Site Templates

36

Using the Form Template Library

Many Microsoft Office users know about Microsoft's InfoPath product, but few know what it can actually be used to do. InfoPath is a tool that can be used to create electronic forms. Forms can be simple, such as a company feedback form on a website, or more complex, such as a form that is connected to and displays information from a corporate database. Every InfoPath form starts as an InfoPath template that is used to create the form you eventually use. The template is then published to SharePoint forms libraries for use.

The form library gives you a place to publish forms; using InfoPath Forms Services, users can work with forms in a browser without needing the InfoPath client application. If a user does have InfoPath installed, the form opens in the client.

InfoPath can also be used to customize SharePoint list forms. Figure 36-1 shows a SharePoint tasks form that has been slightly customized with InfoPath Designer 2010.

Default SharePoint list forms can also be customized in InfoPath without the use of SharePoint Designer. InfoPath is sprinkled throughout SharePoint before you even get to use it to build electronic forms for your users. One of the benefits of using InfoPath for forms is that control validation is available via InfoPath. For example, you can set the control background color to change to red if a valid entry is missing.

OVERVIEW OF FORMS SERVICES

SharePoint 2010 uses Forms Services to provide you with the infrastructure to open and use InfoPath forms in the browser. Forms Services is a service application that is set up and configured within SharePoint 2010 Central Administration. It is different from other service applications in that it is configured and managed from the General Application Settings page in Central Administration, as opposed to under Manage Service Applications. Several categories of information are available to you on this page, including the following:

➤ **Manage Form Templates:** Manage existing InfoPath templates already stored on the server. You will find a number of templates already listed. SharePoint workflows usually use these templates, and you can upload additional form templates to the server.

➤ **Configure InfoPath Forms Services:** Does just what it says on the tin. This is the area in which you configure the services and the following settings are available:

> ➤ Use Browser-Enabled Form Templates: Enable the use of InfoPath in the browser.

> ➤ Data Connection Timeouts: Set the timeout values for data connections.

> ➤ Data Connection Response Size: Set the maximum size of responses for data connections.

> ➤ HTTP Data Connections: Enable SSL connections.

> ➤ Embedded SQL Authentication: Enable the use of embedded user name/password pairs in connection strings used with SQL Server.

> ➤ Authentication to Data Sources (User Form Templates): Allow form templates to use embedded user name/password pairs in connections to external data stores.

> ➤ Thresholds: Set limits for user sessions and post-backs.

> ➤ User Sessions: Specify time and data limits for user sessions. User session data is stored by the Microsoft SharePoint Server State Service.

> ➤ Upload Form Template: Upload a new InfoPath forms template to the server.

> ➤ Manage Data Connection Files: Manage database connection files that contain connection information for reuse by your users.

➤ **Configure InfoPath Forms Services Web Service Proxy:** Pass credentials to other systems using Web Services.

PUBLISHING TEMPLATES

After a template has been created, it can be published to your SharePoint site. Publishing is a fairly straightforward process that requires only a couple of mouse clicks. If your form template contains a connection to an SQL Server database, for example, remember that the connection file must be stored within the same site collection as the form itself.

When you are working in InfoPath, you have two main options for SharePoint: a SharePoint list template for when you are working with list data, and a SharePoint form option. The SharePoint list option enables you to view and edit data held within a SharePoint list. The SharePoint form option enables you to build very complex data-driven forms and store them for execution within a SharePoint form library.

The form library is much the same as other libraries in SharePoint and you will find that it contains many of the same features and functionality.

It is a requirement at times to publish the same InfoPath form to multiple site collections; in such a case, the form must be approved and installed by your SharePoint administrator during the publishing phase of the process. The InfoPath template is saved locally, then uploaded to SharePoint and approved by the administrator for use in multiple site collections. This is a common way to use complex InfoPath forms that have been created by programmers to solve specific business needs.

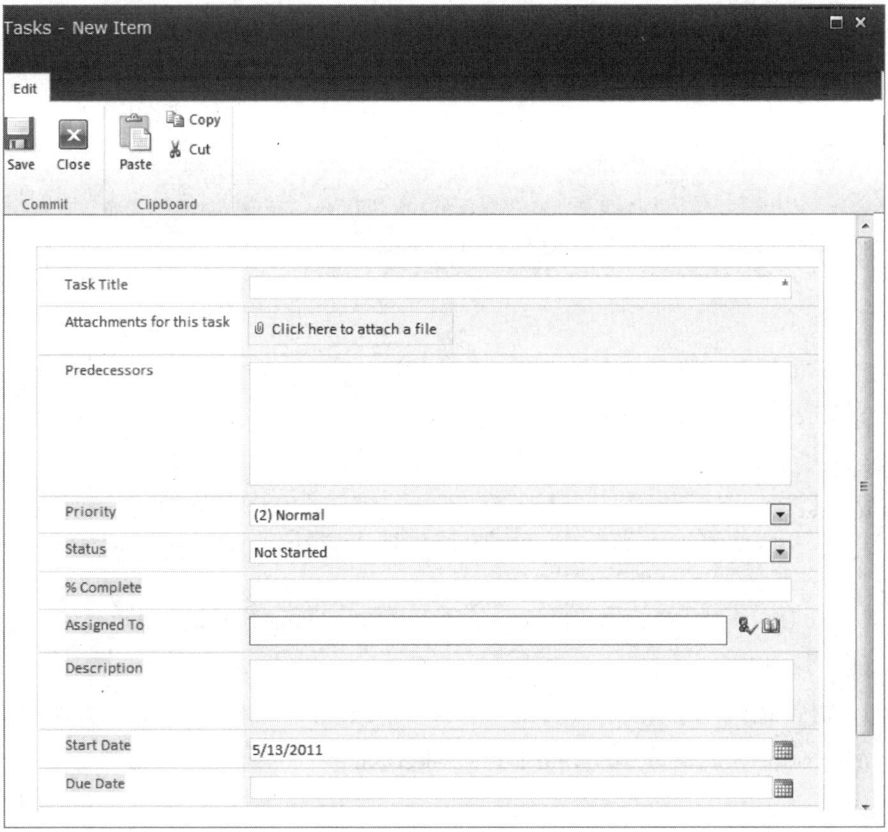

Tasks - New Item					□ ×

Edit

Save Close Paste 📋 Copy ✂ Cut

Commit   Clipboard

Task Title	☆
Attachments for this task	📎 Click here to attach a file
Predecessors	
Priority	(2) Normal ▾
Status	Not Started ▾
% Complete	
Assigned To	🔍📖
Description	
Start Date	5/13/2011 📅
Due Date	📅

FIGURE 36-1

TRY IT

In this Try It exercise, you will create a SharePoint list form, which requires a list. You also create a SharePoint form that can be completed in the browser and saved within the form library. You will create a more sophisticated form that demonstrates additional features of InfoPath and SharePoint when they are used together. At any point in the form design process, you can click the Preview button located on the far right side of the ribbon to view the form in preview mode.

 I advise completing this Try It section in conjunction with the Lesson 36 video. InfoPath is a complex application and it is impossible to cover it adequately in a single lesson. The DVD lesson contains additional information that will assist you in completing the Try It that follows.

Lesson Requirements

To follow this example, you need to create a custom list to store details of DVDs that you collect. The list should have the following columns:

➤ Title

➤ Genre drop-down list (Horror, Thriller, SF, Factual)

➤ Date Released

➤ Director

➤ Studio

You should also have Microsoft InfoPath 2010 Designer installed.

Step-by-Step

To begin the process, open Microsoft InfoPath Designer 2010.

1. Click the SharePoint list template.

2. Click Design Form.

3. Return to your custom list and copy the URL from the browser. Copy the URL only to the end of the list name. Ignore the rest of the URL. In this case, it is `http://dev/sites/Adminbook/Lists/DVD%20Collection/`.

4. Paste the URL into the text box on the screen of the Data Connection wizard.

5. Click Next.

6. Click the Customize an Existing SharePoint List radio button.

7. Click the list name you created for your DVD collection.

8. Click Next.

9. Click Finish.

Figure 36-2 shows the new form in the InfoPath Designer.

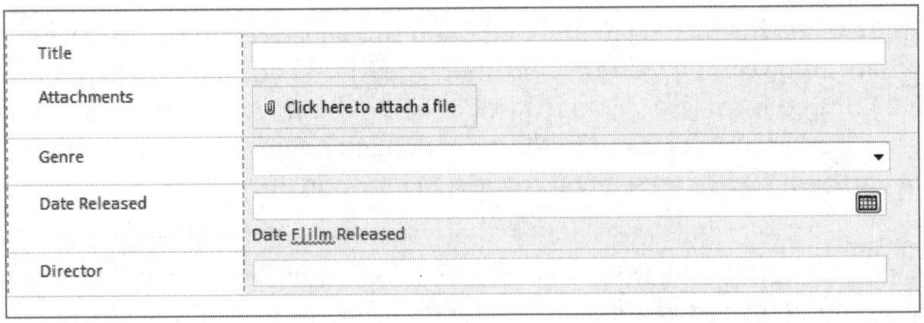

Title	
Attachments	📎 Click here to attach a file
Genre	▼
Date Released	📅
	Date Flilm Released
Director	

FIGURE 36-2

To publish the form to the SharePoint List, do the following:

10. Click the InfoPath File menu.

11. Click Publish.

12. Click SharePoint List. (Note the name of the list that will be published is next to the Publish button.) Your new form will be published to the SharePoint site and list.

13. Return to your custom DVD collection list and click the Add New Item link to continue and see the form in operation.

Figure 36-3 shows the Add New Item form in the list.

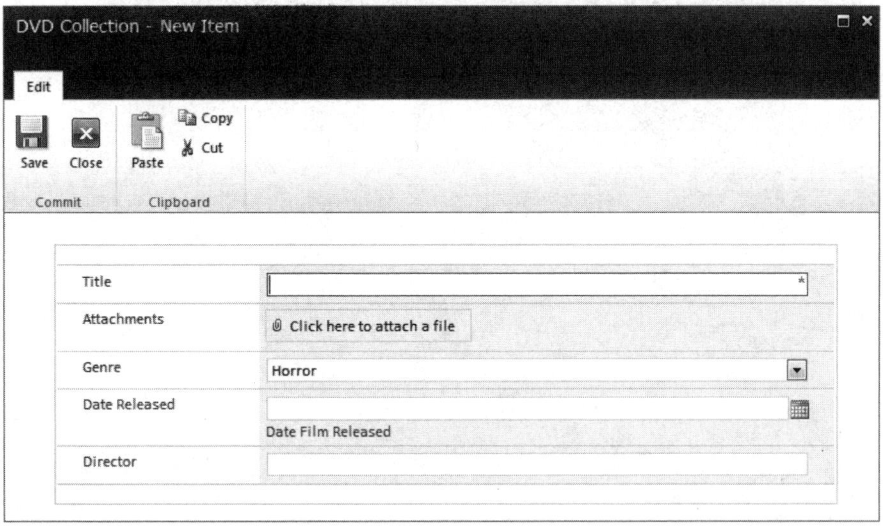

FIGURE 36-3

To further customize the form, return to InfoPath, where your form template should still be open, and the follow these steps:

1. Click the Genre text box. The text box should now be showing a set of handles — small white squares that when clicked can be used to resize the text box.

2. Resize the text box by clicking a handle and dragging the text box to the right.

3. Repeat the process for each object you want to resize.

4. Click within the white space above the word Title.

5. From the ribbon, select the Insert tab.

6. Click Clip Art.

7. Enter **Movie** in the Search For box and click Go.

8. Drag any of the movie clip art images into the white space above the word Title on your form and resize as required.

9. Click File.

10. Click Publish.

11. Click SharePoint List.

Your edited form is published to your SharePoint site. Figure 36-4 shows the new form that displays in the browser when the Add New Item link is clicked in the list. As you can see, this is a simple example that opens the door to creating customized forms within your SharePoint libraries.

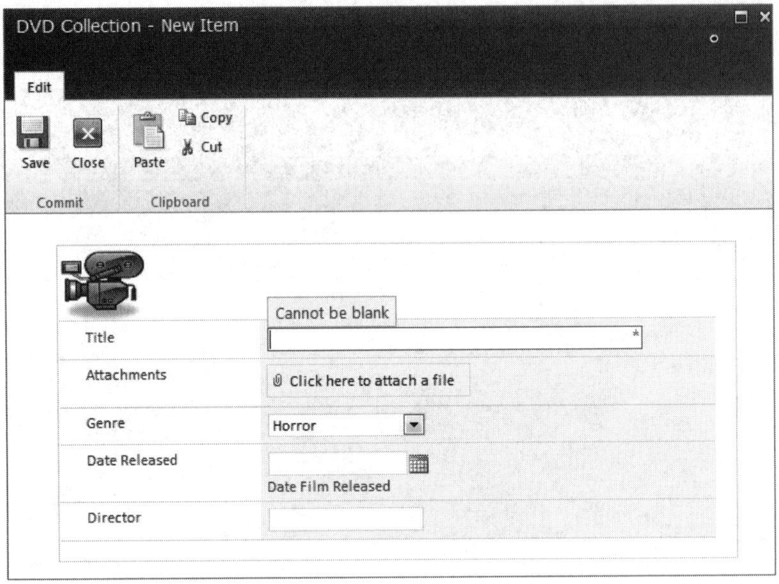

FIGURE 36-4

Now you will create another form, but this form will enable users to request a team site be created. This is a simple form but one that can be used to display some of the additional features of InfoPath 2010 when it is used to build forms for SharePoint. To create the form using Microsoft InfoPath Designer 2010, proceed as follows:

1. Click File.

2. Click New.

3. Click SharePoint Form Library.

4. Click Design Form. Your new form opens, ready for you to begin customization.

5. Click the text "Click to Add Title" and enter **Team Site Request From**.

6. In the Add Heading cell, enter **Welcome**.

7. Click the first cell marked Add Label and enter **Name**.

8. Click the adjacent cell and click Text Box on the design ribbon to add a text box.

9. In the cell below Name, enter **Email Address**.

10. In the adjacent cell, select the Person/Group Picker from the Input Objects to insert the control. Just as in SharePoint, this control enables you to search for a user to add to the form.

Figure 36-5 shows the completed form with the new objects added.

FIGURE 36-5

After you have completed the form, you need to publish it to a SharePoint form library. To do this, follow these steps:

1. Click File.

2. Click Publish.

3. Click SharePoint Server.

4. Click OK in response to the Save dialog that appears. (You must save the form template before publishing.)

5. Enter a name for the template, for example **SiteRequest**.

6. Click Save.

7. Enter the URL of your SharePoint site.

8. Click Next.

9. Accept the default on the next step in the publication process, Enable This Form to be Filled Out by Using a Browser, and accept the From Library default.

10. Click Next.

11. The wizard connects to your SharePoint Server. At this point, you can place the form template into a new forms library or create a new library for this form. In this case, accept the default, Create a New Form Library, and click Next.

12. Enter a name for the library, for example **Site Request Forms**.

13. Click Next.

14. Click Next.

15. Click Publish.

16. Check the Open This Form in the Browser box once the form has been published.

Figure 36-6 shows the form available in the browser on SharePoint.

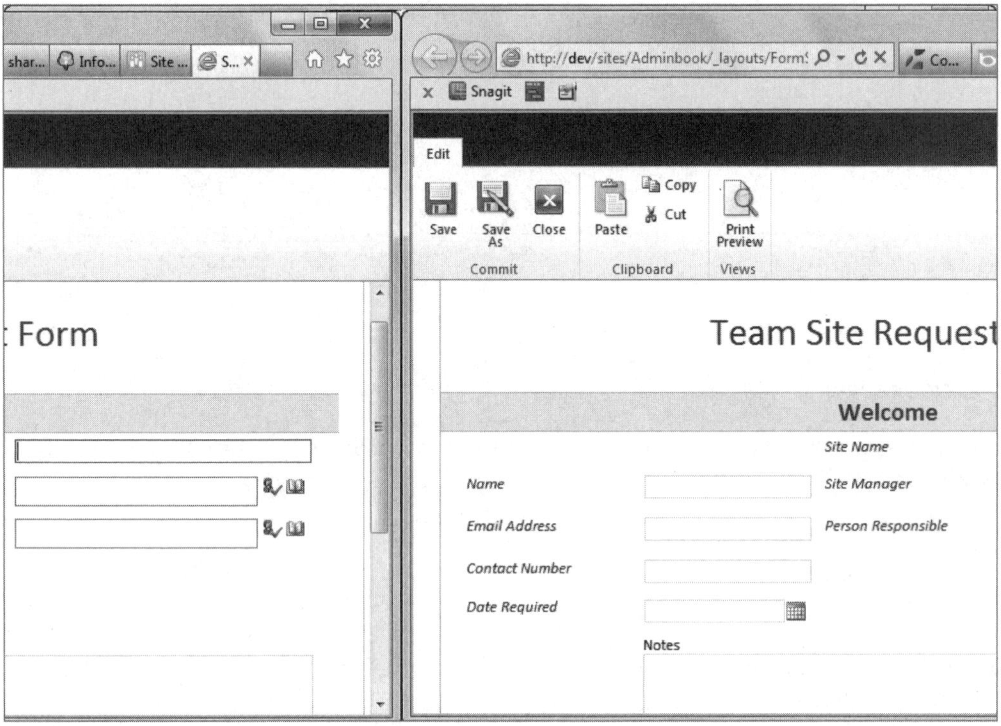

FIGURE 36-6

Now that you have a form published you should fill it in to see how it works within the form library. Complete the form by entering the required data. In this case you can use the People Picker Control (used for Site Manager and Person Responsible) to look up information. Each completed form is saved within the library as a distinct object. You will of course be prompted for a form name when saving.

> Please select Lesson 36 on the DVD or visit www.wrox.com/go/sp2010-24 to view the video that accompanies this lesson.

37

Using the Records Center Site Template

In this lesson you look at the uses of the records center site template. In Lessons 14, 16, and 17 you looked at several record management features. The records center is a preconfigured site created using the records center site template that uses many of these features and packages them together into a specialized site for the long term storage of digital records. The records center is useful for many tasks, including the following:

➤ Moving older records from an everyday portal site to a permanent storage location to reduce the amount of data that resides on the day-to-day portal.

➤ Saving records for the long term for legal or regulatory reasons in a location subject to more strenuous security requirements.

➤ Holding documents in a way that makes them difficult to modify and easy to audit.

In this lesson, we are going to examine using the records center site to perform a variety of record management functions. The specifics of many of these functions have been discussed in previous lessons, so the focus of this lesson will be to demonstrate how the records center site enables this functionality in a more centralized manner than using the record-management features individually in other sites.

FEATURES OF THE RECORDS CENTER SITE

The records center is configured with the following features, most of which are available on any given site, but are active by default on a records center site:

➤ The hold and e-discovery site-level feature is activated.

➤ Metadata navigation and filtering are activated.

➤ Offline synchronization is activated to pull records to offline clients.

➤ The Content Organizer is activated.

➤ The Document ID search box is available on the front page to enable users to find documents by individual ID. The Document ID service is a site collection–based feature.

➤ A special link called Manage Records Center console page is added to the Site Actions menu. This link connects to a special page that offers the site administrator some hints about how to set up the records center. The page is titled, "Records Center Management," and uses the page name of `rcconsole.aspx`.

Using the Records Center Management Console Page

The records center management console page lists several steps used to configure the records center site. In this section, we will discuss each configuration step and refer to previous lessons, where appropriate, that discuss the item in detail. This page includes two main columns. The left column is for general set up and planning, including:

➤ Create a New Record Library: This is a document library with one special feature. Any documents placed in it are automatically declared as "records." The concept of record declaration is described in Lesson 17.

➤ Manage Content and Structure: use this tool to rearrange the location of sites, libraries, and folders within the records center.

➤ Create Content Organizer rules: This is a repeated link from step 3 above.

➤ Discover and Hold Records: The topic of e-discovery and holding is described in Lesson 16.

➤ Generate a File Plan Report: This link allows you to create an Excel-based report that summarizes the content and policies (such as retention schedules) for a given document library.

➤ Generate an Audit Report: Opens the auditing reports page for the site. The auditing reports page is a series of Excel-based reports that specifies what sort have operations have been performed on files in the site collection. This is one reason that records center sites are frequently created in their own site collections or web applications, so that the auditing report information is specific to the records center documents, and is not mixed with other items in other sites.

The right column is used for configuring specific records management settings, including:

➤ Create Content Types: Content types are discussed in detail in Lesson 12. Content types are used in records management to define different types of documents, to which different policies may be applied.

➤ Create Records Libraries: This step involves creating normal libraries and folders, and assigning them retention schedules. Lesson 17 discusses the concept of retention schedules in detail.

➤ Create Content Organizer Rules: A records center site automatically configures the content organizer feature. This is discussed in detail in Lesson 14. The process is the same in a dedicated records center site as described in that lesson.

➤ Design the Site Welcome Page: Use the built in content editor web parts, or add your own to customize the home page and explain the use of your site.

TRY IT

In this walkthrough, you will be creating a records center site and performing many of the functions listed above.

Lesson Requirements

To perform this lesson, you need a SharePoint site with SharePoint Server.

Hints

Activate the Document ID feature at the site collection level before creating a Records Center.

The steps in this walkthrough are not all dependent on previous steps. The steps cover a range of activities you can perform on a records center site that aren't all connected.

Step-by-Step

1. Create a records center site. Go to the Site Actions menu on any site and select the option to create a new site. If you do not see the option for creating a records center site, check the features activated in your site. You should have the SharePoint Server standard site features activated on this site. Activating features is covered in Lesson 2. See Figure 37-1.

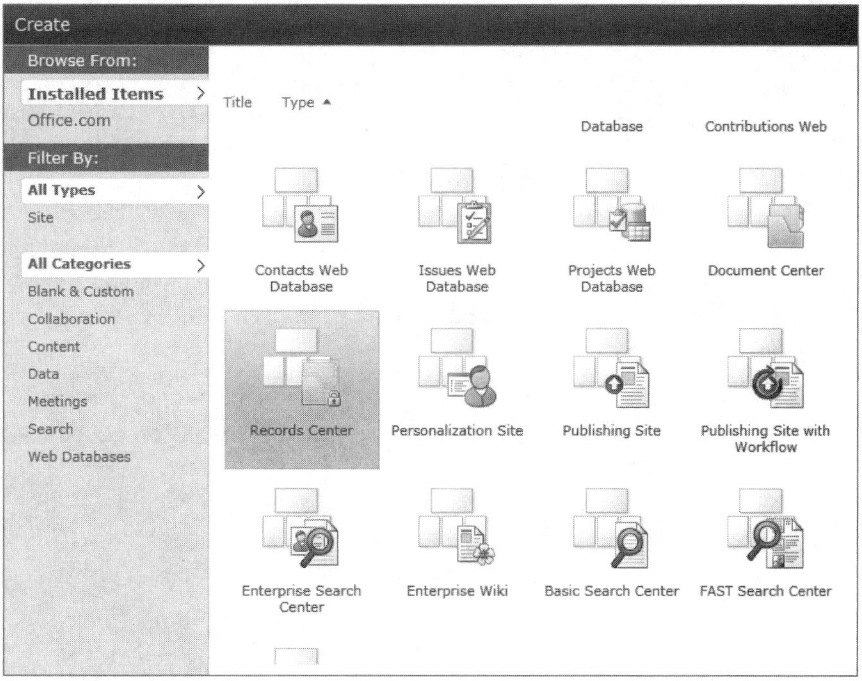

FIGURE 37-1

2. Once the site is created, look at the special item added to the Site Actions menu for managing the Records Center, shown in Figure 37-2. Click it and view the suggestions for using the Records Center.

Site Settings
Access all settings for this site.

Manage Records Center
Manage record keeping
settings on this site.

FIGURE 37-2

3. Set up routing options in Central Administration. You can set up a special connection to the records center that enables you to manually send any record to it from any document library in the farm by using the document's right-click menu. By setting this routing, a user can send any document in the farm to this record storage site with a simple command in that document's right click drop down menu.

In Central Administration, click General Application Settings. Then, under the External Service Connections link, click Configure Send to Connections.

4. On the Configure Send To Connections page there are several options. The first is a checkbox (shown in Figure 37-3) that enables the connection to cross subscription barriers. This allows the connection to be used across tenants in a multi-tenant architecture. Multi-tenant architecture is an advanced form of configuring a SharePoint farm and is beyond the scope of this book. The explanation here is simply to inform you of the meaning of this checkbox.

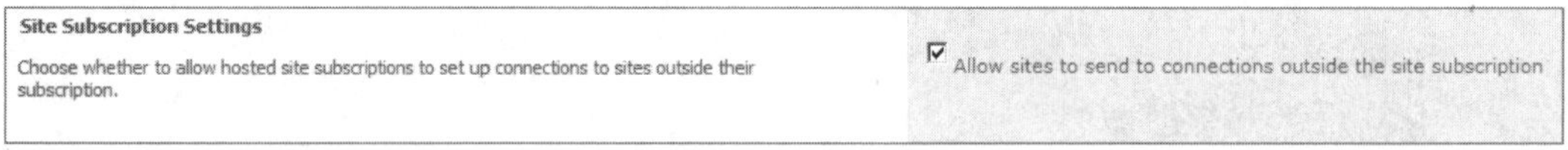

Site Subscription Settings

Choose whether to allow hosted site subscriptions to set up connections to sites outside their subscription.

☑ Allow sites to send to connections outside the site subscription

FIGURE 37-3

5. The Send To Connections list box shows you all the connections available on the farm. Select a connection choice from the list box. The choice you make here will be the record center used when you use the right click "send to" command from a document in a document library. See Figure 37-4.

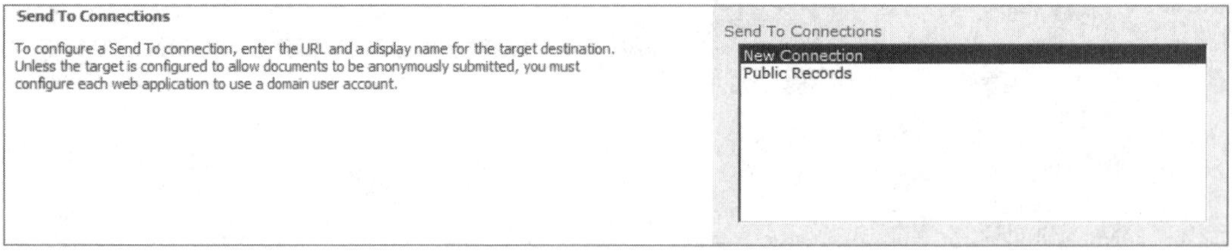

Send To Connections

To configure a Send To connection, enter the URL and a display name for the target destination. Unless the target is configured to allow documents to be anonymously submitted, you must configure each web application to use a domain user account.

Send To Connections
New Connection
Public Records

FIGURE 37-4

6. Under Connection Settings, as shown in Figure 37-5, you can set the settings for the connection you chose in Step 5. Specifically, you need to enter a display name and URL. Display name is what shows up in the Send To menu of a document in a library, on the Items drop-down menu. The URL is the actual URL of the records center site. Notice the note below the URL box, showing you the protocol for entering a URL. If you do not follow this protocol precisely, the connection will fail. For example, if your records center site is called "archives" at server "foo" (`http://foo/archives`), then your URL should read `http://foo/archives/_vti_bin/officialfile.asmx`.

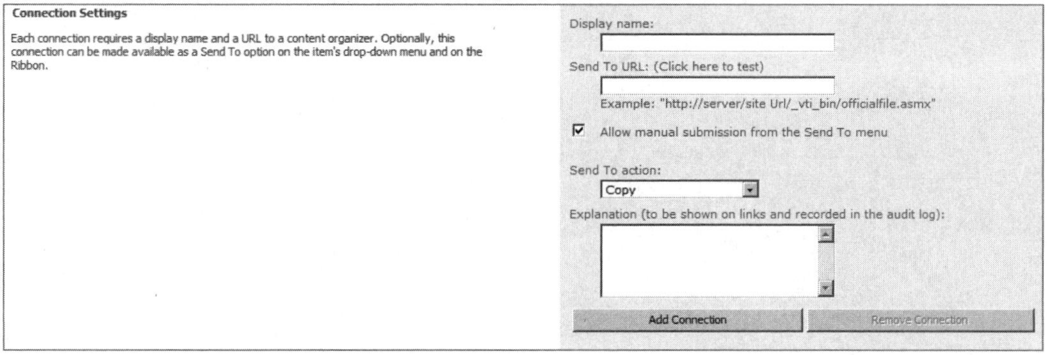

FIGURE 37-5

The Send To URL should be the full URL of the records center site followed by `/_vti_bin/officialfile.asmx`.

Allow Manual Submission from the Send To menu allows the option to appear in the drop-down menu of a document. If this option is not enabled, items can be directed to the records center only via workflow or policy.

Finally, the Send To action dictates whether the submission will send a copy, move the document, or move the document and leave a link to its new location. Figure 37-6 shows an example of how the Send To menu looks on a document. This is the menu you can access from any document in your SharePoint site.

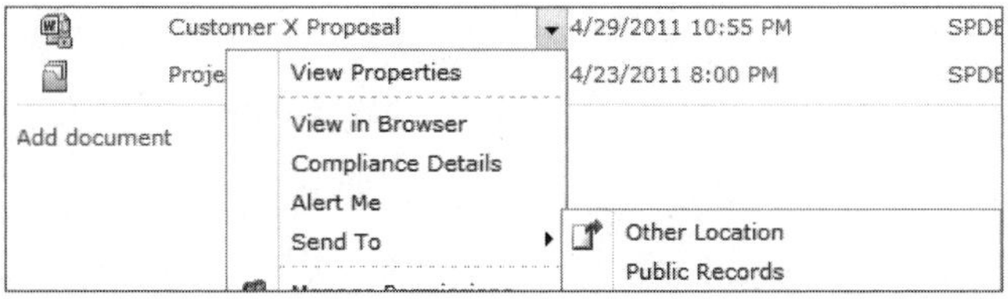

FIGURE 37-6

Please select Lesson 37 on the DVD or visit www.wrox.com/go/sp2010-24 *to view the video that accompanies this lesson.*

38

Creating a Meeting Workspace

Meeting Workspaces are useful templates for creating sites that meet a common need: the need to record information about meetings, such as the attendees and the topics discussed. The other nice feature of a meeting workspace is that you can easily link it to a calendar of events on your intranet and/or in your personal Outlook calendar. In this lesson we examine creating a meeting workspace and attaching it to a calendar of events.

CREATING A MEETING WORKSPACE

There are several Meeting Workspace templates to choose from when creating meeting sites. They differ in the combination of pre-created lists and libraries that are provisioned when you create the workspace. When you create a Meeting Workspace, you are creating a separate sub-site, and not just a list or library.

Unlike typical SharePoint sites, Meeting Workspaces can be directly connected to an events list and calendar on their parent site. This feature will be shown in detail in the Try It section of the lesson.

There are four out-of-the-box Meeting Workspaces:

➤ **Basic Meeting Workspace:** Use this template for everyday business meetings. It has a few pre-created lists and libraries to track meeting agenda, attendees, etc.

➤ **Blank Meeting Workspace:** Use this template if you like to make your own sites for meetings, and don't want pre-created lists and libraries. It includes only an attendee list, which is a special type of list you cannot create outside of the workspace templates. Otherwise, you will have to add all of the other elements that you want on the site.

➤ **Multipage Meeting Workspace:** This is the same as the Basic Meeting Workspace template, except that a few extra pages have been pre-created. Use this type of site for really large meetings for which you may need multiple pages for the agenda.

> ➤ **Social Meeting Workspace:** Use this template for creating a site to hold information about the company picnic, the sales conference, and so on. It includes pre-created libraries for image uploads.

Other than the ability to connect to event lists and calendars, and the attendees list type, Meeting Workspace sites operate just like any other SharePoint site. Any user that can create a SharePoint site can create a Meeting Workspace. The other list types used in Meeting Workspaces, such as the document library, or the agenda list, are available in other sites as well. In the Try It section below, we will examine the unique feature of workspace sites; connecting them to event lists and calendar views.

TRY IT

In this walkthrough, we will create a Meeting Workspace site and examine how you can connect it to an event list to create multiple unique meeting instances using just one workspace site.

Lesson Requirements

To perform this lesson, you need a SharePoint site with SharePoint Server or SharePoint Foundation installed.

Step-by-Step

1. Select New Site from the Site Actions menu on a SharePoint site. Select Multipage Meeting Workspace, give it a name and URL, and then click Create. You should see a page similar to Figure 38-1.

FIGURE 38-1

2. Fill out the provided list and libraries, such as the meeting objectives, agenda, and attendees. You can also add a document library if you want to provide the materials for the meeting. Also note the additional pages provided on the left navigation menu, as shown in Figure 38-2. The pages are empty and each contains three columns for adding Web Parts. If you are holding a large conference or meeting, these additional pages, Web Parts, and list views can contain information about each day's events, for example.

FIGURE 38-2

3. Now that you have a meeting workspace, let's link it to events on a calendar. Go back to the site from Step 1 and create a calendar list.

4. Create a new event on the list you just created. Give it a name and start and end times and, as shown in Figure 38-3, select a Category.

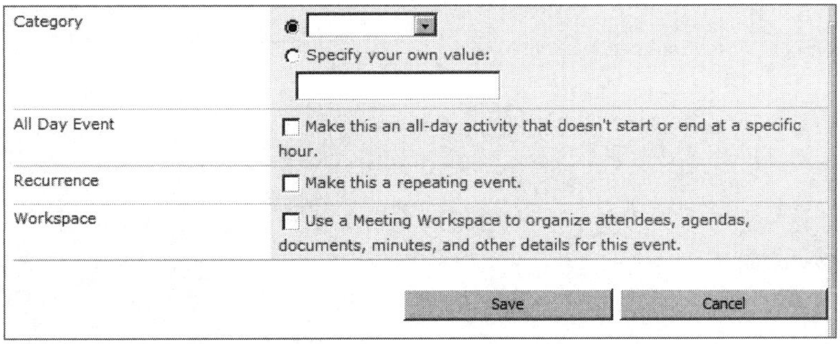

FIGURE 38-3

Check the Make This a Repeating Event checkbox. This creates multiple instances of the meeting on a schedule you can determine. When you select the checkbox for a recurring event, more controls display. Select a weekly occurrence. See Figure 38-4.

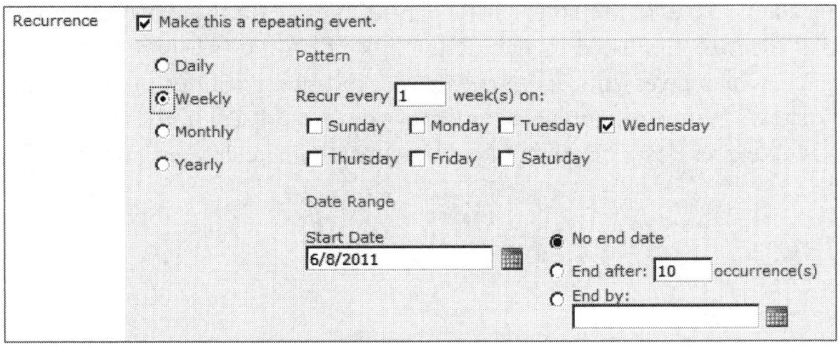

FIGURE 38-4

The category field is added to a calendar list by default. Select a category. Check the All Day Event checkbox if you would like to block out the entire day on the SharePoint calendar or your outlook calendar.

5. Also select the checkbox with the caption Use a Meeting Workspace to Organize Attendees, Agendas, Documents, Minutes, and Other Details for This Event. Finally, click Save.

6. On the next page there should be a section titled Create a Link, where you can choose from existing workspace sites to link to the recurring event. Select the site you used in Step 1. The rest of the page will be grayed out. Click OK. See Figure 38-5 to see a view of the form.

Keep in mind that if you do not have a meeting workspace already created, you will not see Figure 38-5. Instead, you will be taken to a slightly different screen without the option to choose an existing site. Figure 38-6 shows this form.

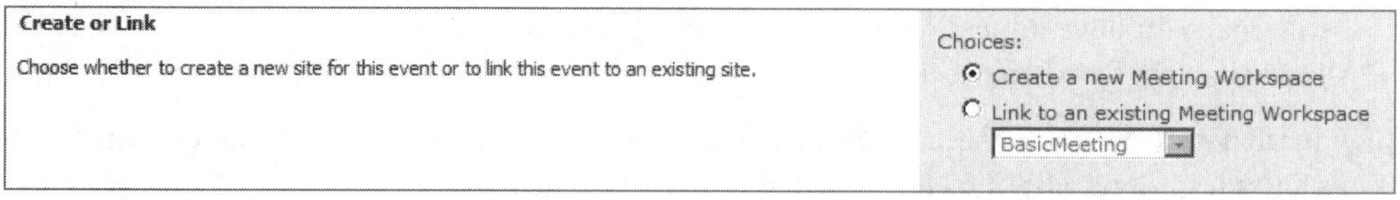

Create or Link

Choose whether to create a new site for this event or to link this event to an existing site.

Choices:
- ● Create a new Meeting Workspace
- ○ Link to an existing Meeting Workspace
  [BasicMeeting ▼]

FIGURE 38-5

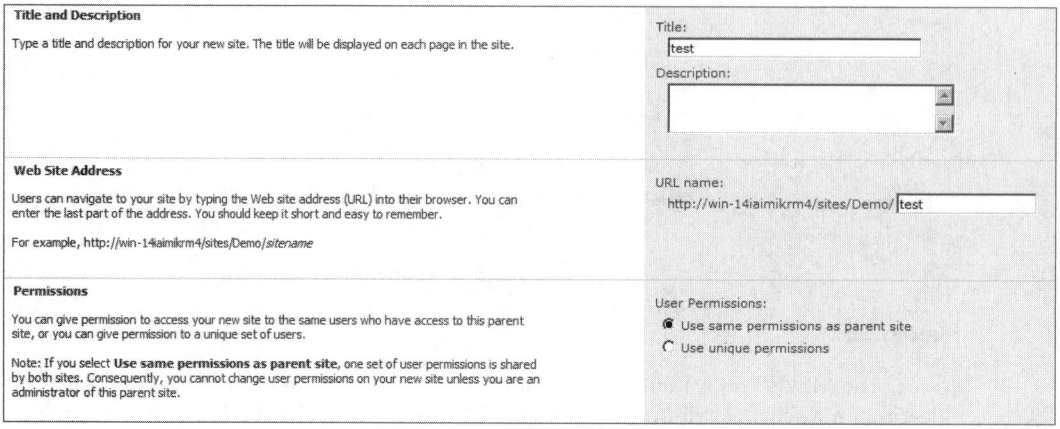

Title and Description

Type a title and description for your new site. The title will be displayed on each page in the site.

Title:
[test]

Description:
[   ]

Web Site Address

Users can navigate to your site by typing the Web site address (URL) into their browser. You can enter the last part of the address. You should keep it short and easy to remember.

For example, http://win-14iaimikrm4/sites/Demo/*sitename*

URL name:
http://win-14iaimikrm4/sites/Demo/ [test]

Permissions

You can give permission to access your new site to the same users who have access to this parent site, or you can give permission to a unique set of users.

Note: If you select **Use same permissions as parent site**, one set of user permissions is shared by both sites. Consequently, you cannot change user permissions on your new site unless you are an administrator of this parent site.

User Permissions:
- ● Use same permissions as parent site
- ○ Use unique permissions

FIGURE 38-6

7. The meeting site you created in Step 1 is displayed. Notice on the left side a link for each occurrence of the meeting, listed by date. Each link opens a different version of the meeting workspace, which gives you a convenient way to track meetings in your organization. Figure 38-7 shows the meeting navigation dates you should see on the left side of the screen. Each date listed represents a new instance of the meeting site created until the final date as configured.

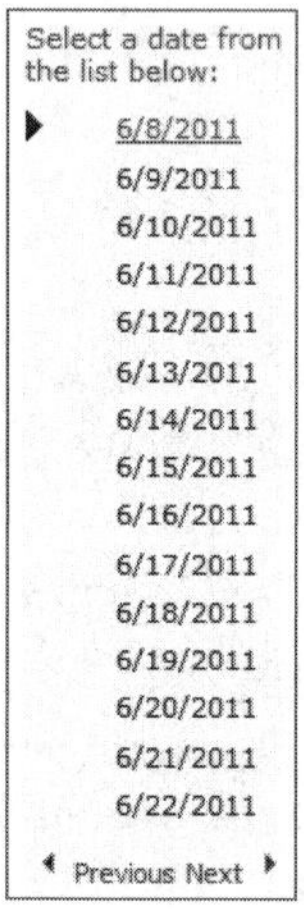

Select a date from the list below:
- ▶ 6/8/2011
- 6/9/2011
- 6/10/2011
- 6/11/2011
- 6/12/2011
- 6/13/2011
- 6/14/2011
- 6/15/2011
- 6/16/2011
- 6/17/2011
- 6/18/2011
- 6/19/2011
- 6/20/2011
- 6/21/2011
- 6/22/2011
- ◀ Previous Next ▶

FIGURE 38-7

Please select Lesson 38 on the DVD or visit www.wrox.com/go/sp2010-24 *to view the video that accompanies this lesson.*

39

Personalization Sites

This lesson covers one of the most powerful and least used features in all of SharePoint, the *personalization site*. A personalization site is a special kind of site template. Its purpose is to create sites inside your portal, but present each of these sites as an individual experience to each user, with content customized for her.

Imagine for a moment you have a company portal. This portal has a human resources site. You would like people to have a personalized view of the site. For example, you would like to arrange it so each person sees state income tax documents based on the ZIP code of his home address. Or perhaps your business has different employee bonus schedules for different types of employees. Salespeople get one bonus schedule and the janitor another. You can present a bonus schedule to each employee based on job title.

For another example, you could have a collaboration site in which everyone is uploading documents related to some large project. A personalization site could present a special view that shows only those documents authored by the user who is logged in. It could also show a view of the logged-in user's tasks for a project as assigned on a task list and imported into Outlook and presented on a site in the portal. There are endless possibilities for content that is presented differently for each user. That is the purpose of a personalization site.

A personalization site can be built anywhere within the portal, just like any other site template. Note that the User Profile Service must be active in order for the personalization site template to be available for use. Starting and configuring a User Profile Service is beyond the scope of this book, but you should be aware of this important prerequisite to avoid the confusion of not seeing personalization sites as an option on your SharePoint farm. If this is the case, check with your farm administrator to make sure a User Profile service application is running.

LINKING TO MY SITE

You can link a personalization site to the top navigation bar of a user's My Site by setting some properties in the User Profile service in Central Administration. Figure 39-1 shows the links to the MY HR site created in another section of the portal but pushed to the My Site navigation bar for the logged-in user.

FIGURE 39-1

PERSONALIZATION WEB PARTS

There are a number of Web Parts that are particularly suited to placement on My Sites. They include the following list:

➤ **Outlook Web Parts:** This list includes MyCalendar, MyInbox, MyTasks, etc. These Web Parts show information from Outlook.

➤ **Colleagues Web Part:** This shows coworkers as set in the user profile properties.

➤ **SharePoint Documents:** Aggregates a list of documents authored by the user. It will reach across sites to collect the information.

➤ **RSS Feed:** This can be used to collect favorite feeds from the Internet or other SharePoint lists.

TRY IT

In this lesson, we will create two Personalization sites. We will examine the options available for personalizing each site to reflect different views based on the identity of the logged in user.

Lesson Requirements

To complete this Try It exercise, you need the following:

➤ A SharePoint site with SharePoint Server.

Hints

This walkthrough assumes a User Profile service application has already been created and configured. It also assumes you can perform some minor tasks such as adding and editing Web Parts on a page.

Step-by-Step

Follow these steps in order to complete the goals of this lesson:

1. Create a personalization site from any other site, using the Create Site command from the Site Actions menu. Select the personalization site template. Once the site is created, copy the URL from the browser address bar. You will paste the link in Step 5.

2. Access the Central Administration site to set up the user profile service. At a minimum, you need rights to manage the User Profile service. The easiest way to access the Central Administration site is by logging into the server, clicking the Start menu and the All Programs link, and then opening the Microsoft SharePoint 2010 Products folder. In this folder is a link to open the Central Administration website.

3. From the home page of the Central Administration site, click the Manage Service Applications link under the Application Management heading.

4. From the list of service applications highlight the User Profile Service Application, and click the Manage toolbar on the ribbon. The User Profile Service management page should be displayed. Figure 39-2 shows the page and highlights the Configure Personalization Site link.

People
Manage User Properties | Manage User Profiles | Manage User Sub-types | Manage Audiences |
Schedule Audience Compilation | Manage User Permissions | Compile Audiences | Manage Policies

Synchronization
Configure Synchronization Connections | Configure Synchronization Timer Job | Configure Synchronization Settings |
Start Profile Synchronization

Organizations
Manage Organization Properties | Manage Organization Profiles | Manage Organization Sub-types

My Site Settings
Setup My Sites | Configure Trusted Host Locations | Configure Personalization Site |
Publish Links to Office Client Applications | Manage Social Tags and Notes

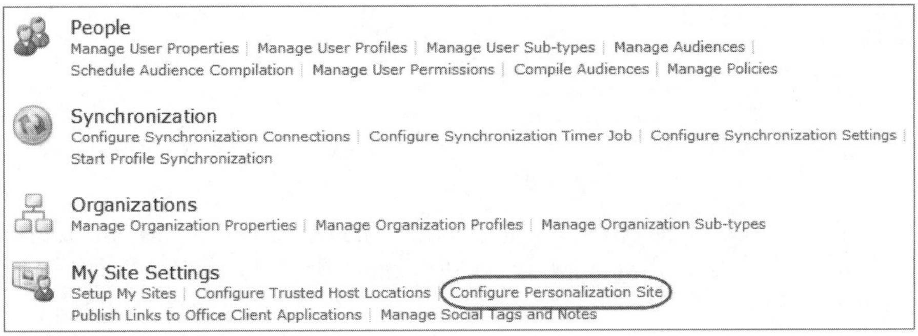

FIGURE 39-2

5. Click the New Link button on the Personalization site links page. Paste the value you copied in Step 1 into the URL field. Enter a description. What you type in the description field will show up as the link on the user's My Site. The Owner field will usually contain the name of the personalization site owner or a farm administrator. Finally, you can target the link to show up only in the My Sites of users who belong to certain audiences. Audiences can be compiled on the User Profile Service Management page under the People heading by clicking on the link titled Manage Audiences. However, this task is not the focus of this lesson. If no audience is specified, the link will be visible for all users. Click OK after completing the form. Figure 39-3 shows a form filled out for a site link called MY HR, which links to an HR personalization site.

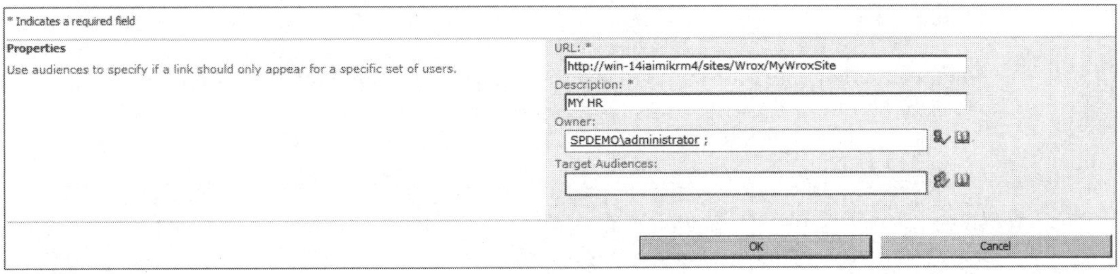

* Indicates a required field

Properties
Use audiences to specify if a link should only appear for a specific set of users.

URL: *
http://win-14iaimikrm4/sites/Wrox/MyWroxSite
Description: *
MY HR
Owner:
SPDEMO\administrator ;
Target Audiences:

OK   Cancel

FIGURE 39-3

6. In the upper right corner of any site, you will see a control that shows the logged-in user and a drop-down menu, as shown in Figure 39-4. Click the drop-down menu and select My Site.

FIGURE 39-4

7. On the My Site, in the upper left-hand corner, you will see the top navigation bar, which should include the link you have just added. Figure 39-5 shows the MY HR link on the navigation bar.

FIGURE 39-5

8. Create a new personalization site, as you did in Step 1. This example features another personalization site called My Projects. In this case we will not add a link in Central Administration, but will see how an individual user can pin a link to her individual My Site, which will be seen only by her. Figure 39-6 shows that we have navigated to the new My Site. By hovering over the link you enable the option to pin it to your personal My Site.

FIGURE 39-6

9. Return to the My Site and you will see the site you just pinned to the top navigation bar. No one else who doesn't also pin this link will see it.

 Please select Lesson 39 on the DVD or visit www.wrox.com/go/sp2010-24 *to view the video that accompanies this lesson.*

40

Creating an Enterprise Wiki Site

Wikis are a very useful means of creating documentation and sharing knowledge in an organization. They are more user-friendly for storing frequently accessed and updated information than lots of files on a hard drive or network folder. The information on a wiki is presented as a web page and is very easy to edit directly from a browser: users can easily add text, links, multimedia, and other content. By contrast, documentation and procedure-related content that sit in word-processing files may be accessed rarely and be less pleasing to use. Users have to open file after file to browse this information, and the files may soon become outdated or contradictory.

A wiki site is a good choice when you have content that will have many editors and many readers. Some of the types of content that wikis are particularly suited for include the following:

➤ Process documentation.

➤ General rules and procedures.

➤ Frequently asked questions.

➤ Technical documentation.

➤ Department policies.

WIKI FEATURES

There are two different ways to implement wiki functionality in SharePoint 2010. One is to create a wiki page library, which can be created on any site. The other is to create a site using an Enterprise wiki template. The basic functionality of a wiki is the same for both. The Enterprise wiki site has additional features conducive to large-scale use, such as the following:

➤ **Custom page layout:** Enterprise wikis are built using the SharePoint publishing infrastructure. This enables site developers to create more advanced layouts and customized page branding for a more refined user experience.

➤ **Ratings:** Each page is preset to allow ratings, to encourage user feedback on the content.

➤ **Category tags:** Wiki content can be tagged with descriptive terms, making it easier to filter and search information contained in larger wikis with many categories.

➤ **Approval workflow:** Content can be set to require approval before it becomes available for general users. This level of control over content may be more appropriate for corporate-wide communication than use by an individual department or project team.

There are differences between creating a site with an Enterprise wiki site template and creating a wiki document library on a SharePoint site. Wiki document libraries are typically created for smaller audiences, are less closely monitored and less likely to be accessed by the general employee population, and are more focused in scope. Consider a library created to document how to install software in an IT department. The wiki may be used only by the IT department, and there probably isn't much concern for page layout, approval, or other advanced features.

On the other hand, a corporate-wide information portal to be used by a majority of the company's employees is more likely to be an Enterprise wiki site. It includes preconfigured features for rating and tagging content, and supports customized page layouts to make it easier for users to create and lay out content. In addition, an approval workflow can easily be added to enable content review before publishing. These features will be demonstrated in the Try It section of this lesson.

TRY IT

In this walkthrough, we will create a site with the Enterprise wiki site template and examine some of the key features.

Lesson Requirements

To complete this exercise, you need the following:

➤ A SharePoint site with SharePoint Server.

Hints

This walkthrough will demonstrate some common features of SharePoint wikis and some features that are specific to the Enterprise wiki site template.

Step-by-Step

1. On a SharePoint site, create a new site (using the Site Actions menu) and use the Enterprise Wiki site template, as shown in Figure 40-1.

2. Edit the page. On the home page of the newly created wiki site, click the Edit This Page link shown in Figure 40-2. You can freely edit the page using the edit toolbars shown in Figures 40-3 and 40-4.

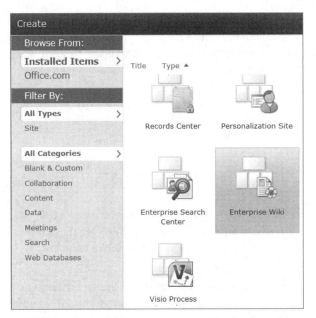

FIGURE 40-1

Last modified at 6/10/2011 11:49 PM by SPDEMO\Administrator   [Edit this page]

Use the Enterprise Wiki to create a single, go-to place for knowledge sharing and project management across the enterprise. Enterprise Wikis are simple to use, flexible, and lightweight in features. They are quick and easy to create, and you can easily add links to other information systems, corporate directories, or applications.

By using an Enterprise Wiki, you can avoid e-mail overload, provide structure to new and existing information, and encourage collaboration. This helps build consensus among team members.

Working with content - text, graphics or video - is as easy as working in any word processing application, such as Microsoft Word. Use the Rich Text Editor to enhance the formatting of content, apply styles to text, reorganize or spell check your content, insert and format tables, and embed graphics or video. You can do all these things without leaving the wiki page.

Other things you can do when working with Enterprise Wikis:

- Collaborate on wiki pages with other users
- Comment on a wiki page to enable discussion about the contents of the page
- Rate a wiki page to share your opinion about its content
- Categorize wiki pages to enable users to quickly find information and share it with others

FIGURE 40-2

FIGURE 40-3

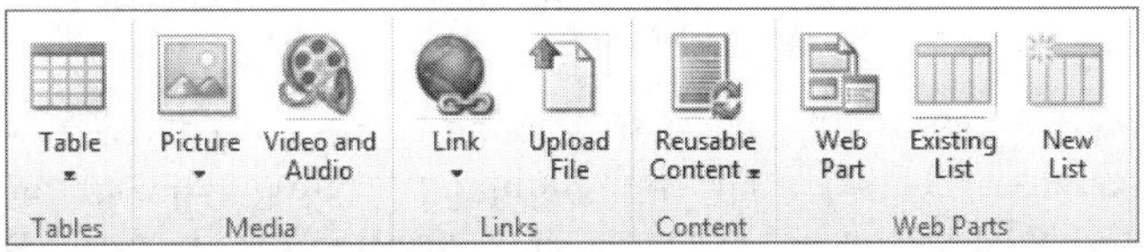

FIGURE 40-4

3. Somewhere in the editable area, type the following: "[[new page]]". Surrounding text with double brackets creates a link to a page. If the page does not exist, the user will be prompted to create it. Click Save and Close in the page options on the toolbar. Figure 40-5 shows how the newly created link should appear on the page.

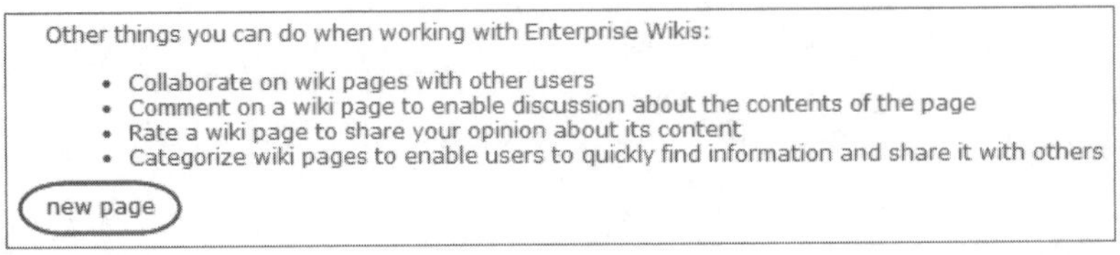

> Other things you can do when working with Enterprise Wikis:
>
> - Collaborate on wiki pages with other users
> - Comment on a wiki page to enable discussion about the contents of the page
> - Rate a wiki page to share your opinion about its content
> - Categorize wiki pages to enable users to quickly find information and share it with others
>
> (new page)

FIGURE 40-5

4. Click the new page link. A dialog will appear asking you to create the new page. Click Create. Boom! A new page is created, ready to go. Isn't this drastically easier than navigating endless word processing documents in a folder to create documentation and content? Return to the home page of the wiki site.

5. Notice that along the top navigation bar you can see the pages in the site as navigation elements. Over time, using the top navigation bar will become impractical, as it may contain dozens or hundreds of pages. You can modify this behavior by changing the navigation options in the Site Actions menu. For more information on this, see Lesson 3.

6. Use the page rating stars on the right side of the page to rate it. Page ratings are updated using a timer job that can be set by administrators to run on varying schedules. The update could take minutes, hours, or even days. Therefore, don't fret if your ratings aren't instantly reflected on the page.

7. Edit the page again. On the right-hand side, click the tag icon to the right of the category text box, shown in Figure 40-6. This will open a dialog box where you can add tags or choose from existing tags to describe the page's content. Save the page after applying a tag.

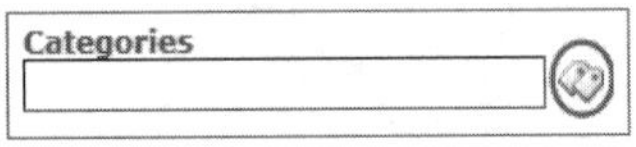

> **Categories**
> [_____] (⊕)

FIGURE 40-6

8. You will notice that if you click the tag you just created in Step 7, a page will open to display all pages using that tag. This gives you an easy way to browse content related to a certain topic.

9. In the toolbar, click the page tab and then the Page History toolbar link. A new view will appear on the left side of the screen, showing the history of the page versions. In the middle of the page you will see a limited view of some of the changes made to the page in each version. Figure 40-7 shows this view of the page history.

10. On the Page History view, shown in Figure 40-7, click the Version History toolbar. You will see an in-depth view of each version of the page. The time stamp on the modified column contains a drop-down menu that will allow you to view, delete, or restore the given version of a page. Figure 40-8 shows this menu.

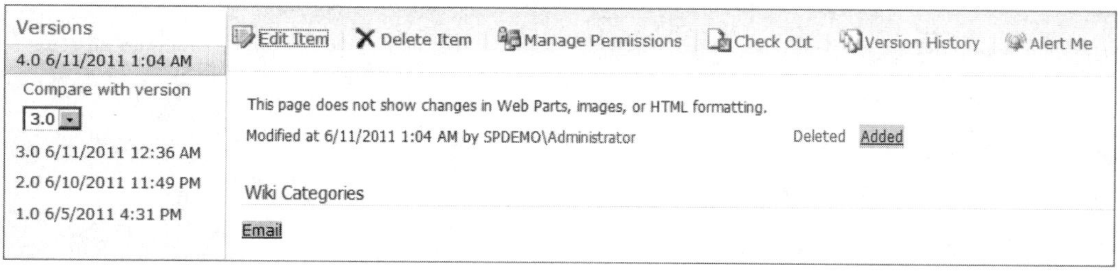

Versions	Edit Item	Delete Item	Manage Permissions	Check Out	Version History	Alert Me
4.0 6/11/2011 1:04 AM						

Compare with version

3.0 ▾

3.0 6/11/2011 12:36 AM

2.0 6/10/2011 11:49 PM

1.0 6/5/2011 4:31 PM

This page does not show changes in Web Parts, Images, or HTML formatting.

Modified at 6/11/2011 1:04 AM by SPDEMO\Administrator   Deleted Added

Wiki Categories

Email

FIGURE 40-7

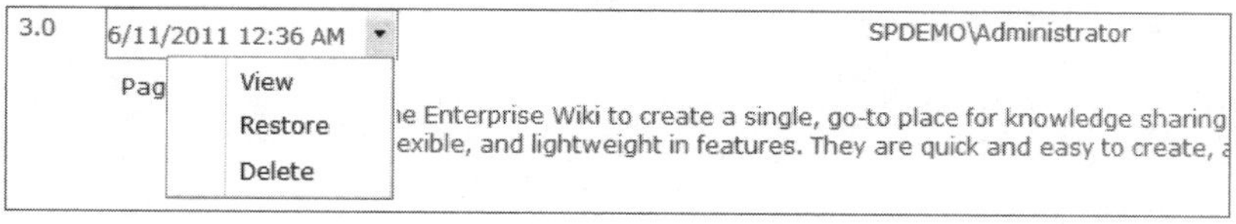

3.0	6/11/2011 12:36 AM ▾		SPDEMO\Administrator
	Pag	View	
		Restore	
		Delete	

he Enterprise Wiki to create a single, go-to place for knowledge sharing
exible, and lightweight in features. They are quick and easy to create, a

FIGURE 40-8

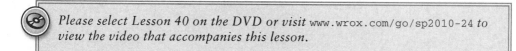

Please select Lesson 40 on the DVD or visit www.wrox.com/go/sp2010-24 *to view the video that accompanies this lesson.*

What's on the DVD?

This appendix provides you with information on the contents of the DVD that accompanies this book. For the latest and greatest information, please refer to the ReadMe file located at the root of the DVD. Here is what you will find in this appendix:

- ➤ System Requirements
- ➤ Using the DVD
- ➤ What's on the DVD
- ➤ Troubleshooting

SYSTEM REQUIREMENTS

Most reasonably up-to-date computers with a DVD drive should be able to play the screencasts that are included on the DVD.

USING THE DVD

To access the content from the DVD, follow these steps:

1. Insert the DVD into your computer's DVD-ROM drive. The license agreement appears.

*The interface won't launch if you have autorun disabled. In that case, click Start ⇨ Run (for Windows 7, click Start ⇨ All Programs ⇨ Accessories ⇨ Run). In the dialog box that appears, type **D:\Start.exe**. (Replace **D** with the proper letter if your DVD drive uses a different letter. If you don't know the letter, check how your DVD drive is listed under My Computer.) Click OK.*

2. Read through the license agreement, and then click the Accept button if you want to use the DVD.

3. The DVD interface appears. Simply select the lesson number for the video you want to view.

WHAT'S ON THE DVD

Each of this book's lessons contains a Try It section that enables you to practice the concepts covered by that lesson. The Try It includes a high-level overview, requirements, and step-by-step instructions explaining how to build the example program.

This DVD contains video screencasts showing my computer screen as I work through key pieces of the Try Its from each lesson. In the audio I explain what I'm doing step-by-step so you can see how the techniques described in the lesson translate into actions.

I don't always show how to build every last piece of a Try It's program. For example, if the requirements ask you to do the same thing multiple times, I may only do the first one and let you do the rest so you don't waste time watching me do the same thing again and again.

I recommend using the following steps when reading a lesson:

1. Read the lesson's text.

2. Read the Try It's overview, requirements, and hints.

3. Read the step-by-step instructions. If the code you write doesn't work, use the code provided to find your problem. Look for places where my solution differs from yours. In programming, there's always more than one way to solve a problem, and it's good to know about several different approaches.

4. Watch the screencast to see how I handle the key issues.

You can also download all of the book's examples and solutions to the Try It's at the book's websites.

TROUBLESHOOTING

If you have difficulty installing or using any of the materials on the companion DVD, try the following solutions:

➤ **Reboot if necessary.** As with many troubleshooting situations, it may make sense to reboot your machine to reset any faults in your environment.

➤ **Turn off any anti-virus software that you may have running.** Installers sometimes mimic virus activity and can make your computer incorrectly believe that it is being infected by a virus. (Be sure to turn the anti-virus software back on later.)

➤ **Close all running programs**. The more programs you're running, the less memory is available to other programs. Installers also typically update files and programs; if you keep other programs running, installation may not work properly.

➤ **Reference the ReadMe**. Please refer to the ReadMe file located at the root of the DVD for the latest product information at the time of publication.

CUSTOMER CARE

If you have trouble with the DVD, please call the Wiley Product Technical Support phone number at (800) 762-2974. Outside the United States, call 1(317) 572-3994. You can also contact Wiley Product Technical Support at `http://support.wiley.com`. John Wiley & Sons will provide technical support only for installation and other general quality control items. For technical support on the applications themselves, consult the program's vendor or author.

To place additional orders or to request information about other Wiley products, please call (877) 762-2974.

INDEX

WILEY PUBLISHING, INC.
END-USER LICENSE AGREEMENT

READ THIS. You should carefully read these terms and conditions before opening the software packet(s) included with this book "Book". This is a license agreement "Agreement" between you and Wiley Publishing, Inc. "WPI". By opening the accompanying software packet(s), you acknowledge that you have read and accept the following terms and conditions. If you do not agree and do not want to be bound by such terms and conditions, promptly return the Book and the unopened software packet(s) to the place you obtained them for a full refund.

1. **License Grant.** WPI grants to you (either an individual or entity) a nonexclusive license to use one copy of the enclosed software program(s) (collectively, the "Software") solely for your own personal or business purposes on a single computer (whether a standard computer or a workstation component of a multi-user network). The Software is in use on a computer when it is loaded into temporary memory (RAM) or installed into permanent memory (hard disk, CD-ROM, or other storage device). WPI reserves all rights not expressly granted herein.

2. **Ownership.** WPI is the owner of all right, title, and interest, including copyright, in and to the compilation of the Software recorded on the physical packet included with this Book "Software Media". Copyright to the individual programs recorded on the Software Media is owned by the author or other authorized copyright owner of each program. Ownership of the Software and all proprietary rights relating thereto remain with WPI and its licensers.

3. **Restrictions on Use and Transfer.**

   (a) You may only (i) make one copy of the Software for backup or archival purposes, or (ii) transfer the Software to a single hard disk, provided that you keep the original for backup or archival purposes. You may not (i) rent or lease the Software, (ii) copy or reproduce the Software through a LAN or other network system or through any computer subscriber system or bulletin-board system, or (iii) modify, adapt, or create derivative works based on the Software.

   (b) You may not reverse engineer, decompile, or disassemble the Software. You may transfer the Software and user documentation on a permanent basis, provided that the transferee agrees to accept the terms and conditions of this Agreement and you retain no copies. If the Software is an update or has been updated, any transfer must include the most recent update and all prior versions.

4. **Restrictions on Use of Individual Programs.** You must follow the individual requirements and restrictions detailed for each individual program in the "About the CD" appendix of this Book or on the Software Media. These limitations are also contained in the individual license agreements recorded on the Software Media. These limitations may include a requirement that after using the program for a specified period of time, the user must pay a registration fee or discontinue use. By opening the Software packet(s), you agree to abide by the licenses and restrictions for these individual programs that are detailed in the "About the CD" appendix and/or on the Software Media. None of the material on this Software Media or listed in this Book may ever be redistributed, in original or modified form, for commercial purposes.

5. **Limited Warranty.**

   (a) WPI warrants that the Software and Software Media are free from defects in materials and workmanship under normal use for a period of sixty (60) days from the date of purchase of this Book. If WPI receives notification within the warranty period of defects in materials or workmanship, WPI will replace the defective Software Media.

(b) WPI AND THE AUTHOR(S) OF THE BOOK DISCLAIM ALL OTHER WARRANTIES, EXPRESS OR IMPLIED, INCLUDING WITHOUT LIMITATION IMPLIED WARRANTIES OF MERCHANTABILITY AND FITNESS FOR A PARTICULAR PURPOSE, WITH RESPECT TO THE SOFTWARE, THE PROGRAMS, THE SOURCE CODE CONTAINED THEREIN, AND/OR THE TECHNIQUES DESCRIBED IN THIS BOOK. WPI DOES NOT WARRANT THAT THE FUNCTIONS CONTAINED IN THE SOFTWARE WILL MEET YOUR REQUIREMENTS OR THAT THE OPERATION OF THE SOFTWARE WILL BE ERROR FREE.

(c) This limited warranty gives you specific legal rights, and you may have other rights that vary from jurisdiction to jurisdiction.

6. Remedies.

(a) WPI's entire liability and your exclusive remedy for defects in materials and workmanship shall be limited to replacement of the Software Media, which may be returned to WPI with a copy of your receipt at the following address: Software Media Fulfillment Department, Attn.: *SharePoint Server 2010 Administration 24-Hour Trainer*, Wiley Publishing, Inc., 10475 Crosspoint Blvd., Indianapolis, IN 46256, or call 1-800-762-2974. Please allow four to six weeks for delivery. This Limited Warranty is void if failure of the Software Media has resulted from accident, abuse, or misapplication. Any replacement Software Media will be warranted for the remainder of the original warranty period or thirty (30) days, whichever is longer.

(b) In no event shall WPI or the author be liable for any damages whatsoever (including without limitation damages for loss of business profits, business interruption, loss of business information, or any other pecuniary loss) arising from the use of or inability to use the Book or the Software, even if WPI has been advised of the possibility of such damages.

(c) Because some jurisdictions do not allow the exclusion or limitation of liability for consequential or incidental damages, the above limitation or exclusion may not apply to you.

7. **U.S. Government Restricted Rights.** Use, duplication, or disclosure of the Software for or on behalf of the United States of America, its agencies and/or instrumentalities "U.S. Government" is subject to restrictions as stated in paragraph (c)(1)(ii) of the Rights in Technical Data and Computer Software clause of DFARS 252.227-7013, or subparagraphs (c) (1) and (2) of the Commercial Computer Software - Restricted Rights clause at FAR 52.227-19, and in similar clauses in the NASA FAR supplement, as applicable.

8. **General.** This Agreement constitutes the entire understanding of the parties and revokes and supersedes all prior agreements, oral or written, between them and may not be modified or amended except in a writing signed by both parties hereto that specifically refers to this Agreement. This Agreement shall take precedence over any other documents that may be in conflict herewith. If any one or more provisions contained in this Agreement are held by any court or tribunal to be invalid, illegal, or otherwise unenforceable, each and every other provision shall remain in full force and effect.

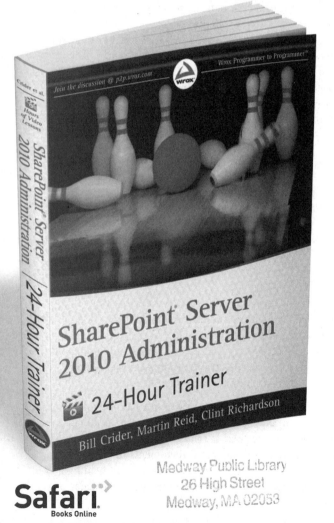